Making Money with Your Computer at Home

SECOND EDITION

Other Books by
Paul and Sarah Edwards

Best Home Businesses for the 90s

Finding Your Perfect Work

Getting Business to Come to You
(with Laura Clampitt Douglas)

Home Businesses You Can Buy
(with Walter Zooi)

Secrets of Self-Employment

Teaming Up
(with Rick Benzel)

Working from Home

Jeremy P. Tarcher/Putnam
a member of
Penguin Putnam Inc.
New York

Making Money with Your Computer at Home

SECOND EDITION

**The Inside Information You Need to Know
to Select and Operate a Full-Time,
Part-Time, or Add-On Business
That's Right for You**

Paul and Sarah Edwards

Most Tarcher/Putnam Books are available at special quantity discounts for bulk purchases for sales promotions, premiums, fund-raising, and educational needs. Special books or book excerpts also can be created to fit specific needs. For details, write or telephone Putnam Special Markets, 200 Madison Avenue, New York, NY 10016; (212) 951-8891.

Jeremy P. Tarcher/Putnam
a member of
Penguin Putnam Inc.
200 Madison Avenue
New York, NY 10016
http://www.putnam.com

Library of Congress Cataloging-in-Publication Data

Edwards, Paul, date.
Making money with your computer at home : the inside information you need to
know to select and operate a full-time, part-time, or add-on business
that's right for you / Paul and Sarah Edwards.—2nd ed.
p.   cm.
Includes index.
ISBN 0-87477-898-0
1. Home-based businesses—United States—Technological innovations.
2. Microcomputers.   I. Edwards, Sarah (Sarah A.)   II. Title.
HD2336.U5E38   1997   97-19612 CIP
658'.041—dc21

BOOK DESIGN BY DEBORAH KERNER
COVER DESIGN BY TANYA MAIBORODA

Printed in the United States of America
1   3   5   7   9   10   8   6   4   2

This book is printed on acid-free paper. ∞

Acknowledgments

A new edition of a book gives us a chance to update content and tweak format. In the frenetically moving world of personal computers, a new edition of this book required that and more. For help, we turned to Walter Zooi, the co-author of our book *Home Businesses You Can Buy.*

We especially acknowledge our assistant, Joyce Acosta, whose good cheer enables us to complete the manuscripts that come from our home office and who makes the hundreds of phone calls to verify telephone numbers and other information.

We thank the supportive team of people at Tarcher/Putnam, including our publisher, Joel Fotinos, with whom we delight in working; the editors upon whom we rely, David Groff and editor-in-chief, Irene Prokop; Coral Tysliava and Claire Vaccaro and the people who work with them to turn our manuscripts into finished books; publicists Joanna Pinsker and Ken Siman; and marketing coordinator Maria Liu.

We hope the cumulative contributions of these people will lead you to finding ways to earn money with your computer in the comfort and enjoyment of your home.

PAUL AND SARAH EDWARDS

Contents

Introduction

Computers are becoming as everyday as appliances in people's homes. But unlike most appliances, a computer can be used to make money. It can help you supplement your income so that the month is not too long for your money. A computer can be the key tool for starting a business at the peak of your life or it can serve men and women seeking a new opportunity following a career move or a layoff. It can enable the homebound to find dignity in producing income and provide alternatives to low-paying work requiring long hours standing on hard floors for seniors seeking to supplement retirement funds.

Year after year, surveys tell us that most people wish they could be their own boss. The computer makes the realization of that wish within the reach of virtually everyone attracted by:

- **the freedom to set your own hours**
- **working in a less stressful environment free of office games, doing work of your choosing, in the way you want**
- **the opportunity to spend more time with your family**
- **the ability to earn more on the basis of your own abilities**

Because of computers, there are literally dozens of new things you can do cost effectively from home. It's also become fashionable to work at home. A recent *Wall Street Journal* article discussed the advantages and etiquette of holding power lunches at home. Meanwhile, the personal computer, along with the Internet, printers that produce high-quality output, and sophisticated telephone services, make the home-based entrepreneur an equal competitor, for all intents and purposes, with just about any company or corporation in the world. And the good news is, it's only going to get better for home-based businesspeople. In the years ahead, the continued miniaturization of microprocessors and leaps in their speed will continue to whittle away the difference in capabilities between large companies and small ones.

In this book we aim to help you tap into the excitement and opportunity of this revolutionary change in two ways. First, we show ways you can use your personal computer to make money. In Part I of this book, we profile one hundred home-based businesses that generally use a personal computer as the focal point of the business. Many of the businesses we cover can easily become full-time careers, either replacing a job you already have or slowly developing into full-time work over time. Other businesses we review are income-enhancing activities that you can do on a part-time basis or that you might add on to expand an existing business you may already run from your home.

The second chapter in Part I contains forty-seven critical questions together with answers or ways to develop answers that will guide you in starting and positioning yourself successfully in a home-based business. Chapter 2 also includes tips to help you understand how to make your decision about which business may be right for you as well as reminders and advice about the legal, financial, and personal aspects of initiating a home-based business. We answer such questions as: how to assess your business interests; how to test the market; how to learn about potential competition; and how to capitalize your business. Because some of these issues deserve a fuller discussion of your options, at times we refer you to our other books, where you can find more in-depth information.

In Part II of this book, we explain how you can set up your home office so that your computer and its peripherals, such as multifunction devices, enable you to perform the most basic as well as sophisticated marketing, administrative, and financial functions. We will describe, for example, how you can connect into the online world, which provides you with up-to-the-minute market research, business news, consumer trends, and other important information. We also will categorize and discuss dozens of powerful software packages such as contact managers, database programs, and word-processing/desktop publishing software that can help you track customers, produce attractive mailings to potential new clients, and create top-notch letters and proposals. As you will learn, the well-equipped home office need suffer no disadvantage from the larger office, as long as you know how to take advantage of the knowledge and capabilities available to you with your computer.

Who This Book Is For

We believe this book can assist all those who are looking for a way to earn a living, raise their income, expand an existing business, or simply fulfill a dream of being their own boss. But if there is any single identifying factor that describes the person for whom we've written this book, it is the term "propreneur." We've been using this word for years in our seminars and in other books, and for a good reason. When we say propreneur, we distinguish today's self-employed individual from the traditional entrepreneur, who is usually in business primarily to make money and build a business. A propreneur may never have wanted to run a business but has discovered for one reason or another that he or she is driven to learn something new, to follow a passion, or simply to try out a dream about making a better livelihood doing what he or she enjoys. The propreneur, therefore, starts a home business based on curiosity, personal interest, and a desire for fulfillment rather than a more impersonal inclination to create a business per se.

We have written this book therefore for both entrepreneurs and propreneurs. We have chosen an eclectic group of businesses, covering a diverse assortment of fields, including publishing, math, science, communications, finance, real estate, the arts, and many other areas. Whatever your interest, we are sure that you will be able to find something that strikes you as a business to consider. Even if you don't like the businesses we've described, we believe you will find grist for the mill in the sense that the profiles may motivate you to think about and discover other opportunities you might explore or invest in. Each person has one or more areas of expertise, and so finding your niche simply requires asking yourself the right questions and finding the right answers.

One additional issue you may be wondering about is how computer literate you need to be to read this book . . . and profit from it. While we do not want to suggest that you must be a computer fanatic or have extensive previous experience in computers and software, this book is definitely based on the premise that the future is upon us and that future includes computers. As long as you are willing to learn new things, and have an open mind, nimble fingers, and at least some degree of curiosity for what computers can do, you can take advantage of the opportunities described in this book.

How to Use This Book

We suggest that you begin by reading or skimming the profiles of the businesses in Part I. Alternatively, you might examine the lists in the Appendix at the back of the book that categorize the businesses in various ways, such as word businesses vs. numbers businesses, full-time businesses vs. part-time vs. add-on businesses, and so on. Using these lists, you can then pick out the businesses you might be most interested in, and read only those selections.

Once you identify a few businesses you want to know more about, you can move on quickly to check out the various resources for additional information that we have cited. You may also need more information about how to select or start your computer business. Chapter 2 is for this. It contains forty-seven questions you should explore and answer to select, set up, and position your business most successfully. As stated above, this chapter reviews many critical issues in selecting a business and getting it up and running. It covers various legal and financial issues you need to consider, as well as ideas about marketing your business and finding your first clients. We urge you to read Chapter 2 if you do not have prior experience in business or if you have never really given serious thought to running a home-based business and are essentially starting from scratch. Once you've answered these questions, you will have a viable business plan you can begin to implement immediately.

Whether you are in business already or just beginning to think about it, we suggest that everyone read Part II of the book. Here you will find valuable information on setting up a home office that works, one that facilitates, rather than hinders, your work. Each chapter details how your computer and its peripherals can support you in many critical ways, from tapping into online databases to performing powerful mail-merge functions for sending out your marketing materials.

Some people may find the information in Part II a breeze to follow, while others may feel overwhelmed since on the surface reading about hardware and software sounds highly technical and often refers to topics and machinery you may not know existed. Our experience is, however, that the more you read about technology, the easier it becomes to fathom. With experience comes knowledge. You will find yourself quickly picking up the vocabulary and even tidbits of conceptual understanding about the inner workings of your computer or software programs. Although you may never become a hacker from reading computer magazines and books, we have known more than one person who began their career as nearly computerphobic and over time developed a real fascination and love for computers. It can happen to anyone!

Actually, if you feel confused and frustrated about not understanding some of the material in Part II, you can take solace in knowing that you are not alone. Think of it this way: there is an entire computer industry that wants people like you to use computers and buy their products. They are trying day by day to make computers easier to operate, to write software manuals in plain English, and to make everything about using technology intuitive or flexible. When you sit down to use an accounting program, and you press a key because it seems like the right thing to do, and it works, you have just re-created what some company may have spent thousands of dollars to program so that it works the way the average person would have wanted it to. So don't fret: the computer industry aims to be either right alongside you, or at most only one step behind you.

Once you have completed this book, we would encourage you to read widely in many additional sources of information. Any time you devote to doing additional research is "money in the bank" if it saves you from making a wrong decision for your business or buying a needless item. Naturally, we enthusiastically recommend our other books that provide different gateways to becoming self-employed (*Finding Your Perfect Work, Best Home Business for the 90s, Home Businesses You Can Buy*) and that provide guides through the stages of self-employment (*Working from Home, Getting Business to Come to You, Secrets of Self-Employment,* and *Teaming Up*).

We counsel you to keep in mind that technology enables people to have their grasp equal and even exceed their reach, but to realize that, it's up to you to extend yourself with energy and persistence. We wish you success in achieving your goals.

PART I

Using Your Computer as a Business

IN RESEARCHING THIS BOOK, we reviewed over 175 computer-related businesses from the over 1,600 self-employment careers we concisely profile in the appendix to our book *Finding Your Perfect Work.* Of course, new businesses came to our attention and these were also considered. The task of selecting from an overwhelming set of choices and paring them down to the "best" of the best therefore demanded that we establish a group of criteria by which we would assess a business for inclusion in this book.

Obviously, the first and most natural was: Does the business truly need to use a computer per se, or is the computer an ancillary tool used for bookkeeping or writing letters? After all, computers, in one form or another, have become so extensively used in nearly all aspects of business today that one could classify practically any business as a candidate. Our goal, however, was to identify those businesses that depend significantly on the computer as their lifeblood. For example, a person doing Web-site design or desktop publishing clearly requires a computer at the heart of the business, while an export agent may use a computer in running the business, but it isn't central to exporting.

Additionally, we also included businesses in which using a computer to conduct the essential tasks involved makes the business substantially more profitable than trying to do it without one. A property management service, for example, can be much more effective and efficient by using a spreadsheet program to track their clients' income, expenses, and tax information than trying to rely on pen, paper, and calculators.

Beyond this logical parameter, however, several other criteria influenced our decisions, as follows:

Income Potential

Given the title of the book, we were next interested in businesses that would truly offer the opportunity to provide a meaningful income to the owner. In general, we searched for businesses in which the income potential would either be enough to categorize it as the equivalent of a full-time job, or enough to remunerate the person who does the business part-time and is counting on a certain level of income to make working worth the time. The figures we've quoted for income reflect reliable information from interviews with people in the field, or are reasonable estimates based on our knowledge and information about the field. Please note, however, that the fees and hourly rates we mention may vary due to a person's skill, experience, geographic location, and many other factors, so you will need to consider your personal circumstances in assessing your income potential.

We've also included several businesses that one might do on a less-than-part-time basis, but which we feel are worthwhile as add-ons to an existing business. For example, we review the business called "data conversion service," in which you assist companies that are changing software or upgrading computers and therefore need to convert massive amounts of old data to a new format without losing it. Chances are that if you're already running a related business, you could at least find clients over the course of a year who need this work and would hire you once they know that you offer the service. By adding "data conversion" to your letterhead, writing some news columns, or giving speeches or seminars, you may therefore get some business income you would not have had otherwise. This is true of all the add-on businesses we've included.

Last, we also included a few "idea businesses." These are possible businesses that reflect the fact that computers, and especially the Internet, often generate new ways to make money. These businesses are simply ideas for businesses; they're not yet tested. As far as we know, no one is actually doing them, unlike all the other businesses we included, which a substantial number of people are not only doing but doing successfully. While some other books mix hypothetical businesses with real ones and leave you wondering which are which, we have clearly identified these businesses as "ideas" with the lightbulb icon. We've included them in the book because our experience suggests that each one could be a good business for the person who has the right mix of skills to make it work.

Reasonable Ease of Entry

Our next criterion involved selecting businesses that for the most part are relatively easy to start and do not require special academic degrees. In the majority of cases, the business depends not on a diploma but on knowledge, experience, and ability. For instance, while it may help to have a B.A. or M.A. in finance to do business-plan or proposal writing, the degree is not at all necessary to succeed, since one's knowledge and experience in many different areas are likely to be much more critical in getting clients and performing well in the business.

It is important to mention, however, that most of the businesses we've included do work best if you can bring some background or experience to the table.

Actually, we believe that this is true for any business venture, computer based or not. The person who has previously worked in the medical field, for example, will be able to start a medical billing business more quickly than the person who has never seen an ICD-9 code; similarly, the person who has worked with numbers before is probably better equipped to open a financial planning or billing and invoicing service than the person with a speech therapy background.

In short, the experience you already have is usually proportional to how long or short a learning curve you will experience and how many barriers you will encounter along the way. If you know little about a field, you will probably need to read a great deal, talk to people in the business, and take more time getting your business off the ground. You will also be more likely to struggle through the initial stages, especially when it comes to figuring out how much time it takes to get a job done and what you can charge for your work. In fact, novices frequently underestimate how long it takes them to complete a task, or they make mistakes and spend double or triple the time they expected to spend, and so end up earning much less money per job.

Although the businesses we've included generally have a reasonable ease of entry, we caution you to fully explore the specific personal issues that may have an impact on your success. We'll also address this issue more completely in chapter 2.

Variety

The expanding use of computers and software in recent years into vastly differing areas of work has meant that many, many fields are now computerized to some extent. We therefore aimed to include a wide variety of ways in which people of diverse interests could make a living and work using computers. We've selected a broad assortment of professions, from writing and publishing to health, finance, real estate, allied medical fields, teaching, design, business administration, marketing, music and various other artistic endeavors.

Demand

In the past decade, tens of thousands of people have started home businesses, many of whom did so by purchasing a "business opportunity." (See the box on page 6.) We have met people who have been successful with business opportunity programs, especially computer-oriented opportunities. Always check out a business opportunity thoroughly before buying it. Consult our book *Home Businesses You Can Buy,* written with Walter Zooi, for in-depth information on the types of business opportunities available for purchase and how to make sure you're getting what you pay for.

Although most home businesses are started from scratch, a variety of the businesses we discuss in this book can be started through a "business opportunity," a presumably complete blueprint you purchase from a company already in the business or that has some experience in the field. As you read this book, the question will naturally arise: Is it worth your money to buy one of these business opportunities or should you go it alone and rely on your own resources? Well, our response is that business opportunities are sometimes useful, and sometimes not, and you will need to do some homework to learn which is which. Here's why.

First, on the positive side, business opportunities, also known as "seller-assisted marketing plans," are simply a matter of people selling their expertise to help others start a business. Unlike a franchise, their value is that you are seldom obliged to pay continuing fees or a percentage of your income year in and year out, nor are you required to use their company name and adhere to strict internal rules about how you run your business. With a business opportunity, all you are doing is paying someone to sell you the ways and means to start your business and operate it in a way that has supposedly proved successful. The seller of the opportunity has presumably made all the mistakes a start-up business makes and through trial and error has come up with a business that works consistently. When you buy a business opportunity, you receive the benefit of years of groundwork which, hopefully, you won't have to repeat.

However, on the negative side, we emphasize two key operative terms that we feel people need to consider if they are interested in a business opportunity package. The first is "expertise." We believe you must ask plenty of questions about the seller's true expertise in this business. How long has he or she been in business? Is the seller currently involved in performing the same business in another area, and if so what are the results? How much does the seller really know about this business? The second operative term is "opportunity," meaning that you need to assess who is really getting the opportunity here, you or the seller? Is there really a market for the business large enough to fulfill your expectations and financial needs, or is the seller of the business opportunity getting the only real opportunity?

Unfortunately, since the business opportunity market exploded in the past decade, there have been highly reputable vendors, but there have also been many others who crossed the limits of honesty and integrity in selling or pricing their packages. As a result, increasing numbers of states are monitoring the industry, with about half the states specifically regulating seller-assisted marketing plans that have a purchase price of over $500; a few states have lower thresholds. Most of these regulations are fairly weak, but they often require that businesses must register with the state attorney general's office, that each prospective customer must be given in advance an offering prospectus listing the executives of the company and stating specifically what is included in the price of the business opportunity, including any goods, services, and training. In many states, the buyer also gets a period of time, such as three days, in which to change his mind and obtain a refund of his purchase price. Last, many states bar the seller from making representations about how much income you can earn, or if allowed to do so, he or she must report how many prior purchasers of the plan have made back their initial investment.

Ultimately, our advice to you is:

1. Check out as many references as possible before buying a business opportunity. Use Dun & Bradstreet, previous buyers, current operators, state, county, and city consumer protection offices, Better Business Bureaus, the Federal Trade Commission, and U.S. postal inspectors to find out if the company has a good reputation and a record of honest dealings. Furthermore, if you live in California, Connecticut, Florida, Georgia, Indiana, Iowa, Kentucky, Louisiana, Maine, Maryland, Michigan, Minnesota, Nebraska, New Hampshire, North Carolina, Ohio, Oklahoma, South Carolina, South Dakota, Texas, Utah, Virginia, or Washington remember that a business opportunity company that sells in your state, no matter where it is headquartered, must be registered and follow your state's guidelines. Call your state's attorney general's office to get information about the regulations affecting any contract you may sign.

2. Find out specifically what you will get with your purchase in terms of training, materials, and hardware/software. Ask also about how many other people in your area may already own the business or will be allowed to purchase it, since you want to avoid entering an already saturated market. Do your own checking in the community as well.

3. Don't hesitate to negotiate on price. Some business opportunity companies advertise a high price but will drop it if you bargain with them.

4. Don't expect that you will necessarily be more successful by starting your business through the purchase of an opportunity than

you would be if you began on your own. In fact, buying an opportunity can even be deceiving, leading you to think you can work a little less hard or that you have a backup system to support you through hard times. In reality, although you may have a blueprint for how to do your business, getting it successfully under way will still require hard work, long hours, and creative thinking to bring it into the real world of cash flow from satisfied customers.

So watch out for myths about business opportunities. Getting any business off the ground requires dedication, good personal skills, and business acumen, all of which business opportunities cannot truly provide. Also, the great number of companies selling these opportunities have in some cases saturated the country with a particular business to the point that a new entrant today would have a hard time competing profitably.

In mentioning this warning, we are not intending to focus on or blame any particular company selling a business opportunity. Clearly the demand for any business varies greatly from community to community, but we wanted to make sure that the businesses we included in this book were generally, to the best of our knowledge, not saturated but actually had a good probability of being reasonably in demand. As a result, we have excluded several popular businesses that we believe are oversaturated at this time, including personalized children's books, credit repair, 900 phone numbers, laser cartridge repair, and scholarship matching.

CHAPTER 1

100 Computer Home Businesses in Profile

A t the beginning of each profile below, you will note a group of as many as four icons that identify various characteristics of the business. The key to the four groups of icons is as follows:

GROUP 1: Type of Business Category

ABC **Word Business**—The alphabet block refers to businesses that are related to word processing, writing, and publishing.

**Numbers Business**—The # sign identifies businesses that are related to number crunching, like bookkeeping and auditing.

Database Business—A set of Rolodex cards refers to businesses that are based upon creating and maintaining a database, such as a referral service or a software locator service.

Graphics Business—A T-square/triangle identifies a business that is based primarily upon using graphics software like desktop video or market mapping.

Computer Service Business—A floppy computer disk indicates businesses that involve providing a service to help others better use or maintain their computers, such as computer consulting or a computer repair service.

Communications Businesses—A telephone symbolizes modem and communication-based businesses like Web site publication, information broker, and electronic clipping services.

MS **Multimedia Business**—Interlocked *MS* indicate that the businesses involve producing or managing multimedia content including sound, video, graphics and animation.

Multiple Application Businesses—A series of interlocking rings represents businesses that rely upon multiple applications like association management, which may involve word processing, number crunching, and database functions.

GROUP 2: Income Potential

 Full-Time—A full glass identifies businesses that have sufficient income potential to provide a full-time income. However, most full-time businesses can be operated part-time as well.

 Part-Time—A crescent moon refers to businesses like keeping sports league statistics or creating computerized astrological charts that are most suitable as a sideline business for supplementing other income and most likely would not yield a full-time income.

 Add-On—A plus sign indicates a business like a disk backup service that makes an ideal add-on service to an existing business. While these businesses most likely will not produce sufficient revenue to become a full-time or even part-time, stand-alone business, they can be an excellent way to attract initial customers for a related business or as additional services you provide for your existing customers.

GROUP 3: Location of Work

 At-Home—A house indicates that the business can be done AT home. While you will probably need to go out of your home for client meetings, or to market these businesses or even to pick up work, you will be able to do the actual work of these businesses in your home.

 From-Home—A car indicates that while you can run these businesses FROM home you will actually do most of your work elsewhere. In these businesses, your home can be your base of operation, but they will take you away from home to deliver your product or service.

GROUP 4: Noteworthy Characteristic

In this last group, we have identified one major characteristic we believe distinguishes a particular business, as follows:

Idea Business—A lightbulb highlights an idea that we believe could become a good business. Such listings aren't actually proven businesses; they are bright ideas for how you could use your computer to make money. As far as we know, no one is doing them as yet, but they hold the potential for becoming successful businesses.

 High Income Potential—These businesses can potentially produce a six-figure income without moving out of the home or adding more than one staff person.

 Evergreen—These businesses have been around for many years and will undoubtedly be around for many more. We call them evergreen businesses.

 Recession-Resistant—These are businesses that tend to weather or even prosper during economic downturns.

 Up and Coming—These are relatively new businesses that are on the rise in popularity.

 Low Start-Up Costs—These businesses do not require much up-front investment to get under way.

Using the Resources in This Book

At the end of each profile, we have listed resources that can be useful to you in learning about or actually operating each business. This information is intended as a starting point. Most of the resources are not specifically about how to start such a business.

So, unless otherwise indicated, DO NOT phone these resources, especially the associations and organizations, expecting that they will help you get started in a business. Some may provide you with general information and others may be useful for networking, but unless indicated, none are in the franchising business or offer actual business plans to get you started.

The resources are generally listed in the following order:

- Books
- Magazines/Journals
- Web Sites
- Software
- Associations/Organizations
- Courses
- Franchises/Business Opportunities
- Newsgroups

As we stated earlier, the businesses listed here do not require an advanced degree or years of formal study. Many, however, do require expertise. With the proper background and experience, perhaps a course or two, extensive research and initiative you can be up and running with even the most complicated of businesses, such as CGI or Java Programming, in six months' time. Also, please note, these descriptions are presented only as "thumbnail" sketches, simple overviews, of the main aspects involved in starting and running each of the businesses. They are provided as starting points from which you can begin the journey that might lead you to an exciting and rewarding home-based business.

1.

Abstracting Service

Behind the scenes of the 6,000-plus online database services available today are scores of abstracting services whose job is to condense information of all kinds into a brief format for storage and review. Culling from professional journals in medicine, engineering, science, and other technical fields to more common periodicals and books, the professional abstracting service turns lengthy material into digestible tidbits of ten to fifteen sentences. These synopses then facilitate the work of researchers and browsers, who obtain this information online or on CD-ROM products.

In addition to database applications, abstracting services also frequently work with corporations, creating summaries of books and articles of interest to the companies' executives and technical people, as well as to their customers. Some corporations make extensive use of abstracting in order to stay up to date with our burgeoning information-based society. Considering that information is doubling every year, the market for abstracting services will grow and grow and grow.

Running an abstracting service requires an ability to synthesize and consolidate information and, of course, excellent writing skills. It also helps to have a background in and first-hand knowledge of the areas in which you work, since much of the material is specialized in scientific and technical fields. Finally, given that the profession feeds into online information services, you must also have or acquire a familiarity with database services, CD-ROM publishers, and other companies that supply and deal with information.

The best way to get business as an abstracting service is to write several samples that you can use in a portfolio to show database publishers and others. Many database publishers hire only local freelancers. To find publishers in your area, decide which type of database you want to work with and search a directory like the *Epsco Index and Abstract Dictionary* or *Cuadra Directory of Online Databases* to identify publishers in that field by address. To get corporate work, contact corporate librarians and the department responsible for technical writing.

An abstractor can normally charge $4 to $14 per abstract. This business is also a good add-on to an indexing service, or an editing or technical writing service.

Resources

Abstracting and Indexing Services in Perspective, published by Information Resources Press, 1993, ISBN: 0878150439, 1110 N. Glebe Road, Arlington, VA 22201, (703) 558-8270.

The Information Broker's Handbook, by Sue Rugge and Alfred Glossbrenner. The Information Professional's Institute, 46 Hiller Drive, Oakland, CA 94618, 1997, (510) 649-9743, Web: *http://www*.ipn.net/ipi, E-mail 76220.454@compuserve.com. Although this book covers a somewhat different career, it contains much valuable information about abstracting, databases, and the electronic information industry.

AMERICAN SOCIETY FOR INFORMATION SCIENTISTS, 8720 Georgia Avenue, Ste. 501, Silver Spring, MD 20910-3602, (301) 495-0900.

NATIONAL FEDERATION OF ABSTRACTING & INFORMATION SERVICES, 1429 Walnut Street, Philadelphia, PA 19102, (215) 563-2406.

Newsgroups: misc.int-property
sci.finance.abstracting

2.

Answering/Voice Mail Service

There's no shortage of answering services for businesses and professionals who need telephone coverage when they're away from their offices, but most services simply take brief messages in a cold, impersonal fashion. Therefore, a home-based business can fulfill a need by providing a truly personalized answering service that operates like a knowledgeable administrative assistant. Such an answering service is particularly useful for small businesses and individuals such as plumbers, contractors, and repairmen who often miss new opportunities by not returning a call or responding to a need immediately. Other potential clients include businesses that need or want to have a "live" person answering their phone because their customers expect it or would be put off by a pager, an answering machine, or voice mail, as well as people on the move like salespeople and long-distance truckers, military personnel, students, and, if you think about it, people in jail such as white-collar criminals and other individuals who don't have their own phones and need a private answering line. Still other businesses need twenty-four-hour answering for orders on their 800 phone numbers.

The logistics of operating an answering service are perfect for the home-based person. Most phone companies can now set up your phone to ring differently for each incoming phone number, so you can answer the calls with whichever business greeting identifies the client being called. You can then take messages for your clients using your computer and word-processing, database or contact-management software program that allows you to keyboard a complete record of the information. With an internal fax/modem board, you can then immediately fax the typed transcript of the call to your client's office so that the message awaits the person upon return, or you could call or page the client if immediate action is required. The advantage to this kind of operation is the level of support a home-based person can supply her or his clients. You will screen calls, decide what's important and what's not, take messages, give responses to the client's customers, and in general represent his or her business more fully than a typical answering service.

An additional option in running an answering service is to offer a sophisticated voice mail system for new business clients who will pay you rather than purchasing and setting up their own voice mail system when they're just starting out. Voice mail has many advantages over a traditional answering machine, since it can recite multiple outgoing messages using a menu system ("press 1 for x, 2 for y," and so on), and it can direct incoming messages to specific mailbox locations for privacy. Running a voice mail system requires a dedicated PC with a large hard drive (because of the space required to convert voice to digital form), a voice mail board, and software. You may also need to reconfigure and possibly add to your incoming phone lines to handle the needs of your clients.

The fees you can charge for this business will depend on your locale and the type of clients you get, but many small businesses will pay for a high-quality answering service if you can help them win a few additional customers. If you had five or ten clients, each paying you a $100 to $200 per month, you could conceivably earn between $5,000 to $25,000 per year just by putting your phone to work!

The best ways to get business include networking and advertising in the yellow pages and in local business newspapers. It helps to get clients to sign on for several months at a time. Additionally, referrals from satisfied clients can significantly expand your business, so you should also consider offering a promotion that gets clients to refer others to you in exchange for a discount.

Resources

BIGMOUTH (Talking Technology) is a voice mail board for a single line. 1125 Atlantic Avenue, Ste. 101, Alameda, CA 94501, (800) 934-4884, *http://www*.tti.net

THE RESOUND FROM DIGITCOM CORPORATION is a sophisticated PC-based voice mail system available for under $5,000. The price includes a dedicated PC. Contact Jimmy Chin at 2190 Colorado Avenue, Ste. B, Santa Monica, CA 90404, (310) 584-0750, *http://www*. digitcom.com

V/M, INC. VOICE COMPUTER PRODUCTS. You can hear an example at (800) 714-9192 or (408) 365-8601.

Newsgroups: comp.dcom.telecom
alt.voicenet
alt.dcom.telecom
comp.dcom.telecom.tech

3.

Association Management Services

People love to belong. As a result they join associations, clubs, and organizations of all kinds, organized around the sharing of hobbies and economic interests as well as religious and fraternal affiliations. In many cases, such associations are small enough that their members can take care of all organizational and administrative needs. But when an association grows beyond the size that its volunteer officers can effectively handle, they often turn to an association management service (also called an executive director service) to provide organizational and financial continuity.

As an association manager, you will probably find yourself responsible for keeping the files on membership and dues, paying bills, sending out frequent flyers and announcements to a mailing list, and possibly writing and publishing a monthly newsletter. As you might imagine, the more services you can offer, the more you can charge, and the higher class of clientele you can command. Similarly, the more efficient you are at performing these tasks, the more clients you might be able to handle. So running an association management service requires good management skills, a flexible communication style, and, in today's PC-based environment, a fair amount of hands-on skill with many kinds of software: accounting and bookkeeping packages, contact and database management systems, and word-processing/desktop publishing programs.

Home-based association managers can earn up to $50,000 per year, billing out at $35 an hour and working from thirty hours per week to full-time. If you start a new association yourself, you might earn an additional $20,000 to $30,000 by paying yourself a salary rather than an hourly wage.

If you already have a background in management, finance, or administration, some of the best ways to get into this business are to contact the presidents of professional and trade associations directly, network with professional organizations, or offer to do a seminar on administration for volunteer organizations. Alternatively, you might begin this business more informally until you gain a track record by volunteering to administrate a small group you belong to yourself, and then with experience you can survey the officers of other organizations in your community to locate paid opportunities.

Resources

The Encyclopedia of Associations, by Gale Research, Detroit, MI, ISBN: 0810361795, is available in the reference section of most libraries. This three-volume set lists literally thousands of local, state, regional, and national associations, both large and small. It can be one of your primary sources for locating prospective clientele.

AMERICAN SOCIETY OF ASSOCIATION EXECUTIVES (ASAE), 1575 I Street, N.W., Washington, DC 20005-1168, (202) 626-2723, has useful publications and local chapters.

THE SOCIETY FOR NON-PROFIT ORGANIZATIONS, 6314 Odana Road, Ste. 1, Madison, WI 53719, (800) 424-7367, (608) 274-9777. A resource center for nonprofit organizations of all types, including associations, throughout the country.

4.

Astrology Charting Service

If you believe that your fate and destiny are determined or influenced by the stars and are willing to serve other people who believe and will pay for this information, you can use your home-based PC to run an astrological charting service. Computers are actually the perfect tool to track astrological databases, such as the movement of the stars and planets around the zodiac, along with a client's birthday and other relevant information.

Today even businesspeople consult astrologers about their businesses. In fact, a French business school (HEC) reports that 10 percent of French businesses use astrologers, usually for a second opinion about job applicants.

By tapping into the astrological databases now available on several software packages, you can prepare in ten minutes what formerly took hours of time: an astrological chart with interpretations about future events. Astrological forecasting software requires only the customer's date, place, and time of birth. With this information, it will determine the configurations of the heavens at that moment and place and compile a star chart from which a forecast is drawn. Then, depending on your equipment, you can print out the client's information as a simple table or, if you have a color plotter or printer, like the Hewlett-Packard 820CSE, you can produce a high-quality full-color chart with beautiful graphics and designs.

The going rates for a charting service range from $25 to as much as $75 for a comprehensive astrological chart. The most successful marketing aims at getting people to buy a chart at special turning points in their lives like a birthday, wedding, or birth when they wish to know what the future holds in store for them. Advertising in local "New Age" publications, on the Web, and through word of mouth are your best sources of customers. You might also want to consider offering a discount package, such as two-for-one specials, once-a-month clubs, and so on, in order to bring clients in and keep them coming back. In addition, you can do group, organization, or family charts and, using a laptop computer and portable ink-jet printer, do charts at parties and other events.

Resources

The Astrologer's Handbook, by Louis S. Acker and Frances Sakoian, New York, HarperCollins (paper), 1993, ISBN: 006272004X.

THE AMERICAN FEDERATION OF ASTROLOGERS, Inc., P.O. Box 22040, Tempe, AZ 85283-2040, (602) 838-1751, fax: (602) 838-8293, Web: *http://www.*astrologers.com.

ASTROLABE SOFTWARE produces over thirty software programs for astrological charting for both Windows and DOS. Programs include the Astrolabe's Professional Natal Report and the Complete Forecaster Report, and a wide range of other charting services. 350 Underpass Road, P.O. Box 1750, Brewster, MA 02631, (800) 843-6682; (508) 896-5081, Web: *http://www*.alabe.com

Newsgroups: alt.astrology
　　　　　　　alt.astrology.marketplace

5.

Backup Service

Most businesses take little or no precautions when it comes to backing up their computers. They fail to think about the financial loss and operational problems they would incur if their files were damaged or destroyed due to fire, theft, or hardware failure. Even businesses that make backups usually do not do it regularly nor do they keep their backup files off-site for safekeeping. So if you are a technically oriented computer buff, and especially if you already have a computer consulting, training, or repair/maintenance service, you could have a ready-made group of clients for whom you could provide backup services as a profitable addition to your business.

You can run a backup service in any of several ways. Some services go to the client's place of business and perform the backup on-site, using a portable external hard drive or tape drive, taking the data away to a vault or to their home office for safekeeping. Other backup services do the work over the phone lines in the evening when the client's business is closed, using remote communications software and a modem to back up the data to a hard drive on their home computer. Depending on your client's needs, you can perform the backup as often as every night or as infrequently as once a month. Still another idea is to provide data archiving and backup using CD-ROM. The latest thing, but producing the least revenue, is to refer customers to an Internet-based backup service.

The technology for backup services is continually improving, with many new devices on the market that offer very high-speed backups and complete accuracy. For instance, recent generation tape drives costing less than $300 can back up a 1.2-gigabyte hard disk on one tape. Removable hard drives, like Iomega's popular Jaz drive and SyQuest's SQJetSX offer storage capacities of up to 1.3 gigabytes as well. Additionally, communications software such as *PCAnywhere* allow the backup process to run quickly and smoothly, and data compression programs can cut a file down to a quarter of its original size, thereby saving valuable tape or disk space, while services like Connected Online Backup (*http://www*.connected.com), operating over the Internet, make it possible to back up only new and changed files.

Potential clients for a backup service range from the administrative departments of large companies in need of regular backups or off-site safekeeping to small businesses and stores, doctors' offices, and others who don't want to spend the time or don't have the expertise. The way this service is priced varies. Some charge a flat monthly fee; others charge by the megabyte; still others by the minute. On average, expect to realize about $50 per client per month. You can also beef up your fees by adding other services, such as encryption of data, and maintenance services, such as defragmentation and cleaning of hard drives, virus checking, laser printer maintenance, and renting out hardware for companies with temporary problems or growing needs.

We can recommend this business and its allied services largely as an add-on to any existing computer business, because our research indicates that the costs of marketing and operating a stand-alone backup business are apparently not worth the income. The business can be good, however, if you have clients for whom you already provide related computer services. Also, you may expand this business by offering other computer preventive maintenance services, such as checking for viruses, cleaning the heads of floppy disk drives, and defragmenting hard disks.

Resources

Biz Kit, Rob Cosgrove. Quantum Tech, 376 South Mendenhall Road, Memphis, TN 38117, (901) 682-0732, (800) 552-7814, *http://www*.alice.net.

Includes book, software marketing kit, technical support bulletin board, and backup service through the Internet.

Newsgroups: umn.local-lists.techc-backup

6.

Billing and Invoicing Service

Repeatedly we hear that billing is the most time-consuming administrative task successful home-based businesses have. As a result they, like many other small businesses and independent professionals, frequently get behind schedule in mailing their bills and invoices out to their clients. Often this is because many small businesses still do invoices inefficiently by hand, but most are simply too busy to stay on top of their bookkeeping needs. Other people have psychological hang-ups about taking care of themselves around money. This reality opens the door for the person who can specialize in billing and invoicing and who understands how to bring in the cash when a company needs it.

The best way to operate your billing service is to arrange a regular daily or weekly pickup, either by fax or in person, of all your client's transaction reports. Then, using any one of today's sophisticated billing software packages, you keyboard each transaction received, update the customer's total balance, and print out the invoice for mailing. Finally, as checks are mailed in either to your address or directly to the business, you record the payment and do any account maintenance required. In the case of tardy payments, you might also perform "soft" collections such as issuing reminder invoices or calling the customer in accordance with your state laws on dunning.

A billing and invoicing business is easy to start and requires only a small investment in equipment. You will need a personal computer with a hard disk for file storage, a reliable dot matrix printer with a wide carriage and ability to print three-part invoice forms, and one of the professional billing and invoicing software packages such as *TimeSlips* (for Windows), *TimeSlips* (for Macintosh), or *WinVoice*.

Although you don't need to be an accountant to perform billing and invoicing, at the minimum, you should be very organized and efficient, have excellent math skills, and be familiar with your computer and software. Additionally, we believe this business works best as an add-on to an existing bookkeeping or other business service where you are already providing work for a client who can afford to hire you. The risks of the business include not getting enough clients to keep your business profitable and spending too much time getting the invoices done to make it worth your time.

The fees you can charge for billing and invoicing depend on the type of clients you find and the time it takes you to do the work. If your client is a small professional practice, such as a design firm or law office, you can probably charge between $15 and $30 dollars per hour. On the other hand, some billing services are able to negotiate taking a percentage of any unpaid invoices that they manage to collect through their efforts.

Resources

See chapter 3 for references to *TimeSlips* and *WinVoice*.

7.

Bookkeeping Service

This numbers-related business is an "evergreen" business, because bookkeeping is a required business activity, not a discretionary one. The need for outside bookkeeping services is changing. On the one hand, the number of small businesses, customary users of outside bookkeeping service, is growing. On the other hand, low-cost and easy-to-use accounting software makes bookkeeping an increasingly do-it-yourself function. Do they still need help? The answer is often "yes" because they encounter problems using their software, and some people recognize that they have psychological blocks when it comes to managing their finances. If they are using a single-entry system, their bank statements and check register may not balance. So enter the bookkeeping "consultant."

Traditionally, a bookkeeping service performs such tasks as keeping a client's financial records (accounts receivable and payable), reconciling bank statements, doing payroll and invoicing, and preparing financial reports (profit/loss statements and balance sheets) for tax or accounting purposes. In other words, the bookkeeper carries out all the tasks of doing the books, up to the point where an accountant can step in to interpret the financial information for the client and provide business and tax-planning advice.

Many excellent software packages are available today to fully computerize a home PC–based bookkeeping service, including Intuit's *Quick-Books Pro, Peachtree Complete Accounting, M.Y.O.B.,* and others. The decreasing cost of laptop computers and the popularity of removable disk drives also make it possible to perform your work at the client's place of business, or at your own home office, depending on your client's needs.

To succeed in this business you must enjoy doing detailed, accurate, and reliable work. While you don't need a degree in accounting to be a bookkeeper, it helps to have had several basic academic or vocational courses if you are putting yourself in a position to manage financial issues for people who aren't good with numbers and who don't have a suitable background.

Typically a bookkeeping service can gross from $20,000 to $60,000 a year, charging from $15 to $50 an hour. There are many ways to expand a bookkeeping service, however. For example, you can branch out into doing tax preparation or billing and invoicing for your clients.

The best way to build a bookkeeping service is to focus your marketing on businesses within a twenty-to-thirty-minute drive from your home. Networking through personal contacts and business and trade organizations such as the chamber of commerce can be a valuable source of business. You should also definitely have a yellow-pages advertisement, as new businesses are constantly starting while others often switch bookkeepers. Finally, you might also explore obtaining overload or referral business from CPA firms, other bookkeeping firms, and financial planners.

Resources

Keeping the Books: Basic Recordkeeping and Accounting for the Small Business, by Jerry Jinnett and Linda Pinson, Dover, NH, Upstart Publishing Co., 1996, ISBN: 1574100289.

Simplified Accounting for Non-Accountants, by Rick Stephan Hayes and C. Richard Baker, New York, Wiley, 1986.

Small Business Accounting Handbook, Small Business Administration Publications, Box 15434, Forth Worth, TX 76119. The SBA also has many other free or low-cost publications. Call them at (800) 827-5722 to obtain information and a catalog.

THE AMERICAN INSTITUTE OF PROFESSIONAL BOOKKEEPERS, 6001 Montrose Road, Ste. 207, Rockville, MD 20852, (800) 622-0121. A professional association providing news, education, and training services for bookkeepers.

Franchises

AFTE Business Analysts, 2180 North Loop West, Houston, TX 77018, (713) 957-1592.

General Business Services, 1010 University Park Drive, Waco, TX 76707, (800) 583-6181.

Newsgroups: biz.comp.accounting

8.

Bulletin Board Service (BBS)

While most bulletin board service operators have switched their activity to the Internet, bulletin board systems are still being established in countries where Internet access remains limited. Jack Rickard, publisher of *Boardwatch* magazine, observes that hobbyists have gone to the World Wide Web while people who pursued BBSs as moneymaking ventures have largely become Internet Service Providers (ISPs).

So if you are now operating a BBS, consider becoming an Internet Service Provider (see #45, Internet Service Provider that follows). You can still operate in a spare bedroom or a corner of your living room and you will still be billing people for providing local dial-up access.

If you are in a location that does not yet provide reasonably priced access to the Internet, you can still obtain one of the specialized BBS software programs such as *TBBS* (eSoft), *Wildcat!* (Mustang Software), *Major BBS* (Galacticom, Inc.) or *PCBoard* (Clark Development) that allows your callers to communicate and also keeps track of the time people spend online.

Resources

The BBS Construction Kit: All the Software and Expert Advice You Need to Start Your Own BBS Today/Book and Disk, by David Wolfe, New York, Wiley, 1994, ISBN: 0471007978.

Boardwatch magazine, 8500 West Bowles Ave., Ste. 210, Littleton, CO 80123, (800) 933-6038, *http://www*.boardwatch.com, monthly magazine published by Jack Rickard and Gary Funk containing articles of interest to

BBS operators and Internet service providers and others personally and professionally interested in the online world.

Directory of Internet Service Providers. Lists Internet service providers by area code. Comes out bimonthly. Published by *Boardwatch* magazine.

Newsgroups: fido7.bbsnews.talk
comp.bbs.majorbbs
alt.bbs.wciv
ieee.bbs.help
alt.binaries.bbs
alt.bbs
alt.bbs.ads
alt.bbs.internet

9.

Business Plan Writer

A business plan writer helps develop a road map for where a business is headed, laying out the estimates and projections of expenses and revenues that will predict whether the business is feasible. If you understand what's involved in the financial, marketing, and administrative aspects of taking a business idea from concept to reality, you have the basic know-how to become a business plan writer. While business plan writers depend heavily on word processing and spreadsheets, helping a client successfully develop a business plan is as much a communications process as a writing task.

Most experts advise that you develop plans on your own. Your clients are paying you to develop a plan that will stand out in terms of presentation, organization, and unique focus on the company. Specialized software is available to help the business plan writer analyze and present alternative projections for a business, use spreadsheets, and develop "what if" scenarios. These programs are helpful in helping you organize the content of a business plan, but we do not recommend that you use them exclusively to develop the plan. Here are a few such packages:

BizPlanBuilder (Jian Tools for Sales) has more than thirty file templates and linked financial work sheets to use as the basis for your plan.

Business Plan Pro (Palo Alto Software) offers a customizable, easy-to-navigate package plus a directory of sources of loans and venture capital.

Success, Inc. (Dynamic Pathways) is a comprehensive package that links to spreadsheet programs for financial analysis.

Tim Berry's Business Plan Toolkit (Palo Alto Software), a favorite of Macintosh users, works with Excel's spreadsheet.

As we said, these packages can be helpful to you in preparing the business plan, but you should not rely on them to do a standard plan for your clients. The best business plan writers create a unique plan for each client.

New businesses provide a good market for business planners, but often the best clients are those businesses that are well established and are seeking funding to expand. Other occasions when a business plan can be a necessity are when a business is wanting to franchise or to be acquired.

Business plan writing can be lucrative. Fees can range from $2,000 to $5,000 or more per plan, and annual gross earnings can exceed $100,000. Developing a professional relationship with bank-lending officers and organizations like Small Business Development Centers that work with new entrepreneurs and can refer business to you is one of the best ways to market yourself. Networking through trade and business organizations can also be effective, as well as giving speeches or teaching courses on starting and running a business. Showing a sample of your own business plan or other plans you have developed can be more important than having a brochure.

Resources

The Business Plan Guide for Independent Consultants, by Herman
    Holtz, New York, Wiley, 1994, ISBN: 047159735X.

10.

Clip-Art Service

As desktop publishing and Internet publishing expand into more and more areas of business, trade, and professional communications, one corollary development will be the increase in the need for generic and specialized illustration that publishers can turn to when they need inexpensive and quick artwork. Many published pieces require visual material, from spot illustrations to large, colorful scenes, to accompany the written word or simply to spice up the layout.

If you have an artistic bent, and are interested in learning to use design and drawing software, starting a clip-art business can earn you some extra income. You might focus your talents on doing specialized artwork, such as religious or technical drawings, or you might try to develop a unique style of art which you can then self-syndicate or sell to a clip-art software publisher.

The challenge in running a clip-art business is marketing your work. If you want to go big-time, you might consider packaging your diskette or CD-ROM of clip art and selling it retail in as many outlets as you can get. Alternatively, you could pursue the smaller self-publishing route and simply advertise your work in computer magazines or publications as a mail-order product, or try to sell it as shareware over the Internet from which users can download it. You could also sell subscriptions for a year-round clip-art service and provide monthly diskettes of new art. Your clients could include advertising agencies, graphic designers, in-house art departments, and any organization that produces regular newsletters or other publications using illustrations.

There is no standard pricing for clip art in the industry, but if you have a distinctive or unusual style, you might be able to earn from a few extra thousand dollars per year to much more.

Resources

Books, Books, Books: A Treasury of Clip Art, by Darcie Clark Frohardt, Englewood, CO, Libraries Unlimited, 1995, ISBN: 1563082659.

Clip Art: Image Enhancement & Integration, by Gary Glover, New York, McGraw-Hill, 1993, ISBN: 0070235686.

GRAPHIC ARTIST'S BOOK CLUB, P.O. Box 12526, Cincinnati, OH 45212-0526, (800) 937-0963, a book club with a monthly newsletter, a main selection, and discounted special offers.

Newsgroups: alt.binaries.clip-art
comp.graphics.misc

11. 🗑 🏠 ☀

Collection Agency

Many businesses rely on collection agencies to collect on delinquent accounts, and there is no reason to think this need will diminish. In fact, during tough economic times, collections become even more vital. According to the *Los Angeles Times,* the number of business collection agencies goes up 20 percent during recessions.

Today the collection business is changing in ways that give a home-based collection service a distinct advantage in serving small businesses. While large collection agencies cannot afford to take on smaller accounts, or give up on some small accounts after three letters, a home-based service can take on such business and, by operating efficiently, obtain reimbursements for its smaller clients and still make sufficient money to prosper.

To succeed in this business you need to have good communication skills and the ability to write a good collection letter. You must also be able to walk a fine line between being firm and understanding when you deal directly with the people who owe money. Above all, you must know the laws in your state about collections, and you may need a state license and a bond. In addition, you must operate within the 1977 Fair Debt Collection Practices Act.

The quickest way to develop your business is to solicit professionals and businesses by phone or in person, including medical practices, small retail stores, and even nonprofit associations that have conducted donation campaigns. Health-care providers are an especially good market for a collection agency because three out of every four dollars sent out for collection are for hospital and medical bills not covered by insurance. Other markets include day-care providers, cable TV operators, companies who sell infomercial products in installments, and the growing number of spouses who need help collecting child-support money.

The collection business is now computerized with several specialized software packages on the market such as *Cash Collector* or *Debtmaster*. Their prices range from $100 to over $2,000. You will also want a good printer, since the professional quality of your letter can have an impact on a forgetful or negligent payer.

Home-based collection agencies earn up to $60,000 a year, although the typical average is $30,000 to $50,000. The competition is steep in this field, but by finding your niche, you can make a good living at it.

Resources

THE FAIR DEBT COLLECTION PRACTICES ACT, U.S. Code Annotated, St. Paul, MN, West Publishing Company. Updated annually. Available in libraries.

CASHCOLLECTOR software, Jian Tools for Sales, Inc., 1975 W. El Camino Real, Ste. 301, Mountainview, CA 94040, (415) 254-5600, (800) 559-5426, *http://www.* jianusa.com

DEBTMASTER software, Comtronic Systems, 205 N. Harris Avenue, Cle Elum, WA 98922, (509) 674-7000, *http://www.*debtmaster.com

Newsgroups: misc.business.credit

12.

Composer/Sound Designer

You hear it everywhere. Television programs, cable programs, commercials, promotional videos, training videos, CD-ROM and multimedia programs, computer games—even on the Web. Never before has such a wide variety of music been used in so many media. Where does all this music come from? It can come from you. Whether you're an accomplished, trained musician or composer, or an intuitive, creative lover of music, today's computer-based music-making technology makes it possible to compose and record music, right at home and with sound quality technically superior to the best recording studios used in the 1960s. And with the growth of many new media and markets that require fresh, new sounds we feel that this is an excellent climate for home computer–based composers.

The home-based digital studio doesn't require extensive soundproofing or costly renovations to living quarters. Many successful composers work out of a spare room, garage, basement—even bedroom. The reason for this is that, due to MIDI technology, you can write music that will be performed electronically by electronic keyboards, sound modules, and sound cards. An entire sixty-six-voice symphony can be written and realistically performed electronically and recorded without a single microphone. No outside noise gets in, and—especially important to apartment dwellers—no noise gets out, either.

Now, if you're interested enough to be reading this, chances are you already know something about MIDI and digital recording, so we won't get into much detail in terms of the technology. In addition to creating music through your computer, you can also record it. With a fast enough processor (Pentium, 133Mhz minimum or Power Mac), large enough hard drive (three Gigabyte, minimum), and the right sound card, you can also record music at CD quality or better resolution. This is especially helpful for providing music for multimedia or Internet-related projects.

The best way to get business always starts with a good demonstration tape. Put together a short tape of least five examples of your best work. Put the emphasis on short. Three to five minutes total. Select pieces that show your range or specialties. Potential clients look for one thing in original music: originality. The better you demonstrate your originality, the better your chances of getting the work. Another thing producers, directors, and other prospects look for is range. Even if you specialize in one style of music, create your demo tape to reflect the range you cover; i.e., fast, mid, and slow tempos and emotional ranges including exciting, calm, uplifting, and dramatic. When your demo tape is complete, put together a biography that includes a brief description of your experience, credits, and working style. The better your materials look, the better your chances. Invest in nice-looking labels and J-cards for your demo cassettes and make sure your bio is well designed and is easy to read.

For advertising and commercial work send your package to local advertising agencies, cable television stations, radio stations, and independent producers. It is helpful to call each of your prospects beforehand to find the name of the person responsible for selecting music. For soundtrack work your choices are myriad. For corporate and "industrial" productions (a great market in and of itself) send your package to the directors of media services or corporate communications departments of the larger corporations in your region. Again, call first to get the proper name and department. For multimedia work, your choices include corporate communications directors, independent producers, and multimedia production houses. Check the latest edition of *Songwriter's Market,* published yearly by Writer's Market Books for more prospective outlets for your work.

The income you can earn as a home-based composer varies considerably. When you're first starting out, you may even find yourself doing some work for free. Composers we spoke with vary greatly in terms of how they bill for their services. Bigger projects, such as a soundtrack for a program ten minutes or longer, are usually on a complete project basis. Shorter pieces such as commercial jingles are usually billed on a per-piece basis.

Composing for a living is a difficult undertaking, but do we know people who are doing it. You may wish to offer composing services in conjunction with a desktop video or multimedia production business. As your composing credits and contacts pile up, you can make the switch to full-time composing if you wish.

Resources

General Midi (Computer Music and Digital Audio Series, Vol 11), by Stanley Jungleib, Book and Disk Edition, A-R Editions, 1995, ISBN: 0895793105.

Songwriter's Market: Where & How to Market Your Songs (Annual), by Cindy Laufenberg, Cincinnati, Writer's Digest Books, ISBN: 0898797950.

The Virtual Musician: A Complete Guide to Online Resources and Services, by Brad Hill, New York, Macmillan Library Reference, 1996, ISBN: 0028645839.

Electronic Musician magazine, 6400 Hollis St., Ste. 12, Emeryville, CA 94608, (510) 653-3307.

ASCAP (AMERICAN SOCIETY OF COMPOSERS AND PUBLISHERS), 7920 Sunset Boulevard, 3rd Floor, Los Angeles, CA 90046, (213) 883-1000; 1 Lincoln Plaza, New York, NY 10023, (212) 595-3050.

BMI (BROADCAST MUSIC INCORPORATED), 8730 Sunset Boulevard, 3rd Floor, Los Angeles, CA 90069, (310) 659-9109.

Newsgroups: comp.multimedia
alt.binaries.sounds.midi
alt.music.midi
comp.music.midi

13.

Computer-Aided Design

From architecture to printed circuit board design and from fashion to product engineering, the expanding field of computer-aided design (CAD) has completely changed the way inventors, builders, electricians, plumbers, and creators of all kinds visualize new ideas. For example, using computers, scanners, and specialized software, a fashion designer can scan in a fabric pattern, place it on a dress design, and sketch a model in 3-D all on the computer screen. Similarly, an interior designer can construct an office or conference room, paint colors or scan in wallpaper for the walls, and reconfigure the placement of furniture until the most attractive combination is achieved. And a civil engineer can produce a layout of every street in a city and show the effect on traffic of installing a new set of lights at a busy intersection.

As a result of this technology, there will be tremendous growth over time in the need for specialists who can work with people in many fields integrating the hardware and software of CAD with the needs of the profession. Depending on your background and interest, you might therefore explore establishing a CAD-based company specializing in any of many design fields: architecture, civil engineering, electrical or plumbing layout, fashion, interior design, landscaping, mechanical engineering, and many others.

To be in this business, you will need, however, to invest heavily in high-quality hardware, including a minimum of a Pentium or Power Mac computer with at least thirty-two megabytes of RAM. You will also be most efficient with your CAD software if you have a 3.2 GB or larger hard drive, a mouse, a light pen or graphics tablet with a puck, and a high-resolution graphics video card. For printing out blueprints or designs, you will also need a laser printer with at least 2 MB of memory and the capability of printing out in eleven-by-seventeen-inch format.

This career may require specialized training for a few months, but you can find such training in many technical schools and community colleges. The opportunities for success are enormous if you can offer special expertise in a particular field and you know your way around the hardware and software. CAD designers can be paid $50 and more per hour for developing computer models of a design, blueprints, and even three-dimensional animated sequences that simulate the item, be it a building, a room, or a product being used. This is also one field where the technology is rapidly changing, so you will need to stay abreast of changes in the field on a continual basis.

Resources

Learn Autocad 12 in a Day, book and disk, by Ralph Grabowski, Plano, TX, Wordware, 1994, ISBN: 1556223390.

Autodesk AutoCAD Forum on CompuServe provides support as well as demos of applications for AutoCAD, a widely used CAD program.

Newsgroups: comp.cad.autocad
comp.cad.microstation
alt.cad
alt.cad.autocad
comp.cad.i-deas
comp.cad.pro-engineer

14. [icons]

(CAI) Computer-Assisted Instructional Design

Computer-Assisted Instruction (CAI) is used to teach practically any field to almost anyone. You might think of CAI as the equivalent of a textbook or a self-study course, except that the information is designed as interactive software to be delivered on a computer screen, often enhanced with graphics, diagrams, simulations, and quizzes that make the instruction more interesting and useful.

CAI programs are being used to teach nursing, carpentry, technical repair, employee safety, sales techniques, accounting, and many other skills. Other CAI programs help people learn home repair, crafts, foreign languages, and even cooking. In short, whatever people may want to know, a CAI program can be designed to teach it.

Furthermore, unlike writing other kinds of software publishing, you do not need to be a programmer or know how to do custom programming to be a CAI designer. So if you have a strong background or expertise in a specific area that other people may want to learn, then consider becoming a CAI designer. Only your expertise and ability to teach are necessary. This is because most CAI packages are developed using special software programs, called authoring systems, that provide you with templates for designing screens, drawing diagrams or illustrations, and writing any accompanying text. The authoring systems then help you sequence the material and tag screens indicating such things as optional material, points where readers may skip ahead, and interactive question/answer material.

The best way to get into this business is to ask yourself what expertise you can share or what market might benefit from a CAI course you could develop. Once you have targeted an area, find out which authoring system works best for you, as each system is slightly different in its approach to CAI and what it requires to run on your hardware. Then you can approach companies directly and offer to create a customized CAI tutorial for them to use in teaching their employees the material. Or you can develop a CAI program and market it directly to companies via telemarketing or flyers. Another option is to develop your program and offer it as shareware (see "Software Publishing," page 141) through the distribution channels used for such kinds of programs. What you can earn as a CAI designer will vary, depending on the nature of your tutorials, the market niche you select, and how much you charge for your product. Some CAI designers who produce customized training materials for corporations can earn from $2,000 to $10,000 for a single tutorial. Other CAI designers who work on consumer-oriented products earn similar amounts as the authors of a shareware product.

Resources

Hypermedia Learning Environments: Instructional Design and Integration, by Piet A. M. Kommers (editor), Scott Grabinger (editor), Joanna C. Dunlap, Lawrence Erlbaum Associates, 1996, ISBN: 0805818294.

Intelligent Design of Computer-Assisted Instruction, by Richard Venezky and Luis Osin, Longman Group United Kingdom, 1991, ISBN: 0801303907.

TUTORIALWRITER is a shareware authoring system for producing computer-based tutorials and documents in multimedia; designed for nonprogrammers by a psychologist. It's available in Library 15 of the Working from Home Forum on CompuServe under the file name TW30.EXE.

AMERICAN SOCIETY FOR TRAINING AND DEVELOPMENT, 1640 King Street, Alexandria, VA 22313, (703) 683-8100, (800) 628-2783, *http://www.*astd.org

INTERNATIONAL SOCIETY FOR PERFORMANCE IMPROVEMENT, Suite 1250, 1300 L Street, N.W., Washington, DC 20005, (202) 408-7969, *http://www.*ispi.org. Has a newsletter and national conference.

15.

Computer Consulting

Computer consulting is second only to management consulting as the largest specialty in the consulting field. The downsizing that is occurring in American corporations only further stimulates the trend to make use of outside consulting services. According to Raj Khera, who tracks computer consulting trends and operates two highly successful Web sites, areas of significant growth for computer consultants over the next five years are interfacing existing databases with the Internet and intranet-working.

A computer consultant might work in a single area or multiple areas of expertise, including analyzing a business's needs and recommending how to set up a range of hardware and software systems such as local area networks, workstations, and commercial or customized software. Because today's options in computerization are so extensive, the demand for assistance is extremely high and will continue to be so as the competition in hardware tools brings about more and more products, and software applications become increasingly sophisticated.

Technical knowledge and expertise are obviously musts for the person interested in becoming a computer consultant. The most successful consultants today will, in fact, have both a broad knowledge of the field and a specialty that distinguishes them from other consultants. One consultant, for example, might focus on working with law firms or medical offices, while another specializes in retail stores.

Many people start out as computer consultants by learning about the needs and operation of one particular business field and how computer systems can solve their problems. They may do a few small consulting jobs, and then build their business over time with word-of-mouth referrals. If you are a generalist and have an interest in working in many areas, however, you would benefit from getting certified by a vendor or software publisher. This can require a significant cash and time investment but can be a key to building your business. Networking is an excellent route to building this business. Helping people at computer and software user-groups, answering questions on online computer services and local bulletin board systems, and joining business networking groups are several good avenues. Publicity, direct mail, yellow page listings, and ads are among the many ways computer consultants market themselves.

Potential earnings for the skilled computer consultant can easily exceed $100,000 a year, and even consultants who are able to bill only twenty hours a week can anticipate earning $50,000 a year by billing out at $50 per hour.

Resources

The Computer Consultant's Guide: Real-Life Strategies for Building a Successful Consulting Career, by Janet Ruhl, New York, Wiley, 1997, ISBN: 0471596620.

Computer Consulting on Your Home-Based PC, by Herman Holtz, New York, Windcrest/McGraw-Hill, 1994, ISBN: 0070296693.

How to Be a Successful Computer Consultant, by Alan R. Simon, New York, McGraw-Hill, 1994, ISBN: 0070576173.

INDEPENDENT COMPUTER CONSULTANTS ASSOCIATION, 1131 S Towne Square, Ste. F, St. Louis, MO 63123, (800) 774-4222, *http://www.*icca.org. The ICCA sponsors the Consult Forum on CompuServe Information Service.

INSTITUTE FOR CERTIFICATION OF COMPUTER PROFESSIONALS, 2200 East Devon Avenue, Ste. 247, Des Plaines, IL 60018, (847) 299-4227, fax: (847) 299-4280, Web: *http://www.*icca.org

BROKERS AND JOBSHOPS
Day and Zimmerman, Inc., 1818 Market Street, Philadelphia, PA 19103.
Tad Technical Corporation, 639 Massachusetts Avenue, Cambridge, MA 02139.
Volt Information Sciences, Inc., 101 Park Avenue, New York, NY 10017.

Newsgroups: alt.computer.consultants.adds
alt.computer.consultants
alt.computer.consultants.moderated
alt.computer.consultants.ads.norecruiters
misc.business.consulting

Web Sites:
*http://www.*govcon.com publishes the contents of the *Commerce Business Daily* without charge to users.
morebusiness.com is operated by Raj Khera, cited above.

16.

Computer Programming

The Bureau of Labor Statistics has identified programming as one of the fastest-growing occupations in this decade. The number of programmers is expected to grow by 45 percent between now and the year 2000, equaling 250,000 new programmers, just about equivalent to the 1990 population of Las Vegas, Nevada. Much of the demand for programming is being provided by freelancers because as companies reduce the number of core employees, more programming work is being "outsourced," to outside contractors.

Freelance computer programmers may create customized, one-of-a-kind programs to help clients run their businesses, or they may modify or develop macro programs with off-the-shelf software so that the client can avoid the cost of creating a program from scratch. A programmer will begin by developing an understanding of the tasks the client wants the computer to perform, how much data will be processed, and in what form it will be needed. Once the programmer has a full understanding of what needs to be done, he or she may design and write code to fit the platform used by the client, or modify a commercial program for a PC that will do the job to the customer's satisfaction and pocketbook. Then they test, debug, and implement the software, including training personnel to use it.

Ideally you should have two to five years of programming background in several languages and platforms if you want to strike out on your own. This experience will help you know how long it takes to complete various projects so you can make accurate estimates of what you will need to charge your clients. You also need to be able to understand and speak knowledgeably with clients about their business needs so you can do what they want and inspire trust in your abilities. Many of your clients may have little or no technical background and often will expect you to do a perfect job the first time.

Programmers' fees range from $25 per hour for students to more than $125 per hour for experienced professionals. If you were to bill out at $40 an hour working twenty hours per week, your gross annual income would be $40,000, but many programmers do better than that.

Making personal contacts through business and trade associations, getting referrals through computer stores, and teaching classes on programming for businesspeople are effective ways to get business.

Resources

Make Money Selling Your Shareware, book and disk (Entrepreneurial PC Series), by Steven Hudgik, New York, McGraw-Hill, 1994, ISBN: 0070308659.

Visual Developer, Coriolis Group, 14455 Hayden Rd., Ste. 220, Scottsdale, AZ 85260, (602) 483-0192, *http://www.coriolis.* com

Databased Advisor, Advisor Publications, 5675 Ruffin Rd., Ste. 200, San Diego, CA 92123, (619) 278-5600, (800) 336-6060, *http://www.* advisor.com

Dr. Dobb's Journal, written by professional programmers for professional programmers. 411 Borel Avenue, Ste. 100, San Mateo, CA 94402, (415) 358-9500, Web: *http://www.ddj.com/ddj/index.htm*

CNET, a comprehensive online database and news publication dealing with computing and Internet issues and updates. Web: *http://www.cnet.com*

ZDNET, Ziff Davis publications' online resource site. Web: *http://www. ZDnet.com*

SOCIETY FOR TECHNICAL COMMUNICATION, 901 North Stuart Street, Ste. 904, Arlington, VA 22203, (703) 522-4114.

Newsgroups: rec.games.programmer
               comp.programming
               comp.os.msdos.programmer
               comp.lang.c
               comp.sys.mac.programmer
               comp.sys.mac.programmer.help
               comp.os.ms-windows.programmer
               alt.msdos.programmer
               comp.os.msdos.programmer
               comp.unix.programmer

17.

Computer Sales and Service

Although there's no shortage of retailers and mail-order companies selling computers, the market for computer systems and peripherals is still huge, with over fifty million homes not yet computerized and millions of businesses that buy equipment year to year. And since many people and companies need extensive assistance or prefer to work one-on-one with a consultant when they buy a system, opportunities for a home-based computer sales and service business are good in the coming years.

There are two keys to being successful in this business. First, even if you generalize and work with many clients, we recommend that you have a specialization in one or more specific areas such as a certain kind of office system, or in one technology such as intranetworking or accounting. Having an area of expertise adds value to your service and gives you a market cachet that many others lack. Second, you should be able to provide a wide range of services to your customers, including system customization, software installation, and ongoing support. In this sense, you want people to consider you more as a computer consultant than as a salesperson.

Getting into the sales and service business is actually quite easy, given that the field of hardware suppliers is teeming with companies looking for business. You begin by contacting manufacturers and vendors of computer equipment around the country and finding out about bulk pricing options for prebuilt systems or parts that you can assemble into a system yourself. If it suits your business, you might also arrange to become an exclusive agent for a manufacturer as a Value Added Reseller (VAR) for their equipment or software, a useful approach if you specialize. Becoming a VAR also adds to your credibility and sometimes gives you a higher profit margin, since you are usually selling a complete package to a customer rather than just one component of a system.

To obtain clients, you can advertise in the yellow pages and do telemarketing directly to businesses. However, your most effective methods should focus on getting business to come to you, and so networking both face-to-face and through the Internet and online services, giving speeches, and encouraging referrals will save money and time. As is true of any computer consultant, your satisfied customers are your best source of new business, since customers prefer to know that you have been successful in helping others.

Earnings for a sales and service business can be considerable. Some consultants can make as much as $300 to $500 on a single equipment sale. Furthermore, you can also charge hourly fees for consulting, customization of software, and other services that businesses often need when they buy equipment.

Resources

The Computer Industry Almanac, by Karen Juliussen and Egil Juliussen. New York, Brady Publishing. A yearly guide listing company officers' names, trends, forecasts, and interesting miscellanea.

Microcomputer Marketplace, by Steven J. Bennett and Richard Freierman, New York, Random House Electronic Publishing. A comprehensive guide to vendor information, trade shows, and much more.

COMDEX, the major computer show for the trade, is held twice a year. The fall show is in Las Vegas; the spring show in Atlanta. Contact Softbank Comdex for more information, 300 1st Ave., Needham, MA 02194, (617) 449-6600, *http://www.*comdex.com

COMPUTER RETAILER ONLINE MAGAZINE: weekly news, trends, and updates, Web: *http://techweb.cmp.com/crw/*

Newsgroup: nj.market.computers

18.

Computer Training

Learning to use computers, software programs, and getting around on the Internet is fast becoming a necessary aspect of running a successful business. Rather than wasting time reading manuals and groping in the dark in cyberspace or with new software programs, many companies recognize the value of bringing in professional trainers to teach executives and support staff the basics of word processing, spreadsheets, databases, networking, and specialized or customized software.

Computer trainers generally teach groups of individuals in a classroom style on the premises of a company. They may also teach public computer seminars or offer corporate training classes off the company premises. Classes can range from small groups of two to six individuals to workshops with twelve to twenty people paired up on PCs.

As a computer trainer, stand-up training and presentation skills are essential. You must be able to command your audience's attention, communicate instructions clearly, and handle group dynamics. A background in teaching or educational design is useful, as this helps you know how to sequence and present new information to people in "chunks" so that they can understand and assimilate it efficiently.

Income potential for computer trainers is good, ranging from $40,000 to over $100,000. This is a business that is easily expanded without significantly increasing overhead because you can subcontract with other trainers to teach your classes once you are selling more training than you alone can deliver. You need to price your fees at just the right rate so that the client perceives a savings over and above what it would cost their employees to sit at their desks and try to learn on their own. For example, if employees are earning $15 an hour and your program is sixteen hours long divided into four four-hour classes, you might charge $50 per student per class period, hence $200 per student for the four classes.

Directly soliciting companies that need computer training and speaking before business and professional groups on computerizing are effective routes to getting work doing in-house training. Direct mail and print advertising will most likely be necessary if you intend to offer and fill public seminars. Another alternative is to arrange to teach courses under the sponsorship of business or educational institutions that will promote and administer the seminars.

Resources

The Accidental Trainer: You Know Computers, So They Want You to Teach Everyone Else (Jossey-Bass Business and Management Series), by Elaine Weiss, San Francisco, Jossey-Bass Publications, 1996, ISBN: 0787902934.

The Computer Trainer's Personal Training Guide, by Gail Perry, Bill Brandon, Paul Clothier, Shirley Copeland, and Patty Crowell, New York, Que Corp., 1996, ISBN: 1575762536.

The Micro Computer Trainer, 696 Ninth Street, P.O. Box 2487, Secaucus, NJ 07096-2487, (201) 330-8923, monthly newsletter for the professional.

THE AMERICAN SOCIETY FOR TRAINING AND DEVELOPMENT, 1640 King Street, Alexandria, VA 22313, (703) 683-8100, (800) 628-2783, *http://www.astd.org* offers a professional journal, a catalogue of resources, local chapters, and a train-the-trainer certificate program.

COMPUTER TRAINING FORUM ON COMPUSERVE Information Service is a special-interest group for computer trainers (GO DPTRAIN).

Newsgroups: alt.computer.consultants
                comp.edu
                uk.comp.training

19.

Computer Tutoring

While there are many computer trainers and training companies, independent computer tutors have an advantage over other methods of becoming computer literate because they bring the training to their clients and customize it to their needs. Computer tutors generally work on the client's premises, providing in-depth, one-on-one coaching. They may go into a company to help an office automate, assisting in setting up the entire computer system and teaching the responsible employee to use the hardware, software, and the Internet.

Most successful tutors specialize in working with particular industries like law firms, health professionals, construction companies, and so on. Alternatively, they may specialize in particular software applications like spreadsheets, database management, or desktop publishing and graphics software as well as the Internet.

To be a computer tutor you must have a thorough knowledge of at least one software program that a sufficient number of people need to learn. Some software manufacturers actually offer training courses and will certify you to teach their software. Once you're certified, the manufacturer may also become a referral source for clients. You must also be familiar with the field in which you decide to work so you can understand your clients' particular needs and uses for computer technology. Finally, you need to have tact, patience, and good communication and presentation skills and be able to convey technical ideas in a nonthreatening, easy-to-understand style.

Income potential for a good computer tutor is excellent. Fees range from $50 to $125 an hour, with annual gross incomes ranging from $40,000 to $125,000. Giving speeches about computerizing a business and networking through professional, trade, or business associations in the field you choose to serve are the best routes to building your business.

Resources

The Computer Training Handbook: How to Teach People to Use Computers, by Elliott Masie and Rebekka Wolman. Minneapolis, 1996, Lakewood Publications, (800) 707-7769, ISBN: 0943210372.

The Micro Computer Trainer, 696 Ninth Street, P.O. Box 2487, Secaucus, NJ 07096-2487, (201) 330-8923, a monthly newsletter offering practical solutions and strategies for the microcomputer training professional. Also, E-mail loretta@panix.com and request to subscribe to free weekly how-to training tips.

Franchises

COMPUTERTOTS—this award-winning company offers franchises for a business teaching children to use computers. 10132 Colvin Run Road, Great Falls, VA 22066, (703) 759-2556, (800) 531-5053, *http://www.* computertots.com

20. # C 🚗 💡

Construction and Remodeling Estimating and Planning Service

With the high cost of new-home construction, do-it-yourself home-improvement projects are the rage. American Demographics rports that 55 percent of adults do interior painting; 50 percent do minor plumbing repairs; 49 percent do minor electrical work; 42 percent do exterior painting; and 30 percent do minor repairs of appliances.

So if you are wanting to expand an existing contracting or repair business, consider the following idea. Since such a large percentage of people want to save money by doing their own home-improvement projects, why not create a home-repair and -improvement business that goes into customers' homes or offices not to do the work yourself but to teach your customers how to do the job properly or to help them through a job they're stuck on? You might call your business "Do It Yourself Plumbing [Carpentry] Assistant," or "We Help You Do It Carpentry," or "Fix It Yourself Consulting."

You could charge much less than someone who actually does the repair and still help clients feel that they've saved money since they've received professional advice to help them complete their current job as well as learn for future tasks too. You can also add on other services, such as providing special supplies or materials they may need. The computer aspect of this idea is that you can use costing software to provide cost estimates for your clients. And you might offer a finder's service by which you locate the best source and price for construction materials using a database you develop from various supply sources in your area.

Your fees might range from $35 to $50 per hour plus any extra services the customer requests. The best methods to get customers may include advertising in local community newspapers and yellow pages, direct mail, and particularly networking with salespeople in building supply stores who can pass your business card to people who are purchasing materials and inevitably ask how to do the work properly. For a person already in the home-construction or -repair business, this service can also be an excellent way to make money from lost query calls when the people decide they can only afford to do the job themselves.

Resources

BID MAGIC software is a graphically oriented estimating package for making rough estimates on a room-by-room basis. Turtle Creek Software, 118 Prospect Street, Babcock Hall, Ste. 201, Ithaca, NY 14850, (607) 272-1008, *http://www.* turtlesoft.com

INUIT'S PROJECT ESTIMATING package interfaces with both CAD and *Quicken,* (800) 446-8848.

TURBOCAD DESIGNER is a computer-aided design and drafting program that provides automatic dimensioning and hatching and will generate a bill of materials by IMSI, 1895 Francisco Boulevard East, San Rafael, CA 94901-5506, (415) 454-7101. IMSI also offers a library of symbols for use with TurboCAD that includes electronics, home design, and furnishings, *http://www.* imisoft.com

Newsgroups: alt.construction
alt.building.construction

21.

Copywriter

Businesses and organizations often have a need to sell their products or services using written materials that represent them to the world. From advertising slicks and brochures to direct-mail sales letters, newsletters, and Web sites—everything they put out not only needs to be written clearly and concisely but also must capture attention, impress, and motivate the reader to buy or to call for further information. And given the high cost of direct mail and advertising today, it is extremely important that the writing for such materials sparkle.

As a result, small-business owners rarely have the time, talent, or know-how to prepare such sparkling materials themselves. Since they usually don't need (and often can't afford) to employ a full-time copywriter to do it for them, they instead turn to freelance professional copywriters.

Copywriters prepare the text and sometimes the design for a wide variety of materials, including ads, brochures, Web sites, instructional manuals, media kits, created feature stories, catalogs, company slogans, consumer information booklets, captions for photographs, product literature, annual reports, product names and packaging labels, marketing communication plans, speeches, telemarketing scripts, video scripts, and storyboards. The copywriter's clients may include major corporations, independent professionals, small manufacturers, banks, health clubs, consumer electronics firms, direct-mail catalog companies, and newsletter publishers.

Copywriters use word-processing and sometimes desktop publishing software to produce their work. CD-ROM disks loaded with reference material are a boon for copywriters, allowing them to find in a flash millions of well-known quotes, look up rules of usage, or incorporate clip art in their material.

Robert Bly, author of *The Copywriter's Handbook,* has surveyed copywriters across the country and found that serious freelance copywriters typically gross from $20,000 to $40,000 a year during their first two years but can then increase their income up to $80,000 to $175,000 in subsequent years when they become "real pros" and begin writing for major companies.

If you are interested in copywriting as a career, the best way to build your business is to develop samples of your work to show to everyone you know. Also, begin networking through business organizations, especially in industries with which you are familiar, and develop affiliations with related professionals such as graphic designers, desktop publishers, photographers, copy shops, and printers who can refer business to you.

Resources

Advertising Copywriting, by Philip Ward Burton, Lincolnwood, IL, NTC Publishing Group, 1997, ISBN: 0844232068.

Persuading on Paper: The Complete Guide to Writing Copy That Pulls in Business, by Marsha Yudkin, Plume, 1996, ISBN: 0452273137.

Secrets of a Freelance Writer: How to Make Eighty-five Thousand Dollars a Year, by Robert Bly, New York, Henry Holt, 1990.

Writing High Tech Copy That Sells, Janice M. King, New York: Wiley, 1995, ISBN: 0471058467.

Write on Target: The Direct Marketer's Copywriting Handbook, by Floyd Kemske and Donna Baier Stein, Lincolnwood, IL, NTC Publishing Group, 1997, ISBN: 0844259144.

WRITER'S DREAMTOOLS, a software package for copywriters available from Slippery Disks, P.O. Box 1126, Los Angeles, CA 90069 (mail order only).

INTERNATIONAL ASSOCIATION OF BUSINESS COMMUNICATORS, 1 Hallidie Plaza, Ste. 600, San Francisco, CA 94102, (415) 433-3400, (800) PROIABC, *http://www.*iabc.com

22.

Coupon Newspaper Publishing

Have you recently received a booklet, flyer, newsletter, or magazine composed of advertising coupons for local business services? If so, you are undoubtedly familiar with the concept of this business idea.

Thanks to desktop publishing technology, you can start a business publishing and distributing an advertising newspaper service. Your goal in this business is to sell space in your coupon booklet to small businesses that will benefit by having a chance to advertise at relatively inexpensive rates to a clearly targeted audience. You operate the business by contacting local businesses, helping them compose ads or discount coupons, and then putting the coupon booklet together using your computer, desktop publishing software, and a laser printer. You then provide camera-ready art to your print shop and have your booklet printed in two colors. Once the booklets are printed, you can either drop them off in bins at stores where neighborhood people can take them for free, distribute them by hand, or purchase a specific mailing list or develop one yourself which you use to mail the booklets.

The earning potential in this business is good. For example, as a sideline or add-on business, you can make $600 in just a few days by taking an 11-by-17-inch page, breaking each half into eight equal parts or sixteen blocks total, selling each square (which will measure 23/4 by 3/1 inches) to local retailers, doing the ad design and pasteup, getting them printed in two colors, and distributing 5,000 copies by hand over a holiday weekend. Or as a full-time venture, you could create a twelve-page coupon newsletter (with three coupons per page) every month for thirty-five advertisers in it at $150 each and generate $5,250 in gross revenue, while your production costs could be as little as $600 to $1,000.

One angle that you may wish to pursue if you are interested in this business is to organize your booklet around a specific niche, such as wedding services (florist, caterer, bridal boutique, wedding makeup, etc.), cleaning services (carpets, windows, venetian blinds, air ducts, etc.), health (chiropractors, health-food stores, diet programs), or new parents (diaper service, day-care center, parenting class, children's clothing store), etc.

Advertisers pay in advance, and if you do this as an add-on business you can reserve one of the coupons for your own business. This way you not only make a profit, you also get free advertising!

The two major qualifications for operating this business include good telephone sales skills and desktop publishing savvy. However, it would also help to have some retail business experience, a knowledge of marketing and advertising, and excellent writing and visual skills, since your clients may expect your assistance in designing an effective advertisement or coupon.

It pays not to skimp on equipment when you start this business. You will need a fast computer with a large-capacity hard drive, a good monitor (perhaps even a seventeen- or twenty-inch oversized color monitor) that allows you to see complete pages clearly, word-processing and desktop publishing software including clip-art programs, and a high-quality laser printer. You may also wish to own a scanner that allows you to scan in photos, logos, and other items that retailers may want you to reproduce.

The most difficult aspect of the business is selling space for the first issue, since most businesses will repeat their ads several times if your prices are reasonable and the ads are even slightly successful. Your selling points, however, can be that the material is hand-delivered to a guaranteed number of targeted customers, you sell to no two competing businesses in a given booklet, and their coupon appears in a well-designed, two-color publication.

Resources

Consult any of the many books and Web sites dedicated to desktop publishing, typography, and principles of advertising.

Newsgroups: alt.coupons
　　　　　　　alt.consumers.free-stuff

23.

Creativity Consultant

How often do you hear about a business wishing it had a winning idea for a product, a press release, an ad campaign? How often do you hear executives and entrepreneurs say: "If only I could find the right angle . . . the missing piece . . . the new idea." It's not unusual for most of us to find ourselves groping for something clever, only to find our thoughts to be hopelessly mundane.

Well, if you're a person who enjoys developing creative ideas, why not make use of today's new idea-generating software and package yourself as a creativity consultant and sell your services to companies looking to brainstorm their way to the winning product idea, marketing campaign, or service? Although it may sound strange, creativity is fast becoming the science of the future, as businesses explore every avenue to expand revenues or cut expenses.

What makes a creativity consultant different from an ordinary consultant is that this person specializes in using specific tools and techniques to jar people into thinking differently and to abandon their inhibitions and customary habits, such as constant nay-saying or nit-picking. In fact, the creativity consultant intentionally aims to produce unusual and silly ideas, since these are often the basis for brilliant, cash-producing winning products.

Not so strangely, computers have now become one of the tools used by creativity consultants. One program, IdeaFisher by Fisher Ideas Systems, Inc., allows the user to generate ideas for marketing strategies, advertisement and promotional materials, new products and product improvements, speeches, articles, stories and scripts, solutions to problems, names for products, services and companies, or any other task requiring the creation of new ideas. The results can be interlinked with a personal information manager program to follow through on an idea.

We've been told by public relations and advertising firms that they don't want their clients to know that their best ideas come as a result of using IdeaFisher, for fear that their clients might conclude they don't need them anymore. But although anyone can buy and learn to use such software themselves, learning it takes time, so employing a creativity consultant who specializes in using such software can be a cost-effective way for many companies to design an ad campaign, problem-solve an issue, name a product, or create a new business.

It would probably be easiest to market this service if you are already doing consulting, business plan writing, copywriting, or other work that brings in business clients on a regular basis. Nevertheless, don't automatically dismiss this as a business possibility; be creative and see if you can make it work!

Resources

A Whack on the Side of the Head, by Roger von Oech, New York, Warner, 1983.

The Path of Least Resistance, by Robert Fritz, New York, Ballantine, 1989, ISBN: 449903370.

IDEAFISHER, Fisher Idea Systems, Inc., 2222 Martin Street, Ste. 110, Irvine, CA 92612, (800) 289-4332, (714) 474-8111. *http://www.*ideacenter.com

IDEA GENERATOR PLUS, Experience in Software, Inc., 2000 Hearst, Ste. 202, Berkeley, CA 94709, (800) 678-7008, (510) 644-0694. *http://www.* experienceware.com/Creativity Forum on CompuServe (GO CREATE).

24.

Data Conversion Service

If you have a good technical background in data storage and retrieval, you may enjoy a business in data conversion. This business encompasses four types of activities: converting data from one software platform to another, transferring disk drive storage to CD-ROM, converting archival data, and converting databases for use on the Internet.

Companies and professional offices occasionally change software and then must convert their word-processed documents, spreadsheets, and databases to the new software so that they will be continuously usable. As an expert in this service, you implement the needed conversion and assist in making sure that no data is lost, destroyed, or improperly converted. While many software packages have the built-in capability to perform conversions, most are imperfect and therefore require a certain amount of supervision and manual intervention. For example, in transferring a large spreadsheet, some cell definitions and macros that the user may have defined in the original software may not translate accurately into the new program without a knowledgeable professional tweaking them just right to allow the conversion to proceed. Similarly, converting large and complex databases often requires hand-holding to be sure that data is not scrambled or lost.

Conversion of data into CD-ROM provides another market for this business. As many companies expand their information requirements and resources (databases, research materials, and so on), they surpass the capabilities of ordinary hard disk storage and retrieval, and need to put their data on CD-ROM disks. Therefore a conversion service can assist in the evaluation of the appropriate technologies and in the actual data transfer itself as well.

As you might imagine, both of these services require an excellent command of hardware and software, as well as a fair amount of expensive equipment such as scanners, tape drives, disk drives, etc. In particular, you need to be completely competent and confident in your ability to complete conversions successfully, as you run the risk of making serious errors and/or losing valuable data, and you could be held liable for damages. Regardless of your skill level, obtaining liability insurance is smart.

Converting data can be a profitable add-on business for computer consultants or trainers specializing in spreadsheet programs, databases, and in high performance hardware. Your fees can range from $35 to $125 per hour for skilled advice and work.

Resources

Newsgroups: comp.programming
comp.databases.ms-sqlserver

25. Databased Marketing Services

Although mailing list services have been around for a number of years, a rapidly expanding extension of the business is developing that can be called a databased marketing service. In brief, the general concept behind this business is to make mailing lists and direct marketing lists much more precise so that mailings or telemarketing offers can be more closely customized to the actual needs of customers. This is done by learning more about customers and their purchasing habits and customizing lists accordingly. The benefits of a databased marketing service are therefore twofold: first, to provide highly targeted mailing lists that have substantially higher returns than even a qualified list, and second, to learn how to project the psychological and demographic profile of potential new customers in order to expand a list.

Databased marketing grows out of the increasing sophistication of both database management software to cull information and mail-merge software to facilitate personalized mailings to customers. It reflects the need to reduce the costs of marketing, and to improve a company's ability to perform "narrowcasting," whereby they can find the market for their product among the smallest audience of likely customers (the opposite of mass marketing). Databased marketing also points to the growing recognition that every customer is an individual and has personal needs and desires. It therefore allows a business to locate niches faster and to understand customers better so that they can address them with exactly the right products and services at the right time.

Getting into databased marketing will be easiest if you have a background in marketing, sales, or computers, but anyone who has worked with database software can probably enter the field without much difficulty. You will need a personal computer with a large hard drive and one of the professional database management programs such as *Paradox,* Microsoft *Foxpro,* or Microsoft *Access.*

Your clients can include any businesses that have their own mailing lists and need assistance in developing, targeting, managing, and regularly contacting their lists. You might also be able to perform subcontract work from mailing-list services and mailing-list brokers who can benefit by allowing you to massage their mailing lists to create more accurate marketing databases. In such a case, you can likely command $50 to $100 per hour for your professional expertise in developing mailing-list databases.

Resources

Databased Marketing: Every Manager's Guide to the Super Marketing Tool of the 21st Century, by Herman Holtz. New York, Wiley, 1992: probably the best basic introduction to the field.

The Complete Database Marketer: Second-Generation Strategies and Techniques for Tapping the Power of Your Customer Database, by Arthur M. Hughes, New York, Probus, 1995, ISBN: 1557388938.

Targetsmart!: Database Marketing for the Small Business (Psi Successful Business Library), by Jay Newberg and Claudio Marcus, Grant's Pass, OR, Oasis Press, 1996, ISBN: 155571384X.

DBMS, Miller Freeman Publications, 411 Borel Avenue, San Mateo, CA 94402, (415) 358-9500, a magazine for database professionals.

AMERICAN MARKETING ASSOCIATION, 250 South Wacker Drive, Ste. 200, Chicago, IL 60606, (312) 648-0536, (800) AMA-1150, *http://*www.ama.org

Newsgroups: comp.databases.olap
comp.databases.orical
comp.databases.ms-sqlserver
comp.databases

26.

Desktop Publishing Service

Desktop publishing (DTP) grew out of improvements in word-processing software that little by little helped to computerize many of the steps of preparing printed materials. In the past decade, in fact, desktop publishing has virtually taken over the fields of typesetting, design, page layout and pasteup, illustration, and even printing. With such advances, nearly every major type of printed document, from books, magazines, and catalogs to newsletters, brochures, corporate annual reports, and even Web sites are now prepared using desktop publishing hardware and software.

Desktop publishers provide services for organizations of all kinds that need printed material both for their internal and external communications. While some DTP companies do any kind of work that comes their way, others carve out their own niche and specialize by serving only particular industries or doing only particular types of documents like newsletters, proposals, books, or directories. Some specialize even further, doing only newsletters for law firms or catalogs for mail-order craft companies.

Of course, this business requires that you become skilled at using desktop publishing hardware and software. You must also have a sense for design and layout and a feel for fonts, illustration, printing, and paper. Additionally, if you are creating or editing text for your clients' documents, you obviously need the ability to write good copy, edit, and proofread. You can, of course, also use the services of a fellow home-based copywriter, technical writer, or proofreader.

Fees vary in this business, depending on the job, and work can be charged by the hour, by the page, or by the project. A small business can gross from $20,000 to $100,000 if you can maximize your billable hours or add additional services like complete design, copywriting, editing, graphics, or high-resolution output. Of course, to do this kind of work, you may need to invest between $5,000 and $20,000 to purchase a laser printer, scanner, CD-ROM drive, external drive such as a SyQuest or Jaz drive, a powerful PC or Power Mac with at least 32MB of RAM as well as desktop publishing and graphics software such as *QuarkXpress, Aldus PageMaker, Adobe PhotoShop,* and *Adobe Illustrator,* to name a few.

Effective ways to get business as a desktop publisher are to directly solicit small businesses, independent professionals, and nonprofit organizations and to advertise in the yellow pages and local newspapers. Contacting businesses directly through their Web sites can also be effective. The business has become competitive, so networking and word of mouth through professional and business organizations is critical to your success.

Resources

Desktop Magic: Electronic Publishing, Document Management, and Workgroups, by John M. Wood and James Wood, Solomon Press, 1995, ISBN: 0442017723.

Desktop Publishing: Dollars and Sense, by Scott R. Anderson. Hillsboro, OR: Blue Heron Publishing, 1992. ISBN: 0936085517.

Pricing Guide for Desktop Publishing Services, Brenner Information Group, 9282 Samantha Court, San Diego, CA 92129, $49 plus $3 shipping and handling.

Publish magazine, monthly, 501 2nd Street, San Francisco, CA 94107, (415) 243-0600, *http://www*.publish.com

DESKTOP PUBLISHING FORUM, CompuServe Information Service, 5000 Arlington Centre Boulevard, Columbus, OH 43220, (800) 848-8199. Once online, enter "GO DTPFORUM."

BUSINESS MEDIA GROUP, 462 Old Boston Street, Topsfield, MA 01983, (508) 887-7900. Publishes a monthly magazine, *Desktop Publishers Journal, http://www*.dtpjournal.com

Newsgroup: comp.text.desktop

27.

Desktop Video

The impact of the rapidly growing field of desktop video in the world of video production has been as dramatic as that of desktop publishing in the world of print. Essentially desktop video refers to using computer technologies to edit and add effects to full-motion video at a fraction of the cost of more traditionally shot and edited video programming. Desktop video is actually a wedding of video and computer technology and can be considered to be a branch of the larger field of multimedia production. The following are some of the types of applications made possible with desktop video.

Presentation Videos—creating low-cost videos for use in presentations that would previously have relied on still slides and overheads, or if produced with analog equipment would have cost over $5,000.

Computer Graphics—integrating computer-generated graphics and special effects into video productions.

Video Production Services—turning raw videotapes shot from a camcorder into professional-looking productions good enough for broadcast television.

Creating Television Commercials for Local Cable Companies—producing professional-quality commercials for local businesses at a fraction of their normal cost.

Self-Publishing Special-Interest Videotapes—producing how-to and local-interest videotapes.

Corporate Video—producing full-motion video for marketing, sales, training, and annual reports.

Video-on-Demand for World Wide Web Publishing—any of the above can now be incorporated into a Web site where it will be instantly available to be played using applications such as *VDO, Real Video* and *Stream-Works* by Xing technologies.

To get started in this exciting field you will need to spend between $4,000 and $20,000 to outfit yourself with the proper equipment. There are two ways to go here: traditional linear editing and total computer-based nonlinear.

Linear video production uses your PC to essentially enhance the way video has always been produced. Your "raw" footage remains on your source videotapes and you use your computer to add effects and otherwise manipulate images as you edit them. A nonlinear system requires a computer with a large hard disk (at least three gigabytes), with thirty-two MB of RAM, a genlock video card, a digitizing tablet, an optical scanner with appropriate desktop presentation software, two high-quality or professional videotape recorders, an edit controller unit, two color monitors, time-base correctors, a camcorder, and video printer, and more.

Nonlinear desktop video production utilizes much more of your computer's processing ability for much more dramatic results. Your raw video footage is immediately stored in the digital domain, usually to a hard disk. (That is, unless you shot the footage with a digital camera in the first place.) All editing then takes place within your computer. A nonlinear system costs more in computer hardware but eliminates the need for editing VCRs, outboard edit controllers, and effects. Nonlinear systems require the fastest PCs available, at least thirty-two MB of RAM, six to ten gigabytes of hard disk space, a good multimedia video card, an editing program such as *Adobe Premier,* and a VCR onto which you can download your finished programs.

Once you get to know your equipment and establish your reputation, the income potential is high, up to $100,000. To do well in this business, you should have good visual abilities as well as computer know-how. Networking and directly soliciting clients needing the type of work you specialize in are the best routes to building the business. You can also establish a multimedia Web site on which you can post short clips of your work.

Resources

Desktop Video World, TechMedia Publishing, 80 Elm Street, Peterborough, NH 03458.

Operating a Desktop Video Service on Your Home-Based PC, by Harvey Summers, New York, Windcrest, 1994, ISBN: 007062545X.

Videography magazine, PSN Publications, 2 Park Avenue, Ste. 1820, New York, NY 10016.

PC PRESENTATION PRODUCTIONS, an online magazine by Pisces Publishing Group, (203) 877-1927, Web: *http://*www.cadvision.com/nolimits/pcpp. html

Newsgroups: rec.video.desktop
rec.video.production

28.

Diet and Exercise Planning Service

You've probably heard about statistics that show that millions of Americans are overweight and, for one reason or another, usually cannot maintain a diet or exercise program. But have you ever thought about making a business out of helping people through a computerized diet and/or exercise program custom-tailored to their needs?

A wide array of software is now available for such businesses as "personal nutrition planners" or "body designers." There are programs that analyze a person's eating preferences and habits, and then recommend a specific nutritional plan to follow; programs that contain thousands of recipes with a complete breakdown of calories and nutritional content; and programs that can track a person's exercise workouts and help maximize their utility. While most of these programs are commercially available for the home market, many people don't have the time to learn to use them and would gladly pay a consultant to help them find the right diet and exercise program for their specific needs, be it to lose weight or to build muscle mass.

You don't need to be an expert to run this business, but a strong personal interest in the field and background in nutrition and/or exercise will help your professional credibility. To get clients, you might begin by advertising in local and community papers and on bulletin boards in fitness centers, supermarkets, and other public locations. With luck, you will also find that word of mouth from satisfied customers is a major way to bring in new business.

Fees for your service will depend on the extent of your work for a client. You might prepare a one-time diet or body-building plan for $50 to $250, but you might also offer monthly, quarterly, or biannual updates for maintenance diets or workout programs coupled with your ongoing personal support and motivation.

Resources

Your Health: Total Healthcare Planning on Your Computer, book and CD-ROM, Alan Neibauer and Barbara Neibauer, Ziff Davis Press, 1995, ISBN: 1562763024.

Food/Analyst Plus, CD-ROM database, Hopkins Technology, LLC, 421 Hazel Lane, Ste. 200, Hopkins, MN 55343-7116, (612) 931-9376, fax: (612) 931-9377, Web: *http://www.hoptechno.com*

SANTÉ, software for weight control and diet and exercise planning, Hopkins Technology.

Newsgroups: alt.support.diet
alt.support.diet.zone

29.

Digital Photography/Image Manipulation

Digital photography and digital image manipulation technology have made profound advances over the past five years. Today's digital cameras, scanners, and image manipulation software serve a wide variety of needs on a number of different levels. On the highest level, digital photography is beginning to gain ground on traditional photographic methods. High-end digital cameras now boast resolution quality on a par with 35-millimeter film and don't require film developing or prepress preparation for printing. Image manipulation software, like Abode's ubiquitous *Photoshop,* allow for complete photo retouching and image enhancement as well as a galaxy of special effects and editing procedures. The money-making possibilities utilizing these new technologies, especially using image manipulation software, are only limited by your creative ability to find ways to use them.

One enterprising example of a creative use of color scanning and image manipulation software is the Vancouver (British Columbia) based photo service DivorceX. Featured in the *New York Times,* DivorceX, founded by Keith Guelpa, specializes in "manipulating memories." Keith's clients bring him wedding and other memorable photos for "updating." Keith then scans in the photo and uses image manipulation software to cut out an ex-mate or add someone to the photo who should have been there in the first place. He can also fix bad-hair days, trim a few pounds, or change the entire location background of a photo. Happy clients pay him between $75 and $150 per photograph. Another example is Los Angeles–based Eclectica Media works. Founder Dee Louzginov uses digital photography as well as scanned photographs to help schools compile interactive year-books on CD-ROM. Other digital image entrepreneurs are putting their ideas to work on the World Wide Web, in traditional printing, corporate communications, and just about any other area where images are a primary component.

If the possibilities of this kind of business intrigue you, you will want to conduct some more research into the latest digital photography and image manipulation technologies. Start with the resources listed below. The capabilities of the technology itself should open doors to creative ways in which you can use it to create a specific service. You will also need to purchase the necessary hardware and software. If you are considering a computer upgrade, purchase a Pentium pro model with MMX if you can afford it. MMX greatly enhances the computer's ability to deal with images and multimedia content. You will also need good image manipulation software such as the earlier mentioned *Photoshop, EasyPhoto* by Storm Technologies, or *PaintShop Pro* from JASC. For greater flexibility, you will need a color scanner as well. If your primary market is multimedia or the Web, you will not require a high-resolution machine. Six hundred dpi will be more than enough. If your primary market is the printed media, you will need a scanner capable of 1,600 dpi or greater.

This is a well suited for being an add-on business for Web Designers, Scanning and Digitizing Services, Graphic Designers, and Desktop Video Services. With the right idea, like DivorceX, it can become a thriving full-time venture as well. To obtain clients, you must first determine the exact nature of the service you wish to provide. The more targeted, the better. When you have determined your market, begin finding work by networking online in discussion groups, newsgroups, bulletin boards, and users' groups. If your service is unique, small advertisements in the appropriate trade magazines and newsletters might be helpful. If this is an add-on business, let your current clients know what you're up to and show them examples of your work. You might also consider establishing a Web site that demonstrates your capabilities.

Resources

Digital Photography, by David Busch, New York, M & T Books, 1995, ISBN: 1558284486.

Digital Photography: A Hands-On Introduction, by Philip Krejcarek, book with CD-ROM, Albany, NY, Delmar Publishing, 1996, ISBN: 0827371314.

Professional Photoshop: Color Correction, Retouching, and Image Manipulation with Adobe Photoshop, by Daniel Margulis, New York, Wiley, 1995, ISBN: 0471018732.

PHOTO-ELECTRONIC IMAGING, online magazine. Web: *http://www.peimag.com*

Newsgroups: comp.graphics.apps.photoshop
rec.photo.darkroom
comp.graphics.misc

30

Digital Recording Studio/Service

"**P**eople are now sending in demos that they made in their bedrooms, even closets, that sound technically as good as what the top studios were producing ten years ago" is how KCRW Music Director Chris Douridas describes the effects of the home digital studio phenomenon. Now, with a large hard drive, a Pentium or Power Mac with a sixteen or thirty-two bit recording sound card, the right software, and some reasonable-quality microphones, a package costing far less than $10,000, you can turn a spare room in your house into a top-quality, professional recording studio.

Depending on the physical size of the room you use, you can record almost anything, from a single voice-over narration to a small choral group. Digital recording technology is far cleaner and quieter than its analog predecessor. This means that soundproofing is far less of a consideration than before (unless your neighbors mind the extra noise!). The market for high-quality digital recording is extremely large and includes small advertising agencies, local radio and television stations, independent multimedia producers, desktop video producers, composers, musicians, actors, publishers of books on tape and instructional audio programs, church and civic groups, and many more. If you purchase a portable DAT (Digital Audio Tape) recorder, priced from about $600 to $1,400, you can double your potential business by recording events, speeches, concerts, ambient location sounds, news, and interviews "in the field."

The technology required to set up a digital recording studio is rather straightforward. In addition to the Pentium or Power Mac computer, you will need a high-quality sound card which allows you to record sound to your computer's hard disk as well as translate the stored material so it can be played back in real time. There are many excellent choices for sound cards, including Digital Audio Lab's Card D Plus and Digidesign's Audio Media Design which enable you to record from two to sixteen "tracks" of music or sound. You will also need software that will allow you to record sound onto your hard disk, then edit it. Programs such as Digidesign's *Pro-Tools* have interfaces that work just like analog reel-to-reel recorders and mixing boards, so if you're familiar with these technologies, the transition to digital will be seamless. You can record multiple tracks, then quickly and easily cut, paste, splice, loop, compress, equalize, and otherwise manipulate the material to your liking. This software also enables you to "mix" multiple tracks together, which eliminates the need and expense of traditional analog mixing boards. There are also all-in-one hard disk recording systems available from manufacturers such as Akai and Alessis that include a dedicated computer, hard disk, sound card, and recording/editing software.

To find customers for your digital studio, first identify which market you wish to serve. Although the best results come from servicing one market well, there is no law saying you can't go after a number of markets when you're first starting out, then see which responds the most positively. This will also allow you to find out which kinds of clients and work you enjoy the most. No matter which market you target, you first have to produce a demonstration tape of your capabilities. Keep your tape short, about five minutes, and include a wide variety of recording situations, such a short narration, solo instrument, instrumental group, sound collage or ambient "soundscape," and a larger musical group, if your physical space permits. To find work from small advertising agencies, local radio and television stations, publishers of books on tape and instructional audio programs, approach them directly, preferably by phone. Find out who is responsible for audio production and try to develop a relationship with that person. For independent multimedia producers and desktop video producers, try networking online in user groups and professional forums. To find composers, musicians, and actors in need of recording services, place ads in local newsletters and publications that cater to these people. Also try leaving flyers in music stores and local theaters.

Most audio studios we know charge by the hour. The rate you charge should be commensurate with the capabilities you offer. Straightforward, high-quality digital recording and editing runs between $25 and $50 per hour. More complicated recording projects like those that require SMPTE lock-up, many tracks with multiple effects can be billed from $60 to $125 per hour.

Resources

The Audio Workstation Handbook (Music Technology Series), by Francis Rumsey, Newton, MA, Focal Press, 1996, ISBN: 0240514505.

The Billboard Guide to Home Recording, by Ray Baragary, New York, Watson-Guptill, 1996, ISBN: 0823083004.

Principles of Digital Audio, by Ken C. Pohlmann, New York, McGraw-Hill, 1995, ISBN: 0070504695.

Mix magazine. *Mix* is a magazine for commercial and project studio recording, concert sound, audio for film and video and more. Web: *http://www.mixmag.com*. Also available on newsstands.

Newsgroups: rec.audio.pro
rec.music.marketplce
comp.sys.ibm.pc.soundcard.misc

31.

Disk Copying Service

While we haven't found anyone earning a full-time income copying disks, we have found people copying disks as an add-on business or service. Disk copying can be an additional source of revenue for software companies, computer consultants and tutors, and someone providing backup services as well as someone already in the audio and video copying business. As a disk copying service, you can handle any combination of the following tasks for a software developer for an agreed-upon price:

- Duplicate diskettes
- Duplicate CD-ROMs
- Attach diskette labels
- Prepare retail boxes (fold, make inserts)
- Put diskettes, manuals, warranty sheets, etc., in boxes
- Attach Universal Product Code labels to boxes
- Shrink-wrap boxes
- Put retail boxes in shipping boxes
- Prepare shipping documents
- Ship merchandise and send copy of shipping documents to clients for invoicing

Your clients would be software companies that fall in between those large enough to have their own staff to carry out these functions and the very small companies that can only afford to handle these tasks themselves. There are thousands of software publishers that may fill a few thousand or even tens of thousands of orders a month split among various products. These production runs are simply not long enough to support a large-scale minimum-wage staff. Some companies use diskettes as a marketing tool to acquaint customers with their product. Others use diskettes to teach clients how to use their product.

The best part of this income generator is that it's extremely easy. Tasks like attaching labels and assembling boxes can be done, for example, while you're watching TV or waiting for dinner to cook. Also, the entry cost is low. It does require attention to detail and correctness and a sincere ambition to satisfy the customer. Using software like EZ-DISKKLONE, you can format, copy, verify, and serialize disks and print labels at the rate of better than one a minute on an inexpensive computer. Dedicated duplicator machines costing thousands are also available, but an ordinary computer can be outfitted with four disk drives so that it can produce as many as 300 disks per hour. One person can manage six to ten computers.

Typical prices for duplicating disks in quantities of 100 to 1,000 are approximately $1.10 to $1.75 each.

Prices may or may not include a label and disk sleeve. Additional charges can be made for packaging, customized printing of labels, and binding.

Resources

EZX Corp. EZ-Forms Automation Company offers two inexpensive disk-copying software packages: *EZ-DiskCopy PRO* and *WinDiskKlone.* 917 Oakgrove Drive, Ste. 101, Houston, TX 77058-3046, (281) 280-9900. Web: *http://www.ezx.com*

Newsgroups: comp.sys.mac.system
comp.sys.mac.misc
comp.os.ms-windows.win95.misc

32.

Drafting Service

Personal computers may not have replaced every drafting table, but they can automate much of the drafting work required for architecture and mechanical engineering. Computers make it increasingly possible to do this work at home.

Home-based drafting services work with companies that aren't large enough to employ someone full-time to do their drafting in-house. For example, small contractors doing room additions and swimming pool contractors often hire a drafting service to turn a design into a rendering for customers.

You need a background in drafting or architectural design. Training in drafting is available through a community college, or it can be learned through practical experience. Most of the work can be done at home, and there is usually not a great deal of competition. The work can be seasonal, however—swimming pools in the summer, remodeling during good weather. During these peak times, everyone wants renderings immediately, so you may be working under the pressure of deadlines. You also must make sure to get deposits up front before doing this type of work.

Pricing for work may be by the square foot or based on flat rates; for example, $500 for a swimming pool design. Gross earnings may reach six figures. The best way to get business is through personal contacts with contractors or homeowners. Start-up costs for computer and equipment including drafting tools, a blueprint machine, and drafting table run around $3,000 to $7,500.

Resources

Easy AutoCAD, by John Hood. New York, Windrest/McGraw-Hill, 1993.

AMERICAN DESIGN DRAFTING ASSOCIATION, P.O. Box 799, Rockville, MD, 20848-0799, (301) 460-6875. Publishes a bimonthly newsletter. *http://www.adda.org*

QUICKCAD software by Softdesk offers a powerful, low-cost program aimed specifically at building contractors.

Newsgroups: comp.cad.autocad
comp.sys.mac.graphics
comp.graphics
comp.cad.microstation
alt.cad
alt.cad.autocad
comp.cad.i-deas
comp.cad.pro-engineer

33.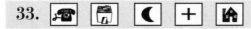

Electronic Clipping Service

In today's competitive world, businesses and professionals need to keep up with the constant flow of information about their field, their competitors, and their own products. Each day, in fact, hundreds of periodicals, newspapers, and journals publish articles that might contain useful data, product reviews, and inside information about competitors that many businesses simply miss.

An electronic clipping service is one answer to this dilemma, and a fascinating business for those who enjoy reading and learning about many fields. As a clipping service (also called an Alert Service), you track articles in many publications that are of interest to your clients. In the past, this service was performed manually, and so a clipping service would subscribe to hundreds of publications, read through them, and actually cut out the appropriate articles.

Today, however, a clipping service can be entirely computerized, using online databases and fast searches using the keywords and phrases that a client gives you. Any wire service story or article that uses those keywords or phrases is then delivered in original form or in an abstract to your computer or in print through the mails. In this way, you can help a business stay current with every article that mentions whatever subjects they want to follow.

To run a clipping service, you must enjoy sleuthing and investigating information, as well as have a solid expertise in computerized database searching, using online information services such as Dialog, America Online, CompuServe, Prodigy, Microsoft Network, and Mead Data Central (Lexis and Nexis). One area you need to be aware of, however, is that you may need to pay copyright fees for any articles that you clip or copy.

Clipping services usually charge a flat monthly fee that takes into account the costs they will incur on behalf of their client for using online services. These costs depend on how many documents the client is likely to receive and which database services you will be using, since you pay for these according to the amount of time you spend online, and each service varies in its per-hour fees.

Resources

The Information Broker's Handbook, by Sue Rugge and Alfred Glossbrenner, the Information Professional's Institute, 46 Hiller Drive, Oakland, CA 94618, 1997, (510) 649-9743, Web: *http://www.*ipn.net/ipi E-mail: 76220.454@Compuserve.com

The Lexis Companion: A Complete Guide to Effective Searching, by Jean McKnight, Reading, MA, Addison-Wesley, 1995, ISBN: 0201483351.

Starting and Operating a Clipping Service, by Demaris C. Smith, Babylon, NY, Pilot Books, ISBN: 0875760902.

COMPUSERVE EXECUTIVE NEWS SERVICE provides access to the Associated Press, United Press International, Reuters, and OTC NewsAlert, (800) 848-8990. Web: *http://www.*world.compuserve.com

AMERICA ONLINE also offers access to the Associated Press, United Press International, Reuters, and many more news organizations, (800) 827-6364. Web: *http://www.*aol.com

34.

Electronic Public Relations and Publicity Service

The number of online publications, newsletters, and news services will soon outnumber that of traditional print media. Even more significantly, a growing number of businesspeople, educators, civil employees, and consumers are turning to online publications as their first choice for news, learning about new business and social trends, technological and product updates, even entertainment. All these publications must meet the burgeoning demand for new content. One of their main sources for information is Online Public Relations and Publicity Services.

We see a steady growth in the demand for Online Public Relations and Publicity because there are actually two markets who need the service: 1) online media who publish information, and 2) those who create the information—the companies, individuals, government and civic organizations, and anybody else who benefits from having an audience find out about what they are doing or have done. If a software company creates a new accounting program that's easier to use and more powerful than what's currently available, that's worthwhile news to anyone who needs the product. Online publications whose content deals with computers, technology, or accounting know this and are always looking for this kind of news. As an online Public Relations and Publicity specialist, your job is to bring the news to the publication for the benefit of its readers. The other beneficiary is the software company who created the product. The more people who know about the product, the more people are likely to buy the product. It is always the information provider who will be your client and pay for your services. Your services will include E-mail press releases, company profiles, articles for online publication, E-mail letters, and electronic media kits which can even include multimedia content such as video, audio, graphics, and animation.

By specializing in online Public Relations, also know as PR, and Publicity you create a niche for yourself that allows you to stand out from the many established PR firms and publicists who do not concentrate on the online world. The online publications and media are also rather different from the print media. The online landscape changes continuously. New publications and media are constantly springing up, and the technology required to deliver information changes frequently. Toyota, for example, launched a promotional campaign for its new line Lexus luxury cars through a targeted E-mail campaign to 30,000 registered visitors of its Web site. By making the online world your specialty, you will have the time, focus, and expertise to stay abreast of the latest developments. This will make you a valuable resource for your clients.

To do well in online PR and Publicity you need to be creative, to write well, and be eager to learn about and enjoy the challenge of a quickly changing business landscape. It is helpful if you have public relations or corporate communications experience, but it's not essential. In terms of equipment, you will need a business-level PC, 33.6 modem (minimum), a reliable Internet Service Provider (ISP), bulk E-mail software, contact management software, and a database program to keep track of clients, publications, etc.

Within your specialty as an online PR and Publicity service, you can concentrate even further in terms of the type of clients you serve. Areas of concentration include high-technology companies, manufacturers, entertainment companies, nonprofit organizations, even celebrities.

Earning potential is similar to that of traditional PR agencies. As an independent practitioner, you can expect to earn between $35,000 and $75,000 annually. Networking online is a good place to pick up clients. You might also try contacting large PR agencies and asking them to outsource their online PR work to you. You can also contact companies directly, either through a direct "snail mail" or a targeted E-mail campaign.

Resources

Electronic Public Relations, by Eugene Marlow and Janice Sileo, Belmont, CA, Wadsworth, 1996, ISBN: 0534262449.

IDG LIST SERVICES provides E-mail lists of high-tech users who subscribe to online magazines. These users have agreed to accept promotional E-mailings. (508) 875-5000, *http://www*.idglist.com

NEW RESI DATA provides E-mail lists of segmented users, such as lawyers, accountants, doctors, etc., and many other business lists. These users have agreed to accept promotional E-mail. (201) 476-1800, *http://www*.newresi.com

NETMAILER, by Alphatel Communications, allows you to send as many 2,000 personalized E-mailings per hour. (508) 475-2900, *http://www*.alphasoftware. com

PR NEWSTARGET, by Arial Software, offers electronic news distribution to high-tech editors. (503) 646-4515, *http://www*.newstarget.com

PUBLIC RELATIONS SOCIETY OF AMERICA, the largest organization for public relations professionals. 33 Irving Place, New York, NY 10003-2376, (212) 995-2230, E-mail: hdq@prsa.org, *http://www*.prsa.org

35. | ABC | 🗑 | + | 100,000 |

Employee Manual Development and Writing Service

One specialized area of business consulting is helping companies write comprehensive, informative, and legally passable documents that serve as their employee manuals. Nearly every company that employs more than ten or fifteen people will want to have available standard and consistent information that spells out for employees the policies and procedures for performance appraisals, sexual harassment, vacation and benefit terms, regulations on safety and substance abuse, dress codes, employee development, and many other issues.

Most of this work can be done using standard word-processing and desktop publishing software, but one company, JIAN Tools for Sales, has also developed a software package specifically for this purpose. Called the *EmployeeManualMaker,* the software provides formats and templates that allow you to create manuals more easily and accurately.

The qualifications for running this business should include a good background in human resources, organizational behavior, and personnel development. You also need to have at least some knowledge of the various federal and state government laws about equal opportunity employment, harassment, hiring and firing regulations, insurance requirements, and so on. Excellent writing skills and personal communication habits are also critical, since you will be working directly with company presidents and directors of personnel.

Fees for this service can be quite lucrative, ranging from $5,000 to $20,000, depending on the length of the document and amount of time you need to spend developing the material with the executives. Such manuals are often vital pieces in a company's public relations and hiring procedures and are, therefore, worth their cost.

The best ways to get business include networking in professional organizations and among business planners and consultants who specialize in working with small companies. You might also consider sending out direct-mail announcements to companies in your area, being sure to follow up with a call and samples of your work. This business is a good add-on business if you are already operating a consulting or business-planning company.

Because of the legal aspect of these manuals and the frequency of lawsuits filed against employers, you will want to have a contract for any job you take that eliminates and minimizes your liability in the event of an employment lawsuit. You might also wish to have errors and omissions insurance to protect you against any mistakes you might make in developing manuals.

Resources

DESCRIPTIONSWRITENOW! Knowledge Point Software. Available in retail software stores, this program aids in writing job descriptions that might be part of an employee manual. About $75.

EMPLOYEEMANUALMAKER, JIAN Tools for Sales, Inc., 1975 West Camino Real, Ste. 301, Mountainview, CA 94040, (800) 346-5426, (415) 245-5600. A personnel handbook on disk that contains more than 110 prewritten policies and 30 employee benefits, a new employee orientation guide, interview questions, and an employment application form. About $99. Web: *http://www*.jianusa.com

Newsgroup: alt.publish.electronic

36.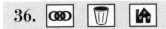

Event and Meeting Planner

If you enjoy planning and organizing events of all kinds and have an excellent track record for getting things done without forgetting even the slightest detail, this business may be the one for you. Although the field has become very competitive in recent years, a good event planner can work steadily with a variety of companies that need to attend trade shows or put on sales conferences, create product announcements, set up seminars and training workshops, and even stage employee parties.

Event planners today are no longer simply well-paid socialites; they are highly trained and professional individuals who know where to find high-quality goods and reliable services at the best prices. Whether it's catering services or clowns, musicians or multimedia equipment, the event planner has names and numbers of suppliers at his or her fingertips.

This need for professionalism and contacts is, in fact, one of the driving forces in including event planning as a computer-based business. The most effective event planners will not hesitate to use their computers to make sure that the job is done efficiently and well. Software such as project management and scheduling programs, database programs, and contact managers all allow an event planner to keep track of the myriad arrangements behind the scenes of an event, thereby avoiding slip-ups and mistakes.

Getting started in this business is easiest if you have a public relations or communications background and perhaps have done event planning for a company, volunteer organization, or association before. If you don't have a background, you might wish to work with an existing company to get experience. You should also join your city's convention and visitor bureau as a membership often entitles you to inside information about trade shows and a free listing of your company's name in any materials they send out to prospective attendees.

Another aspect of event planning is contest organizing, in which you help companies set up sales contests for the general public. To do this, you need to be familiar with your state's laws about contests, and it also helps to have a statistical background so you can deal with the mathematics behind designing successful contests.

A top-notch event planner can work for a wide range of corporations, planning important functions that might make or break a product announcement or sales conference. As a result, fees for event planning can range from $40 to $60 per hour and up to thousands of dollars per event.

Resources

MEETINGTRAK, Phoenix Solutions, 39560 Stevenson Place, Ste. 112, Fremont, CA 94539, (800) 779-7430, (510) 713-2685, a software program costing $29.95 that enables you to plan meetings, seminars, and conventions by computer; manage registration, people, exhibitors, and speaker needs; and produce confirmation letters, badges, tickets, and marketing labels. Web: *http:www.*psitrak.com

MEETING PROFESSIONALS INTERNATIONAL, 4455 LBJ Freeway, Ste. 1200 Dallas, TX 75244, (972) 702-3000, a trade association for meeting planners. Web: *http://www.*mpiweb.org

37.

Expert Brokering Service

An expert location service matches businesses that need highly specialized professional help with the people who can meet their needs. Two growing work force trends are converging to make expert location services an up-and-coming computer-based business. First, with many companies operating leaner and meaner, they are turning to freelance outside experts for ad hoc consulting services rather than keeping expensive experts on staff. Second, with a growing number of middle- and upper-management executives being laid off, many highly skilled professionals are now self-employed and need help marketing their services.

The expert broker therefore puts the two parties together as needed for either a short-term job or an ongoing consulting or training contract. For example, an expert service might provide a client with a direct-mail specialist, a lawyer with specific expertise in exports, a materials engineer specializing in plastics, or a toxic waste manager. Whatever the situation, the expert would then perform a job for the client or teach specific skills to their employees.

Success in this business depends on creating a pool of reliable, respected experts you can count on and attracting companies that are looking for such truly specialized assistance. Using your own contacts is the best way to get started, but you can also turn to telemarketing and/or direct-mail pieces addressed to the directors of appropriate corporate departments, such as engineering, manufacturing, finance, human resource development, training, etc.

Start-up costs to become an expert location service are low and income potential is good, since you take a cut of the fees paid to the expert, typically as much as 25 percent. Some expert location services can earn as much as $60,000 a year. To get started you need a computer with a hard disk; contact management, database, or personal information software; and other basic business software, a fax, and a telephone headset. You will also need to write contracts with your clients, so you may wish to explore the many prewritten contract software programs available.

Resources

The Encyclopedia of Associations, published annually by Gale Research in Detroit, is available in the reference section of most libraries. This three-volume set lists professional and trade associations of all kinds, which are an excellent source for locating consultants and experts in most fields.

Newsgroups: biz.marketplace
biz.marketplace.computers
alt.business.career-opportunities.executives
misc.entrepreneurs

Also see chapter 6 for information about using online sources to locate prospective clients.

38. Fax-on-Demand Services

A fax-on-demand service is an exciting marketing and information concept that is both a tool for anyone with a home office to consider and a home business in itself. The technology required to turn fax-on-demand into a business consists of multiple telephone lines, a modified computer with a special fax board, and customized software that makes the system into an automatic fax delivery machine that can assist with sales, marketing, customer support, and "fax publishing" for large numbers of clients. Large companies are setting up such systems in-house to speed customer requests for information while reducing their costs of providing it. A fax-on-demand service can provide this for smaller companies and professionals.

Generally a fax-on-demand service works as follows: First, a typical system holds up to 1,000 extensions that the fax-on-demand service "leases" to other businesses or individual professionals who want their clients or employees to have information available twenty-four hours a day, seven days a week. These people can call the fax-on-demand service at any time, listen to a synthesized voice telling them what's available, or punch in an extension they've already been told to ask for, and they then leave their fax number on the computer. A few seconds later, the computer calls the person back and immediately faxes several pages of up-to-date product literature, a newsletter, or whatever document the lessee wants delivered.

Here are a few examples of the possible uses of a fax-on-demand service. A bank can give customers the special phone number to call to obtain current information about its daily loan and investment rates; busy retailers, wholesalers, and manufacturer's agents can have their prospects and customers call the service for product information; plumbers or carpenters can enable new callers to obtain rate information and schedules while away at another job; a restaurant can have customers call the number to receive a copy of that day's menu; and a mail-order company can offer more in-depth or up-to-the-minute product descriptions than their catalog does for customers who want more information on an item.

The fax-on-demand software can also be programmed to perform automatic broadcasting services whereby faxes are delivered to large groups of people on a regularly scheduled basis. Such services are useful for companies that need to communicate regularly with sales reps or employees to update them on products or specials, and for associations and trade groups that must communicate with members or associates around the country.

Fax-on-demand is a good add-on service for answering-service and voice mail businesses, as many of today's voice mail systems also have a fax-on-demand option or component.

Fax-on-demand can also be used in conjunction with a 900 number as a way of selling information such as a newsletter or a specialized report. Buyers get charged on their telephone bill for the material they receive by fax with no postage stamps and no collections on your part.

Running a fax-on-demand service requires an initial investment ranging around $10,000 to $15,000 for the hardware (including a scanner needed to scan in the documents that your clients want to have available on the system) and software to record the incoming calls, track them, and bill your clients. You may also choose to use an 800/888-number or 900-number phone line for incoming calls and additional lines for outgoing faxes. One important concept to keep in mind is that your customers, too, can make money through the service; for example, a restaurant can lease a line from you and charge people for calling in to receive a special recipe by fax, or a plumber might send faxes to do-it-yourselfers for a small fee.

Revenues from this business vary greatly, depending on the number of clients you can get and how extensively they use the system. Some services charge from $150 to $300 per month for each client to cover incoming calls with unlimited fax responses. Other services charge a lower monthly fee but place a cap on the number of faxes allowed without additional charges.

A fax-on-demand service is also a good add-on business for an answering/voice-mail service or a consultant who may work with businesses in marketing or sales.

Resources

Teleconnect magazine, (212) 691-8215, *http://www.*flatironpublishing.com/tc–home.html

Sarah Stambler's Marketing with Technology Newsletter, 370 Central Park West, #210, New York, NY 10025, (212) 222-1713, voice; or (212) 678-6357, fax. Web: *http://www.*mwt.com, E-mail: sarah@mwt.com

ALTERNATIVE TECHNOLOGY CORPORATION (ATC) sells a turnkey system for computer novices called *MarketFax* that includes all hardware and software for $12,500 or a kit with everything you need for $7,000. The creative founder and owner, Tom Kadala, is constantly dreaming up ways to use the business. One North Street, P.O. Box 357, Hastings-on-Hudson, NY 10706, (914) 478-5900. For a demo, call (800) 783-SEND, ext. 103.

Newsgroups: comp.dcom.fax
comp.sys.misc

39

Financial Information Service

Because large numbers of baby boomers are now into their peak earning years when they are investing their savings for retirement, a growth in the number of financial products is all but inevitable. People will need help sifting through the competing alternatives as well as a predictable glut of information focused on this lucrative market.

Selling financial products is one way to go in this growing field, and there are other ways to exploit an ability to analyze financial matters. You may become licensed as a financial planner; you may publish a financial newsletter; or you may be able to gain the confidence of clients, both companies as well as individuals, and sell your expertise as an analyst or adviser. Your computer will be the means to access information and do your research and analysis.

While you don't need an M.B.A. to operate in the financial arena, you do need a solid background in the financial markets so you know where to look for information and how to get the inside story on investment opportunities. You should be familiar with software that can handle the analysis of business data or be able to develop your own spreadsheets and formulas for projections about a company's future profitability. You should also be a facile user of the information available on the Internet, conversant with numerous online databases like Dow Jones News/Retrieval, Disclosure II, Company Analyzer, and TRW Business Credit Reports, to do research and analysis. Finally, you might be a member of a local bulletin board system, from which you can get tips and information by chatting with others.

The one caveat about providing financial information and services is that you must be extremely careful about how you promote your business to avoid coming into conflict with the federal and state licensing and regulatory laws. You must maintain a reputation for honesty and integrity, in addition to your credibility as a researcher and information mogul.

Fees for your service might range from $100 to $250 per month per client for supplying daily or weekly reports, charts, graphs, and articles. With forty clients at $100 per month, you will be earning $48,000 a year. The best way to get business is word of mouth, since this is a field in which trust counts a great deal. One way to begin your business is to offer free information to friends or a few clients over two or three months until you can begin charging them comfortably once they see how much information you can obtain. From there, you can build up a larger list of accounts using their referrals or endorsements.

In addition to a personal computer setup, you will need a high-speed modem, a laser printer, and a good spreadsheet or word-processing package that allows you to generate tables, charts, and graphs in your reports to clients.

Resources

THE AMERICAN SOCIETY OF CERTIFIED LIFE UNDERWRITERS AND CHARTERED FINANCIAL CONSULTANTS, 270 South Bryn Mawr Avenue, Bryn Mawr, PA 19010-2195, (610) 526-2500, offers correspondence courses for certification. Web: *http://www*.agentsonline.com

NATIONAL ENDOWMENT FOR FINANCIAL EDUCATION, 4695 South Monaco Street, Denver, CO 80237-3403, (303) 220-1200, offers self-study courses to become a certified financial planner. $1995, including books and the cost of the tests. Web: *http://www*.nefe.org

THE INTERNATIONAL ASSOCIATION FOR FINANCIAL PLANNING, 5775 Glenridge Dr., N.E., Ste. B300, Atlanta, GA 30328, (404) 845-0011. Publishes a monthly magazine. Web: *http://www*.iafp.org

THE INSTITUTE OF CERTIFIED FINANCIAL PLANNERS, 3801 E. Florida Avenue, Ste. 708, Denver CO 80210, (303) 759-4900, (800) 282-7526, Fax: (303) 759-0749, Web: *http://www*.icfp.org

40.

Form Design Service

If you are thinking about starting or are currently operating any kind of desktop publishing or graphic design business, take note that you can expand your customer base and income by also offering a professional form creation and design service. The market for this business includes companies and services of all kinds that have special needs for forms such as invoices, purchase orders, customer forms, questionnaires, or other paper documents they may use frequently and need to print in large quantities. An important area of form design is designing computer forms for online use where receptionists or operators keyboard information into grids on the screen.

Form design is in some ways akin to the field of ergonomic designing, in that it's becoming recognized by many businesses as a previously overlooked factor in reducing errors, increasing efficiency, and ensuring that a business transaction is properly done. A poorly designed form can take a salesperson much longer to fill out or cause an employee to process information incorrectly, and thereby cost the company money.

Like most graphics and publishing work, form creation used to be done manually using paste-up type, rules, and screens, but now a personal computer and specialized software such as *PerForm* (JetForm Corp.) make designing forms a sophisticated process that can be done on screen with many graphic options from which to choose. The created form can then be printed out in high-resolution type on a laser printer or linotronic machine or be transferred directly to a file as a graphic image that can be stored online by a computer system.

To market yourself as a form designer, you should have a good background in graphics, type design, and color. You also need to have good communication skills so that you can interview your clients to understand their needs and create the best form for them.

Fees for form designing range from $25 to hundreds of dollars for complex jobs that require color separations and special printing.

Resources

HotDocs from Capsoft Development is a software program that allows you to create customized templates for any kind of form. *HotDocs* works with *Microsoft Word,* Corel *WordPerfect,* and Lotus *Word Pro* word-processing programs.

PerForm (JetForm Corp.) is available in retail software stores. Some form designers also use desktop publishing software such as *Ventura Publisher* or *Aldus PageMaker.*

BUSINESS FORMS MANAGEMENT ASSOCIATION, 319 S.W. Washington Street, Ste. 710, Portland, OR 97204, (503) 227-3393. Professional association that publishes books and a directory. Web: *http://www.bfma.org/~bfma*

Newsgroup: comp.text.frame

41.

HTML Programmer

HTML (Hyper Text Markup Language) is the international language of the World Wide Web. HTML allows text, graphics, and now video and audio to be combined in a Web page or site, then posted on the Internet where it can be accessed by anyone with a browser and a connection. Programming in HTML is a much-needed skill whose demand is growing with the size of the World Wide Web itself.

Although HTML is a programming language, it is actually very easy to learn. Anyone with an aptitude for computers and logical thinking can become fluent in HTML in less than a month. If you remember the older DOS-based word-processing programs like *WordPerfect 5.1* and were able to master them, HTML should be a piece of cake.

As we stated, the need for good HTML programming is extremely widespread. People who are not outright experts in the language, such as graphic designers, Web masters, MIS (management information system) staff, or corporate communications people, often wind up doing their own programming when developing their Web sites. We see opportunity for those who become experts in HTML to provide services to these people. As an HTML expert, you will be able to provide sophisticated solutions to your clients and save them a great deal of time and aggravation in the process. Because of your focus on the language, you will always be aware of the latest developments in features and capabilities. You will be on top of all the capabilities available and will be able to incorporate them into your client's Web sites.

The World Wide Web, despite all the hoopla it's been getting these last few years, is still developing. There are a great many generalists out there who wear many hats: typically a Web site designer also writes the text, programs the HTML, secures the server on which the site will reside, submits the site to popular search engines, and often is responsible for promoting the site as well. You can take considerable advantage of this situation by being among the first to make a business of a Web-based specialty.

You will need an up-to-date computer system with a minimum 33.6 modem. You will also need to research what the latest version of HTML is. At the writing of this book, the current version is 4.0. You will need a good Web editor, such as Adobe's *PageMill* (Mac) or Softquad, Inc.'s *HotMetal Pro.* In addition to your programming skills, part of the value you will offer to your clients is your up-to-the-second knowledge of the Web and

HTML programming developments. Your best source for this information is the Web itself. Use search engine databases and online service providers such America Online and CompuServe religiously to keep yourself in tune with the industry.

Good strategies for finding clients include networking with the graphic designers in your area who design Web sites. Tell them you'll do all their HTML programming. Watch their faces light up. Contact local ISP (Internet Service Providers) and tell them what you do. Network with user groups in your area and online. You can even contact MIS, corporate communications, and media services departments of corporations you find online and ask them to outsource their HTML programming to you.

You can charge on an hourly basis or by project. This is a very new area, and industry standard rates have not been set yet. You can comfortably charge at least $20 per hour when you start out and see what the market will bear from that point forward.

Resources

How to Use HTML3, by Scott Arpajian, New York, Ziff Davis, March 1996, ISBN: 1562763903.

HTML and the Art of Authoring for the World Wide Web, by Bebo White, Dordrecht, Netherlands, Kluwer Academic Publishing, May 1996, ISBN: 079239691X.

THE AMERICAN MULTI-MEDIA INSTITUTE is a nonprofit, international association serving professionals who promote, produce and use the World Wide Web. *http://www.*ami.org

HTML WRITERS GUILD, the first international organization of World Wide Web page authors and Internet publishing professionals. Offers a wide range of HTML tools and resources. *http://www.*hwg.org

*http://www.*CNET.COM is one of the many great sources of daily news about the Web, the Internet, and computer technology and culture.

ZDNET, another excellent Meta-site offering the latest news and developments. *http://www.*zdnet.com

Newsgroups: alt.html.webedit
alt.programming.html
complang.html

42.

Indexing Service

Indexing services can be divided essentially into two different fields. The first type of indexing service serves the publishing industry. This kind of indexer reads page proofs and prepares the index that you see at the back of most nonfiction books. To be in this business, you must obviously enjoy reading a variety of books and have the ability to read quickly and categorize information into appropriate topics and subtopics according to stylistic conventions. Many authors do not have the time or desire to index their own books, and some publishers don't want them to, so publishers frequently hire independent indexers.

The second type of indexing service serves the field of online computer database publishers. Currently there are over 6,000 databases that are accessible either directly or through database vendors such as Dialog, BRS, Dow Jones, and CompuServe. Most databases store what are called "bibcites," which are bibliographic citations to thousands of articles according to the title, the publication name and date, the author's name, and usually a brief summary (abstract) rather than the full text of the article. To speed up searches on articles, each "bibcite" includes several descriptors or keywords that quickly identify the major topics covered in the original article. When a researcher is trying to locate information, he or she therefore tells the computer, "Find all articles that are about this or that topic," and the computer searches through just the keywords to produce a list very rapidly.

As you might guess, it is indexers who read original articles and decide which keywords to use. (The indexer is often the same person who prepared the abstract of the article, which this book covers under the category of "Abstracting Service.") This kind of database indexing is a more specialized profession than book indexing, because often each database producer has a specific list of allowable keywords that the indexer must use.

Whichever kind of indexing you do, you must be a detail-oriented person and enjoy working with words. It also helps to have a background in the subject areas you are indexing or a broad enough general knowledge and interest to ferret out central ideas and relevant information. The computerization of this business comes in the form of software that allows you to build an index using specialized software that helps you categorize, alphabetize, and keep track of page references.

Generally computer database indexing pays better than book indexing. While book indexers may earn only $15,000 a year, those indexing computer databases may earn $30,000 to $35,000.

The best way to get business is to contact publishers or database services directly and send them a sample of your work. Many database publishers only work with local indexers, so to find database publishers in your area, decide what type of databases you could work with and then search a directory like *Epsco Index* and *Abstracting Dictionary* or the *Cuadra Directory of Online Databases.* To locate book publishers for whom you might work, check into *Writer's Market,* by Writer's Digest, or *Literary Marketplace* published by Bowker.

Resources

The Art of Indexing, by Larry S. Bonura, New York, Wiley, 1994, ISBN: 0471014494.

A Guide to Indexing Software, by Linda K. Fetters, Maria Coughlin, and Ty Koontz, American Society of Indexers, Seattle, WA, 1994, ISBN: 0936547278.

Indexing from A to Z, by Hans H. Wellisch, Bronx, New York, H.W. Wilson, 1996, ISBN: 082420882X.

Marketing Your Indexing Services, by Anne Leach (editor), American Society of Indexers, Seattle, WA, 1995, ISBN: 0936547286.

Running Your Indexing Business, American Society of Indexers, Seattle, 1995, ISBN: 0936547324.

AMERICAN SOCIETY OF INDEXERS, P.O. Box 48267, Seattle, WA 98148-0267, Fax: (206) 727-6430, E-mail: asi@well.com, Web: *http://www.*well. com/user/asi/

EDITORIAL FREELANCERS ASSOCIATION, P.O. Box 2050, Madison Square Station, New York, NY 10159-2050, (212) 929-5400. A trade association that includes editors, writers, researchers, proofreaders, indexers, and others. The association produces a survey of members' rates and operates a "job phone," *http://www.*the-efa.com

UNITED STATES DEPARTMENT OF AGRICULTURE, GRADUATE SCHOOL, Independence Avenue, South Agriculture Bldg., Washington, DC 20250, offers a correspondence course in indexing.

Newsgroups: comp.databases.visual-dbase
comp.databases.ms-access

43.

Information Brokering

Our society is drowning in information, yet finding the particular information we need when we need it is increasingly a challenge. In the past ten years, the new career of information broker, or information retrieval service, has developed to meet this challenge. Information research is now a multibillion-dollar industry that is growing by 12 to 14 percent a year, with hundreds of companies, small and large, offering search and retrieval services.

Like a detective, the information broker tracks down and locates any information a client needs, be it market research for a company investigating a possible new product idea, a legal search about government regulations for a law firm, or an erudite biography search for a movie producer. Going far beyond what even a specialized librarian does, the information broker does far more than look up information in books and periodicals. The main tools for the professional information broker are interviews with experts and tapping into any of the 6,000 or more databases on more than 500 online computer systems that hold millions of documents in their original form or as abstracts (summary form). In fact, with so many databases and online systems, each with its own set of passwords and methods of use, today's information broker does best by specializing in a particular type of research such as high technology, business, manufacturing, or whatever.

To do well in this business, you do not necessarily need a degree in library science, although it may help some people. You must have, however, an absolute love for information and a never-say-die attitude in sleuthing through whatever sources you need to find what your client wants. Because this is still a relatively new field, you must also have an ability to sell your service, since many people are not used to paying for information; still others consider it a commodity available free on the Internet. And last, it helps to be somewhat familiar with the many online information services available, at least to the point of knowing how to do a computer search cost effectively and how to get help when you need it.

Information brokers typically charge between $20 and $100 per hour, or they hire themselves out on a monthly retainer for businesses that have frequent need of information searches. Typically, full-time brokers gross between $17,500 and $75,000 per year. Some brokers command fees as high as $200 an hour and produce significantly more income. Networking and personal contacts in organizations, such as trade and business associations in the industries or fields in which you specialize, are the best sources of business. Speaking and offering seminars on information searching at meetings and trade shows or writing for trade journals can also be effective.

To be in this business, you will need a personal computer, a high-speed modem, a large-capacity hard disk for storage of information you retrieve, a CD-ROM drive, a fax machine to receive copies of original documents, and a good printer for your reports to clients. In all, you might spend about $5,000 to set up your home office. Do not forget that you will also need to pay monthly fees to all the online information services to which you subscribe.

Resources

The Information Broker's Handbook, by Sue Rugge and Alfred Glossbrenner. The Information Professional's Institute, 46 Hiller Drive, Oakland, CA 94618, 1997, (510) 649-9743, Web: *http://www.*ipn.net/ipi E-mail: 76220.454@Compuserve.com

The Prentice-Hall Directory of Online Business Information, by Christopher Engholm and Scott Grimes, Englewood Cliffs, NJ, Prentice-Hall Trade, November 1996, ISBN: 0132552825.

The Online 100: Online Magazine's Field Guide to the 100 Most Important Online Databases, by Mick O'Leary, Online, 1996, ISBN: 0910965145.

ASSOCIATION OF INDEPENDENT INFORMATION PROFESSIONALS, contact (609) 730-8759, E-mail: 73263.34@Compuserve.com for information and membership; the association can also be contacted online in Section 4 of the Working from Home Forum on CompuServe.

INFORMATION BROKER'S RESOURCE KIT, $13.50. The Information Professional's Institute, 46 Hiller Drive, Oakland, CA 94618, 1997, (510) 649-9743, *http://www.*ipn.net/ipi

Making Money in the Information Business at Home, by Sue Rugge and Seena Sharp. Two audiotapes. (800) 561-8990.

Newsgroups: biz.marketplace.services.discussion
biz.marketplace.discussion

biz.marketplace.computers.discussion
biz.marketplace.international.discussion

44.

Internet Consultant

Many organizations are recognizing that the Internet and the World Wide Web offer many advantages over traditional communications media and are more cost-efficient. Although they understand the basic advantages, even today, many businesses still don't have a firm grasp on how the Internet actually works, or specifically how it can help them achieve their goals. These businesses are prime candidates for the services of an Internet Consultant.

Internet Consultants are somewhat different from computer consultants. Internet Consultants are specialists whose domain is, of course, the Internet and its component parts. Additionally, Internet Consultants must have a feel for marketing and communications. Most companies turn to the Internet to add strength to their marketing and to improve the efficiency of their communications. Specifically, Internet Consultants help companies and organizations understand and implement Internet-based solutions in the following areas:

- Internet connectivity and access
- Intranet/Internet connectivity
- Internet communications and transactions such as E-mail, video conferencing, interactive forms, secure transactions, digital money (or Ecash).
- Internet applications such as Archie, Veronica, FTP, telnet, gopher, *http://www.* wais
- "Netiquette" and rules for proper and appropriate network usage.
- How to research, including finding addresses, databases, vendors, bulletin boards, and service companies

If you believe your experience with and knowledge of the Internet and your understanding of the basics of marketing and general business knowledge would be of help to a company getting its feet wet in the cyberpond, you may have what it takes to be an Internet Consultant. Your potential clients will include businesses who are either considering putting up a Web site or have just done so. Potential clients also include companies and organizations who have had a basic Web site up for a while but wish to expand their Internet presence. You can prospect for clients in both the virtual and actual domains. Virtually, start by putting up your own Web site that explains your experience, services, and areas of expertise. Then publicize your site through targeted E-mail and online networking in user groups, newsgroups, and discussion groups. Try to avoid "spamming," which is overtly advertising yourself. Rather, contribute useful information to newsgroups and discussion groups and try to establish yourself as an expert. This will be far more effective. In actuality, networking at your local chamber of commerce and other civic and business organizations is quite helpful. You can also host free Internet or World Wide Web seminars for prospective clients in public meeting rooms, etc. In addition, you can write articles on relevant Internet and business issues and get them published in business, computer print, and online magazines. These activities will establish you as an expert whom people will want to turn to.

A successful, well-known Internet Consultant with a track record can charge up to $200 per hour and up to $2,000 per day, even more. If you're starting out, your rates will need to be much lower. The average range for Internet consultants with a year or two of experience is about $40 to $125 per hour. Day rates vary from $350 to $600. Contact other Internet and computer consultants and try to find out what they charge, then set your prices accordingly—somewhere in the middle of the figures you are quoted.

Resources

Internet Access Essentials: Everything You Need to Know, by Ed Tittel and Margaret Robbins, San Diego, CA, AP Professional, 1995, ISBN: 0126913935.

The Online Business Atlas: The Best Online Sites, Resources and Services in—Management, Marketing and Promotion, Sales, Entrepreneurial Ventures, by Douglas Goldstein and Joyce Flory, New York, Irwin Professional Publishing, October 1996, ISBN: 0786308885.

Telecommunications in Business: Strategy and Application, by John Vargo, Ray Hunt, and Richard D. Irwin, New York, Irwin Professional Publishing, 1996, ISBN: 0256197873.

Tricks of the Internet Gurus, by Philip Baczewski and Billy Barron, Indianapolis, IN, Howard W. Sams and Company, 1994, ISBN: 0672305992.

BUSINESS.NET ONLINE magazine: *http://www.iworld.com/business*

Internet World Online Magazine: *http://www*.internetworld.com

The Web Developer's Virtual Library. A good resource site that contains an extensive list of bookmarks, reference material, and software useful to Web consultants. *http://www*.wdvl.com

Independent Computer Consultants Association. U.S. nonprofit professional organization for computer consultants. (800) 774-4222, *http://www*.icca.org, E-mail: 70007.1407@compuserve.com

Newsgroup: comp.help

45.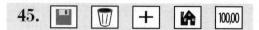

Internet Service Provider

The Internet and the World Wide Web is not a nebulous collection of sites that exist in a mysterious dimension called cyberspace. What we call "the Web" is actually a complex network of servers (host computers) linked together through routers and high-speed communications lines that share common protocol languages. Every site you've ever accessed on the Web actually resides on a server somewhere on the network. These servers, in many cases, aren't the large mainframe or mini computers you might imagine. That site you browsed last night may well have been "served" on a Pentium PC. And you might be surprised to find out that these servers don't reside in the upper floors of corporate high-rises or communication towers. There are more than a few servers on the World Wide Web residing in people's living rooms and dens.

Running a server on the World Wide Web as a home business has a number of clear advantages. Your income is derived from "renting" space on your server. The larger the Web site, the more space it takes up and the more you can charge for rent. In addition to occupying space, Web sites also generate "traffic." The more a site is accessed and viewed, the greater its traffic. Higher traffic takes up more "bandwidth." Bandwidth is the second resource you have to sell as a server, and the greater a site's traffic, the more you charge for it. The great thing here is that once a site resides on your server, all the income you derive from it is passive. It's like owning real estate; you can charge rent for its use.

The technical requirements for running a server are straightforward. You will need a high-speed Pentium, 200Mhz minimum with at least thirty-two MB of RAM. The more storage space you have, the more "real estate" you can rent out. We recommend a minimum of eight Gigabytes. As your business grows, you may need additional storage space, or even a second computer. You will also need a high-speed telephonic connection to the Web. Running a server over regular phone lines with a 36.6 modem won't cut it. You will need to lease a special line from your local phone company to gain greater bandwidth. Bandwidth is the essential commodity in Web hosting. The more bandwidth you can offer, the more competitive you will be. Do some research into this area; we don't have the space to devote to it. As a baseline recommendation, we strongly suggest that you lease at least a T1 digital phone line and highly recommend that you lease a DS3 line, the fastest available. After you buy the computer hardware, the phone line will be your greatest expense. Expect to pay at least $2,000 to $3,000 per month for your high-speed connection. You will also need a specialized operating system, in most cases UNIX, communications and protocol (http, FTP, etc.) software. Most of these resources are available on the Web itself. Configuring a server and maintaining it can get rather technical. You may want to consider hiring a consultant to get you up and running and to be a phone call away in case of problems.

If the idea of actually owning a physical server and leasing a connection seems overwhelming, you can offer Web site hosting on a virtual server. A virtual server is where you don't have a physical computer—you just "rent" space on somebody else's and configure it to resell to clients as Web server space. The only disadvantage to this is that you are at the mercy of someone else's space limitations, service schedule, and general business fortunes. If the owner of the physical server upon which you rent space goes out of business, so do you, at least temporarily.

Once you've got your server and high-speed connection up, or have a virtual server deal in place, you can market your service to a wide number of potential clients. Web site designers and design agencies are always looking for new, competitively priced high-speed servers. Send an E-mail to every Webmaster you come across when browsing sites. Network with local Internet Service Providers. They generally serve their own sites, but sometimes these sites get full and you can take their overload. You may even want to consider a small ad in a national computer or Internet-oriented magazine.

The income potential for Web server hosting is quite good. Competitive rates for hosting a twenty-five MB site, served over DS3 lines is about $40 per month. If you rent out one Gigabyte of space, that's $1,600 a month. If you rent out eight Gigabytes, that's $12,800 a month! This doesn't count the income you will derive from charging for bandwidth. As we said, busy sites take up more bandwidth, and you can charge accordingly. Bandwidth charges tend to fluctuate. To determine current competitive rates for bandwidth, call your competitors and find out what they charge.

As you can see, a Web serve host business can work well as a stand-alone business. It is also an excellent add-on for a Web site design business or a specialty Web programming business and is a great way to finance a Web publication.

Resources

Boardwatch magazine, 8500 West Bowles Ave., Ste. 210, Littleton, CO 80123, (800) 933-6038, *http://www*.boardwatch.com

Directory of Internet Service Providers. Lists Internet service providers by area code. Comes out bimonthly. Published by *Boardwatch* magazine.

THE INTERNIC, http://rs.internic.net. Leading registrar of domain names and provides tools and resources to the Internet community.

NETGUIDE ONLINE MAGAZINE, *http://www*.netguidemag.com. Also available on newsstands.

INFORMATION WEEK ONLINE MAGAZINE, *http://techweb.cmp.com/iw*. Also available on newsstands.

UNIX WORLD ONLINE MAGAZINE, *http://www*.wcmh.com/uworld

The Web: http://www.boardwatch.com. Offers the current and back issues of *Boardwatch* to 1994 with key word search.

46.

Internet Trainer

The Internet is the fastest-growing communications medium since television. At the time of this writing, there are over fifty million sites on the World Wide Web alone. More and more businesses, schools, and civic organizations are going on the Internet every day, if they're not on already. Yet, most of the people within these organizations are not familiar with even the basics of the Internet and how it can be used effectively. Many of these companies and organizations are turning to Internet Trainers to teach their employees about the Internet and how it can be utilized to help serve the company's needs.

The need for knowledgeable Internet experts who also have an affinity for teaching is definitely on the rise. There has been an increase in the number of both midsized and smaller firms that provide Internet Training, but the market is still growing.

To set about becoming an Internet Trainer, you must, of course, possess a great deal of knowledge about the Internet and how it works. You must also know the basic principles of instructional design so that you can develop cohesive course content outlines. In addition, you must be able to relate to the students in your classes and one-on-one sessions. Your students will most likely be technical novices. There are a number of Internet textbooks you can purchase and teach from, but we recommend that you develop your own coursework. This will give you an added benefit in the marketplace.

The basic subject areas that companies are paying to be trained in include:

1. *How to Use the Internet:* how to access Internet resources and find information using E-mail, mailing lists, and newsgroups (Usenet), Telnet, FTP, Gopher, and the World Wide Web.

2. *Navigating the World Wide Web:* how to use Web browsers and Internet search tools to locate, view, and download different media types.

3. *HTML (Hypertext Markup Language):* how to create Web pages and use HTML to format documents and make them available via the Internet.

4. *Doing Business on the Internet:* how large and small organizations are using the Internet to enhance visibility, increase productivity, improve customer relations and support, reduce costs, advertise effectively, and sell creatively.

There are many other subject areas that clients may desire instruction in. If there is enough demand in a specific area, develop a course to teach it.

As an Internet Trainer you may find yourself teaching large classes at your clients' facilities. You may also be asked to work one-on-one with specific employees. In either case, you will have to have your coursework developed before you begin teaching. Materials you will need include course outlines that you can send to prospective clients as well as hand out at the beginning of a class or session. You will also need detailed teaching plans that outline what subjects will be covered during each session. Teaching plans are for your own use and should not be given to clients or students. You will need at least one textbook for each of the classes you teach. You can use a published textbook and include it in your teaching plan, or you can develop your own. Your own textbook need not be a professionally bound and published book. You can use a word processor and a desktop publishing program to produce the book, then print it out on a laser printer. Take the printout to a copy shop and have it photocopied and bind just the number of books you will need for each class.

To find clients, start by developing a Web site of your own. Be sure to include a form on your site that allows visitors to request further information. In most cases, you will need to go to a client's location to do your training, so you will, at least at first, have to confine your marketing efforts to your immediate region. Networking at your local chamber of commerce and other business organizations is a great way to market locally. Try calling your local Internet Service Provider and arranging a deal whereby you train the business customers who request it. Since Internet Training is a fairly new and specialized service, advertisements in local business publications might also bring you some results. You may also consider giving free seminars to business on the "Power of the Internet," or "Internet Business Solutions" to attract local clients.

Income potential as an Internet Trainer is quite good. Hourly fees range from $50 to $125 for class instruction and $40 to $100 per hour for individual instruction. You can also charge by class. Fees for an eight-week class of twenty or more students range from $2,000 to $3,500.

Resources

The Complete Guide to Teaching a Course: Practical Strategies for Teachers, Lecturers and Trainers (Complete Guide to Teaching a Course), by Ian Forsyth, Alan Jolliffe and David Stevens, London, UK, Kogan Page Ltd., 1995, ISBN: 0749415290.

Instructional Design Fundamentals: A Reconsideration, by Barbara B. Seels, Educational Technology Publications, April 1995, ISBN: 0877782849.

Learning the Internet: A Workbook for Beginners, by John Burke, New York, Neal Schuman Publishing, March 1996, ISBN: 1555702481.

GESTALT SYSTEMS, INC. 2070 Chain Bridge Road, Ste. 040, Vienna, VA 22182, (703) 748-1817, fax: (703) 748-1553, E-mail: learn@gestalt-sys.com, Web: *http://www*.gestalt-sys.com. Gestalt offers coursework for classes in various aspects of Internet training.

SYLLABUSWEB ONLINE magazine. Information on computing, Internet, and education news and technologies. *http://www.*syllabus.com

Newsgroup: comp.training

47.

Inventory Control Services

We first saw an inventory control service in operation at a health-food store—a man we were acquainted with was using a bar code reader and a laptop computer to inventory the shelves of his "mom-and-pop" store. A few months later we were giving a workshop in the second-floor meeting room of another health-food store and were telling the group about this business. The owner on the floor below overhead us and shouted up, "If any one of you wants to get into that business, I'll be your first customer!"

Many businesses need inventory control, which embraces not only merchandise in stores and warehouses but also office equipment and vehicles, as well as other kinds of equipment used by businesses, nonprofit institutions, and governments. Small businesses in particular need to know their inventory and when to reorder, but often they lack the technology or the staff to do it efficiently.

While inventory can still be done with a bar code reader and laptop using either a database program or special inventory control software, the technology for doing inventories has advanced in a number of ways that enhance its potential as an add-on, part-time, or even full-time business. For example:

A TimeWand II hand-held code-scanning device will read "buttons" attached to vehicles or equipment that will withstand weather and handling. This product, made by Videx, will also read other types of media with bar codes too.

A software package called *PC Census* eliminates manual scanning of all equipment and software attached to a LAN to produce an inventory.

A bar code printer might be the basis of a service for colleges, small cities, or companies in which you provide printed bar codes on permits that then can be assigned to vehicles, allowing law enforcement or parking officers to instantly identify a vehicle from the bar code placed on the windshield.

Fees for inventory services may be established for doing the inventory on a regular, recurring basis, or if you help the business computerize its inventory control system, you can likely obtain a consultant's fee for selecting, installing, and setting up the hardware and software as well.

Resources

BEAR ROCK TECHNOLOGIES is one of many companies that offer bar coding software for PCs and Macs so that you can produce your own bar codes. 4140 Mother Lode Drive, Ste. 100, Shingle Springs, CA 95682-8038, (800) 232-7625, (916) 672-0244, fax: (916) 672-1103, Web: *http://www.* bearrock.com

BONAFIDE MANAGEMENT SYSTEMS, 7618 Variel Avenue, Woodland Hills, CA 91367, (818) 999-9888, (800) 822-4999, fax: (818) 999-9895 E-mail: bonafide@bonafide.com offer a number of different PC-based inventory control software packages.

NET CENSUS, Tally Systems Corporation, P.O. Box 70, Hanover, NH 03755-0070, (800) 262-3877, (603) 643-1300, Web: *http://www*.tallysys.com

TIMEWAND II, Videx, Inc., 1105 N.E. Circle Boulevard., Corvallis, OR 97330, (541) 758-0521; Web: *http://www*.videx.com

48.

Local Area Network (LAN)/Intranet Consultant

One of the real areas of development in the past few years, in both software and hardware, has been in networking. Networking offers all the computers in an office, or throughout an entire company, the ability to share programs and allows users to work on the same document simultaneously and access the same data files. LANs (local area networks) can also be connected to the Internet, giving several computers access simultaneously. Once the province of large corporations, the power of LANs is being put to use by small firms, even home-based businesses. Although a great many small-business people recognize that networking their computers into a LAN would be of great benefit, most of them don't have the time or expertise to do it themselves. This creates a demand for independent LAN consultants who are expert at configuring and maintaining local area networks.

Most LAN consultants today focus their energies on serving larger and midsized businesses who have twenty-five or more computer users. We believe that by focusing on the home-based office and small-business market, LAN consultants will have a relatively untapped market. Even if a home office only has two computers, efficiency of operations will greatly increase if those machines are networked. Software developers know this and that's why most of the newer versions of the major word-processing, database, spreadsheet, and presentation graphics programs are all designed to accommodate networked situations. Even printers and scanners by manufacturers such as Hewlett Packard offer low-cost network-ready models. By helping home offices and small offices utilize the power of networking, you will help them take advantage of the power of the technology they already possess.

Lower-cost and less complicated networking software, such as ArtiSoft's LANtastic, is designed specifically with the small office in mind. These are known as "peer to peer" networks. Even Windows95 allows for peer-to-peer communication, but according to Doug Savarese, MIS manager of Analysis Group, a Los Angeles–based financial consulting firm, "most people will definitely need to hire a LAN consultant to get it working right." Peer-to-peer networks do not require a dedicated server and allow each machine in the network to communicate equally. In addition to the networking software, networks with more than two computers will require the installation of network cards, known as Ethernet cards. The most common Ethernet cards for smaller networks, and the least expensive, are 10Base-T cards. 100Base-T cards are also available. They offer ten times the speed but cost considerably more. One of the other great advantages of LANs for small businesses is the ability of several computers to share a single printer. Hewlett Packard offers a network interface called JetDirect that will turn any printer into a network printer.

As a LAN consultant for the home-office and small-business market, your potential clients are businesses that utilizes two or more computers in their daily operations. You can find clients by networking, in person, that is, at your local chamber of commerce, business events, users' groups, and trade organization events. If you can afford it, try running small advertisements in your local business journal that emphasize your focus on the home-office and small-office market. You can comfortably charge from $60 to $100 per hour, depending on the complexity of the project and your level of experience and skill.

Resources

Connect Your Lan to the Internet: Cost-Effective Access for Small Businesses and Other Organizations, by Thomas Madron, New York, Wiley, 1996, ISBN: 0471140546.

Ethernet Networks: Design, Implementation, Operation, Management, by Gilbert Held, New York, Wiley, 1996, ISBN: 047112706X.

LAN Tutorial With Glossary of Terms: A Complete Introduction to Local Area Networks, by the editors of *Lan* magazine, San Mateo, CA, Miller Freeman Publishing, 1996, ISBN: 0879303794.

Networking the Small Office, by Patrick Campbell, Alameda, CA, Sybex, 1996, ISBN: 0782117902.

LAN TIMES ONLINE, a daily online publication that provides the latest news and developments in local area networks. *http://www.*wcmh.com/lantimes

ZDNET, the online source for many useful computer and networking magazines and products. Especially helpful to LAN issues is *PC* magazine, which is also available on newsstands. *http://www.zdnet.com*

49.

Law Library Management

In the course of any given day, a lawyer usually refers to many law books, so many in fact that law firms usually maintain their own private libraries. The problem is, books in a law library must be kept current with the continual stream of updates on the latest legal rulings, which are supplied on a regular basis by publishers. Keeping the library updated, however, is an important but time-consuming task.

As a result, medium-sized law firms and corporate legal departments that are not large enough to employ a full-time law librarian contract out the management of their law libraries to a law library management firm, which keeps the physical law library up-to-date. This business requires that you acquire or already have a background in legal reference work and have a system for keeping the library current that is flexible enough to be adapted to the needs of a variety of clients. Since many firms also do on-line computer research, you should also know how to use the online services such as Lexis, Nexis, and Westlaw efficiently.

Once established, this business provides steady work because updating is an ongoing enterprise. Your hours can be long, however, and the work can be repetitive. Typical gross revenues range from $35,000 to $80,000 a year.

Networking in librarian associations and personal contacts with legal librarians can be a source of business as can direct mail addressed to the managing partners of law firms. Mail, however, needs to get through the secretary, so it needs to look like news or an announcement. We suggest having an informative, professional brochure to leave with people you meet. Also, you need a visual identity so as lawyers repeatedly see your logo you will develop name recognition. Once you have a few clients, you are likely to make many other contacts in the field while working in clients' offices.

Resources

Legal Information Alert is a newsletter published by Alert Publications, Inc., 399 West Fullerton Parkway, Chicago, IL 30614.

THE UNITED STATES DEPARTMENT OF AGRICULTURE GRADUATE SCHOOL offers a reasonably priced correspondence certificate course in library technology. Graduate School, USDA, Independence Avenue, South Agriculture Bldg., Washington, DC 20250, (202) 720-2077.

THE AMERICAN ASSOCIATION OF LAW LIBRARIES, 53 West Jackson Boulevard, Ste. 940, Chicago, IL 60604, (312) 939-4764, publishes a newsletter and the *Law Library Journal. http://www.*aallnet.org

Newsgroups: misc.legal.computing
law.school.legal-proofs
misc.legal

50.

Legal Transcript Digesting (Deposition Digesting)

Transcript digesting, also called deposition digesting, is an important part of the complex practice of law in this country and a potentially well-paying career as well. The transcript digester assists lawyers by summarizing documents that they need to read as background to their cases.

The need for transcript digesting services arises from the way legal cases flow through the court system. First, lawyers don't like to be surprised in the courtroom when someone takes the stand, and they are entitled to know what the opposition has as evidence. So prior to a trial, lawyers take testimony from those involved under oath in what is called a deposition. Depositions are recorded by a court reporter and then the entire testimony is transcribed into a document, which the lawyers must study carefully before the trial. As you can imagine, the transcripts are quite long, so to save time for the lawyers (many of whom now charge up to $400 an hour), transcript digesters identify relevant points and summarize the transcript. Each page of testimony is reduced to a paragraph. Depositions are also carefully indexed for the lawyers.

Digesters can also digest trial transcripts during the course of a trial, such as when an attorney needs a transcript of a previous day's proceedings to prepare for cross-examination. In lengthy trials that can last for months, digests of prior testimony are essential. Digests are also used in making appeals.

Sometimes digests are prepared by trained paralegals. In fact, digesting transcripts is part of paralegal training, but a digest can also be done by someone who has the ability to analyze and write succinctly. And today more and more law firms, from the solo practitioner to large firms with over 100 lawyers, are using outside digesting services.

Provided that you have the ability to write clearly, this is a business that takes a minimal amount of time to learn, costs little to start, and has the potential for earning good money. Typical gross revenues for a digester range from $38,000 to $100,000 or more per year.

Resources

Mary Helm's Transcript Digesting Manual, complete with WordPerfect macros on disk, P.O. Box 3911, Tustin, CA 92681.

TUTORIALS: THE WORKING FROM HOME FORUM ON COMPUSERVE INFORMATION SERVICE offers files covering the basics of digesting transcripts, a sample deposition, and sample summaries in various formats. This material is available in Library 5.

Newsgroup: misc.legal

51. |ABC| 🗑 |🏠| |-$|

Legal Transcription Service

Although most state and federal courts employ court reporters with computers or stenography machines at trials and legal proceedings (see page 111, "Notereader-Scopist"), many other trials, as well as various kinds of legal hearings such as arbitration negotiations, worker's compensation, and law enforcement interrogations use tape recorders and sound tapes that must later be transcribed. This job is done by a legal transcriptionist who, like a medical transcriptionist, frequently works at home using transcribers and computers to produce the documents that are used for record keeping and reference.

While technology has improved how the work of legal transcription gets done, the basic work attorneys need to have done remains much as it has been for years. This ranges from transcribing one-on-one interviews recorded on tape to transcribing tapes dictated remotely into taping equipment in the legal transcriptionist's home office.

Legal transcription requires excellent typing ability and a devotion to accuracy and perfection. You will need to know the special vocabulary of law and the formatting conventions used in typing up legal motions, cross-examinations, summations, hearings, and other proceedings. Strong listening skills are critical, since you are transcribing from tape and must sometimes identify up to four voices—the judge, a witness, and two attorneys. Finally, you must also be able to work well under pressure, since some projects have short turnaround times.

Since it is the courts who hire most legal transcriptionists, to get started you can contact the state and federal courts in your area to find out about transcription needs and any certification requirements. Transcriptionists are usually paid on a per-page basis, and a diligent and accurate legal transcriptionist can generally type sixty to eighty or more pages a day. Average annual earnings are between $15,000 and $35,000.

Resources

(PRODUCTIVITY PLUS) LEGALEASE SYSTEM is resident software that allows you to automate repetitive and complicated keystroke operations by automatically expanding abbreviations of legal terms into full definitions as you type. This program includes a beginning list of 2,500 legal terms. Each abbreviation can represent as many as 4,000 characters. Productivity Software International, Inc., 211 East 43rd Street, Ste. 2202, New York, NY 10017-4707, (212) 818-1144.

Newsgroup: misc.legal

52. MS ◗ + ⌂ 👍

Lifestyle and Hobby Resource Web Site

One of the great benefits of the World Wide Web is that it provides a way for participants of any lifestyle, hobby, or trend a way to find one another and exchange information, opinions, news, etc. From stamp collectors to fans of Charlotte Rampling, ballroom dancers to cigar devotees, and no matter where in the world, people with similar interests are connecting through the Web. A small, but forward-thinking group of cyber entrepreneurs and enthusiasts have recognized the Web's unique strength in this regard and have, in turn, provided an income for themselves and helped the cause of their interests and passions. For example, we recently met a young Web consultant in the course of our online travels. Conrad came to the U.S. from Belgium about two years ago. He brought with him a love of dance music and rave music in particular. He was active in the Los Angeles dance club scene and kept in touch with his European connections via the Internet. One day he was struck with an inspiration: "Why not create an online environment where everyone can be updated on dance events, new clubs, new releases, fashions and exchange information, too?" Thus Conrad's concept of "Web Clubbing" was born. The concept is based on his Web site the *Rave Network* (*http://www.*ravenetwork.com). On the site, people find dance events in major U.S. and European cities, downloadable samples of the latest releases, fashion trends, and more. He initially hoped to build enough traffic on his site so that he could sell advertising to record companies, but the idea has surpassed his original plan. He is currently in negotiations with radio stations in each of the major cities where he lists events, clothing manufacturers, and printed music publications—all who wish to sponsor his site. He is also in the process of netcasting video feeds from featured dance clubs around the world. Conrad was able to achieve this on a part-time basis, evenings and weekends when not servicing his consulting clients.

As you can see from Conrad's example, the World Wide Web provides exciting opportunities to pursue a passion and perhaps turn it into a viable business. The possibilities are virtually endless but should conform to the Web's unique strengths and characteristics:

- The more unique the content or subject, the better chance you will have of attracting online traffic. For example, a site that covers all aspects of jazz in America might not do as well as a site dedicated to American avant-garde jazz or the work of Charles Mingus.

- The more interactive you make the site, the better. Include a "chat" room where visitors can interact with one another in real time and discussion groups where visitors can post messages for others to read and respond to.
- Include audio and video content, if appropriate.
- Include a well-thought-out page of links to other sites relevant to your content.
- The more frequently you update your content, the better. Do it once a day, if possible. This gives visitors a reason to return frequently.

Unless you go into production of your Resource Site with a sponsor already in place, this enterprise may take awhile to generate any income. We definitely recommend that you start off on a part-time basis. A Resource Site works very well for Web site designers, Web writers, Web consultants, and Web server hosts. Although the Resource Site might not create an instant revenue stream, it can help attract business to your main money-making activity. Once you have built a fairly high level of traffic on your site, there are several ways to generate income. You can sell advertising at a rate of $50 to $75 for every 1,000 daily visitors you can demonstrate. You can also approach potential sponsors such as equipment manufacturers, print magazines who cater to your visitors' interests, or any company or organization that provides products or services of interest to your visitors.

Resources

Running a Perfect Web Site with Windows, by Mark Surfas, David M. Chandler, Tobin Anthony, and Rick Darnell, New York, Que Corporation, 1996, ISBN: 0789707632 (also available for Macintosh).

Spinning the Web: How to Provide Information on the Internet, by Andrew Ford, New York, Van Nostrand Reinhold, 1995, ISBN: 0442019963.

The Web after Hours (Online), by Bill Mann, Rocklin, CA, Prima Publications, 1996, ISBN: 0761503773.

HOTWIRED ONLINE magazine, one of cyber culture's premier publications. *http://www.*hotwired.com

WEBWEEK ONLINE magazine, a good source for new technology news, marketing and promotion trends, and design issues. *http://www.*webweek.com

53.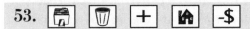

Mailing-List Service

A mailing list service is an evergreen business that's relatively easy to enter and costs little to start up once you've purchased your computer and printer. It makes a good sideline business or an excellent add-on service for a wide variety of other businesses. It can also grow into a substantial full-time venture.

As a mailing-list service, you can put your computer to work providing at least three different services:

1. Compiling and maintaining mailing-list databases for clients, using their invoices or receipts of current customers. Since many businesses don't make use of their existing list of names, your job is to help them turn these names into a valuable mailing list, since it's always easier to get more business from existing customers than it is to find new ones.

2. Selling specialized mailing lists which you develop or purchase from others. While you can't compete with large mailing-list companies that sell tens of thousands of names in thousands of categories, you can create lists that are tailored to your local community or area of specialization. For example, you can contact new residents or businesses in your community, or make lists of solo practitioners such as doctors and dentists, or lists compiled from local associations, clubs, and groups. You can then sell these lists to companies in your area that seek sales leads and names for direct-marketing or mail-order businesses.

3. Since many companies don't have the expertise or equipment to do direct mail, you can design a campaign, using their list, a rented list, or your own list, and take charge of the printing, sorting, addressing, and mailing of the items to be sent out. Or consult with companies to help them do direct mail themselves.

To get started as a mailing-list service, you will need a personal computer with a large-capacity hard disk, a high-quality laser printer that can handle mailing labels, and a database program, preferably a relational database program, such as Microsoft Access, Paradox, or FoxPro, that allows you to store and sort through names and listings in many ways. You may also wish to have your own folding and sorting equipment in the event that you manage direct mailings for companies. As for marketing your business, approaching owners of small local stores that are collecting customer names is the quickest route to getting maintenance or consulting business, and networking and advertising in the yellow pages are effective methods for selling lists you've compiled yourself.

Income potential for a full-time mailing-list service ranges from $10,000 to $75,000 a year. Depending on your services, you can charge monthly fees for database maintenance, set fees (usually per thousand names) to do mailings, or establish per-hour charges for professional consulting in direct-mail techniques. You can also increase your earnings by adding additional services such as pickup and delivery, twenty-four-hour turn-around time, high-quality printing, or folding and sorting capability.

While this business has few requirements, you will be most successful if you have some experience using database management systems that handle mail merge and relational sorting. You also should be familiar with all postal regulations regarding mass mailings and software such as *ArcList* and *AccuMail,* two of the best-selling products that are vital in the direct-marketing business for sorting addresses and applying zip +4 codes to addresses and bar coding of envelopes.

Resources

Direct Mail List Rates and Data, the bible of the business on direct-mail list prices and who offers what lists, published by Standard Rate & Data Service, Willamette, IL (available in most libraries).

How to Make Money in the Mailing List Business, by Katie Allegato. An audiotape album available from Here's How, Box 5091, Santa Monica, CA 90409, (800) 561-8990.

List Broker Manual and Complete Business System, Synergetics International, 857 Orchard Avenue, Moscow, ID 83843.

Newsgroups: comp.mail.misc
　　　　　　comp.mail.list-admin
　　　　　　comp.mail.list-admin.software

54.

Market Mapping Service

Market mapping is a fast-growing and exciting field that helps companies track their customer demographics and dramatically improve their understanding of patterns such as sales potential and market penetration. The field merges sophisticated mapping software with database management systems so that what was formerly difficult-to-decipher alphanumeric data and statistics can be turned into clear, captivating visual information in the form of maps. And now, thanks to low-cost but powerful PC-based mapping software, the field has become a viable desktop business that can be operated from home as easily as a desktop publishing or word-processing service.

Market-mapping services can assist many kinds of clients. You might consult with a marketing director trying to decide the best location for a new franchise store, or a restaurateur wanting to find the right spot for a new restaurant with the most foot traffic at lunch. Or you might work with a CEO needing to relocate an office but not wanting to disrupt employee drive patterns, or an advertising executive trying to decide where to place a billboard or in which newspapers a client should advertise. Even mail-order companies and small businesses can benefit from an analysis of their customers' location and purchasing habits.

Getting into this business does not require a special degree in geography or cartography, since the field focuses more on marketing concepts and the use and analysis of data. You do need a good understanding of market-mapping software and the applications it can perform, and a strong interest or background in marketing, sales, and data management. Equipping your office can be done for around $7,500 including a personal computer with a one-gigabyte hard drive and a CD-ROM drive, a seventeen-inch or larger SVGA color monitor, a scanner, a digitizing tablet with pen or puck, and the desktop mapping application software such as *ArcView for Windows* (Environmental Systems Research Institute) and *Atlas GIS* (Strategic Mapping, along with any various geographic-based maps you may need for your work.)

Earnings in this field will vary depending on the volume and depth of your assignments. Given the professional nature of the work and the expertise you can bring a client, however, your fees can easily climb in the $50- to $100-per-hour range.

Resources

1995 Commercial Atlas and Marketing Guide (updated annually), New York, Rand McNally, ISBN: 0528814125.

Market Mapping: How to Use Revolutionary New Software to Find, Analyze, and Keep Customers, by Sunny and Kim Baker, New York, McGraw-Hill, 1993. An excellent introductory book and resource for the entire field.

GIS World is a magazine that publishes an annual sourcebook, which is a definitive overview of companies, technologies, applications, etc., in geographic information systems, (800) 447-9753, *http://www. geoplace.com*

55.

Medical Billing Service

Medical billing services continue to have potential in many parts of the country. This is largely due to the complexity doctors encounter in billing third parties for payment and the difficulty of getting and keeping trained personnel to perform this vital task. Many doctors are still unequipped technologically to submit claims electronically to reduce errors and wasted time checking paper claim forms. In recent years, the private health insurance carriers have also recognized the value of electronic billing, which is a more efficient and preferred way of billing.

As a result, many medical practices now rely on outside services to operate the entire process of electronic billing. A billing service therefore prepares the claims using a personal computer and special medical billing software, and then sends them out over the phone lines to the Medicare intermediaries and insurance companies for evaluation and payment. The medical billing service might also handle other related tasks in billing, such as following up on rejected claims, invoicing the patient for deductibles and co-payments (the 20 percent portion that most health insurance companies don't pay), and generally maintaining patient accounts.

A medical billing service isn't limited to serving medical doctors. Other health professionals that need billing services are cardiac profusionists, chiropractors, commercial ambulance services, dentists, home nursing services, massage therapists, nurse practitioners, occupational therapists, optometrists, physical therapists, physician assistants, psychologists, as well other counselors, respiratory therapists, and speech therapists.

You do need specialized knowledge to succeed in this field, although it can be learned in a few months' time. You must know the rules and regulations for submitting electronic Medicare and private insurance claims, as well as the complex coding systems doctors are required to use on claims to indicate the diagnosis and the procedures implemented. You also need to purchase a medical billing software package that allows for electronic bill submission. Medical billing software can be expensive, running from $500 to $10,000, depending on which company you buy from and how much training you need to get started.

A medical billing service that works with five or six doctors' offices can gross $20,000 to $50,000 per year. To market your business effectively, you will need to solicit doctors' offices directly, as well as to do direct mail announcing your service. Since some doctors prefer to keep the billing in their control, you will need a strategy to convince them that you can do a better job than an in-house billing secretary could.

Resources

Making Money in a Health Service Business on Your Home-Based PC, by Rick Benzel, New York, Windcrest/McGraw-Hill, 1997. Included is a CD-ROM with demonstration versions of popular medical billing software, ISBN: 0079131395.

Directory of Medical Management Software, Resource Books, 175 North Buena Vista, Suite B, San Jose, CA 95126, (408) 295-4102.

MEDICAL MANAGEMENT SOFTWARE, INC. offers turnkey business opportunities in the medical billing industry. Contact Merry Schiff by phone at (415) 341-6101, fax (415) 341-9759, E-mail Merry@nebazone.com Medical Management Software, Inc., 1730 S. Amphlett Boulevard, Ste. 217, San Mateo, CA 94402. *http://www.*medicalbillingbiz.com

Newsgroup: misc.education.medical

56.

Medical Transcription Service

Medical transcription is a specialized field, in which much of the work is done by independent transcriptionists. Medical transcriptionists produce typed reports and documents from dictations that doctors, nurses, and other medical personnel have made regarding their patients. Medical transcriptions are required for many reasons: to create a record for other doctors who work with a patient to review; to serve as evidence in malpractice suits; and to obtain insurance reimbursement, since most insurance carriers require a report before they will pay for surgery and other hospital work.

To be a transcriptionist, you must train for a year or more learning the vocabularies of anatomy, pathology, pharmacology, and other related fields, as well as the format conventions for the various kinds of transcription reports. Many transcriptionists then specialize in only one of several medical specialties, such as orthopedics, neurology, or radiology. Transcriptionists can work for hospitals, private doctors, and clinics, or for other transcription services that hire freelance subcontractors.

Transcriptionists use personal computers with regular commercial word-processing software along with specialized medical spelling correction software. You also need a transcriber unit that takes tapes, or one of the newer machines that uses digital technology whereby doctors can call your machine and dictate over the phone lines to your hard disk. Overhead in this business is low and income potential runs between $30,000 and $75,000 a year. Because of the specialization required, it is difficult to get into the business without working first at a hospital or doctor's office for a few years, but with this experience, you can then start your own business.

Resources

Making Money in a Health Service Business on Your Home-Based PC, by Rick Benzel. New York, Windcrest/McGraw-Hill, 1997. Describes how to start and run a medical transcription business.

AMERICAN ASSOCIATION FOR MEDICAL TRANSCRIPTION, offers free information about the profession. Box 576187, Modesto, CA 95357-6187, (209) 551-0883, fax: (209) 551-9317, E-mail: aamt@sna.com, Web: *http://www.*aamt.org/aamt

AT HOME PROFESSIONS, 2001 Lowe St., Fort Collins CO 80525, (800) 333-2846. Offers at-home courses.

HEALTH PROFESSIONS INSTITUTE, P.O. Box 801, Modesto, CA. 95353, (209) 551-2112, E-mail: hpi@ainet.com, Web: *http://www.*hpisum.com. Offers a course in medical transcription. They also publish reference and workbooks for medical transcriptionists, as well as a quarterly magazine.

Newsgroup: sci.med.transcription
Medical transcription section on Working from Home forum on CompuServe (GOWORK)

57. |MS| |🗄| |🗑| |+| |🏠| |👍|

Meta-Site Service (World Wide Web)

The World Wide Web can be an unruly place. Oftentimes a search through the Web for information will yield a jumbled and confusing array of results. It's touted as the ultimate research tool and information resource, and it really is, but unless someone has a great deal of experience in conducting searches and performing research, or an unlimited amount of time to follow a sometimes endless series of links, finding exactly the information one needs on the Web can be a daunting task. For example, a search for the term "home-based franchise" using Infoseek (*http://www*.infoseek.com), one of the Web's top search engines, yields over 62,000 sites!

One of the services most helpful to researchers on the Web today is what's known as a "Meta"-site. A Meta-site is a site on the World Wide Web that offers little in terms of original content but, rather, offers visitors a well-organized, comprehensive store of resources and "links" to other useful sites, all pertaining to a single area of interest. For example, one of the largest and most successful Meta-sites on the Web today was compiled by Yogesh Malhotra. In the course of his studies at the Katz Graduate School of Business at the University of Pittsburgh, he began to compile an extensive list of resources for various avenues of business and organizational research found on the World Wide Web. The information was built into a Meta-site he called *A Business Researcher's Interests* (*http://www*.brint. com/interest.html). *A Business Researcher's Interests* grew quickly. It has become one of most information-rich, useful places on the Web for business and technological issues. The site itself is searchable for any business topic of interest. It is also organized into a comprehensive series of links by subject matter such as Journals & Magazines (links to over 800 business-related magazines and research journals), IS (Informational Services) Professional Careers (links to positions offered, career trends, etc.), International Business Technology (links to worldwide business entities and organizations, travel resources, and international media), and much, much more. If you are interested in compiling a Meta-site, we recommend you take a look at *A Business Researcher's Interests* to see an example of one of the best.

Running a Meta-site can serve several functions in terms of *your* business interests. If you develop a site that appeals to a large number of people, you can sell advertising space or you can look for sponsors: companies who sell products or services to the market you attract. For example, a

Meta-site that provides an exhaustive series of links to sports teams, sports statistics databases, season schedules, sports news sources, sports equipment manufacturers, etc., would be a great site for beverage bottlers, sports publications, or even professional sports teams to sponsor. A Meta-site is also an excellent way to promote a primary business such as an Internet consultancy or Internet trainer, Web writer, Web site reviewer, Web publication, Web promotions expert, or Web program. Such a site will establish your credibility in any of these areas and draw attention, and perhaps even publicity, to you and your business.

To start a Meta-site, you must, of course, select an area of concentration. Choose a subject that you're interested in, even passionate about. You'll be spending a lot of time conducting research for site content. If you have a high level of personal interest, your research will go more smoothly. Then meticulously search the Web to make sure that there aren't too many such sites in existence. Now you're ready to begin some serious research. The value of a Meta-site is that it saves visitors to your site a considerable amount of time in performing their own research. The time you save them must, however, be invested by you. Your job at this point is to sift through the countless thousands of Web sites that do not provide substantive information about your area of concentration and compile a listing of those that do. You must also organize lists of relevant sites into meaningful categories. The better and deeper your own research, the more value you will offer to your site's visitors. Check other Meta-sites to see how much information they offer and how the information is organized. You will also have to actually design and post your site on the Web. There are many Web designers who can offer you some excellent solutions for fairly reasonable prices. Check for designers online and also ask your local Internet Service Provider if they can design a Meta-site for you, or if they can recommend someone who can. If you want to build up high traffic quickly, you may also wish to engage the services of a good Web publicist or promotions specialist.

Resources

Finding It on the Internet: The Internet Navigator's Guide to Search Tools and Techniques, by Paul Gilster, New York, Wiley, 1996, ISBN: 0471126950.

Researching on the Internet: The Complete Guide to Finding, Evaluating, and Organizing Information Effectively, by Robin Rowland and Dave Kinnaman, Rocklin, CA, Prima Publishing, 1995, ISBN: 0761500634.

INFOWORLD ONLINE magazine, *http://www*.infoweek.com

WEBREVIEW ONLINE magazine, *http://*webreview.com

STARTING POINTS FOR INTERNET EXPLORATION. This Meta-site contains hyperlinks to many common Internet-based information resources. *http://www*.ncsa.uiuc.edu/SDG/Software/Mosaic/StartingPoints/Network-StartingPoints.html

THE YANOFF LIST, compiled by David Yanoff, is a Meta-site's Meta-site and a great place to start research of any sort. *http://www*.spectracom.com/islist/

58.

Mortgage Auditing Service

Have you read any of the news stories over the past several years about lending institutions miscalculating the mortgage payments on adjustable rate loans? The errors range from 20 percent of A.R.M. mortgages from commercial banks to 29 percent from thrifts and 38 percent from credit unions. Some reports have found error rates as high as 75 percent.

How do such miscalculations occur? In a number of ways: improper rounding of a mortgage index, making the adjustment in the payment based on the wrong date, or using an index different from the one in the loan agreement (which may happen when a loan is sold to a bank in a different federal reserve district). These are among the ways buyers can pay their lender hundreds of dollars a year in undeserved loan costs. But a mistake in one year will make all subsequent calculations inaccurate as well, and with many loans going back to the eighties, the claims can be in the thousands of dollars.

The role of a Mortgage Auditing Service is to find these errors for the home buyer. If a miscalculation is found, the mortgage auditor supplies the clients with the information necessary to appeal the payment, or they represent the client in arguing the point with the bank. If a trial is necessary, they will appear as an expert witness.

Mortgage auditing can be a part-time business or it might be an add-on service for financial planners or others providing financial services. It requires a solid understanding of mortgage tables. Software can be used to help calculate the correct payments. You might use a specialized program like *ARM Alarm!* or set up your own formulas on a spreadsheet program like *Excel, Quatro,* or *Lotus 1-2-3.* You can also use one of the many standard mortgage calculation programs commercially available.

Mortgage Auditing Services often charge an audit fee for checking a client's records plus a percentage of the client's savings made from the discovery of errors. Others charge no up-front fee but a higher contingent fee.

Resources

ARM ALARM!, Selfware, Inc., 8618 Westwood Center Drive, Vienna, VA 22182, (703) 506-0400. This software calculates the correct payment for adjustable-rate mortgages and indicates where lender errors have been made. *http://www.*selfware.com

Newsgroups: alt.org.natl-assn-mortgage-brokers
            us.housing
            misc.invest.real-estate
            misc.consumers.house

59.

Multimedia Production

If you have an interest in education, training, communications, or marketing and a real love for advanced graphics and computing technology, you definitely want to explore the exploding field of multimedia services. Growing out of the advent of CD-ROM hardware and software, digitized sound boards, high-speed video cards, and linkages between PCs and video cameras, today's multimedia producer uses the PC as the central tool helping businesses and schools to create truly impressive multimedia presentations for almost any purpose.

Although they've been around for years, faster speeds and lower prices have exploded CD-ROM sales. Although most CD-ROMs are going into people's homes, there is a growing need for independent contractors who can create materials on CD-ROM for training, publishing, and archiving for in-house use.

No longer will audiences need to look at static overhead projections or sit in the dark lulled by slides that can put people to sleep. Today's technology allows you to create animation, three-dimensional graphics, sound, and motion to enhance any demonstration, tutorial, workshop, presentation, or training session. Your output may be a computer disk or CD-ROM disk that your client uses during the presentation, or it may even be a kiosk that your client places in a convention center, hotel lobby, or airport for people to see. One of the most dynamic developments is the utilization of multimedia content on the World Wide Web.

To be in this business, you must enjoy helping people organize information and figure out how best to present their message. You need to understand the various components of multimedia technology and be willing to stay continuously abreast of new developments that affect your business. You will also need good writing, visual, and graphic skills, since you will be likely to help your clients design and write their presentations on your equipment.

Starting a multimedia service will probably require an investment of between $10,000 and $13,000 on a Pentium Pro, with MMX, 200MHz minimum processing speed, a very large hard drive, 40MB of RAM, a high-resolution seventeen-inch monitor, a 10x CD-ROM drive, sixteen- or thirty-two-bit sound board, a video card, color scanner, laser printer, graphic design software such as *Photoshop* and *Illustrator* by Adobe, and an "authoring system" software program such as *MacroMedia Director* that puts the whole thing together. You may also want to consider purchasing a recording-capable CD-ROM drive and a removable storage device such as a Syquest drive or the Jaz Drive by Iomega. (Note that there are certain standards that have been established by the Multimedia PC Marketing Council, which you will want to make sure your equipment meets.)

Your clients can include companies or institutions of any kind that regularly have sales conferences, presentations, workshops, or training seminars. You market your services by advertising in the yellow pages, by sending out direct mail to companies, and by networking among trade and industry groups to make executives and training organizations aware of your capacities. Once you establish your business, word of mouth will bring you new clients if your presentations are unique and effective.

Fees for a multimedia service vary tremendously, but a good operator can get up to $100 an hour for consulting and setting up a multimedia presentation for a business or association. Some multimedia services charge as much as $5,000 for a three-minute presentation.

This is one business that offers ground-floor opportunity for the creative, visually oriented person who can handle the technology involved.

Resources

Director Close-Up: Interactivity & Animation, Versions 4 and 5, by Tim Vaughan and Peter Vaughan, Wadsworth, 1996, ISBN: 053450423X.

Electronic Publishing Construction Kit: Creating Multimedia for Disk, CD-Rom, and the Internet, by Scott Johnson, New York, Wiley, 1996, ISBN: 0471128546.

Making Money with Multimedia, by Caryn Mladen and David Rosen, Reading, MA, Addison-Wesley, 1995, ISBN: 0201822830.

MULTIMEDIA FORUM ON COMPUSERVE Information Service (see chapter 6).

Newsgroups: comp.multimedia
alt.multimedia.director
alt.binaries.multimedia
misc.education.multimedia

60.

Newsletter Publishing

As information proliferates, more and more people realize that their best method of staying abreast of developments in their careers or personal hobbies is through one or more highly focused newsletters. As a result, the number of newsletters is growing. Just about any specialty you can name has a newsletter—innkeepers, coin collectors, medical billing services, users of XYZ software programs. And as the economy, technology, and world markets change, new markets for newsletters are created.

As newsletters increase in popularity, the distinction between newsletters, magazines, and newspapers is becoming somewhat blurred, but usually a newsletter refers to a publication that is two to eight pages in length, no larger than 8-1/2 by 11 inches, and not available on newsstands.

Anyone can start a newsletter or become the publisher of one that another person might write. There are, in fact, three ways you can use desktop publishing software to earn an income in the newsletter business:

1. You can publish your own special-interest business or consumer newsletter, in which case you earn income from subscriptions and possibly from advertising. Prices of newsletters range from $30 to $125 a year for consumer-oriented ones to $300 to $1,000 for business/professional-

oriented ones with highly specialized information. If you can get 300 people to pay you $100 each, that's $30,000 for publishing information or news you gather! You can distribute your newsletter by mail, but increasingly newsletters are being distributed by fax.

2. You can write and produce newsletters for someone else, usually a company or association, who will use it to communicate with their employees or members or as a promotional tool to send to past, present, and potential clients. To do this, you can charge from $200 to $500 a page to write, typeset, and manage the printing and distribution.

3. You can write a template newsletter for a group of clients which you customize slightly for each one. For example, many accountants and lawyers are willing to pay to have a newsletter sent out with their name on it, so you write only one monthly newsletter and customize it with each professional's name on the masthead for his or her clients. Doctors and dentists are also prospects for newsletters. In this business, you can charge each of your customers several hundred dollars to create the newsletter and then a per-name fee of $.35 to $1.00 sent to each mailing.

4. You can write a newsletter underwritten by advertising and distribute it without charge on the Internet.

Newsletter publishing can provide a full-time income, or it can be a sideline to another business you operate like an association or private practice management, or a bookkeeping or mailing-list service. To operate the business, you need to have a PC, desktop publishing software, a laser printer, and possibly a scanner and CD-ROM equipment. As far as qualifications are concerned, you need to be able to write good copy and headlines, have a good sense of layout and design, and have something to say.

The best way to get your newsletter off the ground is to test-market one edition for free to a mailing list of potential subscribers. You can first check in books such as *The Newsletter Directory* (Gale Research) or *Hudson's Newsletter Directory* to find out about competition. During the first year of publication, you can expect to spend from $3,000 to $100,000 sending out sample copies, purchasing mailing lists of potential subscribers, and advertising.

Once under way, continue sending sample issues to prospects. Some newsletter publishers have found it smart to sell a subscription of six issues instead of a year. That way, they can begin publishing bimonthly and then move to monthly and obtain renewals.

Resources

Newsletters in Print, Detroit, MI, Gale Research, annual (available in libraries).

Publishing Newsletters, by Howard Penn Hudson, New York, Scribner, 1988.

The Newsletter on Newsletters, the Newsletter Clearinghouse, 44 West Market Street, P.O. Box 311, Rhinebeck, NY 12572, (914) 876-2081, *http://www*.newsletter-clearinghse.com

THE NEWSLETTER FACTORY conducts one-day seminars on how to design, edit, and write a newsletter, 1830 Water Place, Ste. 120, Atlanta, GA 30339, (770) 955-1600, *http://www*.nlf.com. The Newsletter Factory also operates the Desktop Publishing forum on CompuServe.

THE NEWSLETTER PUBLISHERS ASSOCIATION, 1501 Wilson Boulevard, Ste. 509, Arlington, VA 22209, (800) 356-9302, (703) 527-2333, *http://www.* churchstreet.com/npa

61.

Notereader-Scopist

Court reporters are the people who take down testimony in courtrooms or lawyers' offices using a stenograph, a special machine that encodes words phonetically. You may recall seeing Perry Mason movies showing a stenograph spewing out those narrow strips of paper, called stenotype, although today's newer machines record the data on floppy disks or tapes. The problem is, however, that court reporters must convert the stenotype into a fully written transcript, a time-consuming task. And since they make more money when they are in the courtroom, they often hire outside transcriptionists to produce the finished pages; these people are called notereaders or scopists.

The notereader-scopist may work in any of several ways. If the court reporter uses a computer to translate the stenotype automatically (called Computer Aided Transcription), the notereader-scopist reviews and edits the testimony for accuracy and spelling of proper names as it appears on the screen. Some stenotype is not automatically translated, in which case the notereader-scopist may work from the paper stenotype or audiotapes made by the court reporter. We've also been told that some computerized court reporters are handling all the editing themselves again, so before beginning in this field, check out how court reporting is being handled in your community.

Notereader-scopists are hired either directly by self-employed court reporters or by court reporting agencies. In either case they may do their work from home. Notereader-scopists are widely used and readily accepted in most parts of the country. However, in areas where court reporters have not yet used scopists, they must be educated about the scopist's ability to produce high-quality work and to enable the court reporter to earn more money.

The notereader-scopist profession does require some special training, including learning legal terminology and sometimes medical terminology, but much of this can be learned in a short time. A notereader-scopist can typically earn between $18,000 and $45,000, depending on such factors as typing speed and how much work you can generate.

Resources

At Home Professions offers a sixteen-week study-at-home course that provides you with the knowledge and expertise you need to be a notereader-scopist. For more information contact: At-Home Professions, 2001 Lowe Street, Fort Collins, CO 80525, (800) 359-3455.

62.

Payroll Preparation

If you are already doing bookkeeping, accounting, or any other kind of administration for a business, you might consider taking on the payroll preparation function and earn some additional income. Although payroll modules for programs *Peachtree Complete Accounting* or Intuit's *Quick-Pay* (used with *QuickbooksPro*) make doing payroll for a small business much easier, many business owners still find the task tedious and difficult because of the frequent changes in federal and state tax rates, social security, and other deductions a company might need to make. Also, some business owners don't want employees to know what their co-workers earn, and by having the payroll preparation done on an outside contract, they can maintain secrecy.

Many large payroll service companies compete in this business, but as a home-based operation, you can win some business by offering personal attention, pickup and delivery, and a good price. You can also gain an edge by being willing to customize your service to the needs of your clients and by having a background in their field.

While you could get by in this business using the payroll module for the standard bookkeeping or accounting programs your small business clients might be using, you will be able to provide better service with a dedicated payroll program like *B.A.S.S. Payroll System.* Accountants praise *B.A.S.S.'s* more understandable reports and its security features. In part, this is because you do not need to keep your client's blank checks in your home, which clients may resist anyway. You are able to use blank check stock because *B.A.S.S.* will print out the electronically readable bank account codes on each client's checks.

You'll most likely be able to underprice larger payroll services by charging approximately $8.50 to $10.00 a week for three to six employees. In return, your clients will reduce the time they spend on payroll from hours each month to minutes. Be certain, however, to have a written contract with your clients that includes provisions that relieve you of liability for mistakes caused by the client.

The best ways to get payroll clients is by advertising in the yellow pages or local newspapers, and directly calling small businesses in your neighborhood.

Resources

ADVANTAGE PAYROLL SERVICES, a payroll preparation franchise, P.O. Box 3188, Auburn, Maine 04212-3188, (207) 782-2844.

B.A.S.S. PAYROLL SYSTEM, B.A.S.S., 7322 Newman Blvd., Dexter MI 48130, (800) 748-1964. This software is designed for payroll services and will handle companies with employees in multiple states.

Newsgroup: alt.payroll

63.

People Tracing Service

Whether it's trying to locate an old buddy or sweetheart, track down a long-lost relative, obtain a private credit report, or find a person who has "skipped" out on a payment, the personal computer is changing the way missing person and skip-tracing searches are done today. Technology such as modems connected to online information databases and

CD-ROM disks that contain phone books for the entire country allow access to massive amounts of data formerly available only to large companies, collection agencies, and private detectives. It is now relatively easy to obtain instant information on a person's address, phone number, credit reports, driver's record, and even bank balances.

As a result of the decreasing cost of technology, this entire field of investigative work is now open to home-based businesses. If you are interested in this field, however, you must first check to determine if tracing people is regulated by your state's laws. You may find, for example, that in some states like Michigan you must be a licensed private investigator to provide tracing services. In other states you may need to obtain certification and be bonded. You should also be familiar with the various federal and state laws about privacy and the use of credit reports and financial information.

Beyond these important matters, you will need a personal computer with a modem, an ISP, a CD-ROM drive, and the ability to work professionally and creatively to find those people whom your clients are seeking. You should also be prepared to use the telephone as well as to search public documents at courthouses and city halls in order to complete searches that can't be found through your computer.

Marketing your business works best if you can serve both business and consumer markets, so advertising in the yellow pages under "Investigators" is a useful outlet. Again, check your state law before doing this because it may regulate how you can advertise such a listing. You may also wish to contact directly retail businesses that use investigative services, as well as make speeches to private clubs and associations to inspire people to use your services who might like to find old friends.

Fees for investigative searches vary greatly, depending on the extent of the search and the cost of logging on to the databases you need. Some agencies charge from $15 to $25 for an online search in one state to a few hundred dollars for national searches. At that rate, if you perform ten searches per week working part-time, you can earn an additional $10,000 or more per year.

Resources

How to Investigate by Computer, by Ralph D. Thomas with Leroy Cook. Thomas Publications, 1992. Thomas Publications offers several other publications, including *How to Find Anyone Anywhere* and *Advanced Skip Tracing Techniques,* P.O. Box 33244, Austin, TX 78764, (512) 719-3595, *http://www.pimall.com/nais*

64. # ☾ + ⌂

Personal Financial Management Services

This business will work well as on add-on to an existing financial planning or bookkeeping service. You help people manage their personal finances. You assist them in establishing a budget, pay their bills, balance their checkbook, file their records, etc. Your clientele would be people living on a fixed income who don't have the time, the desire, or the health to take care of these tasks. You have their bills sent to your address. You pay the bills, maintain their account, keep tax receipts filed, and provide a monthly statement.

Establishing a budget for your clients is the key to this business, because you will want to show how you can save them some money and still have money left over to pay your fee, possibly 5 percent of the total monthly expenses. You set up a special trust account in which you deposit clients' monies and from which you pay bills, including your own fees. You manage the account, using bookkeeping or accounting and check-writing software. Assuming that you pay bills monthly, once the budget is established you should be able to handle a typical customer's needs in about two hours a month.

Because of the level of trust involved, personal referrals will be your best route to finding clients. You might get referrals, for example, from your bank or your clergyperson. Doctors might be another source of referrals. Also, adult children of senior citizens might arrange for your services for their parents, so you might consider giving free seminars on financial issues involved in caring for aging parents.

Resources

Newsgroup: misc.invest.financial-plan

65. ⊙⊙ 🗑 🚗 100,000

Professional Practice Management Service

Managing a professional practice such as a medical or dental office requires an entirely different set of skills from the training most practicing professionals receive. As a result, an increasing number of dentists, doctors, chiropractors, osteopaths, podiatrists, psychotherapists, and other professionals are turning to professional consultants for help in managing the business and financial aspects of their practices.

Full-service private practice consultants help their clients with virtually any aspect of running their offices. They may hire and fire personnel, train new staff, prepare payroll, handle billing and collections, manage the building, oversee investments and retirement programs, and select computer hardware and software when the business needs it. They may also use their organizational skills to improve productivity among the staff and the professionals themselves, such as studying the scheduling of patients to help the professional increase business.

To succeed in this business, you need to have had some solid experience in office management and a background in or knowledge of the professional field in which you intend to work. Typical annual gross revenues run from $50,000 to $200,000, depending on how many practices you consult with. If you are just beginning in the profession, you may be able to charge $50 to $75 per hour for your time, while experienced consultants can earn $150 per hour and more.

The best way to get business is through contacts in the field. Networking, building a referral base from your own professional clients, and speaking and writing about practice management are also effective methods.

Resources

Encyclopedia of Practice and Financial Management, by Lawrence Farber. Oradell, NJ, Medical Economic Books, 1985.

Practice Management for Physicians, by Donald L. Donohugh. Orlando, FL, W. B. Saunders, 1986.

INSTITUTE OF CERTIFIED PROFESSIONAL BUSINESS CONSULTANTS, 330 S. Wells Street, Ste. 1422, Chicago, IL 60606, (800) 447-1684.

SOCIETY OF MEDICAL-DENTAL MANAGEMENT CONSULTANTS, 3646 E. Ray Road, Ste. B16-45, Phoenix AZ 85044, (800) 826-2264, fax: (602) 759-3530, Web: *http://www.*smdmc.com.

The Consultant, a newsletter published by the Institute of Professional Business Consultants (see above).

Franchise

PROFESSIONAL MANAGEMENT GROUP, P.O. Box 1130, Battle Creek, MI 49016, (800) 888-1932, *http://www.*thepmgroup.com

66

Professional Reminder Service

We first heard of the concept of a reminder service about twelve years ago, but despite its appeal, we haven't met many people who are actually doing it successfully. The problem seems to be that few people or companies are willing to pay to be reminded about birthdays, anniversaries, special occasions, and the like, especially in today's age of computers with calendar and scheduling software as well as handheld electronic devices that can keep track of these items.

The most feasible idea for a reminder service, however, we think makes dollars and sense. Think for a moment about the medical or dental appointment you have; don't you generally receive a call beforehand to remind you about the appointment, to be sure the doctor doesn't end up with a "no-show" that costs him or her money? Well, herein lies the idea behind this business. Also consider wholesaling this service to a seller of gifts for them to offer free to their customers.

While many larger practices have a front office staff to make these reminder calls each day, many solo practitioners, and there are three-quarters of a million of them, don't have sufficient help and probably suffer from a lack of time to make such calls themselves. But as many as 20 percent of patients don't keep appointments, so as a result, thousands of chiropractors, dentists, podiatrists, psychotherapists, massage therapists, facialists, and other professionals are excellent candidates for a homebased "professional" reminder service. This business could take advantage of high technology in many ways too. For example, the doctor could fax directly into your computer's fax/modem board, or send you an E-mail of the list of appointments to be called for the next day, or allow you to use software like Norton *PCAnywhere* (Symantec) to log onto his or her computer each night and retrieve the list yourself. You could use autodialing programs to save on finger work, or even a voice mail system to make the announcement automatically.

This business would make an add-on business for an answering service or a part-time business for a home-bound person. The requirements are few, with attention to detail and excellent communication habits topping the list. You could charge by the call or by the day. As for revenues, if you enlisted six to ten doctors and were making sixty to one hundred calls per day at $1 or so each, you might generate the equivalent of $20 to $30 per hour, a nice payoff for a business with very low overhead. You could also target this service to other businesspeople who operate on appointments; i.e., hairstylists, service personnel, repair people, etc.

67.

Proofreading Service

We know firsthand (boy do we know!) that where there's writing, there are typos. Few things are more frustrating than sending out or posting to a Web site a report, prospectus, business plan, technical manual, or even a business letter and finding out later that a word was missing, or misspelled, or that something was punctuated incorrectly, or worse, the grammar itself was wrong. No matter how well written, thoroughly researched, or professional appearing a document is, one little typographical error will greatly diminish its overall impact.

Large publishing houses and newspapers have proofreaders on staff, but most midsized, smaller, and certainly sole-proprietor businesses do not. Yet all these businesses must communicate well and represent themselves as professionally as possible. We see a large demand for the services of independent proofreaders and copy editors.

If you enjoy language, have an eye for detail, and are knowledgeable in the rules of grammar, you may want to consider starting a home-based proofreading service. Almost every written communication these days is generated on a word processor, so the proofreading and editing of documents can be greatly assisted by a number of software solutions. Most people are familiar with the spell-check features in their word processor, but few take the time to run the other feature common to most programs: the grammar check. You can choose to run the grammar check as a starting point or, better yet, you can opt to use your own skill in language and structure.

There are many secretarial and typing services who claim to offer proofreading and copy editing, but oftentimes their level of expertise in these areas falls short, as does the time they have available to devote to these highly specialized skills. By promoting yourself as an expert in proofreading, with a solid background in grammar, usage, style, and syntax, your perceived, and actual, value in the marketplace will be assured.

Proofreading is a candidate for a stand-alone business. It also will work well as an add-on to a word-processing, copywriting, or technical-writing business. Potential clients run the gamut from small publishing houses to independent newsletter publishers, freelance writers, authors, Web writers, public relations firms, and just about any other business or professional who relies on the published or printed word in his or her business. Networking online is a great way to get business. Find discussion groups for any of the aforementioned businesses and let them know about what you do. It also might be worth your while to place small ads in local publications relevant to any of your target markets. In your communications with potential clients, emphasize your attention to detail and your depth of knowledge in grammar and syntax. This will differentiate you from many of the less specialized secretarial and word-processing services vying for the same business.

Resources

21st Century Grammar Handbook, by Princeton Language Institute, Joseph Holland (editor), New York, Dell Publishing Company, 1993, ISBN: 0440215080.

Think about Editing: A Grammar Guide, by Allen Ascher, Boston, MA, Heinle & Heinle Publishing, 1993, ISBN: 0838439764.

68.

Property Management Service

Although real estate property management can be a rewarding business, it is not as simple as many people think. In addition to watching over properties, the professional manager maintains records on tenants, tracks income and expenses, audits and pays utility bills and taxes, contacts various personnel for repairs and inspections, and performs a host of other duties. The computer can help track all this information effectively, however, and therefore we've included real estate property management as a home-based business for someone who knows how or is willing to learn how to work with spreadsheet and database programs or specialized software dedicated to property management.

Property management combines several managerial skills with a diversified day-to-day schedule. For example, the professional property service that handles several buildings might spend the morning working on a rental lease for a new tenant, using a word processor template and then developing an income projection using a spreadsheet program. During lunch hour, she might next show properties for rent, logging the prospective tenants' names and phone numbers into a database, and then make phone calls to various repairmen in the afternoon, finally collecting rents and updating the financials into an accounting program at night. As you can see, the more adept the property management service is at using a full range of computer software, the more efficient and professional the business can be.

You do not need a real estate license to get into this business, but since you will be working for property owners who want to feel secure in their choice of management services, it helps to have some credentials in office management, administration, or a field like accounting. Your office equipment needs to include a personal computer, a wide-carriage dot-matrix printer for printing spreadsheets, a fax machine for quick correspondence with owners, and a good telephone system with two or three lines.

If you have not done property management before, the best methods for getting into the business include reviewing the classified section of your newspaper for want ads and making direct contact with landlords in your area. Once you establish your business, word of mouth is your best source of new business. A related business is managing condominium developments too large for volunteers to manage but not large enough to hire full-time staff to run.

Resources

The Guide to Practical Property Management, by John Philip Bachner, New York, McGraw-Hill, 1991, ISBN: 0070028435.

Property Management, by Floyd M. Baird and Robert C. Kyle, Chicago, IL, Real Estate Education Co., 1995, ISBN: 079311067X.

PROPERTY MANAGEMENT ASSOCIATION OF AMERICA, 9700 Wisconsin Ave., Ste. 204, Bethesda, MD 20814, (301) 587-6543, *http://www.* reji.com/ reji/association/pma/non-member/data/

Newsgroup: misc.invest.real-estate

69.

Proposal and Grant Writer

The U.S. federal government annually contracts with thousands of companies based on competitive bids to supply products and provide services to its agencies. It also offers millions of dollars each year in special Small Business Innovative Research (SBIR) grants to companies that have ideas for new technology or products from which Americans can benefit. In addition to government grants, there are thousands of private foundations and other funding institutions that provide grants to individuals and nonprofit organizations for a myriad of civic, educational, and social-welfare purposes.

The challenge with nearly all these contracts and grants is, however, that anyone who wants one must traverse a lengthy, complex application process that begins with a special written proposal. Since most individuals and companies do not have the internal expertise to create this document, there is a growing need for freelance proposal and grant writers who guide individuals and companies through the process. These professionals write well and know the rules and regulations governing the creation and formatting of the proposal. Because of their backgrounds and personal experience, they frequently also advise their clients on how to improve upon the original product or service to ensure obtaining government or foundation approval.

Proposal and grant writers are sometimes generalists with a broad knowledge of diverse fields, but many are specialists in a single area such as agriculture, communications, energy, business, space exploration, or another advanced industry. Most proposal writers are also well versed in using spreadsheets, databases, and desktop publishing software, since their job often includes producing the final document and corollary budget or bidding information for their clients. In addition to these qualifications, you must also have excellent communication skills since you will be working directly with CEOs and presidents of companies.

Proposal and grant writers usually obtain their clients through networking and sometimes through advertising or direct mail to companies that might be interested in government or foundation funding. Once established, they can then count on word of mouth since they have developed a reputation for successfully winning contracts or grants. Earnings for writers range from $45,000 to over $100,000.

Making a living as a proposal and grant writer may require a few years of experience as you learn the ropes and develop contacts. However, if you have first-rate writing skills and enjoy working on a variety of projects, the opportunities are good.

Resources

Catalog of Federal Domestic Assistance, available free online from Federal Assistance Programs Retrieval Systems, (800) 669-8331.

The Consultant's Guide to Proposal Writing, 2d ed., by Herman Holtz. New York, John Wiley, 1990.

Government Assistance Almanac, by J. Robert Dumouchel, Detroit, Omnigraphics, annual.

Proposal Planning and Writing, by Lynn E. Miner and Jerry Griffith, Phoenix, AZ, Oryx Press, 1993, ISBN: 0897747267.

Winning Grants Step by Step: Support Centers of America's Complete Workbook for Planning, Developing, and Writing Successful Proposals, by Mim Carlson, San Francisco, Jossey-Bass Publishing, 1996, ISBN: 0787901180.

Foundation Directory, The Foundation Center, New York: Russell Sage Foundation, annual (available in libraries).

THE GRANTMANSHIP CENTER, P.O. Box 17220, Los Angeles, CA 90017, (213) 482-9860, teaches workshops in writing grants for nonprofit organizations. *http://www.tgci.com*

Newsgroup: misc.writing

70.

Public Relations Specialist

The Bureau of Labor Statistics projects a 25 percent growth in Public Relations Specialists through 2005, because PR, as it is often called, is increasingly recognized as a cost-effective solution for marketing a business, a nonprofit agency, even a government program. Additionally, as corporations and organizations cut back on staffing, they are increasingly turning to outside PR and marketing consultants who, with today's computer and telephone equipment, can do a top-quality job cost effectively.

Public Relations Specialists help their clients establish a high profile in the public eye. Their goal is to obtain as much coverage as possible in the media, thereby alerting potential buyers to the existence and usefulness of the client's product or service. To accomplish this, they produce written materials such as news releases, press kits, speeches, and brochures, and they develop contacts among radio and television producers in order to get their clients on the air.

While many PR professionals work for many kinds of clients, others focus on a special niche such as corporate relations (i.e., preparing annual reports and investor newsletters or fostering employee and community communications), celebrity work (i.e., handling authors, television and movie stars), or certain kinds of businesses (i.e., restaurants, toy companies, or clothing manufacturers). Still others prefer to work for trade associations, nonprofit organizations, or political causes.

To do PR, you need to be creative, exhibit outstanding verbal and written communication skills, and have an outgoing personality that can be both persuasive and assertive. To make your operation run efficiently, today's PR professional uses a personal computer with contact management and database software, since you need to contact many people and keep records of your conversations and actions. It also is necessary to have a laser printer, fax, and modem, since the PR Specialist working independently at home will need to produce the same quality of work as someone housed in a high-rise office.

Potential annual earnings for independent PR practitioners range from $35,000 to $75,000. While experience in a PR agency, publishing company, or corporate communications department is useful, you can enter the business as a solo practitioner through networking and personal contacts, taking on small projects and getting results for your clients, who can then refer you to new opportunities.

Resources

Effective Public Relations, by Allen H. Center, Glen M. Broom, Ph.D., and Scott M. Cutlip, Englewood Cliffs, NJ, Prentice-Hall, 1994, ISBN: 0132450100.

Handbook for Public Relations Writing, by Thomas H. Bivins, Lincolnwood, IL, NTC Business Books, 1996, ISBN: 0844234362.

How to Start a Home-Based Communications Business, by Louann Werksma, Old Saybrook, CT, Globe Pequot Press, 1996, ISBN: 1564406318.

The Practice of Public Relations, by Fraser P. Seitel, Englewood Cliffs, NJ, Prentice-Hall, 1995, ISBN: 0024088404.

Public Relations Journal, 33 Irving Place, New York, NY 10003, (212) 995-2230.

PUBLIC RELATIONS AND MARKETING FORUM ON COMPUSERVE.

PUBLIC RELATIONS SOCIETY OF AMERICA, INC., 33 Irving Place, New York, NY 10003, (212) 995-2230, *http://www.prsa.org*

71

Publishing Services

Publishing services produce books, catalogs, and directories for their clients who may be individuals, companies, or organizations. Projects might range from ghostwriting a book for an author who is under contract with a publisher to consulting with a company that wants to produce a mail-order catalog to editing and typesetting a private directory for a local trade group or association to doing publication design. With the advent of desktop publishing technology, home-based publishing services are also expanding into many additional areas that were once the preserve of small presses and vanity publishers. They may help an executive self-publish a showcase book that adds credibility to his or her name, or work with a company or individual to write, produce, and market a how-to or nonfiction book through bookstores, direct mail, or mail order.

Although starting a publishing service does not require extensive experience in publishing per se, you must have strong writing and editing skills, as well as an excellent knowledge of how books and other publications are created from manuscripts to printed titles. Other important qualities are an eye for layout and graphic design, and an ear for helping clients pick out book titles or rewrite material as needed. If you get involved in marketing matters, it is also important to understand the distribution options for books, guides, or directories.

The main tools needed by a publishing service are a personal computer with at least a three-gigabyte hard drive, a laser printer, and one of the many powerful desktop publishing software programs that allow you to design a book, set type, and produce either camera-ready copy or files that can be used by a type service bureau. Some publishing services also utilize many other devices such as scanners and removable drives that give them greater access to research information and artwork.

Publishing services may charge by the hour, by the day, or by the project, depending on the nature of the services they are providing. Their fees may range from $20 to $50 per hour for editorial consultations to several thousand dollars to edit, typeset, and produce camera-ready copy for an entire book. On this basis, gross annual earnings for a busy publishing service operating full-time can amount to $40,000 or more.

One of the best ways to begin a publishing service is by networking among graphic designers, printers, and even literary agents in your area, all of whom are often approached by people seeking assistance in developing a book or other publication. Other ways to get business include advertising in the yellow pages under Publishing Consultant or Desktop Publishing and working with your own professional contacts to locate people who have long thought about writing a book of some kind but who need help to actually do so.

Resources

How to Start and Run a Writing and Editing Business, by Herman Holtz, New York, John Wiley, 1992. Holtz is one of America's most prolific and successful business writers.

The Self-Publishing Manual, by Dan Poynter. Santa Barbara, CA, Para Publishing, 1991. The name Dan Poynter and self-publishing are almost synonymous. He has written and self-published over sixty books.

Publishers of Books on Publishing

DUSTBOOKS, P.O. Box 100, Paradise, CA 95967, publishes *The International Directory of Magazines and Small Presses.*

EDITOR AND PUBLISHER, 11 West 19th Street, New York, NY 10011.

WRITER'S DIGEST BOOKS, 1507 Dana Avenue, Cincinnati, OH 45207, (800) 289-0963. One of the many books from Writer's Digest is *The Complete Guide to Self-Publishing*, by Tom and Marilyn Ross.

PUBLISHERS MARKETING ASSOCIATION, 627 Aviation Way, Manhattan Beach, CA 90266, (310) 372-2732, E-mail: pmaonline@aol.com, Web: *http://www.* pma-online.org

EDITORIAL FREELANCERS ASSOCIATION, 71 West 23rd Street, Ste. 1504, New York, NY 10159-2050, (212) 929-5400. A trade association that includes editors, writers, researchers, proofreaders, indexers, and others. The association produces a survey of members' rates and operates a "job phone." *http://www.the-efa.com*

Newsgroups: alt.prose
comp.publish.electronic
comp.publish.electronic.developer
comp.publish
alt.publish.books

72.

Online Product Sales

One of the fastest-growing industries in retail sales in America has been direct marketing. Direct marketing is loosely defined as any sale generated by a direct communication to a consumer. Up till very recently, direct communication has been primarily via mail and by phone. Usually direct marketing refers to the mail-order industry. According to a recent study conducted by the Direct Marketing Association (DMA), sales generated by direct marketing in the U.S. were $442.4 billion in 1990, $636.9 billion in 1996, and will be projected at $841.2 billion by the year 2000.

Growth like this means there's money to made in direct sales, but the problem for home-based businesses has always been one of cost. It is incredibly expensive to produce a full-color catalog and mail it to enough people to realize a healthy enough profit to justify such a large investment. Thanks to the online revolution, however, the cost of presenting a line of products to a large number of people has been geometrically reduced. Now, a commercial Web site can reach more people than is possible through traditional targeted mailings. Web sites are in an order of magnitude less expensive to produce than a standard catalog or mailing and can be infinitely updated to reflect new products, pricing, etc. Once a Web site is posted, it is available twenty-four hours a day, seven days a week to what by the end of 1996 were forty-seven million Web users in the United States alone plus millions more in 150 other countries around the world. A well-designed site will encourage a viewer to browse or search through your listing of products, make their selections, fill out a simple order sheet with their credit card number, and submit it to you. While commerce on the Web has been slower to grow than other aspects of the Web, one out of three current Web users buys or is willing to purchase products online.

There currently are two models for businesses selling products on the World Wide Web: the online storefront and the online catalog. The online storefront is exactly what the name suggests. A Web site is designed to suggest an actual store in which products can be bought. Online catalogs are also illustrative in their names, as online viewers can browse through a site resembling a catalog and make selections. When structuring a business around either of these models, your chances of success will be greater if you gear it to the particulars of cyberspace. The World Wide Web thrives on uniqueness and niches. The more targeted your product line is (i.e., hot sauces, children's educational books, Eastern European folk music on 78rpm records, cigars, etc.), the greater your chances of being found by readers worldwide. Structure your virtual "storefront" or "catalog" to be as interactive as possible. Involve your viewers as much as possible, update your content frequently, and be entertaining.

To get your business off the ground, we advise you to enlist the services of a top-flight Web site designer who has experience in these kinds of sites and offers expert CGI programming capabilities (for online order forms). To build "traffic" on your site, the services of a Web promotions expert will provide you with many excellent options. You may also wish to hire an on-line publicist to ensure that your site receives the maximum exposure in the digital community. We also suggest that you spend a considerable amount of time online checking out what others are doing. You may also want to enroll in classes on online entrepreneurship.

Resources

Build a World Wide Web Commerce Center: Plan, Program, and Manage Internet Commerce for Your Company, by Net. Genesis Corporation, New York, Wiley, 1996 ISBN: 0471149284.

Digital Cash: Commerce on the Net, by Peter Wayner, San Diego, CA, AP Professional, 1995, ISBN: 0127387633.

Guerrilla Marketing Online: The Entrepreneur's Guide to Earning Profits on the Internet, by Jay Conrad Levinson, Charles Rubin, Boston, Houghton Mifflin (paper), 1995, ISBN: 0395728592.

Launching a Business on the Web, by David Cook and Deborah Sellers, New York, Que Corporation, 1996, ISBN: 078970871X.

Marketing on the Internet: A Proven 12-Step Plan for Promoting, Selling and Delivering Your Products and Services to Millions over the Information Superhighway, by Michael Mathiesen, Gulf Breeze, FL, Maximum Press, 1996, ISBN: 1885068093.

Selling on the Net: The Complete Guide, by Herschell Gordon Lewis and Robert D. Lewis, Lincolnwood, IL, NTC Business Books, 1996, ISBN: 0844232335.

THE DIRECT MARKETING ASSOCIATION. The DMA is the largest and oldest organization dedicated solely to the evolving practice of direct marketing and the issues facing it every day. 1120 Avenue of the Americas, New York, NY 10036-6700, (212) 768-7277, fax: (212) 719-1946, E-mail: dma@the-dma.org, Web: *http://www*.the-dma.org

http://www.techweb.com/webcommerce/ Weekly news and issues regarding commerce on the World Wide Web.

Newsgroup: comp.databases

73.

Referral Service

A referral service is based on the simple truth that most people today have little time to spend researching the many services or products they use. For example, you've probably seen or heard ads for services that offer referrals to lawyers, doctors, and dentists. This same idea can be applied to almost any area of importance to people: plumbers and contractors, appliance repair servicepeople, tutors, caterers and party locations, wedding suppliers, child care, elder care, baby-sitters, house- or pet-sitters, auto repair, roommates, and dates.

Generally, a referral service works as follows: First, you put together a database of suppliers who pay you a flat fee, annual dues, or a percentage commission of their fee for each referral you bring them. Then, when people call your service, you ascertain their specific needs and refer them at no charge to one of the businesses registered with your service. Some referral services, however, will charge both parties for using the service, especially those that match people with people such as a roommate-matching or dating service.

The keys to a successful referral service are first, the level and quality of the research you do in order to match people with the right service, and second, generating enough referrals to satisfy those who pay to list with your service. Your credibility depends on the accuracy of your information and the reliability of the businesses to whom you refer your customers. It is therefore essential that you gather enough information so that you can refer with confidence or so that the consumer can make an informed decision. You'll also occasionally need to drop vendors from your referral list who don't meet your standards or about whom you get complaints that are not solved to the customer's satisfaction.

To start this type of service, you will need a computer and relational database management software such as *Paradox* (Borland), *Foxpro, Access* (Microsoft) or Lotus *Approach* that allows you to create and search lists of vendors using many criteria: location, price, specialized services, guarantee or warranty policies, and so on. You will also need to create an attractive flyer that you can use in signing up vendors and for notifying potential customers about your service. Print as many flyers as you can afford and post them on bulletin boards such as those in stores. Distributing them widely throughout your market area is critical to your success. You may also wish to advertise on the radio (it's cheaper than you think!) and in local newspapers both to attract customers and to let vendors know you are making an investment in reaching people who want to be referred.

Earnings in this business will vary greatly, but some referral services charge vendors as much as $1,500 or $2,000 per year to be listed with them.

Resources

HOMEWATCH, 2865 S. Colorado Boulevard, #203, Denver, CO 80222, (303) 758-7290. A franchise business you can purchase that provides people to take care of someone's home while they are away and home care for the elderly. Their fee is $35,000 to $40,000.

NATIONAL TENANT NETWORK, P.O. Box 1664, Lake Grove, OR 97035, (800) 228-0989. Sets you up in business as a computerized tenant-screening service working for residential landlords.

74.

Real Estate Brochure Service

If you live in an active urban area where people frequently buy and sell housing, and you enjoy real estate, this business idea might appeal to you. The essential concept of the business is to help real estate agents and companies create effective brochures that help to sell a property. Such marketing devices also serve as good public relations for a company and often help to bring in new business as well.

In particular, many agents don't have the time to do as much marketing as they should and would be willing to pay a service to help them expand their opportunity to sell a house. Your service is therefore to take a high-quality photo of homes listed for sale, and, using your desktop publishing software, a scanner, and a color printer like those from Hewlett Packard, Canon, and Epson, you create color brochures that can be distributed to other agents or to prospective buyers. Agents can also use them to send as direct-mail pieces to entire neighborhoods to show potential clients the properties they have gotten listed and sold.

Such brochures are easy to produce, quickly done, and inexpensive to print if you have the right equipment. If you charge $100 per house for 500 brochures that cost you 5 cents each to produce, you can make $75 for just a few hours' work. This could also be an add-on business for a Copywriter, Desktop Publishing Service, or PR Specialist.

Resources

See Desktop Publishing Service, page 51.

75.

Repairing Computers

If there's a quick, convenient way to get equipment repaired, most businesses and private individuals would prefer to have it fixed instead of spending the money to buy a new one. This is true especially for computers that generally retain most of their functionality and value, so that repairing them makes complete sense. Additionally, businesses can't afford to have downtime on their machines, and when their computers break down, they want them repaired immediately.

As a result, repairing computers and peripheral equipment is one of the fastest-growing businesses in the country, amounting to more than $20 billion in annual sales. Although there is plenty of competition from larger service companies, this is a perfect job to do as a home business because you can offer quicker, more personal service on-site for a lower price.

Computer repair can be a part-time venture, a full-time career, or an add-on business for a computer consultant or trainer. While you don't need a degree in engineering or mechanical repair, you will need a good knowledge of computer hardware so you can provide your customers with total satisfaction on any job you do. You will probably want to have a contract that your clients sign, indicating your warranty policy and limits on liability.

Courses in computer repair are offered at some community colleges and trade schools. The quality of such courses varies, but you should choose one that at least offers you a repair manual for most common OEM boards and sources of quality replacement parts. Alternatively, since most PC repairs require simply swapping components, you can use the hands-on approach. You can buy a couple of old computers and several upgrade/repair books along with a software program like *Checkit Pro* and a decent set of tools and dig in. Finally there is also a home-study course from McGraw-Hill (listed below).

Fees for computer repair range from $60 to $100 an hour, depending on your location and the type of service you offer. To increase your revenues, you might offer an annual contract to clients for a sizable fee, for which you will handle all maintenance and repair within forty-eight hours and/or provide backup computers, hard drives, printers, or whatever equipment they need. You might also expand by selling computer supplies or doing computer tutoring for your clients.

To build a computer repair business, identify what type of computers you want to service and what industries or niches you wish to serve. Then begin distributing flyers throughout the area you are willing to travel for work. Keep your travel area small because most people want and need prompt service. Distribute flyers at user groups, schools, and office buildings. A yellow-pages listing or an ad in the classified section of a local business or trade journal can provide other means of reaching small prospective clients.

Resources

Easy-PC Handbook: PCB Layout and Circuit Design by Computer, by Ian Sinclair, Newton, MA, Butterworth-Heinemann, 1995, ISBN: 0750622814.

How Anyone Can Fix and Rev Up PCs (How It Works), by Carrie English (illustrator) and Ron White, New York, Ziff Davis, 1995, ISBN: 1562762524.

The PC and Mac Handbook: Systems, Upgrades and Troubleshooting, by Steve Heath, Newton, MA, Butterworth-Heinemann, 1996, ISBN: 0750622296.

The Computer Shopper is a source of information about prices and parts. It's available on most newsstands. *http://www.ZDNet.com*

Processor, a traderlike magazine, is a source for finding parts, P.O. Box 85518 Lincoln, NE 68501, (800) 334-7443, *http://www.*processor. com

Service and Support Management is a trade journal for repair personnel and service organizations. 12416 Hymeadow Dr., Austin, TX 78750-1896, (512) 250-9023, *http://www.pcinews.com/pci*

McGraw-Hill, NRI Schools offers a home-study course in microcomputers and microprocessors that prepares individuals to repair computers. It includes a computer and diagnostic hardware and software. 4401 Connecticut Ave., N.W., Washington, DC 20008, (202) 244-1600, *http://www.*mhcec.com. Cost: $3,245.

76.

Résumé Service

It is now estimated that Americans change jobs seven times on the average over the course of their working lifetimes. Despite many books on the subject, job seekers don't all have the skill or confidence to create an effective résumé about their past careers or work and school experience. Growing numbers of people, in fact, head straight for the yellow pages to locate a professional service that can help them create clean, sharp-looking, and concise résumés. As a result, a growing industry of résumé-writing services is mushrooming in every major city.

True résumé writers don't simply type up notes handed them by clients. They interview their clients in order to select and develop the precise content for the résumé, write descriptions of the person's background, and lay out and design an impressive résumé that focuses the reader on the person's strengths and capabilities.

The growth of the Internet and the World Wide Web has changed the format and presentation of résumés as well. More and more job seekers are looking for jobs online. Jobs listed online ask that résumés be E-mailed to the prospective employer. Today's résumé service must be prepared not only to create effective printed résumés; they must also be able to prepare winning electronic versions as well. This also means preparing portfolios and multimedia résumés for distribution disks and CD-ROMs.

To be in this business, you will need exceptional writing skills, an ability to interview people and learn what they are good at doing, and some knowledge of how personnel directors and executives read résumés. For your computer equipment, you will want to have a high-quality word-processing or desktop publishing software program, a modem and Internet Service Provider, and a laser printer or access to a service bureau for high-resolution output so that you can produce attractive, well-designed professional résumés. Although template-based résumé writing software is available, most of the packages are too limited for professional use except perhaps in writing a college student résumé. Software such as *ResumeExpert* and *The Resume Kit* for the Macintosh can be helpful in organizing simple résumés.

Résumé prices range from about $50 for a one-page student résumé to over $300 for a full curriculum vitae. The price also depends on the typesetting and design requirements, and the number of copies printed. Some résumé writers offer additional services to increase their fees, such as writing cover letters, handling the mailings, designing letterhead and stationery for the person, and offering post office boxes. Typical gross annual revenue for résumé writers is $39,000.

Résumé services serve two primary groups of clients: university students and people in the business and professional community. As indicated above, yellow-pages advertising is one of the best ways to market a résumé service. Also effective are networking in professional, trade, and civic organizations, both online and in person, and taking out classified ads under the "Employment Professional" sections in college or university newspapers or newspapers read by businesspeople and professionals. A simple Web site outlining your capabilities is also quite helpful.

Resources

Electronic Resume Revolution: Creating a Winning Resume for the New World of Job Seeking, by Thomas J. Morrow and Joyce Lain Kennedy, New York, Wiley, 1995, ISBN: 0471115843.

How to Open and Operate a Home-Based Resume Service: An Unabridged Guide by Jan Melnik, Old Saybrook, CT, Globe Pequot Press, 1996, ISBN: 1564407551.

A Resume Writer's Guide to Asking Effective Questions, Professional Association of Resume Writers (see below).

PROFESSIONAL ASSOCIATION OF RESUME WRITERS, 3637 Fourth Street North, Ste. 330, St. Petersburg, FL 33704, (800) 822-7279, E-mail: parwhq@aol.com This organization provides a newsletter, professional membership identification including name and logo to use in advertising, advertising layouts, and a toll-free consultant line.

77. [icons]

Reunion Planning

As baby boomers enter middle age and beyond, the late 1990s will see literally thousands of milestone high school and college reunions each year for classes that graduated from ten to thirty years ago. But even as nostalgia reigns and alums yearn to return to their youth, most people just don't have time to volunteer to organize their reunion, make phone calls, mail out information, and arrange hotels, child care, catering, and the myriad other details that need to get done for a successful reunion.

Enter the professional reunion planner, a special category of event planner. The job of a reunion planner is to take charge of all aspects and every detail required to make the event successful, well attended, and fun. A reunion planner will locate missing class members, mail invitations, take reservations, hire bands, find food and beverage suppliers, and otherwise coordinate everything involved in the event. Much of this work is extremely time-consuming and requires good investigative abilities, since locating missing classmates may involve telephone calls to previous employers, searching through telephone directories and databases and birth and marriage records, and contacting friends, neighbors, and associates. This volume of research is one of the reasons why reunion planners start their work on a reunion more than a year in advance.

To do this business well, you will want to take advantage of your computer and project management/scheduling software, as well a personal information management program to keep track of your phone numbers, contacts, conversations, and other data on the many companies you will deal with. It can also help to know how to do your own desktop publishing so that you can inexpensively produce your own invitations, brochures, announcements, and other printed materials you can include among your services.

Getting into the business is not difficult, but you should enjoy organizing events, working with people, and attending to details. Reunion planners typically receive a percentage of the registrations as their fee. Full-time professional planners can generate an annual income in the six-figure range if they handle multiple schools and reunions. In addition to high school and college graduating classes, other types of groups that you can approach for business include military units and large families interested in planning family reunions. Reportedly, military reunions are now a growing source of new business for reunion planners.

Resources

Family Reunion Handbook; Reunion Handbook: A Handbook for School Reunions; Activities for Family Reunions and other helpful books published by Tom Ninkovich, Reunion Research, 3145 Geary Blvd., #14, San Francisco, CA 94118, (209) 855-2101, *http://www. reunited.com*

CLASS REUNION, INC. offers small, intensive training programs in how to become a reunion planner. Cost: $2,500, including all materials. Contact Shell and Judy Norris. P.O. Box 844, Skokie, IL 60076, (847) 677-4949, fax: (847) 677-4907.

78.

Scanning Service

A scanning service could be a good add-on for many businesses where customers already come into your home, such as desktop publishing, word-processing, graphic design, or bookkeeping services. You can turn what is now reasonably priced equipment into additional income. Using optical character recognition software like *OmniPage* (Caere) or *Word-Scan* (Calera), image processing software like *Image Assistant* (Caere), or *Photoshop* (Adobe Systems) and a flatbed scanner, you can take documents of any type and turn them into file formats such as JPG or GIF files that your customer's commercial software programs can read and edit.

Many companies can use a scanning service, from law firms to publishers to database producers. They may have old documents that need to be put into computer files but not want to invest the time or the expense to retype the entire document; they may have first editions of books or manuals that need to be updated but the old computer files are lost or damaged; or they may have artwork that needs to be placed into their document and not own a scanner that can handle the type of work they need to do.

Six-hundred-dot-per-inch color scanners are readily available for under $500. However, you can earn from $20 to $25 per thousand characters scanned depending on the nature of the job and the amount of manual intervention it requires. (A single double-spaced typed page contains on the average 2,000 to 3,000 characters.) If you were to charge $2.50 per page, and you scanned only 200 pages per week, that's $500!

No special skills are needed for this business, except the ability to manipulate the software to produce the output desired by your customers and enough familiarity with design and printing terms to know what they need. The best ways to get business are to advertise in the yellow pages and place very small ads in local business newspaper or journals.

Resources

Scanning: Your Personal Consultant, by Jonathan Hornstein, New York, Ziff Davis, 1995, ISBN: 1562762974.

Scanning and Image Processing for the PC, by Frank Baeseler and Bruce Bovill, New York, McGraw-Hill, 1997, ISBN: 0077078195.

Newsgroups: rec.photo.digital
rec.photo.technique
rec.photo.misc

79.

Self-Publishing

Each year, thousands of people publish their own books and sell them through private channels, mail order, and even in bookstores. These individuals do not wait for a big publisher to accept their manuscript; they learn how to publish and market their message themselves, producing everything from children's books and first novels to specialty cookbooks, guides, and how-to books. In fact, many people have been so successful in self-publishing that after their first successful book, they have gone on to establish a publishing company of their own.

Because of sophisticated desktop publishing software, the steps to self-publishing are quite easy today. In brief, you begin by writing and word-processing your manuscript, which you then transform into fully designed pages using a program like *Aldus Pagemaker,* or *QuarkXpress.* Other software such as *CorelDraw* or *Adobe Illustrator* allow you to add your own original artwork, or you can use a scanner and scanner software to import clip art and photos. Next, you either use a service bureau to produce your pages in high-quality type or you can use your own laser printer to produce camera-ready pages. Finally, you must locate a printer who specializes in "short runs" (printings of 3,000 copies and less) who can likely print your book at less than $2 per copy.

Once your book is printed, the next step is marketing it through any of several distribution channels. You can potentially make the most money by selling the book yourself at speeches, workshops, and seminars, and/or through classified or display ads in newspapers or magazines, on the Web, from which people mail a check and order the book directly from you. Alternatively, you can seek a middleman—a distributor or wholesaler—to place the book in retail bookstores and other outlets such as museum and gift shops, although then you will need to sell them your book at a rather steep discount.

Whichever route you take, the self-publishing process can be quite lucrative if you hit upon a subject that taps into a trend or need. Some self-publishers earn $10 and more per book, so a sale of a few thousand copies can pay off handsomely. Do not count on self-publishing to generate quick revenues, however, as it will usually take at least six months to a year before you see a return on your investment. Nevertheless, if you are a creative writer or believe you have special expertise to offer, this is a rewarding full- or part-time business to be in. Of course, self-publishing can also be an add-on business for virtually anyone who wishes to package their expertise in published form.

A paperless route to self-publishing is using the *Expanded Book Toolkit* with a Macintosh computer to produce a complete book together with art, sound, video, and search engines for reproduction on disks, CD-ROM, or for use on online services. The Voyager Company (1351 Pacific Coast Highway, Santa Monica, CA 90401) features some unusual pricing, offering the *Expanded Book Toolkit* for $295 plus a 1 percent royalty.

Resources

The Complete Guide to Self-Publishing, by Tom and Marilyn Ross. Cincinnati: Writer's Digest Books, 1994.

Kirsch's Handbook of Publishing Law, Jonathan Kirsch, Los Angeles, Acrobat Books, 1995. ISBN: 0918226333.

The Self-Publishing Manual, by Dan Poynter. Santa Barbara, CA, Para Publishing, (805) 968-7277, Web: *http://www*.parapublishing.com, E-mail: DanPoynter@aol.com This is a reference book about all aspects of self-publishing, with noteworthy resource lists.

Publishers Weekly, Cahners/Bowker Publication, the leading weekly magazine in the publishing industry, often available in libraries or by subscription, (800) 278-2991, *http://www.*pw.com

Newsgroups: misc.writing
comp.publish
alt.publish.books

80.

Sign-Making Service

Signs, posters, and flyers of all kinds abound in virtually every area of our lives, from storefronts and office buildings to street banners and telephone poles. Most signs are pretty straightforward in delivering their information, but a good sign tells us more than the name of the business or individual doing the advertising; it also says a lot about the quality of the business behind the scenes and the attention they pay to their customers. So if you are a truly "artistically" inclined person, someone who has a superior graphic sense and a feeling for writing and formatting words, you might be able to start a home-based sign business that stands out from the crowd.

Today's signmakers use many computer technologies to practice their craft. Using a software program like *CorelDraw,* you can access hundreds of scalable typefaces and use your computer to add color or clip art to your signs. Printing technology is rapidly advancing with 600 dpi becoming the standard and 1000 dpi available for under $2,000 to print your signs. While some laser printers are capable of eleven- by-seventeen-inch output, you will need access to a printing press. You may either use a local printer or obtain your own printing equipment. There are also computer-based dedicated design systems that control plotters and cutting tables to make the self-adhesive vinyl signs that you see on the sides of trucks, on freeways, offices, and many other places. Having such equipment will increase the scope of your services tenfold. This kind of equipment is available from most sign-making supply stores, Check your local yellow pages. You will also need equipment for mounting your output onto poster boards or other backing, and sundry other tools of the trade.

Customers for your business include new businesses; businesses needing signs for special promotions, exhibits, or trade shows; associations and groups that need signs or banners for meetings, banquets, and other affairs; private individuals who need signs or cards for parties, business, or special occasions; and even florist shops, gift shops, and craft stores, where you might be able to supply a special banner greeting or unique card to accompany a delivered gift. The best ways to market your business are advertising in the yellow pages and local newspapers, approaching new businesses, offering promotions and special arrangements with other people in the gift business, using your existing clients for referrals, and seeking out owners of signs that need refurbishing.

Signs can sell for as little as $15 all the way up to hundreds of dollars for large posters or banners. You can probably price your service for small signs on a per-character basis, while larger signs, banners, and posters can be charged according to an hourly rate that includes a heavy markup for your design input and expertise.

The business can become full-time or a good add-on business for a desktop publisher, marketing or PR specialist, copywriter, or graphic artist.

Resources

Designing and Planning Environmental Graphics, by Wayne Hunt (editor), Eric Labrecque (editor), and G. E. Rosenstwieg, New York, Van Nostrand Reinhold, 1995, ISBN: 0942604350.

Sign Business magazine, a trade publication for the sign-making industry. Online edition: *http://www.nbm.com/signbusiness/homepage.html*

Sign Business magazine, printed edition, P.O. Box 1416, Broomfield, CO, 80038, (303) 469-0424, or fax: (303) 469-5730.

81.

Software Location Service

A software locator service is a cross between a computer consultant and an information broker. Like computer consultants, people in this business help companies solve problems using software, but—and here is the twist—like information brokers, they search through databases to find software that already exists.

The value of software locators is that they can save companies a lot of money. To illustrate how this is so, consider a typical scenario. XYZ Company realizes that their accounting department could improve profits by invoicing customers every two days instead of every two weeks. They are therefore considering hiring a programmer to come in and design a custom program that helps them automate the process. The programmer charges $1,000 a day and expects the job to take three days. Do they need to go to this expense? Might there be a software program in existence already that would do the job for much less than that?

Such situations arise frequently, but many companies don't have the ability or time to find out if software exists that will meet their needs. Before hiring the programmer, however, they could contact a software locator who will search his or her databases and might discover that, indeed, a program does exist that will do exactly what the business needs for only $500.

The software locator must first understand the client's needs and then identify software applications that will do the job. So to be in this business, you must be something of a software junkie as well as a generalist who enjoys learning about many business operations so that you can grasp the nature of a client's problem. You therefore need good communication skills and patience. For your research, you will need a personal computer and database software, a modem for online searches, and a CD-ROM drive, since several new CD-ROM products—one from Ziff-Davis— are now available containing product information on thousands of software programs.

Since this service is relatively unknown, your hardest task will be to educate your potential clients about what you can do and make companies aware of your existence. This means that you will need to do active networking among potential clients or advertise consistently in your local business newspapers and in computing magazines. Another way to get business is to make contacts with other consultants who can use your services when they need assistance in serving their clients. Fees for software locators range from $35 to $75 per hour for searches and consultation.

This business also can be an add-on service for computer trainers and tutors, consultants, and sales and service professionals.

Resources

ONLINE DIRECTORIES

Business Software Database, available on BRS, Dialog, and Knowledge Index (CompuServe). Produced by Ruth Koolish Information Sources, Inc., 1173 Colusa Avenue, P.O. Box 7848, Berkeley, CA 94707.

Micro Software Directory, available on Dialog, and Knowledge Index (CompuServe). Produced by Online, Inc., 11 Tannery Lane, Weston, CT 06883.

Online: The Software Directory, available on Dialog and Knowledge Index (CompuServe), as well as in print from Black Box Corporation, Mayview Road at Park Drive, Pittsburgh, PA 15241.

ZDNET Maintained by Ziff-Davis publications, this extensive site contains every software and product review from the family of Ziff Davis publications. A powerful search engine allows you find information by product name, company name, or type of product. *http://www.zdnet.com*

CHECK THE COMPUTER CATEGORIES OF ANY MAJOR WEB SEARCH ENGINE, such as Infoseek (*http://www.*infoseek.com), Yahoo (*http://www.*yahoo.com), or AltaVista (*http://www.*altavista.com). They all have extensive Metasites that contain thousands of searchable software titles and links to software companies such Microsoft, Adobe, Borland, etc.

PRINT DIRECTORIES

Datapro Directory of Microcomputer Software, 1805 Underwood Blvd., Delran, NJ. Datapro also produces other specialized software directories.

Software Digest Ratings Report, National Software Testing Laboratories, Inc., One Winding Drive, Philadelphia, PA 19131. This company also produces a monthly report containing comparative ratings.

Newsgroups: comp.sys.next.marketplace
comp.software

82.

Software Publishing

Names like Bill Gates, Marc Andreessen, Peter Norton, and Philippe Kahn have become legends in this country and around the world, testaments to the fame and wealth that await the successful software publisher. It may not be as easy today as a decade ago to replicate what these entrepreneurs have done, but it is still possible to become a software publisher who can indeed make money. In fact, more than a few top-selling software programs have taken off from a homegrown start; some have developed into full-blown software companies of note, including Buttonware, Expressware, PKWare, and Quicksoft.

To become a software publisher, your first steps are to identify your audience and develop your program concept. You can decide to create add-on utilities for a hot new program from a major publisher, or maybe your expertise will lead you to develop a program for a specialized engineering or medical application; or perhaps you have an idea for a game with outstanding visual effects for home hobbyists, or an educational program for students using virtual reality. Any of these ideas might fly, as long as the software is well designed, meets a need, and works on the hardware your audience owns.

After you've identified your audience and program concept, the next step is producing your software. You can either learn how to program yourself or you can strike a deal with an experienced programmer to handle the technical side for you. For this, you might either pay a flat fee, or better yet, you might offer a partnership agreement in which you do not pay the programmer any money up front but rather agree to share a royalty on any income earned.

After testing and retesting your finished software, the next step is to launch it into distribution. One of the most popular ways to do this today is through "shareware," a system in which publishers initially sell the software for only a $5 to $10 or even at no fee in order to build a clientele. The real money comes when people who like your software send in a registration card, along with an additional $20 to $80, which entitles them to the documentation and the right to get program updates and new versions.

The concept of shareware has caught on among millions of computer enthusiasts who like to experiment with new programs, or who simply balk at paying high prices for name brands when shareware companies frequently offer similar products for much less. The key to being successful as a shareware publisher is to distribute hundreds of free copies to computer bulletin board systems, computer magazines, user groups, newsletter publishers, and others in order to get people talking about and using your product. Many shareware publishers also attend all the appropriate trade shows where vendors and users may be, and some arrange for consultants and other professionals in their area to resell the program to their clients. Finally, you can also get your programs distributed through several middleman catalog companies that specialize in shareware, such as PC SIG, PC Blue, and Public Brand Software (PBS, now owned by Ziff Communications).

It can take years to become successful in this business, so you shouldn't start out counting on a positive cash inflow immediately. The rule of thumb in shareware is that only 10 to 15 percent of users will register and pay you for your program, but if 10,000 people get your software, for example, you can end up with more than 1,000 fee-paying clients and your earnings can therefore range from a few hundred to tens of thousands of dollars if you have the right program and find the right market. Some shareware eventually finds its way to retail channels and larger distribution as well.

If you are not interested in distributing your software as shareware, many software companies do acquire the work of independent software writers. A smaller publisher with a personal approach to treatment of authors and its marketing techniques is On-Line Resources, 148 West Orange Street, Covina, CA 91723. This company will first evaluate your software for its marketability by the company.

Whether you distribute your software as shareware or through traditional distribution channels, you can create awareness of your products through public relations, sending information about the new program and the availability of review copies to computer publications and broadcast media. You may do direct mail or advertise in specialty publications that target the people for whom you have written your software. Demonstrating your software at computer user groups is a key way of getting word-of-mouth recommendations under way. Even the most well-established software companies spend considerable resources catering to user groups including sending their CEOs to speak to them. Likewise, including the online user groups on your PR list can help publicize your products, particularly those on CompuServe and America Online.

Resources

How to Copyright Software, by M. J. Salone, Berkeley, CA, Nolo Press, 1990.

Make Money Selling Your Shareware (book and disk), by Steven Hudgik, New York, Windcrest, 1994, ISBN: 0070308659.

The $hareware Marketing $ystem, a disk-based newsletter including marketing tips and a database of shareware vendors, available from Jim Hood, Seattle Scientific Photography, Dept. SMS, P.O. Box 1506, Mercer Island, WA 98040, (206) 236-0470.

Computer Shopper magazine (on newsstands) publishes a regular list of computer user groups. *http://www.zdnet.com*

CompuServe offers a Shareware Forum (GO SHAREWARE), managed by the Association of Shareware Professionals.

ASSOCIATION OF SHAREWARE PROFESSIONALS, 545 Grover Road, Muskegon, MI 49442, sponsors an annual conference on shareware.

BRAND SOFTWARE, 3750 Kentucky Avenue, Indianapolis, IN 46261, (800) 343-5737.

SOFTWARE PUBLISHERS ASSOCIATION, the trade association for software publishing, 1730 M Street, N.W., Ste. 700, Washington, DC 20036, (202) 452-1600, *http://www.spa.org*

*http://www.*jumbo.com One of the Web's largest archives of shareware programs.

Newsgroups: comp.sys.next.marketplace
comp.publish.electronic.developer
comp.programming
comp.software

83.

Sports League Statistics and Game Scheduling

Two things Americans love are sports and knowing the ratings of their favorite team or players. Keeping track of sports league statistics combines these American passions. Potential clients for someone making this a business include Little League teams, adult bowling leagues, country club tournaments—any group who sponsors teams, leagues, or tournaments.

Using your computer and reasonably priced software, you can approach coaches, parents, or individual adults themselves and offer to provide them with a weekly tally of how they or their team performed, complete with all the necessary running averages, win-loss records, and so on. You attend the games with your laptop or hire someone to keep paper records, which you later keyboard into your program. Then each week you print out in a nice chart format the various statistics that the league wants you to track, such as each player's batting average or bowling score, the team's history of play against other teams, and whatever other stats are useful to the coaches or parents.

Because many parents may not want their children to feel pressured by someone watching their performance, you might alter this idea by offering to keep records for Little League teams and publishing at the end of season some kind of beautifully printed certificate of congratulations for each child or for the team to accompany the team photo. Each child's certificate would then include a positive statistic to help the child feel good about his or her experiences.

All American Sportsware (see Resources) also offers a software package that allows you to quickly and easily set up graphically appealing schedules for league games.

For your services, you might charge one fee, such as $100, to track an entire team for the season, or you might charge parents $10 to track their child including the certificate. If you are able to get the business for an entire league, your earnings can range from a few hundred dollars to even a few thousand.

Resources

Stats Pack, Baseball/Softball/Soccer/Basketball/Football; League Administration Software, Tournament Time All American SportsWare, 90 High Street, Newtown, PA 18940, (800) 869-8435; (215) 860-8535. These programs will handle team, league, and individual statistics; the lists and reports needed to administer a league; and scheduling single and double elimination tournaments. The programs may be purchased separately or in combinations. *http://www.*voicenet.com/~jenkins

Bowling League Secretary, Mighty Byte Computer, Inc., 6040A, Six Forks Road, Twin Forks Office Park, Ste. 223, Raleigh, NC 27609. This company also publishes *Baseball League Statistics.*

Newsgroup: rec.sports

84.

Technical Writing

As technology becomes more a part of all aspects of our lives, the field of technical writing is seeing tremendous growth. In fact, the Bureau of Labor Statistics projects a 34 percent increase in the number of professional technical writers between now and the year 2000.

Think of it this way: Every new product involving technology needs to be described in brochures, manuals, reference cards, instructional materials, reviews, and press releases aimed at communicating with the many people selling, servicing, and using the product. From salespeople and distributors to training professionals and media reviewers to repair personnel and the final consumers themselves, everyone involved needs to read a document of one kind or another that explains how to install, use, repair, and relate to a myriad of other details about the product.

Each audience creates a need for different types of information. Therefore, technical writing has four distinct markets: (1) writing articles for trade magazines; (2) writing publicity materials, such as press releases and feature articles, for manufacturing and service companies that need editorial coverage in business and consumer publications; (3) writing and editing technical books and instructional materials; and (4) translating technical information about new products and processes into documentation user manuals, instruction booklets, and online help files that can be read and understood by the people who will use them.

Writers for technical magazines are especially in demand as are those who can create high-quality instructional materials, because companies today are often using outside writers to create their user manuals, documentation, training materials, and technical information. It is crucial that you know how to communicate complex ideas in an understandable and easy-to-read manner. Some of your potential clients might object to your writing their documentation unless you are a programmer or engineer experienced in their particular technology or market. A good way to deal to deal with this is to ask them "Would you hire a carpenter to decorate your house?" The carpenter knows how a house is built, but those using the house want their dwelling to be functional, easy to live in, and to look good. The same is true of any end-user of a software program or technical device.

If you have the ability to communicate technical information in an understandable way, you can earn from $300 to $800 a day as a technical writer. Contracts for technical manuals are typically in the $5,000 to $10,000 range. You should be able to write well and be able to use the software intensively to test your instructions. Contacts are best made with the documentation department or, if there is no such department, with the marketing or research and development manager.

Resources

Designing, Writing and Producing Computer Documentation, by Lynn Denton and Jody Kelly, New York, McGraw-Hill, 1993.

Writer's Market: Where and How to Sell What You Write, Cincinnati, Writer's Digest Books. Published annually.

Literary Market Place. New York, R. R. Bowker. Published annually.

Instructional Design Principles and Applications, by Leslie J. Briggs et al. Englewood Cliffs, NJ: Educational Technology Publications, 1977.

AMERICAN SOCIETY FOR TRAINING AND DEVELOPMENT, 1640 King Street, Box 1443, Alexandria, VA 22313-2043, (703) 683-8100, fax: (703) 683-8103, Web: *http://www.*astd.org. Publishes a journal and catalog of resources and local chapters. Of particular interest to technical writers would be their special-interest groups.

INTERNATIONAL ASSOCIATION OF BUSINESS COMMUNICATORS, 1 Hallidie Plaza, Ste. 600, San Francisco, CA 94102, (415) 433-3400, *http://www.* iabc.com

SOCIETY FOR TECHNICAL COMMUNICATION, 901 North Stuart Street, Ste. 904, Arlington, VA 22203, (703) 522-4114. The society has local chapters, some of which have an employment referral service or résumé bank, *http://www.*stc-va.org

INTERNATIONAL SOCIETY FOR PERFORMANCE IMPROVEMENT, 1300 L Street, N.W., Ste. 1250, Washington, DC 20005, (202) 408-7969, *http://www.* ispi.org

TECHNICAL WRITING PAGE. This page aims to provide a set of references (links) to technical writing resources on the Internet and is very comprehensive. *http://*user.itl.net/~gazza/techwr.htm

Newsgroups: alt.books.technical
misc.books.technical
biz.books.technical
bit.listserv.techwr-1
comp.soft-sys.sas

85.

Temporary Help Service

Companies running lean and mean in the style of the late nineties often need the assistance of temporary help services. In fact, temporary help agencies are the third fastest-growing sector of our economy. By specializing in an industry or in a particular type of worker, a home-based temp service can do very well, and even out-compete the big firms with household names by serving a narrow niche market.

You can use your background and expertise to give you a leg up on other agencies by helping companies find qualified workers in a specialized field. For example, you might be able to offer a service in providing paralegals for attorneys and medical front office staff or hospital social workers, escrow officers, pharmacists, short-order cooks, corporate pilots, or printing press operators.

Companies use temporary help services because it saves them the cost and time of looking for someone, training the person, and paying employee benefits. Temporary workers are hired for many reasons: temporary absences, vacations, sickness, seasonal workloads, special projects, and temporary skill shortages. And as many companies continue to experience the need to downsize, they will look increasingly to such services to provide them with temporary help because the regular temporary help agency cannot provide them with the specialized worker.

To succeed in this business, you need to have knowledge of and contacts in the field you specialize in, and you must create a database of reliable skilled personnel. You will need a computer with hard disk, a printer and database, word-processing, and scheduling software. You will also need accounting software with a payroll module (unless you use an outside payroll service), because as a temporary help service, you are the employer of the workers, and so you must pay their wages and taxes, social security, and unemployment insurance. This also means you will need from $5,000 to $20,000 in working capital to start this business, because you will have to pay the personnel you send out while you wait to receive payment from your clients. Income potential from this business is over $100,000 a year.

Resources

NATIONAL ASSOCIATION OF TEMPORARY AND STAFFING SERVICES, 119 South Saint Asaph Street, Alexandria, VA 22314, (703) 549-6287, *http://www. natss.org*

Newsgroup: biz.marketplace.non-computer

86.

T-Shirt and Novelty Design and Production Service

Computer technology is changing how graphic images can be designed and transferred to T-shirts, mugs, plaques, and other gift items, opening up a creative and potentially profitable business for the home-based artist. The technology combines scanners to bring in photos or other art, graphics programs that allow the photos or art to be edited, cropped, enhanced, and color balanced, and either laser printed using dye transfer toners or thermal wax printed using equipment manufactured by Xerox, Tektronix, and other companies. The final output image can then be placed on fabric, using a heat process that takes only minutes and completely eliminates silk-screening, or transferred to gift items of all kinds.

Technology offers many opportunities for the creative graphic designer. You can customize art and text designs to a client's needs or produce unique eye-catching computer-generated art, cartoons, or type for logos, awards, gifts, and premiums. The savvy artist can therefore tap into many lucrative niche markets, including conventions, trade shows, museums, businesses, and private groups that purchase customized T-shirts or other novelty items for meetings, reunions, conferences, or fund-raisers.

Getting into this business requires graphic-design or artistic abilities, good marketing skills, and the creativity to discover a unique product or service. You may also need or want to purchase several pieces of specialized equipment in addition to your computer, including a color scanner, a large-screen monitor (seventeen inches or larger), a drawing program such as *CorelDraw,* and either the specialized laser toner cartridges that work in most standard laser printers or a thermal wax printer and various transfer equipment.

A trap for the home-based T-shirt maker is to try to compete in the traditional retail channels, where volume pricing and cash flow can be overriding obstacles. On the other hand, a more effective strategy can be designing customized items for clients such as sports leagues, reunions, associations, corporate events, art fairs, fund-raisers. Or you might create a design for an attraction like a museum that presents the kind of information synonymous with the museum in a unique way. The museum then becomes your customer and resells your design. A successful design can be sold in this way for years.

Other methods of getting business include advertising in the yellow pages and in trade magazines or newsletters, telemarketing, and networking with meeting planners. Earnings for a T-shirt design business will vary considerably, depending on how many contracts you are able to obtain and the fees you charge for design and manufacturing.

Resources

Flash Compendium, published by BlackLightening, Inc., Riddle Pond Road, West Topsham, VT 05086, (800) 252-2599, a compilation of articles from a newsletter published by this helpful company which manufactures the Transfer Toner cartridges and other supplies used in this business.

How to Print T-Shirts for Fun and Profit, SignCraft, P.O. Box 06031, Fort Myers, FL 33906.

Impressions magazine, Gralla Publications, P.O. Box 801470, Dallas, TX 75380-9945.

RPL SUPPLIES, 280 Midland Avenue, Saddle Brook, NJ 07663, (800) 524-0914, seller of systems for transferring photos and art to T-shirts and novelty items.

87.

Used-Computer Broker

A used computer or laser printer is like a used car, still serviceable long after it is no longer the current model on the showroom floor. Used equipment is sought out by those who can't afford new machines or simply prefer to spend less for their equipment and by third-world countries seeking affordable equipment that is past its prime in the U.S. This demand has opened the way to opportunities in used-computer brokering.

Used-computer brokers can work in several ways. In some cases, they stockpile their own inventory by purchasing equipment from selling parties at one price and then finding buyers in due time to whom they can resell it at a higher price, with the difference being their profit. In other circumstances, they act as a third party who arranges a timely match between a buyer and a seller, fixes a fair price, and takes a commission from the sale. Some brokers also specialize, focusing perhaps on high-end engineering models, desktop publishing equipment, or other specialty areas.

In all cases, the main ingredient in a successful business is maintaining a large database of buyers, sellers, and equipment. This means that the used-computer broker must be constantly on the lookout for new suppliers and customers through advertising, telephone marketing, and word of mouth. Some businesses also network with other brokers to increase their chances of finding a piece of equipment needed by a customer, or a customer for a computer they already have.

While an aggressive broker can easily turn this into a full-time business, brokering can be a part-time business or add-on business as well. Earnings can range from $5,000 to $100,000 per year and more, depending on your ability to get desired merchandise and build a clientele.

Resources

BOSTON COMPUTER EXCHANGE buys and sells used computers. 210 South Street, 6th Floor, Boston, MA 02111, or call (800) 262-6399, (617) 542-4414, *http://www.*bocoex.com

ZDNET, one of the largest information sources on the Web for computers, equipment, etc. *http://www.*ZDNet.com

Newsgroups: misc.forsale.computers
                alt.forsale

88.

Video Animator

Video animation is everywhere. Logos that come flying into view before news broadcasts, soda-drinking polar bears in commercials, sports scores and weather statistics that have more life than the Senate floor during a typical C-SPAN broadcast—anytime you see a bit of programming that doesn't involve actors or landscapes, you're probably watching a video animation. Producing these sequences used to be solely the realm of very high priced, equipment-intensive specialty houses. This is no longer the case.

The increasing power of PCs, market demands, and the power of a new generation of software has changed the video animation, titling, and special-effects business forever. According to Ted Artz, founder and president of the highly successful Amalgamation Haus, and one the first home studio–based animation and effects production houses in the country, "with the advent of more powerful PCs and software there's room in this market for everybody, from the highly sophisticated, high-end products, to very simple, yet effective sequences." For example, only eight years ago the standard technology for producing 3-D video animation was the WAVE-FRONT, by SGI/Alias. A WAVEFRONT system would set you back about $100,000. Today, many animators are using dual processing Pentium machines with MMX and Studio Max software by the Yost Group to achieve faster, even better results. Cost: about $18,000.

Video animation can be a very well paid full-time business. With artistic talent *and* computer graphics, multimedia authoring or digital video production experience you have the basic requirements to begin the process. 3-D video rendering and animation is not something you can learn overnight. You will need six months to a year before you are fully conversant with all the technology and skills involved. We recommend taking classes at your local college or doing an internship with an established business before setting out on your own.

Before purchasing equipment and software for your animation business, it would be helpful to first identify which market you wish to go after. If your aim is broadcast television and high-end corporate video, your investment will be more substantial. A basic setup will include a powerful, dual-processing Pentium-running Windows NT, or two(!), a 3-D animation program such as *Studio Max*, a "paintbox" program such as *Lumina* by Time Arts which will allow you to produce painted effects, logo effects, and so many other kinds of effects that there could be a book written about them alone, a 2-D animation program (although *Studio Max* can operate in 2-D as well), a video card, such as the VISTA card, for digitizing and converting the video signal, and standard video hardware such as a Beta SP video deck and vectorscope. This higher-end system will allow you to produce broadcast-quality animation sequences that can compete with all but the most technologically advanced production houses. Ballpark prices for building such a studio from scratch range from around $25,000 to $45,000 and higher.

If the higher-end market sounds a bit daunting, there is a fairly large, almost untapped market in the middle to lower range. Many producers of CD-ROMs, local television and cable commercials, and corporate training videos would love to include original animation and special-effects sequences in their productions but cannot afford the rates of higher-end studios. With slightly less comprehensive software packages and video output capabilities, you can still provide a dynamic and desirable product at a fraction of the cost of the high-end market. With powerful 3-D–animation software, such as *Strata StudioPro* (Mac) and *Infini-D Production Studio* (PC), available for less than $1,400, and high-quality video digitizing boards, such as the Targa 2000 (Mac) and MicroMotion (PC) available for less then $4,000, you can provide a surprisingly good-quality product. Since your investment will be less, you can pass the savings down to clients who will be surprised that they can afford video animation after all.

Prices vary considerably in video animation. A general figure for high-end, broadcast-quality animation is about $1,500 per *second.* That adds up pretty quickly, but before you put a down payment on that Porsche, be aware that it takes about ten to fifteen hours to produce one second of top-quality animation. Many animators charge by project, as well. The mid-level market cannot bear nearly the broadcast rate. Remember, you are selling a service that people don't currently think they can afford, so you must structure your rates accordingly. Most midlevel producers we know would gladly pay between $500 to $1,500 for a thirty-second animation. Logotype animations and reusable intros and closers can be priced higher, as they are reusable.

Resources

3-D Graphics and Animation: From Starting Up to Standing Out, by Mark Giambruno, New York, New Riders Publishing, 1997, ISBN: 1562056980.

3-D Studio Max Fundamentals, by Michael Todd Peterson, Larry Minton, Frank Delise (illustrator), and Todd Peterson, New York, New Riders Publishing, 1996, ISBN: 1562056255.

The Art of 3-D Computer Animation and Imaging, by Isaac Victor Kerlow, New York, Van Nostrand Reinhold, 1996, ISBN: 0442018967.

Principles of Three-Dimensional Computer Animation: Modeling, Rendering, and Animating With 3-D Computer Graphics, by Michael O'Rourke, New York, Norton, 1995, ISBN: 0393702022.

AV Video and Multimedia Producer magazine, published by Knowledge Industry Publications, Inc., 701 Westchester Avenue, White Plains, NY 10604, (914) 328-9157, *http://www.kipinet.com*

Newsgroups: rec.video.desktop
rec.video.production
comp.graphics.animation

89. MS 🗑 + 🏠 👍

Video and Audio Digitizing Service

For any video footage or recorded audio material to used in any of the multimedia or World Wide Web applications, it must first be converted into a digital file format which can be read and played by a personal computer. The need for digital video and audio files continues to grow as multimedia content is making considerable inroads on the World Wide

Web. Many Web sites now feature video and audio files and more are being added every day. Multimedia and Web designers and developers often don't have the time required to digitize their own media and are increasingly turning to Video and Audio Digitizing Services.

A Video and Audio Digitizing Service, or digitizing service, is similar in concept to a scanning service. As a matter of fact, the two businesses are quite complementary. Clients will come to you with existing video footage or recorded audio. Using your computer along with a video/sound digitizing board and special software, you will convert the material to the digital format your client specifies. This is a fairly straightforward business, but, unlike scanning two-dimensional images, the devil lies in the formats you will receive. You can reasonably expect video footage to come in on VHS, S-VHS, 8mm, Hi-8mm, 3/4 inch, and Beta SP, to name the main video formats. Audio may come to you on cassette tape, CD, long-playing LP (remember those!) half-inch reel-to-reel and DAT, again, to name only the more prevalent formats. Each one of these formats, both video and audio, requires its own playback machine. This can be costly. You can defray some of these costs by searching for used playback equipment.

In addition to playback equipment, you will need the computer equipment and software required for digitization. Start with a fast, late-model PC with at least thirty-two MB of RAM and three gigabytes of hard drive storage. You will also need a special video/sound digitizing board and digitizing/editing software.

Your clients will include Web designers and developers, Webmasters, multimedia producers, and desktop video services. Networking, both online and directly with your potential clients, is the most effective way to get business. A simple Web site that outlines your service, the formats you handle, and your price structure is also helpful. Yellow pages and trade journal ads have been proven effective for digitizing services as well.

A digitizing service can work as a stand-alone business, but we recommend it as on add-on to a desktop video business, scanning service or other media-related venture. Be aware that digitizing audio and video is time-consuming. If the original program material is fifteen minutes long, it will take fifteen minutes to actually digitize. It will also take additional time in the beginning to set the proper levels to ensure the highest quality, and it will take even more time after the material is digitized for you to check to make sure the entire program was completed without glitches or "dropout." Rates charged vary from region to region and market to market, but range, on average, from $50 to $75 per hour of your time, or on a per-project basis.

Resources

Website Sound, by New Riders Development Group, New York, New Riders Publishing, 1997, ISBN: 1562056263.

ITC HOWTO: Digitizing Video

A useful Web site providing an overview of video digitizing written by Joyce See. *http://www.gsu.edu/~http://www.*itc/howto/temp.html

Newsgroups: rec.photo.digital
rec.video.desktop
comp.graphics.animation
comp.misc.music

90.

Webmaster

Outsourcing, the practice of contracting with independent providers to perform a wide number of jobs, has become one of the key words in business in the late 1990s. As companies continue to downsize and streamline, we see this trend increasing and continuing into the next century. The outsourcing trend is providing opportunities for many home-based computer and Internet professionals. Toward this end, we see a growing need in the business community for independent Webmasters.

The job description of "Webmaster" varies a great deal and seems to depend on whom you talk to. Based on our research, a general description of the skills required to call oneself a Webmaster can be described as thus: Webmasters are responsible for proactively developing and maintaining the day-to-day operations of corporate Web sites. Responsibilities include content management and publishing, CGI and Perl scripting, hit/flow tracking and statistical report generation, Web quality assurance and process automation, and Web server administration. Many companies also require Internet programming languages such as Java, system administration in UNIX and Windows NT environments, and knowledge of dedicated-line and dial-up communication protocols. WebMasters' duties rarely, if ever, include the development of the site itself in terms of design, writing, etc.

If you have many of the skills listed above and experience requirements, you are a good candidate for starting a home-based Webmaster service. If you have some Internet experience, but cannot perform many of the skills listed in the previous paragraph, you are not precluded from Webmastering. For any skill you don't know, such CGI scripting, Java, communication protocols, you can find someone to subcontract to. You do need a good general knowledge of the Internet and the World Wide Web in particular, as well as good interpersonal communications skills, strong organization and project management skills, and you should enjoy problem solving.

The market for independent Webmasters, as we see it, is untapped. This is both good and bad. Positively, you will have no real competition at first and you can determine your own modus operandi. On the negative side, you will have to create a market for yourself as most decision makers are unfamiliar with the concept of an independent Webmaster. In the beginning you will have difficulty convincing people to trust the management of their Web site to an outside contractor.

Your potential clients are new businesses and those just putting up their first Web sites, as well as any business that might be downsizing, streamlining, or restructuring. To find clients, we suggest that you team up with a Web designer or Internet consultant. That way, when they pitch a potential client to sell them a Web site, your service will be included in the package of services they can offer. Another way to find clients is to search the literally hundreds of online job listings. Look for Webmaster listings, then contact the company and convince them to outsource the job rather than hire someone to do it in-house. You might also try writing and publishing an article on the benefits of outsourcing Webmaster duties. If you are currently employed as a Webmaster or Web site developer, turn your employer into your first client.

Resources

The Corporate Intranet: Create and Manage an Internal Web for Your Organization, by Ryan Bernard, New York, Wiley, 1996, ISBN: 0471149292.

Web Programming Secrets with HTML, CGI, and Perl, by Ed Tittel (editor), Mark Gaither, Sebastian Hassinger, and Mike Erwin, Foster City, CA, IDG Books Worldwide, 1996, ISBN: 156884848X.

WEBMASTER ONLINE magazine, *http://*www.cio.com/webmaster/wmhome. html

NATIONAL ASSOCIATION OF WEBMASTERS, 9580 Oak Avenue Parkway, Folsom, CA 95630, (888) 564-6279, *http: //*www.naw.org. Provides training, certification, support and an annual conference.

WEBMASTER FORUM, an online forum that provides resources and a panel of experts to help you answer these and related issues about "webmastery." *http://www*.cio.com/forums/career.html

WEBMASTER'S GUILD, a nonprofit professional organization for WebMasters, *http://www*.webmaster.org/ E-mail: guildmaster@webmaster.org

Online magazine, The world's largest circulation magazine for online information for systems professionals, *http://www*.onlineinc.com/online/online/onlinemag/index.html. Printed version also available by subscription.

INTERNATIONAL ASSOCIATION OF PROFESSIONAL WEB DEVELOPERS, a professional association. *http://www*.webpro.org

Newsgroups: alt.webgod
alt.webmaster
shamash.webmasters

91.

Web Site Design

Unless you've been living under a rock for the last few years, you're no doubt well aware of the tremendous growth of the Internet, and especially the World Wide Web. Just about every expert in the field agrees that the Internet is the fastest-growing communications medium since television. Business, to be sure, has been watching closely. To stay competitive, businesses of all varieties and sizes know that now they must have a well-designed, high-impact Web site in addition to the usual brochures and promotional materials.

The market for new or improved Web sites is still far from saturated. According to the latest U.S. Census figures, there are over 11.5 million small businesses in the United States with fewer than 100 employees (your primary market). At the time of this writing, only about half of those businesses have any online presence. Many businesses that already have Web sites are not satisfied with them, which is another market for you.

To be a competitive Web site designer, it is best to come from a background of graphic design or a related field and have a firm understanding of basic marketing concepts. Good-looking, effective sites are still created from the same basic principles that govern top-flight graphic design. There are many programs that offer templates and forms for Web sites, but, in our opinion, you will do far better with solid design talent and marketing experience behind you. Anybody can fill out a template. Your skill and experience are the true assets you will have to offer potential clients.

Web Site Design can be a primary business. It can also work as an add-on business to a graphic-design business. Often a client needing a brochure, ad, or other printed material will need a Web site as well.

Web Site Design requires much of the same equipment as a graphic design business, with a few notable additions. A basic computer system including a Pentium 200Mhz (or better) processor with MMX, at least 32MB of RAM, 10X CD-ROM drive, three-gigabyte hard drive, 33.6 or faster modem, a color scanner of at least 600 dpi, and a color ink-jet or laser printer will get you started. A removable storage drive such as Iomega's Jaz drive or a Syquest drive are also recommended. In terms of software, you will need a solid graphic-design program such as *Quark Express,* and a photo manipulation package like *Adobe Photoshop.* You will also need a Web editor program, which includes the latest version of HTML (Hyper Text Markup Language). HTML is the programming language that allows graphics, text, and other media to be combined and posted on the Web. Don't let the fact that HTML is a "language" scare you. It's quite easy to learn, and with today's powerful editors, like *Adobe's PageMill* for the Mac and *Softquad's HotMetal Pro* for PC, HTML is almost invisible. Subcontracting your HTML programming to a fellow home-based business is also an option. You will also need at least two Web browsers so you can check to see how your sites actually look on the Web. The latest versions of *Netscape Navigator* and *Microsoft's Explorer* are the two most common. When you are ready to actually post a client's site on the Web, you will need to use an FTP (File Transfer Protocol) program that will allow your computer to interface with the computer that will host your client's site.

The great thing about Web Site Design is that you can provide excellent service to any business in the country. The work you do can be immediately posted on the Web for your client to approve. A quick phone conference will allow them to specify any changes, additions, etc.

A good source for finding clients for your Web Site Design business is local Internet Service Providers (ISPs). Just call them up and tell them about your experience and skills. ISPs often offer Web site design and hosting to their customers and they often farm out the design work. Another good way to find clients is networking through local and national users' groups. Artists' temp agencies are also helpful when you're starting out. And of course, using the Internet itself is an ideal way to network as well as demonstrate your capabilities.

Billing structures for Web site designers are by no means universal. Some designers we spoke with charged by the hour ($30–$90), others by the size of the site. Incomes vary as well This is still a fairly new area, and no one can claim to have more than four or five years of experience. Yearly salaries average between $25,000 to $60,000+.

Resources

Boardwatch magazine, 8500 West Bowles Avenue, Ste. 210, Littleton, CO 80123, (800) 933-6038, *http://www.*boardwatch.com

Building Business Web Sites, Adam Blum, New York, Mis Press, 1995, ISBN: 1558284311.

HTML Quick Reference, by Dean Scharf, Que Corporation, 1996, ISBN: 0789707861.

Web Page Design: A Different Multimedia, by Mary E. S. Morris and Randy J. Hinrichs, Englewood Cliffs, NJ, Prentice-Hall, 1996, ISBN: 013239880X.

THE NET online magazine, *http://www.*thenet-usa.com. This publication is also available in printed form on newsstands.

NET GUIDE online magazine, *http://www.*netguidemag.com. This publication is also available in printed form on newsstands.

INTERNATIONAL ASSOCIATION OF PROFESSIONAL WEB DEVELOPERS, a professional association. *http://www.*webpro.org

INTERNET PROFESSIONAL PUBLISHERS ASSOCIATION, professional association. *http://www.*ippa.org

Newsgroups: bit.listserv.techwr-l
alt.webedit
alt.html.webedit

92.

Web Site Publicist

Building a Web site is the easy part for most companies and organizations. The hard part is getting people to visit it. A Web site, like most things in business, needs good promotion to be successful. As cyberspace becomes more crowded, and therefore competitive, we believe that most companies who rely on the Web as an integral part of their marketing plan will turn to experts in Web site and Internet promotion to help them stay ahead of the game. Many already have.

Commercial Web sites are used by companies as part of their overall marketing approach. Their Web sites are as targeted to their specific market as are their advertisements, catalogs, brochures, etc. But unlike print ads and direct mail, once a Web site is completed, the right people need to know it's there. This is where a Web site publicity expert comes in. As a site publicity expert, you will need to understand the intricacies of the Internet and the World Wide Web. You will also need to identify your client's target audience and reach it effectively. Techniques for this include submitting the site in just the right way to the most relevant search engines. Other techniques currently used by top Internet promoters include E-mail marketing, link exchanges, submissions to newsgroups and cross-advertising on related sites. Good publicity also includes E-mail and written press releases sent to print and online media.

To do Web site promotion, it is helpful if you have a background in PR or marketing, as well as a good understanding of the Internet and the World Wide Web. This can easily be a full-time business. Web publicity can also be a synergistic add-on business for Web writers, electronic publicists, Webmasters, and public relations companies. Unless your eventual aim is to promote on a full-time basis, you may wish to limit the number of promotions clients you take on, as publicity campaigns do require a great deal of time and creative energy. Campaigns can also help fledgling Web designers get started by offering additional income, but once a Web design business gets going, the activities involved are too divergent and time-consuming, and you probably won't be able to perform either function effectively. You should focus on one or the other.

The best way to get clients is to demonstrate your promotional skills in your approach to marketing your own business. By this we mean use the same techniques you would use to promote a client's site to promote your services. First construct a simple, high-impact Web site that outlines your services, then submit it to the popular search engines. Post your announcement on the appropriate newsgroups. Send an E-mail message to companies with commercial sites. Other ways to get business include networking with Web designers, Web writers, WebMasters, and other Internet and Web professionals. Convince them that your service would be valuable to their clients. Have them refer business directly to you, or have them offer publicity as part of their menu of services and outsource the promotions to you.

Good online publicity is usually a targeted campaign that encompasses a range of services. Therefore, most Web promotions specialists set their prices in terms of packages. Here's an example of an average promotional package:

- Review of site data for keywords, description, etc.
- Site URL and description submitted to the top 500 search engines and promotional sites.
- Write and submit a press release to 500 press sources, including newspapers, television networks, radio stations, and Internet publications.
- Seek out fifty sites of similar interest and place a targeted link.

Your menu of services, packages, and costs will be unique to your business. Check your competition to find out what they're charging and set your prices accordingly. It is best to not charge lower than all of your competition, nor is it effective to be the most expensive. In general, we believe start-up businesses do the best by charging rates somewhere in the middle.

Resources

Atlas for the Information Superhighway, by Patrick Douglas Crispen and Mark D. Ciampa, Cincinnati, OH, South-Western Publishing, 1996, ISBN: 0538658649.

Advertising Communications and Promotion Management, by John R. Rossiter (editor), Larry Percy (editor), New York, McGraw-Hill, 1996, ISBN: 007053943X.

ADVERTISING AGE'S NETMARKETING ONLINE magazine, *http://www*.netb2b. com

INTERACTIVE AGE DIGITAL ONLINE magazine, *http://techweb.cmp.com/ia/* iad–web–/

ARIAL PUBLIC RELATIONS, E-mail a press release to this service, and for a fee, they will analyze its content and electronically send it to the appropriate editors of relevant online and printed publications. *http://www.newstarget.com*

Newsgroups: comp.edu
comp.publish.electronic
comp.publish.electronic.developer

93.

Web Site Content Promotions Specialist

As the Web develops and matures, businesses and organizations are beginning to expect more in terms of bottom-line results from their Web sites. Marketers on the Web realize that not only can their site bring their company to the market, the market can also give them valuable information about itself. Exciting new ideas and technologies are now available to help any company with a Web site find out detailed information about each person who browses their site. Ethically, the browser him- or herself should volunteer this information. One of the best ways to get them to do this is a clever promotion programmed into the Web site itself. For example, Stu Heinecke's Interactive Features Syndicate (Web: *http://* interactivefeatures.com) offers a Web cartoon that can easily be programmed into any Web site. The cartoon is the first thing a browser sees when logging onto a site. The cartoon includes a "guest register" that asks for a browser's name, address, etc., which is then included into the cartoon itself. This is fun for the visitor and at the same time provides a detailed demographic profile which is automatically stored in a database. Cartoons can be printed out by the visitor (a free premium!) and can even be sent to a friend or colleague. Cartoons change every week so visitors will be encouraged to return again and again. Making your job researching the kinds of promotions available, and perhaps designing a few yourself, we see potential for a new kind of online marketing consultant: Web Site Content Promotions Specialist.

By recommending promotional solutions like the Interactive Features Syndicate you will provide a much-needed service to online marketing managers, WebMasters, and site designers. These professionals have a difficult enough time keeping up with the developments in their fields of expertise and generally do not have the time to stay abreast of the developments in Web site content promotions. By making this your area of expertise, you can offer a one-stop source for a number of different promotion options that will help your clients get the most out of their online marketing efforts. The more deeply you research what's available, the more you will know about the latest techniques and technologies, and the more valuable you will be.

Web promotions include, but are certainly not limited to:

- Free downloadable software
- Free downloadable screen savers
- Giveaways and contests
- Interactive "guest book" type applets
- Special online events such as interviews with experts or well-known personalities

As a Web Site Content Promotions Specialist, you can market your services to any business or organization whose Web site forms an integral part of their overall marketing plan. The best way to find clients is to contact them directly by E-mail through their Web sites. Keep your marketing efforts targeted to specific industries. Search the Web to find a list of sites in an industry. Look through the sites, then send a short, personal E-mail to the Webmaster describing how your service will help attract visitors to his or her site. Also explain that you can provide ways to obtain important marketing and demographic information from each visitor. Choose mid-sized to larger companies to target as they will have the resources, and the need, required to actually institute the promotions you suggest.

This is a brand-new business idea and no fee or price guidelines have been established. The promotional technologies you represent will no doubt cost you a specific amount. You will, of course, need to add a markup in cost to cover your time and expertise. Because it is such a new business idea, we recommend that you start out as an add-on service to a more established business, such as a PR agency, Web publicist business, Web site design or Web site hosting service.

Resources

Web Digest for Marketers, a bi-weekly bulletin or executive summary that reports on the latest marketing sites to come onto the Web. From Chase Online Marketing Strategies, 847A 2nd Avenue, Ste. 332, New York, NY 10017, (212) 876-1096, E-mail: larry@chaseonline.com. Web: *http://www.*wdfm.com

WEB WEEK, a newspaper of Web technology and business strategy, a comprehensive, timely information resource. *http://www.* webweek. com

94

Web Site Reviewer

There are a lot of Web sites out there. By the time this book sees publication there will probably be over sixty to eighty million. The majority of sites are either business or education related. Taken as a whole, these Web sites offer an impressive range of information useful to a vast number of people, but they have to know it's there in the first place, and they have to know where to find it. Search engines are helpful, but many people find the most useful sites on the Web by either reading about them in online and traditionally published publications or through on-site links.

The need to list and review Web sites is creating a new kind of editorial product—Web site reviews—that publishers hope will draw advertisers and viewers to their online and print publications. Most of the Web site reviewing is currently being performed by independent and freelance writers. As publications, both online and printed, devote more of their column space to the World Wide Web, the need for experienced, fast, and dependable Web Site Reviewers will increase as well.

Web site reviews are usually 100 words or less, although publishers sometimes ask for lengthier reviews. Within the review, you should sum up the informative value of the site, define its usefulness, and spell out which audience it will be useful for. Unless specifically asked by a publisher, never include your own opinion in the review. Simply sum up what you see (and maybe hear) on the site.

Currently, the pay scale for Web site reviewing does not make it a good candidate for a full-time business. For example, according to a recent article in the *New York Times:* "the San Francisco-based magazine *The Net,* where one-third of the editorial pages are now devoted to Web site reviews, freelance writers must meet a quota of thirty reviews a week, each about 100 words long, for which they are paid a total of $600 to $750—and this is pretty good pay compared to the going rate elsewhere." We expect these rates to increase as publications become more competitive. For now, Web reviewing can be used as an add-on business for copywriters, technical writers, Web writers, and even Web site designers. In addition to bringing in extra income, reviewing sites will bring you in contact with a wide range of businesses, designers, WebMasters, publishers, and editors. It will give you a greater overview of what's going on out there in cyberspace. If you are given a byline, it will also help to publicize your name and help establish your credibility as a Web expert or journalist.

Potential clients are any online publication or printed magazine that devotes space to the Web itself. Draft a query letter, in which you briefly outline your experience and describe what makes you qualified to review sites on the Web. If you have any specialized experience, such as a concentration in one of the sciences, be sure to mention it. Then send the query directly to the publisher of each publication. If you don't hear back in a week's time, call the publisher and inquire as to the status of your query. It helps if you research each publication before you submit query letters. If the publication has a specific angle or focus area, let the publisher know you've taken the time and done your research by mentioning it in your query. Another approach is to search the many online employment listings for Web Site Reviewers Wanted listings. Contact prospective employers and try to convince them to outsource their Web reviewing rather than hiring someone for an in-house position.

Resources

Writer's Market (annual), Writer's Digest Books, Cincinnati, OH, ISBN: 0898797012.

THE BUSINESS RESEARCHER'S INTERESTS, *http://www*.brint.com/interest.html This Meta-site is packed with literally thousands of links to business-related information. Of interest to Web site reviewers is the extensive listing of online and printed magazines, journals, and other publications.

Use any search engine for "Magazines," "Online Magazines," "Internet Magazines," and you will receive enough listings to keep you busy sending query letters for months.

http://www.zdnet.com. A comprehensive, easy-to-search site that lists all of Ziff Davis's computer-oriented publications.

95.

Web Specialty Programmer: CGI Programming

As the World Wide Web grows and matures, we see a definite trend toward specialization. Web sites are becoming more sophisticated, and their component parts are becoming more complex and involved. Web designers are having a difficult time keeping current with the latest developments and technologies. More and more they are turning into Web specialty programmers and service providers. One hot area of specialization is CGI programming.

Have you ever filled out an order form or survey while accessing a Web site? Have you ever searched through a site using a search engine that's incorporated right into the site? If you have, then you've seen the power of CGI programming. CGI is an acronym for Common Gateway Interface. CGI is a special language that creates interactive forms, guest books, and Web site search engines that work with databases and clickable image maps. CGI is more complex than HTML, but not nearly as difficult to learn as traditional programming languages like C++.

We see the need for CGI programming as being on the increase. "As clients become more knowledgeable about the Web and what the possibilities are, they demand a much more sophisticated Web presence than before," says Chris Richter, founder of Vinnac Media, a home-based Web site design company and virtual server host. Chris, like many other Web designers who want to stay competitive, outsources all his CGI programming to a specialist. Potential clients for CGI programmers are independent Web designers like Chris, WebMasters for companies and organizations, design companies or agencies, and even Internet Service Providers. The best ways to find clients is to directly contact any of the above mentioned and tell them about your service. Two or three busy designers can give you more than enough work to keep you going. As a word of caution, do not rely solely on just a few sources for your livelihood. Even if you have solid, ongoing relationships with a core of clients, losing just one could be devastating. Always network to develop additional potential sources of work.

You have a choice of billing hourly or by project. Hourly, you can comfortably charge from $40 to $70 per hour, depending on the customary rates in your region (which you can find out by calling your competition). Use this hourly scale to determine per-project prices if you prefer billing in this way or your clients request it.

Resources

The CGI Book, by William E. Weinman, New York, New Riders Publications, 1996, ISBN: 1562055712.

CGI Programming on the World Wide Web (Nutshell Handbook), by Shishir Gundavaram, O'Reilly & Associates, 1996, ISBN: 1565921682.

WEB MAGAZINE ONLINE, *http://netweb.com/net/home.html*

WEB DEVELOPER'S RESOURCES, *http://www.sil.org/internet/about_web.html*

Newsgroups: comp.infosystems.*http://www.*authoring.cgi
comp.databases.rdb
comp.datamases.gupta

96.

Web Specialty Programmer: Java

Java programming is another area of specialization in cyberspace, and in Java's case, beyond. Java is a programming language that grew out of more traditional programming languages like C++. Its main function, in terms of cyberspace, is to allow a Web page and its embedded features, such as spreadsheets or calculators, to run on any computer, such as IBM, Mac, Unix workstation, etc. Java allows a developer to actually write independent programs, called applets, and embed them into Web pages. Other uses for Java applets include the scrolling marquees you see on Web sites, animation, moving background, sounds, or music.

Java is a bit trickier to learn than HTML or CGI, but is much easier than C++ and other computer languages. We know many people without previous programming experience who have successfully taught themselves how to program in Java in less than a month. It simply takes solid computer experience, logical abilities, and some practice. There are many helpful books available on learning Java. Java information on the World Wide Web is very helpful, and comprehensive to the point of overload. Many community colleges and extension programs teach courses in Java as well.

The demand for Java programming is definitely on the rise. Some experts predict that Java will become the dominant language on the Web, and beyond, in short order. Web designers and WebMasters are fully aware of the power of Java, but few are expert enough in its use to create Java applets themselves. Java programming, like CGI, is almost always outsourced by smaller organizations. And because of its relative newness, even larger organizations sometimes outsource Java programming to specialists. We don't know of a single independent Java programmer who is currently having trouble finding business.

As a Java programmer, your best sources for work are Web designers, WebMasters, online publications, Internet service providers and Web site hosting organizations. The best ways to approach potential clients include networking, direct contact (calling them up and introducing yourself), and very targeted mailings. To find the names of organizations, decision makers, and independent designers, start with the Web itself. Search for

Web Designers in your geographic region. Consult the various online employment listings and search for Java Programmers Wanted. Contact the organization and ask them if they would consider outsourcing their Java programming instead of hiring a full-time person. You can network in online user groups and on newsgroups. Like other specialty Web programming businesses, you may find that just one or two clients give you more than enough work to keep you busy. This can be a problem, however. If you lose one of these clients, you can find yourself in trouble. Always keep up your networking so that you can replace major clients without too much trouble. You may also want to limit how much work you accept from clients so you can maintain a diverse client base where no one client represents a sizable bulk of your business.

As an expert Java programmer you can easily charge from $40 to $95 per hour, depending on your market, direct competition, and level of experience. You may be asked to bill your services on a per-project basis. In this case, estimate the amount of time you think it will take, then add an additional 20 percent to cover any unforeseen problems. On per-project jobs, you should also include specific language in your quotations that specifies the time period the job will run and includes price contingencies should the job run overtime.

Resources

Teach Yourself Java in 21 Days, by Laura Lemay and Charles L. Perkins, Indianapolis, IN, Sams Publications, 1996, ISBN: 1575210304.

The Java Developer's Toolkit: Techniques and Technologies for World Wide Web Programmers, by Joshua Marketos, New York, Wiley, 1996, ISBN: 0471165190.

JAVAWORLD ONLINE magazine *http://www.*javaworld.com

UNIVERSITY OF TORONTO JAVA DEVELOPMENT CENTER, *http://www.*java.utoronto.ca/. A comprehensive Java resource, including links to publications, software, applets and FAQs.

For the latest Java software: *http://www.*javasoft.com

Newsgroups: comp.lang.java.announce
comp.lang.java.programmer
comp.lang.javascript
comp.lang.java
comp.lang.java.appl

97

Web Site Writer

The unique combination of text and graphics is at the heart of what makes the World Wide Web such a powerful communications medium. Much attention has been given to the graphics side of the equation. The text side, however, is sometimes forgotten in the excitement over developments like the inclusion of animation, video, and sound in Web sites. Many Web sites today look great but leave something to be desired in the way of well-drafted, clear, and organized writing that enhances the unique characteristics of the Web's particular brand of communication.

Web designers, WebMasters, and other Internet communications professionals recognize the need for writing that communicates a site's message while conforming to stylistic and organizational conventions that the Web requires. Writing for the Web is different than writing for any other medium. We see a real need for writers who know how to write well for the Web and make this a specialty.

This is a great add-on business for copywriters, technical writers, freelance journalists, or anyone who enjoys writing, writes well, and can conform their style to the World Wide Web. The primary convention for Web writing is concision: the ability to express an idea or concept clearly, interestingly, and most importantly, in as few words as possible. Unlike with technical documentation, where readers expect to take their time and consider a great deal of detailed information, people "browse" the Web, gleaning just the important facts. Many people viewing Web sites are doing so through services such as CompuServe where they are paying for each minute they are logged on. These viewers especially don't have the time, or credit card limits, to spend poring over minutiae. Copywriting, at the other extreme, tends to deal with short, catchy phrases that convey ideas or feelings about their subjects. This kind of writing doesn't work well on the Web as viewers expect a fair amount of substance from the site they browse. Finding your way between the copywriting and technical writing models is your job as a Web writer.

Potential clients for Web site writers are Web designers, Webmasters, and other communications professionals whose job it is to produce and maintain Web sites. Networking is your best bet for getting work from these prospects. Networking on online discussion groups and user groups is especially effective. Contact Web site designers via phone or E-mail and introduce yourself. You might try browsing the Web and looking for sites that need help in the writing department. Then send an E-mail to the

Webmaster with a well-written, Web-ready letter outlining your experience, skills, etc. If you have a technical or copywriting business already, try to migrate some of your clients over to the Web. Form an alliance with a site designer to help you do this.

At the moment, Web site writer rates are somewhere between copywriting and technical writing fees, with the range being about $20 to $60 per hour. We feel that this rate will go up as Web site design becomes more competitive and clients' expectations rise.

Resources

Cyberwriting: How to Promote Your Product or Service Online (Without Being Flamed), by Joe Vitale, New York, Amacom Book Division, 1996, ISBN: 0814479189.

The Digital Scribe: A Writer's Guide to Electronic Media, by James Ray Musgrave, San Diego, CA, AP Professional, 1996 ISBN: 0125122551.

A Web page from Sun Microsystems that covers a wide range of writing and content strategies for the Web. *http://www*.sun.com/styleguide

WRITERS.COM This site offers online classes, tutoring, workshops, and writers' groups on a number of writing-related topics, including Web site writing. *http://www*.writers.com

WEBSIGHT ONLINE magazine, *http://*websight.com/

98.

Word-Processing Service

Word processing is one of the oldest computer-based home businesses. Because of this you're apt to find a number of other people offering word-processing services in your community, and that could mean they are competing on price. How then can you get your share of the market at a price that will provide you with a full-time income over $20,000 a year?

First, you can distinguish your word-processing service from others with a name that will attract people and suggest that they will pay more because they will be getting more. For example, does a word-processing service with the name "After Hours" or "At All Hours" suggest a benefit that people might be willing to pay extra for? If your reaction is like most other people's, it probably does.

You can also find a specialty market to target with your word-processing service. For example, one woman we know worked in a law office but at night helped her law student husband with his moot court briefs, adding the fine touches she had learned as a legal secretary. Because she did more than simply type his briefs, his friends soon came to her, too. She made them look good and before long she had developed a profitable business typing for law students. Some of her customers stayed with her after they graduated and began practicing law.

Depending upon what industries are nearby, you might specialize in serving graduate students, foreign language students, scriptwriters, government agencies, or fund-raisers.

Resources

How to Start and Profit from a Word Processing and Secretarial Service, two audiotapes with a workbook by Nancy Malvin, former publisher of *Keystrokes* newsletter. Here's How, Box 5091, Santa Monica, CA 90409, (800) 561-8990.

Word Processing Profits at Home, by Peggy Glenn, Huntington Beach, CA, Aames-Allen Publishing, 1994, ISBN: 0936930330.

Starting a Successful Secretarial Service, National Association of Secretarial Services, 18032 Lemon Drive, Ste. C-414, Yorba Linda, CA 92886-3386, (714) 282-9398, (800) 237-1462, *http://www.*nass.com. A 100-page blueprint for starting a secretarial service by Frank Fox.

WORD PROCESSING, NRI, SCHOOL OF HOME-BASED BUSINESSES, McGraw-Hill Continuing Education Center, 4401 Connecticut Ave., N.W., Washington, DC 20008, *http://www.*mhcec.com. This home-study program includes a computer system and software and provides training for starting a word-processing business. No computer experience required. Write for a free brochure.

NATIONAL ASSOCIATION OF SECRETARIAL SERVICES, 18032 Lemon Drive, Ste. C-414, Yorba Linda, CA 92886-3386, (714) 282-9398, (800) 237-1462, *http://www.*nass.com. Has a monthly newsletter and a variety of manuals on topics like pricing, sales and promotion, and the how-to's of expanding into other related services.

NASS/ESN INDUSTRY PRODUCTION STANDARDS SOFTWARE, guidelines for bidding and pricing services (also in print form). National Association of Secretarial Services, 18032 Lemon Drive, Ste. C-414, Yorba Linda, CA

92886-3386, (714) 282-9398, (800) 237-1462, *http://www*.nass.com
Members using these standards report that they increase billings 25 to
50 percent for the same amount of work with no price increase.

99.

World Wide Web Audio or Video Program

The World Wide Web, like television in its formative years, and radio before that, is hungry for content. Most of the commercial sites currently on the Web are just that: commercial. To use the broadcast television model, there are many more "commercials" on today's Web than "programs." With the proliferation of consumer televisions, even telephones, that can browse the Web, what is everybody going to watch? We know one thing: nobody is going to want to watch commercials most of the time!

One of the most exciting aspects of the online digital revolution is the democratization of content distribution. To put it another way: Never before has mass distribution of creative content, such as prose, video, and audio been available to more people. You don't need a radio tower and millions of dollars in equipment to broadcast an audio program. You can record, edit, and distribute an audio program over the Web with equipment that costs less than $500 (if you already have a computer). You don't need a television station and an international broadcast network to get a video program into the homes of people *around the world.* With equipment that costs less than $2,000 (again, if you already have a computer) you can produce and distribute (sometimes called *netcast*) a weekly video-based program. And like broadcast television and radio, you can attract sponsors for your Web program and potentially earn a comfortable income.

The equipment required to record audio and video, digitize the content, and distribute it over the Web is surprisingly low cost. For video, you need a reasonably good quality consumer camcorder. At this stage in its development, the World Wide Web doesn't have the bandwidth to support high-resolution video images. High-resolution cameras costing thousands of dollars would be wasted on the Web. The extra resolution just isn't supported. You will need a high-speed 586-based computer with MMX, a three-gigabyte (minimum) hard drive, thirty-two MB of RAM, and a video board, such as the Targa 2000, for digitization. With Streamworks software from Xing Technologies or other "video stream" software, you can broadcast "live" right over the Internet. If you wish to edit video footage and broadcast a finished program from tape, you will need some sort of editing equipment. You can edit your programs with analog equipment (both Panasonic and Sony, among many others, offer some excellent, low-cost editing equipment. You'll have to research this on your own. Space limitations prevent us from going in-depth). If you wish to use your computer to edit, please see the Desktop Video listing on page 53 of this book. For audio, any of the sixteen-bit stereo digitizing boards will work well. You will also need your own Web site from which to broadcast. When looking for a server for your site, make sure that the company your are considering knows that you intend to use your site to broadcast (or netcast) an audio or video program. This takes up far more bandwidth than nonmultimedia sites, and some servers are not set up to handle the extra load.

Once you have the equipment and the Web site secured, you're ready to start. In terms of content, you're on your own. To build up an audience for your program, you may wish to hire the services of a Web publicist and/or a site content promotions specialist or public relations firm. The more of an audience you can attract to your program, the more you can charge potential sponsors for advertising. Advertising on the Web generally takes the form of a banner ad which any viewer can click on and be taken to the advertiser's own Web site. Once you can demonstrate a sizable, consistent audience for your site, you can approach specialty ad agencies that will sell space on your site during program times. they will keep a percentage of the fees charged to each of your sponsors.

Web-based programs are a very new idea. No real figures exist on what the earning potential actually is, but we believe that it is quite high. Current ad rates for high-traffic sites range from $50 to $75 per 1,000 viewers. In the roughest ballpark estimate: if your program demonstrates regular viewership of 50,000 per program, you could earn between $2,750 to $3,750 per program.

Resources

Increasing Hits and Selling More on Your Web Site, by Greg Helmstetter, New York, Wiley, 1996, ISBN: 0471169447.

The Digital Videomaker's Guide, by Kathryn Shaw Whitver, Michael Wiese Film Productions, 1995, ISBN: 0941188213.

Film and Video on the Internet, by Bert Deivert and Dan Harries, Westport, CT, Michael Weise Productions, 1996, ISBN: 094118854X.

Pre-Production Planning for Video, Film, and Multimedia, by Steve R. Cartwright, Newton, MA, Focal Press, 1996, ISBN: 0240802713.

CYBERATLAS, *http://www.*cyberatlas.com. A commercial site that tracks Web statistics and advertising trends.

*http://*bmrc.berkeley.edu/info/514/how2dovideo/webcont.html This site offers a basic, yet helpful overview of the basics of putting video up on the Web.

XING TECHNOLOGY, 1540 West Branch Street, Arroyo Grande, CA 93420, (805) 473-0145, fax: (805) 473-7440, E-mail: streams@xingtech.com, Web: *http://www.*xingtech.com

100.

World Wide Web Publication

Content is king on the World Wide Web. Industry pundits are almost unanimous (a rare occurrence where the Web is concerned) in saying that the most powerful sites are the ones that consistently offer viewers high-quality information they can use or entertainment they can enjoy. Combine this with the Web's unique and powerful distribution possibilities, and you have the recipe for a fulfilling and potentially profitable business: producing a Web-based publication.

Producing a publication for the World Wide Web is extraordinarily less expensive than producing one for print. There are no prepress and printing costs, no paper costs, and no mailing costs. Design and creative services such as article writing and photography are much the same as producing a printed publication, but if you do the majority of them yourself, these expenses can be greatly reduced. When the publication is ready, you simply post it on the Web. Any corrections or updates can be made instantly.

The content of your publication is up to you. Successful Web-based publications, started by one or two people from their homes, have included *Suck* (*http://www.*suck.com), a satire and social-criticism online magazine now in partnership with *HotWired* and *IUMA* (Internet Underground Music Archive *http://www.*iuma.com). Both publications started small and, within a year, became major players on the Web, attracting a great deal of attention and advertising revenue. Any idea suitable to a print magazine can certainly become a viable Web publication. Publications that fully take advantage of the Web's multimedia capabilities, such as *IUMA,* where viewers can read text, see illustrations and photos, hear music, and watch video will soon be the standard.

To produce a Web-based publication, you will need the same basic equipment and software as a Web designer. If your interest lies more in the editorial aspect of the publication, you will certainly need to team up with a Web Designer. If you're visually oriented, you may want to team up with a wordsmith. Between the two of you, with some creativity and innovation, you have the potential of putting together a high-impact cutting-edge publication that can realistically compete with those produced by much larger publishing entities.

A Web publication, like a Web audio or video program, will require some time to get started and build up an audience. Even then, of course, there are no guarantees of success. If you are able to attract a large, loyal readership, you can sell advertising and sign up sponsors. Advertising and sponsorship rates on the Web change frequently. Based on current fees, advertisers pay between $50 and $75 for every 1,000 readers of your publication for a banner ad. When your readership is up, you may wish to secure the services of an agency that specializes in selling ad space in cyberspace. You may also pitch larger entities to form a strategic partnership with you, as *Suck* did.

A Web-based publication is a synergistic side venture for Web site designers, Web writers, and other creative Web professionals, such as specialty programmers. Although not initially profitable, a publication will give you good exposure in the Web community and establish your reputation as an expert. It is also a great way to generate business for your main moneymaking enterprise.

Resources

How to Publish on the Internet: A Comprehensive Step-by-Step Guide to Creative Expression on the World Wide Web (book and disk), by Andrew Fry and David Paul, New York, Warner, 1995, ISBN: 0446671797.

SLATE Web: *http://www.*slate.com. Slate is perhaps the highest-profile magazine-format online publication on the Web.

HOTWIRED Web: *http://www.*hotwired.com. The online sister publication to *Wired* magazine is a comprehensive online publication that covers a wide range of subjects having to do with cyberspace and cyber culture.

*http://www.*enews.com/monster. A comprehensive site that allows you to search for online magazines by name, subject, or category.

INTERACTIVE PUBLISHING ALERT *http://www.*netcreations.com/ipa. A publication for online publishers offering marketing, production, and industry information. Also provides a comprehensive list of online publications. Printed version available by subscription.

CHAPTER 2

Forty-seven Questions You Need to Answer to Start Making Money with Your Computer

I f you have read through the profiles in chapter 1, you have probably selected a few businesses of interest to you and are already beginning to think about the next steps you will need to take. We have therefore devised this chapter as a guide through the most important personal, financial, and legal issues that you will need to address to actually set yourself up making money in a computer-based business. Answering the following forty-seven questions will take you through a logical sequence of decision making that will essentially become your business plan for success.

Note: You may wish to get a notebook or set up a file in your computer at this time so you can do the various exercises we recommend in this chapter.

1. Why do you want to make money with your computer?

H ow you answer this question will help you answer many of the other key questions below, from which business you will actually want to select, to how you will market and price your products or services—even to what you will tell people when they ask what you do and why.

Additionally, in our experience, we've found that "why" people set out to make money on their own influences how long they will persist and how much difficulty they will put up with. Be it to pursue a passion for programming, the desire to be home with your children, the need to supplement a retirement income, or the dream to become your own boss, having a clear reason to succeed will make you more likely to achieve your goals than someone who, for example, simply purchases a business opportunity on a whim.

In short, your answer to this question can serve as a guiding principle for your entire venture and can help you get past the large and small annoyances you will encounter along the way.

2. Do you want to derive a full-time or part-time income from your computer-based business? Do you intend to work full- or part-time?

Some businesses are more or less likely to produce a full-time income than others. For example, keeping sports league statistics, drawing up astrology charts, or doing data conversion are less apt to generate a regular and sufficient income to serve as the sole source of earnings for a family. They can, however, bring in extra money, supplement a retirement income, or become an add-on to an existing business.

Some businesses like a specialized temporary-help service or a computer-repair service are more difficult to operate as sideline businesses. Others, like word processing, bookkeeping, or Web site design, can easily be done either full-time or on the side.

3. Do you want to continue working in the same field doing the same or similar type of work as you have been doing?

Most likely there is some way for you to make money with your computer in the context of the field in which you've been working. There are several advantages to sticking with a type of work you've had some experience in or at least to staying in the same field. As we mentioned earlier, you'll find getting started will be easier and quicker. Presumably you are already skilled at the work you do, so you won't have to go through a learning curve before you can do a good job for your clients and customers. Also, when you start out fully accomplished at what you're doing, you're able to complete your work more quickly and therefore will be able to take on more clients or customers in the same period of time.

More important, by staying in your existing field, you may be able to capitalize on whatever reputation you've already built. Hopefully you have contacts in the field who can become invaluable sources of referrals or even potential clients. (If you don't have such contacts outside your company, you can begin making them now before you start your business.) And you know the "territory," so to speak. You know who's who, what's what, the lingo, the taboos, the needs, the problems, and the current issues. Otherwise, in order to avoid costly mistakes in entering a new field, you would have to take out time and spend whatever money is needed to acquire such "insider" information.

However, if you don't enjoy doing the type of work you've been doing or you're "burned out" from it, even with these considerable advantages we don't advise trying to "stick it out" in the same line of work just because it would be easier. To really make money on your own full- or part-time, most people need to enjoy what they do, at least enough to look forward to getting up (or staying up) to do it. This is particularly true if you are starting a sideline business and must put in additional hours after coming home from a tiring day on your job. So if you're burned out or bummed out from your current line of work, we urge you to investigate other possibilities you would enjoy more.

The following four questions are designed to help you decide if you can make money full- or part-time on your own doing the type of work you've been doing. If you are certain you do not want to continue in your existing line of work, skip to Question #4.

3a. Are there other people doing something similar to what you would do on a freelance, consulting, or independent basis?

If there are already self-employed individuals doing something similar to what you do, this could be a good sign there will be a market for your services if you go out on your own. You will need to ascertain, however, if there is enough business for one more, or if not, what you could offer that would be sufficiently better or different to beat out your competition. To explore the possibilities further, talk with as many of these individuals as possible. We'll discuss this further in Question #6.

3b. Can your current employer become your first customer?

Would you be a difficult employee to replace? Is what you do integral to the success of your company? If so, you may be able to turn your employer into your first client.

A *Home Office Computing* magazine reader survey found that 49 percent of self-employed individuals responding have done work for their former employers. The best time to approach your boss about such an arrangement is when doing so would clearly benefit the company. Listen and watch for any indication of imminent cutbacks. Be alert to impending layoffs, early retirement offers, or other cost-saving measures. Companies today are looking for ways to get more for less, so one of the surest ways to make the transition into self-employment is to put forth a proposal your company cannot refuse. Demonstrate how much money you can save them (but don't shortchange yourself) and how much work you can produce as an outside consultant, freelancer, or subcontractor for a specified number of hours each week or month.

3c. Could any of the people or companies you currently work with on your job ethically become your clients or customers as well? How many?

For many people, their plans to go out on their own begin when someone they're working with says, "If you ever go out on your own, let me know." When you can do that without a legal or ethical conflict with your employer's interest you need not wait until such a person approaches you. You can approach her, tell her of your intentions, and get her reaction. Clearly, the more commitments you can get, the better the indication that there will be work awaiting you.

3d. Are there other clients for whom you could do your current job on a freelance, consultant, or subcontract arrangement?

Remember, it's important not to put all your eggs in one basket. You should never rely on the income from only one client, because if that client decides to discontinue your contract, you're out of business, at least temporarily. And since it can take one or more months to sign up new clients, even if one contract is keeping you busy, when that contract runs out, unless you have been actively marketing yourself, you will have no business in the pipeline. So always invest some time lining up new clients no matter how busy you may be with one major one.

If you want to stay in your own field, explore these other sources of possible clients or customers:

Large corporations. Many companies are laying off and cutting back staff, and yet they still need to have work done. As a result, they are choosing to contract out whole job functions that were once done by in-house staff. They're "outsourcing," that is, hiring outside consultants, small-business people, freelancers, or independent contractors for everything from marketing and billing to purchasing and technical writing.

Smaller companies. While large businesses are cutting back, the number of small businesses is growing, but often they're not large enough to hire full-time employees to do specialized tasks they need to have done. Instead, they're contracting out for many services like bookkeeping, public relations, cleaning, training, and graphic design.

New fields or industries. Even if there is no market for your services in your own field or industry, another industry or an emerging field may have a need for what you offer. For example, while realty companies or banks may be cutting back on using computer consultants in a tight market, collection agencies and loan brokers may be expanding and therefore have a growing need of such services. Or while advertising agencies may be using fewer freelance graphic designers in a new field like desktop video or online publications, producers and editors may have a growing need for freelance designers to create videos or design Web-based magazine layouts.

Information services or products. Even when the work you've been doing cannot be done outside a large organization, you may be able to successfully turn your expertise from the line of work you've done into a source of income by providing information about it to others. For example, if you are a customer service representative or bank teller, you probably won't be able to do your work on a freelance basis, but you could become a consultant or trainer and use your expertise to help other companies set up and train similar employees. In fact, there are at least fifteen ways you may be able to package the knowledge you have into profitable information products.

FIFTEEN WAYS TO TURN WHAT YOU KNOW INTO INFORMATION PRODUCTS

1. Write a book on the subject.
2. Host an online discussion group on the topic.
3. Publish a Web site on the topic.
4. Speak on the topic.
5. Create educational videotapes.
6. Create audiotape programs.
7. Write articles or a column for magazines, newspapers, or trade publications.

---

  8. Publish and sell a newsletter.
  9. Train or conduct seminars.
 10. Provide consulting services.
 11. Produce prepackaged training programs.
 12. Develop a product.
 13. Design a computer-assisted instructional software program.
 14. Create a television show.
 15. Originate a radio program.
 16. Sell your knowledge as a database online.

If you are now certain you want to continue doing the type of work you have been doing, you can skip to Question #5.

4. If you don't want to, or cannot, do the same type of work you've been doing, what other things do you do well and enjoy doing?

Make a list of your skills, talents, abilities, interests, contacts, and hobbies.

As you can see from the profiles listed in chapter 1 of this book, there are at least 100 ways you can make money using a personal computer. So there is no need for you to feel limited to the type of work that you've been doing. You can use your computer to turn a talent, skill, passion, hobby, bright idea, interest, pastime, or mission into a business. Identifying what you do well and enjoy doing is actually an ideal place to start in finding the best way to make money with a computer.

In fact, we strongly advise against picking a particular computer-based business simply because it's popular or has high-income potential. No matter how promising a particular business is, if you aren't especially good at it or don't particularly enjoy it, you jeopardize your chances of success. You would not want to find yourself in the same predicament as Gary Mc-Clelland, who came to one of our seminars on "How to Make Money with Your Computer."

In introducing himself, McClelland told the class that he had run a highly successful home-based medical transcription business for the past three years. Everyone was immediately curious as to why he had come to this course if he was already making money in one of the best computer-based home businesses. His answer was simple: "I had heard that I could earn a good living in this and I do, but I sit at my desk all day transcribing tapes, and actually I hate it. So I'm now looking for something I can do that I'll enjoy."

The 100 businesses we've profiled are ones that large numbers of people can do, and they should suggest a variety of new avenues for you to explore for matching your talents, skills, interests, ideas, and goals to an income-producing activity. But in addition to these 100, you can use a computer to make money in many other ways that only you can identify because they capitalize specifically on your unique background, skills, contacts, and interests.

It's easy to overlook the income potential of the things we enjoy and do well. We tend to take these abilities and interests for granted or assume everyone can do them. We may even think that if we really enjoy doing something, no one would pay us to do it. Not true. Here are just a few examples of ingenious ways people are using their computers to provide products or services based on the unique combinations of their skills, talents, interests, hobbies, and abilities.

Michael Cahlin turned his love for chocolate into Chocolate Software, a line of computer programs filled with chocolate recipes. Cartoonist Stu Heinecke developed the idea for personalized cartoons and uses his computer to create direct-mail cartoon advertising campaigns for some of the largest advertisers in the world. In addition, he has recruited other top cartoonists in the country and created the Personal Promotion Kit, a desktop micro-ad campaign that puts the power of the personalized cartoon at the fingertips of anyone with a PC.

Rita Tateel turned her interest in celebrities into a database business called Celebrity Source. She matches charity events with celebrities who will attend and endorse their causes. A public relations specialist in Detroit was a tennis pro earlier in her career and still teaches tennis in her spare time. She uses her computer to provide a tennis scholarship matching service.

Ted Artz went from art school into designing custom interiors and furniture where he got in on the PC revolution early by being among the first in his industry to use a CAD system in his work. His love of computers has now brought him closer to his original career vision; his home-based company Amalgamation Haus now produces top-notch video animation sequences for broadcast and industrial video productions. Samantha Greenberg had pounded a keyboard for twenty-five years as a bookkeeper and accountant when she took a particularly demanding job entering medical data. This new job required that she work long days without breaks. Within months she developed a repetitive strain illness and ended up unemployed. Even after surgery she was unable to pick up anything heavier than a paperback book. After researching her disability to learn as much about it as she could, Greenberg started a database business called Computer Injury Network, providing information on the resources available to the 185,000 similarly injured workers who are reported nationwide each year. She also conducts seminars for businesses on VDT-related (video data terminal) afflictions.

Here are a few other examples: Ellie Kahn loves history and she loves to write. She uses her computer to create personalized histories for families, companies, and organizations. Her company is called Living Legacies, and she can provide print, audio, or video histories.

Dee Louzginov has always been a home-based graphic designer. Taking advantage of developments in the multimedia field, Dee has now combined her design experience with her expertise in new media and created her latest home-based business. Eclectica Mediaworks is one of the first companies to create interactive multimedia high school yearbooks on CD-ROM.

Because his passion is boating, Will Milan has developed software for first-time boat buyers. As a professional planner, Wayne Serville was aware of the complexities citizens face when serving on local planning boards, so he has created a business for himself producing a newsletter for lay planners. Susan Pinsky and David Starkman love 3-D photography. They use their computer to run Reel 3-D, a mail-order company selling items of interest to 3-D photographers.

Here is a work sheet to help you discover the gateway to turning your particular talents, skills, passions, hobbies, ideas, interests, and desires into a viable income with your computer:

Work Sheet: Four Gateways to Creating Your Own Job

There are four gateways to identifying and turning what you do well and most enjoy doing into a profitable computer-related business. Answer the following questions to find the best ones for you.

1. Harvesting Your Gifts

Is there anything people readily and spontaneously compliment you on or appreciate you for? It may be a talent, hobby, skill, or interest. It may be something that goes back to your childhood, or it may be something you developed later in life. Such compliments may take the form of people asking you to do something for them because you do it so well, or it may be a more direct comment like "You sure are good at this. People would pay you for doing it!" Someone might have even said something like "You ought to start a business doing that."

If you've had such compliments and you enjoy doing this activity, why not turn your talent, gift, or skill into a source of income for yourself? About one in four self-employed individuals use this strategy as their gateway to self-employment.

This approach has many advantages. First, you already know people appreciate and admire your skill at doing it. Second, you can approach the very people who encouraged you to see if they might become your first clients, customers, or referral sources. Third, since you're already a "master" at this type of work, you'll be able to produce positive results right away for your clients or customers.

If your answer to this question is "yes," describe your talent or skill here and indicate on a scale of 1 to 10 how interested you would be in developing this gift into a business:

My Passion is:

Not Very Interested				*Somewhat Interested*				*Very Interested*	
1	2	3	4	5	6	7	8	9	10

2. Profiting from Your Passion

What do you feel particularly passionate about doing? About one in every six people who work for themselves has found a way to turn his or her passion into a profitable line of work. Some people describe this as having a "fire in the belly." These are the people who say about their work: "I'd do this even if I weren't being paid." Is there anything you feel that strongly about?

Even if your passion is something you'd never think that you could make money doing, don't automatically write it off. Go ahead and describe those things about which you are most enthusiastic. We've seen businesses arise from a love of golf, tennis, pets, model railroading, art, cross-dressing, writing family histories, comedy, matchmaking, music, and even going to parties. One advantage of turning your passion into a living is that your work will often feel like play. You'll get paid for doing what you'd otherwise do for free. And, of course, you'll rarely have problems motivating yourself to get to work.

Some people want to keep work and play separate, so, if your answer to this question is yes, describe your passion here and indicate on a scale of 1 to 10 how interested you would be in developing this passion into a business:

My passion is:

Not Very Interested   *Somewhat Interested*   *Very Interested*

1   2   3   4   5   6   7   8   9   10

3. Earning Your Living from a Mission

Are you the sort of person who is motivated by "wanting to make a difference in the world"? Have you been wishing you could find a way to do more meaningful work than past jobs have provided? Do you have an idea for a new business product, service, or invention that you think could help change the world? Do you want to spend your working life solving a problem or taking on a cause?

Solving problems or turning a "great" idea into a reality can serve as the source for a livelihood. About one in five people who go out on their own have turned such an idea, problem, cause, or mission into a business.

The problems or ideas you want to develop may be of a personal nature, affecting a small percentage of the population, or they may be related to larger social ills that affect many. Write down the your idea or problem here and indicate on a scale of 1 to 10 how interested you would be in earning your living pursuing this idea, mission, or cause:

The problem I'd like to help solve is:

The idea I have to solve it is:

Not Very Interested   *Somewhat Interested*   *Very Interested*

1   2   3   4   5   6   7   8   9   10

4. Choosing an Opportunity

Are you seeking something to do on your own primarily to earn enough money so you can do something else that's important to you? Are you simply wanting to find some way to earn a better full- or part-time income? Are you primarily wanting to be at home more, have greater control of your time, be with your children? Are you developing a career as an artist or entertainer and need a flexible way to support yourself until you break in?

Nearly half the people going out on their own don't have any particular gift, passion, or mission they want to use their computer to pursue. For them, a business is a means to an end, not an end in itself. They are looking for an income opportunity, and their task becomes choosing a financially viable option that they can do successfully. Sometimes they buy a business opportunity or franchise. Sometimes they become active in a multilevel sales organization. Most often, those who succeed either decide to continue in the same line of work if their job ends or they simply *choose* something they can earn money at that already has a proven track record of success.

If this scenario best describes your situation, use chapter 1 of this book as a checklist to make your choice, focusing on businesses that are among the easiest to start and have a strong existing demand. Since you will not be highly motivated by the work itself, you will need to have other reasons for going out on your own to keep you motivated. So write down the other goals that making money will help you achieve and indicate on a scale of 1 to 10, how important it is to you to find a way to pursue them:

My other goals are:

Not Very Interested				*Somewhat Interested*				*Very Interested*	
1	2	3	4	5	6	7	8	9	10

We also recommend two of our books, *Finding Your Perfect Work* (1996) and *Home Businesses You Can Buy* (1997), as well as several other books: *What Color Is Your Parachute?* by Richard Bolles (Ten Speed Press, 1991), *Finding Your Mission* by Naomi Stephan (Walpole, NH, Stillpoint Publishing, 1989), and *Live Your Vision* by Joyce Chapman (North Hollywood, CA: Newcastle Books, 1990).

Whichever pathway you choose to earn a living on your own, there are three alternatives for packaging your gift, idea, passion, mission, or choice into a viable product or service. Consider each of these possibilities:

1. You can sell what you **KNOW** in that area as a consultant, teacher, speaker, seminar leader, or by providing advice on a 900 number.
2. You can **CREATE** an information product or a tangible product related to your gift, idea, passion, mission, or business choice; i.e., books, tapes, novelty, CAI (computer-aided instruction) course.
3. You can **DO** whatever it is you aspire to do as a service for others; i.e., programming, training, financial planning.

5. Who needs the kind of products or services you could offer? Make a list of all the types of people or companies that need them.

Whether you are doing the same kind of work or changing fields, no matter how good you are at what you want to do or how great an idea you have for a product or service, unless there are people who need and are willing to pay for it, it will forever remain a "good idea." We call this the WPWPF Principle—What People Will Pay For. The more precisely you identify what people need and will pay for, the better. If, when you visualize who your prospective customers are, you get no clear picture or your image includes everyone, that's a signal that you have not sufficiently defined your business concept. In today's economy, even large companies are becoming niche marketers.

To determine if your products or services will meet the WPWPF Principle, start by listing all the possible groups of people and companies that you THINK might need and will pay to use them. Then you will need to determine to the extent possible if, in fact, they WILL and start narrowing down those you are uniquely or most advantageously positioned to serve.

The following five questions, 6–10, should help you find out if, in fact, you have selected a viable service or product and narrow down your list of prospective customers to a "target" or niche group you can specialize in serving. Also for help in defining your niche, see our book *Getting Business to Come to You.*

6. Who is your competition? Is anyone else providing similar services or products?

If other people are now providing the products or services you wish to offer, this is a good sign that it is something people will pay for. It's an especially good sign if you determine that your competition has been in business for some time and is doing well. Don't assume, however, that there is room for one more. You'll need to find out if there is enough unsatisfied demand for you to thrive.

You can locate self-employed people doing the type of work you do by looking through the yellow pages and in trade or professional organization directories, by asking for referrals from personal contacts and networking groups, or by talking with likely customers about others they have worked with.

Should you find a considerable number of people are doing what you do, it's important to determine if this is an indication that there's a large demand for such work or whether it means that the market is saturated.

If you discover that no one else is doing what you do on an independent basis, you will need to investigate whether that's because there's not a sufficient need for it or enough profit in it or whether you are simply the first to consider providing these services independently. The best way to determine this is to identify how many people or businesses could use your services and begin talking with some of these potential clients personally.

IS THERE ROOM FOR YOU? TESTING THE MARKET

1. Look in the yellow pages and/or other directories to see how many similar businesses there are.

2. Contact your competition. Find out how long they've been in business and how they're doing.

3. Read business, trade, and professional journals related to your field to identify needs and issues, economic and industry trends, and announcements of business successes and failures.

4. Attend local business, trade, and professional meetings. Listen for needs, complaints, and trends. Discuss your plans with leaders and potential clients in attendance and listen for their reactions.

5. Contact potential customers directly by phone or by attending or exhibiting at trade shows or expos.

If you discover that the area in which you live or the niche you have selected is not large enough to provide full-time support, you may need to branch out by offering related products or services. For example, if there are not enough clients in your community to support a copywriting service, you might broaden your business as Robert Cooper did to include writing of other kinds. Cooper splits his services among copywriting, freelance magazine writing, and writing newsletters for law firms.

7. How is your competition doing? Are they busy? Are they turning away business they could refer to you?

Once you identify your competition, find out as much as you can about what they do, whom they do it for, how they do it, and how long they have been doing it. Actually, your "competition" can be one of your best sources of business. You may be able to do overload for them when they're too busy. You may be able to specialize in doing things they don't provide. You may be able to serve customers or clients whom they are unqualified or unwilling to serve.

One of the best ways to find out about your potential competition and how they're doing is to talk with them personally. Tell them about the products or service you're planning to offer and then listen carefully to their reaction. If they generally are closemouthed or negative about the field, this is not a good sign. If, however, they generally respond positively to your plans, this is an indication that their business is doing well, and they may even become a source of referral business for you. In fact, do offer to set up an overload exchange with them; you can do backup for them and they can back you up when the day comes when you need help with extra business. Likewise, determine what their specialties are as well as whom they don't serve.

8. What specialty or "niche" can you carve out for yourself?

Unless you are one of very few people who do what you do or you live in a very small community, you will probably do best to specialize in a "niche," a target group of clients you will serve. The more specialized or "niched" your business is, the easier and more cost-effective it will be to market yourself. When you specialize, you can focus your marketing activities on the specific groups of people you want to reach. Also, having a niche makes it more likely that people will refer to you because they will be able to remember more easily who you are and what you do.

Here are several ideas about how to find your special niche:

Specialize in one industry that you have unique knowledge of or contacts in. For example, a woman from one of our seminars decided to specialize in providing a billing service for anesthesiologists because her husband was an anesthesiologist. He became her first client and served as a source of referrals to other doctors. As part of his job in the media services department of a major orthopedic teaching hospital, Chris Richter developed an extensive Web site for the facility. So many orthopedic surgeons from all over the country E-mailed him asking for Web sites that Chris now has a thriving independent add-on business developing Web sites.

Offer a service no one else is providing. For example, we mentioned that when systems engineer Wil Milan decided to develop his own software company, he chose to specialize in software for people who, like himself, want to own a boat. He could find no software for prospective or new boat owners, so this became his niche. His first package helps perspective boaters estimate the cost of owning their own boat.

Provide a product or service to a group that has yet to be served. Can you identify a group of people for whom no product or service currently exists? For example, Steve Dworman had been consulting in the infomercial industry and recognized that this was a new and growing industry—so new, in fact, that there was as yet little information or support available for companies producing them. So Dworman decided to offer a newsletter to this new industry, called *Steven Dworman's Infomercial Marketing Report.* He produced the first eight-page issue and sent out a sample with an order form. His thorough knowledge of this industry had earned him the confidence of his potential subscribers, so his list of subscribers has grown to nearly 500, and his newsletter grew to sixteen pages.

9. How will you identify people or companies that need what you can offer?

If you are not already aware of many possible people or companies that need your services, or if the customary pools of clients are well saturated, here are several ways to match up what you enjoy and do well with what people will pay for.

Listen for who's complaining. Complaints are clues to problems people will spend money to solve. Ask yourself: Who is or could be having a problem that my product or service could solve? Attend meetings and other gatherings of the type of customers you wish to serve and listen for their "ain't-it-awful's," the things they're bitching about. Read feature articles and letters-to-the-editor in newspapers, magazines, and trade publications and look for problems, concerns, and issues you might address.

You may read, for example, about how college graduates are complaining about not being able to find jobs. Newspapers have reported that many college graduates still do not have jobs waiting for them upon graduation. Today's graduates are not just in a tight struggle with each other for jobs; they are also competing with some of last year's graduates who are still job hunting and with many people who are still being laid off from their jobs each year. This ongoing problem is creating new clients for résumé-writing services, graphic designers, image consultants, job placement and referral services, and so forth.

Follow trends. Trends suggest possibilities for new groups of customers or clients you could serve. To identify trends that could mean business for you, read and listen for who's doing what. What's coming in? What's going out? Who's moving in? Who's moving away? Who's expanding? And, most important, how could you help them?

As baby boomers age, for example, an increasingly large segment of the population will be over the age of sixty-five, and these older people will have special needs and interests. Lynne Farrell has foreseen this trend and is using her computer to create a referral service to help senior citizens with their housing needs.

Here's another example of a trend that is creating a demand for computer-based business services. As companies downsize, they must turn to outside consultants and freelancers to help them on an as-needed basis. But how do they locate such experts? Jeffrey Day of Boston is an expert service broker, one of the businesses featured in chapter 1. He links companies with the consultants and experts they need.

Managing projects using such "contingent" workers also calls for special project management skills. Philip Dyer of Atlanta is filling this need by providing consulting and training to larger companies on how to accomplish their work on a project management basis. And if the number of expert service brokers or project management consultants continues to grow, they may well need a professional association or a newsletter tailored to their industry—two other computer-based business opportunities featured in chapter 1.

The recent popularity of scuba diving is another example of the business potential that's embedded in popular trends. Scuba diving may be on its way to becoming the next fitness craze. Between 1966 and 1980, the Professional Association of Diving Instructors certified only one million scuba divers. But since 1980, it has certified three million more, and one-third of them are women! These new diving devotees probably are in the market for a wide array of information and services related to their new passion. How about providing a computer bulletin board for scuba divers, or a newsletter for women scuba divers?

Another trend rich with business possibilities is do-it-yourself home-improvement projects. American Demographics reports that 55 percent of adults do interior painting, 50 percent do minor plumbing repairs, 49 percent do minor electrical work, 42 percent do exterior painting, and 30 percent do minor repairs of appliances. So if you're thinking about starting some type of database or referral service with your computer, you might tap into this home repair trend by creating a home repair/home improvement hotline to refer callers to tradespeople who will go into people's homes or offices not do to the work themselves but to teach their customers how to do it or help their customers through a job they're stuck on. For more about this business idea, see p. 128.

Here's another trend that could mean business. *Omni* reported that a new ambulatory-care health clinic opens every day in the country. Predictions are that by the year 2000, such clinics will provide 25 percent of the nation's primary care. If you're providing a business service like public relations, copywriting, or mailing-list management, you might want to specialize in serving these clinics. Find out which other kinds of services or information you could you provide to the patients who use these facilities. Use this kind of analytic thinking whenever you hear about a new trend.

How to Spot a Trend

- **Watch for statistics** contained in news stories and features and "factoid" boxes in *USA Today, Home Office Computing,* and other frequently published print media.

- **Read articles and watch TV news** segments for signs of "what's in and what's out."

- **Watch for "hot" new businesses** or older businesses gaining new popularity.

- **Make links between seemingly unrelated phenomena;** i.e., more older people equals new rules on processing medical claims; traffic on the rise equals more people who have a computer and modem at home; corporations cutting back on staff equals an increased demand for customer service.

- **Pay attention to the news** about segments of the population that have special problems and new laws being passed on their behalf.

- **Read publications that track trends** such as newsletters like John Naisbitt's *Trend Letter* and *Research Alert;* magazines like *The Futurist* and *American Demographics;* and books by futurist authors such as Marvin Citron, Faith Popcorn, and Alvin Toffler.

Find applications for new technology. New technology also opens doors to groups of customers and clients not being served by others. New technology provides the opportunity to offer more to your clients by enabling you to do what you do better in less time than competitors who are still using older technology.

For example, if you've chosen to provide an already established service like word processing or desktop publishing, having the latest high-resolution or color printer or scanner or offering remote printing or downloading into a client's computer can give you a competitive edge. Using your own network of online databases can give a competitive edge to an information broker, a mailing-list service, or a computer programmer. Sometimes new technology also makes it possible to provide new services to clients or to reach whole new groups of clients. For example, a husband and wife in New England have started a highly specialized new business using a color copier. Being horse lovers and owners themselves, they take photographs of clients' horses and put the photos onto T-shirts, using a scanner, a computer, and special software.

Capitalize on new legislation. The passage of new legislation creates an immediate demand for professionals who can educate and train others in how to comply with the new regulations. Needs arise for consulting and referral services. Training materials and manuals must be designed and prepared instructing people how to comply. Newsletters may spring up filling people in on the implications of the legislation, etc.

Aspiring actress Dorene Ludwig has created her business from recent legislation regarding sexual harassment. Ludwig, who had a long-standing interest in women's issues, has combined her skills and interests to become one of a growing number of sexual-harassment consultants. Using dramatic scenes and scripted dialog, she has created a training manual that teaches corporate employees how to deal with sexual harassment on the job.

10. What can you offer that your competition does not offer? Could you do what they do better in some way?

In order to get clients and customers, you will not only need to be able to tell them what you do; you will also need to be able to tell them why they should use you as opposed to another person who offers the same or similar products or services. This is sometimes referred to as your "unique selling advantage."

At first glance, you may not think that you have anything special to offer. But chances are that if you become sufficiently familiar with your competition, you will begin to notice how what you do is, or can be, different. If you listen carefully to what your prospective clients and customers are complaining about, you will uncover many ideas about how you can make what you offer better. You may be more experienced, for example, with a particular type of client. You may be able to do what you do faster, more inexpensively, or more thoroughly. You may be able to offer a more personalized service. Perhaps you can pick up and deliver or provide twenty-four-hour turnaround.

11. How will you let your potential customers and clients know about what you will offer?

At this point, you have zeroed in on your product and service, and considered to whom you can sell it. Now you must let them know about it. No matter how great an idea you have or how good you are at providing a product or service with your computer, unless people know about what you're doing and how they can contact you, you won't have any business. So once you know who needs your products and services and the niche that you wish to carve out for yourself, your next task becomes to identify how you could spread the word about your products and services to those people.

Consider these questions as you build a list of at least ten ways you can inform them about what you do.

- **Where do your prospective clients or customers gather? Could you put materials about what you do in these places? Could you give a speech or presentation?**
- **What other services do they use? Could you get referrals from those other sources?**
- **What do they read? Could you write articles for these publications or take out a small ad?**
- **How could you get a list of their names, addresses, and telephone numbers so you could send them materials or call them?**

List ten ways you could inform your potential clients about what you offer:

1._____   6._____
2._____   7._____
3._____   8._____
4._____   9._____
5._____   10._____

However many hours you plan to work each week (and we recommend that you put in *at least* eight hours a week in a sideline business), you should plan to spend every one of those hours when you are not doing paid work marketing yourself. It can take anywhere from thirty days to several months to obtain a new customer, so you should plan to set aside up to 40 percent of your time for marketing, even after you have ample business.

Fortunately, getting the word out about your computer business need not be expensive. In fact, the majority of the most effective ways very small businesses get business, such as networking, direct solicitation, referrals, and public relations, are not that costly. From our book *Getting Business to Come to You,* written with marketing consultant Laura Clampitt Douglas, here are thirty-eight ways people can successfully get the word out about what they do.

Principle Promotional Methods

1: Word of mouth

1. Networking
2. Online forums and discussion groups
3. Mentors and gatekeepers
4. Volunteerism
5. Sponsorships
6. Charitable donations
7. Referrals
8. Business name
9. Letterhead and business card
10. Product packaging
11. Point-of-sale display

2: Public Relations

12. Writing articles for printed and online magazines and Web sites
13. Letters to the editor
14. News releases: printed and electronic
15. Speeches and seminars
16. Publicity:
    Newspaper
    Magazine

Radio and TV
Business and trade publications
World Wide Web

3: Direct Marketing

17. Sampling
18. Incentives
19. Discount Pricing
20. Contests and giveaways
21. Newsletters
22. Circulars and flyers
23. Trade shows and exhibits
24. Sales seminars
25. Demonstrations
26. Direct mail
27. Promotions on a Web site

4: Inventive Advertising

28. Web site
29. Classified ads
30. Business directories
31. Yellow-page advertising
32. Bulletin boards and tear pad
33. Your own radio show
34. Your own TV show
35. Online networking
36. Fax
37. Direct response ads
38. Card decks

12. Do you know anyone or any company that needs what you offer right now? How many such potential clients do you know?

The more people you know right now who need and will pay for what you have to offer, the better off you are. Some of the most successful computer-based businesses have started almost by spontaneous combustion. In other words, people they knew signed up to do business with them right away.

When Bill Osborne started his newsletter *Only Good News,* for example, ten out of ten of the companies he had worked with in the past as a marketing consultant wanted to take out an ad in his new newsletter. When Bruce Pea started his mail-order catalog of sales-training books and tapes, his first clients were all salesmen he already knew. From those initial contacts, he developed a large and loyal national mailing-list.

To get your enterprise under way, begin with the people you know. Create a list of every possible personal or business contact you can think of who might need what you are offering and call them personally to let them know what you're doing. You don't have to consider this initial contact as a "sales" call. Think of it as an "information" call. You're simply calling to let people you've had contact with in the past know what you're doing and that you will be glad to serve them when they need you.

Listen carefully when you call, however, for any clue that they would be in the market for your product or service now. Such clues are "buying signals." Here are several examples:

- complaints or horror stories about previous experiences;
- comments like "I've been thinking about something like that" or "We could sure use something like that";
- explanations as to why they don't have or are already using a product or service like yours;
- even comments like "Ummm, that's interesting" can be a sign that someone is already starting to imagine him- or herself using your service.

Take such buying signals as a cue to ask if they would like more information and either set up an appointment or agree to send them material. If you send material by mail, make a date on your calendar as to when you will follow up with a phone call to see if they got the material and find out if they have further questions and if they're interested in doing business.

Put the names of everyone you contact who might use your products or services at any time in the future into a computer "contact management" database (see chapter 4) and make periodic contact by phone or mail with your entire list. Continue building this contact list by adding the names of new people you meet. Soon you will have a high-quality mailing list to whom you can send a newsletter or direct-mail pieces.

13. Do you know anyone in other fields who works regularly with the people or companies that need what you have to offer? Such people can become your "gatekeepers."

Gatekeepers are people who in the course of what they do come into regular contact with people who need what you are offering. They can be an invaluable source of ongoing business for you. Here's an example of just how helpful they can be. One January day, a weapons designer was beginning to realize that his position might be eliminated, when he heard us talking about self-employment on KGO radio in San Francisco. After listening to the show, he got a copy of our book *The Best Home Businesses for the 90s* and, realizing he was a competent writer, decided to start a business from home helping others write business plans. This is one of the businesses covered in that book as well. Once he decided to become a business plan writer, he began thinking about who would be in a position to put him in contact with people who need to have business plans. Loan officers seemed like a logical answer and, indeed, loan officers have become his gatekeepers. They send him all the business he needs. In fact,

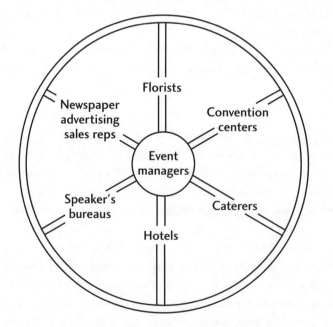

SAMPLE GATEKEEPERS' NETWORK: EVENT CLEARINGHOUSE

Florists

Newspaper advertising sales reps

Convention centers

Event managers

Speaker's bureaus

Caterers

Hotels

Each business represented on a spoke serves the same customers who use the services of event managers and is therefore a potential source of referrals and joint activities.

by late April he became so busy that he had hired two people to work with him, and he's making more money than he did as an engineer designing weapons.

To identify who your gatekeepers might be, create a "Gatekeepers' Network" as follows. Take out a sheet of paper and draw a circle in the center. Write the type of customers or clients to whom you are planning to sell your products and services in the center of the circle. Then draw a spoke off the center circle for each other type of business or service these people might do business with.

Now begin making contact with and collecting names of people who represent each spoke on your gatekeepers' network. Introduce yourself and your product or service to these gatekeepers, then develop a relationship with as many of them as you can. To let them know you're interested in them, ask them questions about their business like "What kind of customers do you like to get?" "How do you like to get referrals?" "Do you have a particular specialty?" Then, after you've established a relationship, maintain a high profile with these individuals so they will think of you whenever one of their clients or customers needs what you have to offer. To keep your name fresh in their minds, create a database of the gatekeepers you identify so you can keep in regular contact with them by mail or phone.

14. How much money do you need to have coming in each month?

To determine how much money you need to have coming in, calculate three things:

- **Living expenses**—How much do you need to make to live on? This is the "salary" you will need to produce to support yourself and your family. Be sure to include taxes and fringe benefits such as health insurance formerly covered by your employer.
- **Direct costs**—How much will it cost you to actually produce your product or deliver your service? This includes the cost of all the travel, phone charges, materials, and supplies used in serving a specific client or customer.
- **Overhead**—How much will it cost you to run your business? This includes all the other costs of being in business like your marketing, utilities, office furniture, and equipment.

Determining Your Salary

To calculate how much your earnings need to be, first identify three income figures. What you need:

- To survive $_____

- To be comfortable $_____

- To thrive $_____

It's important to know these three figures because all products or services you might choose do not have the same income potential. Also, knowing what you need and want to earn will help you set goals, price your services, and determine how many hours you will need to bill out each week.

For example, unless you're looking for a way to pay for a hobby, we don't think you should even consider undertaking a business that will not enable you to at least achieve your survival income. That's why in chapter 1 we classify some of the businesses as merely a part-time or add-on business rather than a full-time venture.

Second, while you might be willing to live at the survival level for a while, over time you probably won't be happy putting in long hours on work for an income that barely keeps you afloat. So you should also project how what you offer can provide you with what you consider to be a comfortable income within a reasonable period of time. And if the business you're considering can never produce what you'd need to thrive, even after several years of working at it, you may burn out in that business within a short time. So make sure that the business you choose has at least the potential to achieve all three of your income targets.

Identifying Direct Costs

Direct costs—those that are directly billable to your clients or customers or which you must spend up front to produce a product—are quite low for many of the businesses you can start with a computer, like résumé writing or computer consulting. Even such businesses as these, however, have some direct costs like the high-quality paper used to print out the finished résumé or the cost of driving to meet with consulting clients, so don't minimize them.

Businesses such as computer-designed T-shirts and novelties, online information research, or producing a newsletter have higher direct costs. You have to pay for the manufacturing of novelties, for example, or the costs of getting online to do the research, which can be expensive. In such cases, you will need to pass these costs along to your clients by making sure you set your prices high enough to cover these costs or in some cases by billing separately for them.

At times, you may need to pay for these costs before you get paid by your clients, so calculating these costs carefully will help you manage your cash flow. Calculating your direct costs enables you to know and plan for the cash you need to have on hand between the time you do your work and when you actually get paid.

Including Overhead

By working from home you will either avoid or reduce overhead costs by nearly 40 percent of the typical expenses required for storefront or office-based businesses. You will, nonetheless, have some overhead costs, which people working from home often fail to build into their fees. Then they wonder why they always seem to be living on less than they expected.

We discovered one reason for this common oversight in the process of interviewing home-business owners for *The Best Home Businesses for the 90s.* We learned that very few home businesses know what their overhead is. But by using money management software like *Quicken, Quickbooks, Microsoft Money,* or *Managing Your Money,* you can quickly and easily track your overhead and therefore make sure your prices account for these costs.

The following work sheet includes standard home business overhead items you can use in making your initial calculations.

HOW MUCH YOU NEED TO MAKE EACH MONTH

Calculating Your Gross Salary Needs

Estimate how much you would need to spend each month on each item for the three income targets you project.

	Survival	Comfortable	Ideal
Auto expenses	_____	_____	_____
Clothing	_____	_____	_____
Food	_____	_____	_____
Health insurance	_____	_____	_____
Home maintenance	_____	_____	_____
Entertainment	_____	_____	_____
Education	_____	_____	_____
Medical and dental care	_____	_____	_____
Personal care	_____	_____	_____
Rent or mortgage	_____	_____	_____

Taxes (federal, state, self-employment)	_____	_____	_____
Utilities	_____	_____	_____
Other living expenses	_____	_____	_____
	_____	_____	_____
Total Living Expenses	$_____	$_____	$_____

Calculating Direct Costs of Producing Your Product or Service

Estimate what each item will cost you.

Cost of materials	_____
Travel to and from client sites	_____
Long-distance phone calls	_____
Cost of services (i.e., printing, design, subcontract services)	_____
Supplies	_____
Other	_____
Total Direct Costs:	$_____

Calculating Overhead Costs for Monthly Operating Expenses

Estimate what each item will cost per month

	Survival	Comfortable	Ideal
Insurance	_____	_____	_____
Interest or loan payments	_____	_____	_____
Marketing costs (i.e., advertising, publicity, marketing)	_____	_____	_____
Maintenance	_____	_____	_____
Office supplies	_____	_____	_____
Postage	_____	_____	_____
Professional fees (i.e., legal and accounting)	_____	_____	_____
Telephone and fax	_____	_____	_____
Utilities (above household usage)	_____	_____	_____
Other	_____	_____	_____
	_____	_____	_____
Total Overhead:	$_____	$_____	$_____

15. How much will you need to charge and how many hours or days will you need to bill for in order to produce the monthly income you need? Is this fee within the range people will pay you?

Once you know your three income targets and have estimated your operating expenses, you are in a position to sit down and calculate the following:

- How much would you have to charge to cover those costs and have enough left over to meet your income goals?
- At that rate, how many hours would you have to work (or how many products would you have to sell) and how many clients or customers would you need to work with per day, per week, or per month to achieve those goals?

!!! ALERT! ESTIMATING BILLABLE HOURS !!!

It is better to be conservative in calculating how many hours you can actually bill out each week, month, or year. One of the common mistakes people make is to assume they will be able to bill out a forty-hour week, week after week, as if they were employed by a firm. They calculate, for example, that if they can charge $40 per hour as a desktop publisher, they will be able to earn $1,600 a week billing out at forty hours per week. That's a gross income of $80,000 a year.

However, unlike working at a job where one can earn $20 an hour, forty hours a week, fifty weeks a year, in most home-based and self-employment businesses you will be spending a portion of each week marketing, doing administrative tasks, and performing other work for which you can't bill your clients. For example, the typical full-time desktop publishers we interviewed were billing an average of four hours a day. So working full-time, they were grossing an average of $800 per week or $40,000 a year.

In like fashion, the typical computer tutor was billing an average of three days of training a week. Information brokers were billing from ten to twenty hours a week. Some successful consultants find they have weeks when they have no billable work. At the other extreme, however, some medical transcriptionists we interviewed were billing thirty hours a week and some computer programmers over forty hours per week. It is the rare business, however, that can bill out a forty-hour week. Even after the business is up and running successfully, many people find they need to spend as much as 40 percent of the week marketing their business and carrying out administrative tasks.

A common mistake people make in a part-time enterprise is to overestimate how many hours each week they will be able to work on their business. They tend to overlook how tired they will be when they get home from their salaried jobs and are overly optimistic about how many weekend hours they will actually be able to put in.

So whether you will be working full- or part-time, be realistic about your schedule and realize you will only be able to bill out a percentage of the hours you will need to work. Then make your income projections accordingly.

Once you have made the calculations necessary to know what you would have to charge, then you must determine if you will actually be able to charge the fees you need to in order to hit your target income. To do this, begin by comparing what you would need to charge with what successful existing competition is charging. Here are a couple of ways to find out what others are charging. First, sometimes national trade and professional associations and trade publications do periodic surveys of what members or subscribers are charging. Second, if there is a local chapter of a trade or professional association for your field, call the chapter president and ask for the range of fees people are charging in your community.

If you find that you would need to charge more than the current going rate, then you need to figure out what you can provide that will add sufficient value to what you're offering to justify the increased cost. If you are more qualified or can do what you offer faster, better, or more conveniently, then you may be able to charge more.

Pricing is always an experiment, however, so ultimately you will need to test the price to find out what people will actually pay. Of course, the most direct way to test your price is to simply ask potential clients what they would expect to pay for what you offer. For example, here's how Bill Garnet found out just how much he could charge when he began offering his Mississippi-based legal research service. Garnet called potential clients and asked them what they were used to paying and what they would like to pay. Based on this feedback, he began charging a lower fee than they expected and then began raising his prices until he started getting complaints. At that point he backed his prices down somewhat to set the optimum fee. If what you are offering is something that can be sold by mail or over the Internet, another way to test your prices is to do a series of mailings or E-mail releases to separate lists of potential buyers offering several different price levels, and then see which price draws the most responses.

Another approach might be to exhibit at a trade show where you can watch and listen for how your prospective buyers respond to your price. Make sure, however, that you know in advance of exhibiting that the people attending the show will, in fact, be the type of people you plan to serve. You can use similar methods to help identify the feasibility of various prices when you're offering something that no one else is providing. In this case, it's also important to identify what potential buyers are comparing your product or service to, because even if it is not actually similar, if they think it is, their perceptions will influence how much they are willing to pay for it.

Should you find that people simply will not pay enough for what you offer so that you can make enough money, then you will need to choose another business or rethink the business you have chosen to make it profitable.

16. How can you support yourself until you have enough business coming in?

As you can see from having calculated the income you will need, your largest expense is not the cost of starting or running the business venture itself. While the cost of your computer equipment and software will probably be your largest business start-up expense, the major costs involved in getting your business under way will most likely be covering your living expenses while you build up your business income. Unless you have plenty of business lined up before leaving your job, you should have an entry plan for supporting yourself for three to twelve months while you build your business. Here are six commonly used entry plans.

SIX ENTRY PLANS FOR STARTING OUT ON YOUR OWN

1. **The Moonlighting Plan.** Keep your full-time job and develop your business as a sideline. When it takes off, you can go full-time. Be sure to work at least eight hours a week on a sideline business.

2. **The Part-Time Plan.** Work at a part-time job to provide a base income while you're building up the business. When your business equals the base income, drop the part-time job.

---

3. **The Spin-off Plan.** Turn your previous employer into your first major customer or, when ethically possible, take a major client with you from your previous job.

4. **The Cushion Plan.** Find a financial resource to support yourself with while you start your business. Your cushion should be large enough to cover your base expenses for at least six to twelve months.

5. **The Piggyback Plan.** If you have a working spouse or partner, cut back your expenses so you can live on one salary until your business gets going.

6. **Do Temporary Work.** Work through a temporary agency or job shop while you build your business. Most such agencies offer enough flexibility that you can take on some "temp" jobs while building your business income.

17. What start-up costs will you have?

You've now estimated your income needs and cash flow. There are, however, undoubtedly one-time start-up costs that you must arrange for in order to get under way. By working from home, your start-up costs will be considerably lower than setting yourself up in an outside office or storefront. Start-up costs for the businesses we identified in *The Best Home Businesses for the 90s,* for example, ran an average of slightly more than $7,500. Purchasing computer equipment and software was by far the major expense involved, ranging from a low of $2,540 for a mailing-list service to $10,000 and up for desktop video service. Part II will provide more detail about the optimal home/office equipment, but in calculating your start-up costs, plan to include funds to acquire at least the following list of what we consider to be the minimum equipment you will need:

- **Office furniture**
- **Computer hardware and software**
- **Printer, fax, scanner, copier, answering machine or voice mail**
- **Business cards, stationery, brochures, other collateral materials, and supplies**
- **Other: separate business phone line, organizational dues, and special requirements of a particular business**

A minimum setup with items purchased new will cost about $2,500 to $3,000, depending on the quality and power of the hardware you buy and the fanciness of the stationery and supplies you choose. Of course, if you already have the equipment you need, you will most likely have only minimal start-up costs over and above the costs of supporting yourself until you get enough business coming in. Use the following chart to estimate your start-up costs. Add more money if you know or think you will need any of the other equipment on the list below. Also, add in an account for cash you will need to cover initial operating expenses until you receive your first income.

Calculating Start-up Costs

Estimate how much you will need to spend on each item for the three levels of income you project:

	Survival	Comfortable	Ideal
Auto expenses	_____	_____	_____
Business cards, letterheads, envelopes, etc.	_____	_____	_____
Business licenses and other fees	_____	_____	_____
Consulting and training fees (legal, tax, computer tutor, etc.)	_____	_____	_____
Initial marketing costs of brochures, Web site, etc.	_____	_____	_____
Miscellaneous office equipment	_____	_____	_____
Answering machine or voice mail	_____	_____	_____
Computer and monitor	_____	_____	_____
Printer	_____	_____	_____
Fax technology	_____	_____	_____
Modem technology	_____	_____	_____
Scanner	_____	_____	_____
Copier	_____	_____	_____
Other specialized equipment	_____	_____	_____
Office furnishings (desk, chair, storage, etc.)	_____	_____	_____
Remodeling of home (if needed)	_____	_____	_____
Software: General	_____	_____	_____
Specialized	_____	_____	_____

Telephone installation	_____	_____	_____
Other start-up expenses specific to your business	_____	_____	_____
	_____	_____	_____
Total Start-up Costs	$_____	$_____	$_____

18. How will you finance the start-up costs involved to adequately set up, equip, supply, and market your business?

While increasing numbers of banks are now offering loans to home-based businesses, usually you will need to have been in operation for several years before you can qualify for such loans. But, in actuality, you will probably not need such a loan to get started. Whereas Jeffrey Seglin, author of *Financing Your Small Business,* claims few traditional small businesses are able to finance their business start-ups themselves, this is not true of full- and part-time home businesses. Because start-up costs are usually so low, most people self-finance, or "bootstrap," their ventures themselves, using personal income, savings, or profits in order to get under way. When necessary, they turn to a variety of less conventional means to cover start-up costs.

Here are several of the more commonly used sources of start-up funds.

SOURCES OF START-UP FUNDS	
Earnings from job	Savings
Credit cards	Life insurance policies
Cash settlements	A line of credit through a home equity loan
Inheritances	Loans from relatives or friends
Retirement funds	Loans from suppliers or colleagues
Credit unions	Microloan programs

A basic adage of making money on your own is that first you must support your business; then it will support you. Starting a business, no matter how small, is like raising a child; you have to invest in it before it can stand on its own. (Fortunately most businesses become self-sufficient much more quickly than the average child does!) But do plan to invest in your business at first. Do it in a way that won't set you back financially. Here are several rules of thumb for financing your start-up costs safely:

1. Be prepared to start and grow your business from funds you have on hand, from your existing income, credit, contacts, or the initial business you generate. If your funds are limited, begin with your "survival" level projections and expand as your business expands.

If you are employed, one way you can finance a sideline business is to reduce the amount of your salary withheld for federal income tax purposes and use the extra income you take home in each paycheck to finance your business startup. As long as you spend this extra money on tax-deductible business expenses, you do not risk owing additional taxes by reducing your withholding. Check with an experienced tax professional or accountant as to how you can best take advantage of the tax benefits that open up to you when you start a business.

2. If you must borrow, borrow the smallest amounts possible (from $100 to $5,000) to finance one-time purchases that will pay for themselves or that can be paid for from work already in progress. Unless you have a considerable amount of work already under contract when you start, or you are someone who performs best under financial pressure, you don't want to burden yourself with the added overhead of having to make large loan payments. Borrow only an amount that you can project specifically how you will be able to repay within a year or less.

Your best source of loans is from relatives, friends, colleagues, or suppliers who are impressed by your character, capabilities, and business prospects and who will benefit either personally or professionally from your success.

In many parts of the country, you may be able to qualify for a microloan program. These programs provide small loans (usually from $100 to $5,000) to low- or moderate-income individuals or to people living in distressed areas. To locate such programs in your area, you can call the Small Business Administration or Small Business Development Center nearest you. A list of microloan programs is also available in Library 2 of the Working from Home Forum on CompuServe.

3. Borrow little or no money to cover your living or operating expenses. Instead make sure you have an entry plan like those described under Question 16 to cover as much of these costs as possible.

Admittedly, the drawback of such a "bootstrap" strategy is that your growth will be limited by the business you generate. But we believe this is a far safer and more reliable way to proceed. In fact, we've seen too many cases where having a lot of money for starting a computer-based venture actually was more of a drawback than an asset. In such cases, people overspent their once ample funds on unnecessary equipment, untested ideas, or marketing methods and lost it all.

By "bootstrapping" your business, however, your growth will be limited only by your results. And, of course, if you suddenly find yourself with signed purchase orders or contracts in hand for more work than you have the cash to produce, then it's time to consider a loan strategy, such as those outlined in *Guerrilla Financing,* by Bruce Bleckman and Jay Conrad Levinson (Boston: Houghton Mifflin, 1991).

19. Do you have a good credit rating?

Clear up your credit if possible before going out on your own. Here's why. Since you will have some start-up costs and direct expenses before you have any money coming in, you may want to delay payment for these cash outlays for thirty days or more. One way to do this is to pay for such expenses by credit card. But, of course, you can't get a credit card unless you have a reasonably good credit rating. Also, vendors will sometimes bill or even finance your purchases, but only if they can determine you have a good credit rating. Otherwise, you'll have to pay cash up front for services or materials.

Sometimes a good credit rating can also help you get business. Depending on the business you've selected, some clients will check into your credit rating before hiring you for a major project.

Don't assume, however, that you're out in the cold if your credit record is less than perfect. You can begin now to repair it. For example, *Vitality* magazine reported that to gain a share of the market, some credit card companies are overlooking the minor credit problems of applicants. They are making credit cards available at favorable rates even to people with slightly blemished credit reports. Getting such a card and using it wisely is a good way to start rebuilding a good credit history.

Another route to building your credit rating is to obtain a secured credit card, which allows you to borrow a minimum amount secured by funds in your savings account. After you use and pay off purchases over a period of time, you may then be able to obtain a regular credit card.

20. Do you have two credit cards: one for business, one for personal expenses?

It seems that most Americans are living beyond their incomes. The U.S. population has run up credit card debt nearing $400 billion. By the year 2000, it is estimated to reach nearly two-thirds of a trillion dollars. In terms of total consumer installment debt, including auto and revolving credit loans, a trillion dollars' indebtedness was passed in 1995.

For small and home-based businesses, however, credit cards can be among one of the only sources of ongoing credit. Therefore we encourage home-based business owners to have and use at least one business credit card to help finance marketing and other costs of business expansion. So if you don't have a credit card, get one. In fact, get two—one that you designate for personal expenses and one for business expenses. A business credit card will allow you to finance initial costs like printing, supplies, equipment, etc. The card you designate for personal use can help you handle unexpected costs you didn't include in your salary projections like having to pay for a costly and unexpected auto repair, a dental emergency, or a roof that springs a leak.

Unlike interest paid on personal expenses charged to a credit card, the interest on business expenses is deductible, but since interest on credit cards is high, make sure you don't end up draining your chances for success by having to pay off large credit card balances month after month. Here are several guidelines for keeping credit card costs down.

KEEPING CREDIT CARD COSTS DOWN

1. **The best credit card policy is to pay off your balance each month.** The most cost-effective use of your cards is to use them to help your cash flow, so you can "delay" payment until you have collected for work you have in progress. Of course, you may not always get the expenses you bill out for paid within thirty days, so here are several additional ideas.

2. **Resist the temptation to run up your credit card balance** with desirable, but unnecessary, charges. Use your business card to finance purchases that you know realistically will pay for themselves (hopefully within six to twelve months) in increased productivity or additional business. This is not an unreasonable goal for many computer-based service businesses when you consider that sometimes just one client will more than pay for the scanner that enabled you to produce the Web site that got you the client in the first place.

---

21. How committed are you to proceeding with your venture?

Now that you've had a chance to ponder your business opportunities, think about how and where you might sell your service or product, and examine the financial side of getting your computer-based business under way, are you still committed to doing it? Indicate on a scale of 0 to 10 how important it is to you to proceed with your plans.

3. Get the best rates. Shop around for the best credit card interest rates. For $5, you can get a list of 500 low-interest rate and/or no-fee credit card issuers. Write Ram Research's CardTrack, Box 1700, Frederick, MD 21702. Related to this, watch out for credit card deals that make you take a cash advance when you get the credit card. Sometimes the rate on the credit card is low, but the rate on the cash advance is much higher, and you will be forced to pay it immediately since you accepted the cash advance. Also, watch out for low introductory interest rates that change to much higher rates six months or one year later.

4. Make sure finance charges on your card are calculated by the ADB (Average Daily Balance). Low credit card rates won't save you much money if the issuer uses the "two-cycle method" to calculate your interest payment. Most issuers compute their financial charges based on the ADB in the prior month. But some issuers are charging interest based on your average balance over the last two months, so if you pay only the minimum balance each month you could end up paying twice on the same charge. Card issuers must disclose their computation method on applications, card-holder agreements, and monthly statements. So check out your existing cards and any future ones you consider and change cards if need be.

5. Pay more than the minimum balance whenever possible. Minimum balance payments cost you the most. For example, if you charge $500 on your card and pay only the minimum each month, at 18 percent interest, the item will actually cost you almost $800 and take six years to pay off. If you pay $50 a month, you'll save almost $250 in interest and be debt-free in only eleven months!

_____ 0 It's better than nothing, but I can take it or leave it.
_____ 3 I need money, but I'd really rather make it on a job, or at least a better-paying one.
_____ 5 I'd like to give it a try; it sounds like a good idea.
_____ 8 I've been wanting to do this for a long time, or I realize I'm ready for this; it's the next step for me.
_____10 I want to do this more than anything else right now.

Your chances of success go up the closer you are to 10. Being highly motivated is the number-one most important variable we've found in those who are able to make money on their own. It's more important than how much money you have to invest in your business; how much experience you've had, even how good you are at what you do. Those who are truly motivated learn what they need to learn, do what they need to do, and persist until they do it.

So if you score 0 to 3, we'd advise that you skip the idea of making money with your computer at this time until it becomes a higher priority.

If you scored 3 to 6 on this scale, we would suggest that you consider starting a part-time venture, almost as if it were a hobby, so you can determine if you like it sufficiently to invest the time, money, and energy involved to become successful.

If you score a 7 or above, you are probably sufficiently motivated to proceed with a full-time venture.

22. Do you have a separate area in your home where you can work productively?

Fortunately most computer-related businesses can be operated just as easily from home as from anywhere. However, we recommend, if at all possible, having a separate area in which to set up your home office. In addition to the considerable savings on overhead it affords you, setting up and operating from a home office offers you a variety of tax benefits. If you set up your home office to meet Internal Revenue Service qualifications, you can take the home-office deduction that entitles you to deduct part of your rent, your mortgage, and other household costs in proportion to the percentage of your home you use for business purposes.

POSSIBLE DEDUCTIBLE HOME OFFICE EXPENSES

- Cleaning a home office
- Depreciation on home (partial)
- Household furniture converted to use in the home office
- Household supplies used in business space
- Interest on mortgage (partial)
- Real estate taxes (partial)
- Rent paid if you rent or lease (partial)
- Repair and maintenance of office portion of home
- Telephone, except the base local service for the first line into your home
- Trash collection
- Utilities attributable to business use of home (electricity, gas, water)

Reprinted from *Working from Home* by Paul and Sarah Edwards (Jeremy P. Tarcher, 1994)

To qualify for these valuable deductions, your home office must be used exclusively, on a regular basis as your principle place of business.

The space you use for your home office need not be a separate room. It can be a portion of a room such as your bedroom, but the portion of that room that you designate for your business must be used only for business. So if you don't have a separate room, we suggest that you clearly demark the portion of the room you use for work space with a divider, screen drape, or furniture arrangement. This is not only useful for tax purposes; it also will help you get to work, stick to business, and keep you from feeling as if you don't have a private life.

Our book *Working from Home* includes additional information on how to claim home business tax deductions.

23. Do you have the support of your family and friends?

Making money on your own, whether you'll be doing it full- or part-time, will be much easier if you have the support of family and friends. Family and loved ones need to be aware and supportive of the changes that starting your business venture will make in all of your lives.

For example, if you plan to earn money part-time as a sideline to your job, those in your life will need to adjust to the fact that you won't be available for personal activities at certain times during evenings or weekends. If you'll be working on your own full-time, you may have to put in longer hours initially than you had been in a previous job. And your income may dip at first while you get your business under way. Once you are working from home, those you live with may also have to adapt to having business calls or even clients and customers coming into your home.

So alert your family and loved ones to all the changes you expect and to the fact that there may be other changes you can't predict. Then make sure you take into account in your plans their concerns and reactions to these changes.

24. Have you checked the zoning regulations in your neighborhood to see if you can legally operate a moneymaking venture from your home?

Every local community has its own ordinances governing what kind of commercial activity can and cannot be done in residential neighborhoods. Unfortunately, some local zoning ordinances still have not been updated since the industrial era, when communities wanted to protect residential neighborhoods from the noise, pollution, danger, and congestion of factories and storefronts. Therefore, you need to find out exactly what you can and cannot do from your home and make your plans accordingly. To check your zoning situation, contact the zoning department at your city hall or county courthouse.

If zoning prohibits you from working from home, you can usually rent a postal address or use an executive suite as an official address while doing your actual work quietly at home.

25. Will your neighbors have any objection to your doing the type of work you plan to do from your home?

Neighbor complaints can cause zoning problems. Therefore, you want to make sure that whatever you do from home in no way interferes with the residential nature of your neighborhood. Fortunately, most computer-related businesses can be virtually invisible, but it's nonetheless important to consider and respect neighbors' rights and concerns.

The kinds of things that tend to bother neighbors include noisy equipment, parking problems caused by too many people coming to your home office, inventory filling your garage, leaving your cars parked on the street overnight, deliveries, or people coming to your home early in the morning, and large amounts of mail clogging communal mailbox areas. Condo or homeowners' associations may also have rules limiting work from home. So check these as well as your zoning.

Ironically, neighbors and people in condo associations that limit work from home may be unaware of the many advantages and the few drawbacks of having people on the premises who do work from home. They may be unaware, for example, that crime goes down in areas where people work from home. They may not have considered that when tenants work from home, there's someone to respond to emergencies like broken pipes, fires, or flooding. These benefits are especially important now that both men and women in most households often work outside the home. So if limitations exist where you live, take steps in concert with others who are already working quietly at home to have the regulations changed to prohibit only those activities that actually interfere with the residential character of the complex.

26. Does what you intend to do require any special state license?

Licensing regulations vary significantly from state to state, and some states license certain computer-related businesses like financial planning, business brokering, skip searching, and tax preparation. Call your state telephone information line to find out which state agency you should contact to ascertain any such licensing requirements in your locale.

27. Have you obtained a local business license?

Most communities require a business license to operate any income-earning enterprise of any size. Going to the trouble to take out a business license says that you take your business seriously. It makes a statement that you want to make your venture official. It reflects a desire to pay attention to details, to dot the *i*'s and cross the *t*'s, to do the homework that will not only get the business off to a good start but also be reflected in other aspects of how you run the business. So make it official. Get your business license.

28. Will you be required to charge sales tax on what you offer? If so, you will need to obtain a sales permit and find out how to pay the tax.

If you are selling a product like software, a shopper's guide, or computer novelties, you will need to collect sales tax on the sales you make to the end user. However, if you sell these same items to a wholesaler or retailer who will in turn sell them to the end user, you do not need to charge sales tax. Instead, you will need to make sure that your buyer has what is variously called, a "seller's permit," "certificate of authority," or "resale certificate" from the state. Keep verification of this on file with their account.

Although most computer service–related businesses do not require that you charge sales tax, some services are taxable. Again, this varies by state, but some services that may require a sales tax include graphic designs and some elements of word processing, desktop publishing, and customized software. Contact the agency in your state that handles sales taxes to determine if any aspects of your service are taxable. If you are troubled by the response you get, consult an attorney.

29. Will you sell your product or service yourself or will you sell it through someone else?

Traditionally there are three avenues for selling products or services: direct sales, wholesalers or brokers, and retailers. To that we've added a fourth: indirect sales. The best route for selling your products or services will depend on a variety of factors such as the nature of your business, your personality, your contacts, the needs of your clients and customers, and the community in which you live. Some businesses sell through multiple channels. Here are some ideas for utilizing each route.

Four Choices for How to Sell Your Products or Services: How to Make the Most of Each

1. Direct Sales

Direct selling involves you or your representative contacting prospective customers or clients directly. It includes "cold calling" by phone or in person as well as other methods of reaching those you serve directly such as networking, advertising, selling by seminar, or using direct mail.

For our book *Getting Business to Come to You,* we surveyed home-based businesses to determine what they find to be the most effective marketing methods. We found direct solicitation to be the fastest, although most personally time-consuming, way to get business. To make the most of direct sales:

Find out as much as you can about the needs and problems of your clients so your sales calls, presentations, ads, and mail pieces can speak "their language."

Warm up your cold calls or direct mail by using public relations to increase your visibility. If prospective clients recognize your name, they'll be more likely to take your calls and keep your direct-mail pieces. Design and maintain a Web site that not only promotes your business but also offers information that's valuable to your customer base and industry. Become an active participant in online forums and Internet newsgroups that are relevant to your customers. Speak at trade and professional conferences in your field. Write a column for the professional and trade publications. Have your own newsletter that educates prospective clients about how you can help them.

!!!! RECOMMENDATION !!!!

You might consider using local television or radio advertising to build your visibility so people will recognize you or your company name when you call or send out a sales letter. You may also consider producing your own cable access show. Cable access gives a low-cost (sometimes free!) access to broadcast-quality video production resources as well as an outlet for your visibility. Access shows are not allowed to be outright commercials, or infomercials, for your business, but, if your enterprise revolves around providing a service, you can frame this information in the form of a how-to show that people can actually learn from. For example, Steve Grody is a martial arts instructor in Los Angeles. To augment his business he not only sells instruction videos through the mail and over the Internet but also produces a self-defense cable access show. To find out more about cable access in your area, simply ask for the Access Department of your local cable provider.

Whether writing or talking about what you do, don't focus on your background, training, or the features of your product or service. Talk about how what you do solves the problems or avoids the disasters your clients and customers know about only too well. Give examples of how you've actually helped those you serve solve problems or achieve goals.

For example, don't say something like "I'm a business plan writer. I worked for ten years in the loan department of Savings Bank where I was a loan officer and ultimately headed up the department. Now I'm helping small businesses write viable business plans." This information may be factual and even impressive, but you want to sell—not just inform or impress. You'll get a much better response if you say something like this: "You know how difficult it is for a small business to get bank loans, especially now with the economy being so tight? Well, I've been a loan officer for many years, and I know what bankers are looking for—what turns them on and what turns them off. I can show a small business how to develop a business plan that will get past a banker's resistance so you'll get the capital you need."

To learn how to talk and write about your business in these terms, we recommend an audiotape program called *Compelling Brief Descriptions,* by Ron Richards, ResultsLab, 2175 Green St., San Francisco, CA 94123, (415) 563-5300, E-mail: ronr@resultslab.com.

!!!! RECOMMENDATION !!!!

Create a portfolio of samples or letters of recommendation from people you've worked with. You can use samples or recommendations of your work from past employers, but do not use a résumé. Simply refer to the individuals or company you worked for by their title, position, or company. If you're going into a new field, get endorsement letters quickly by working on a volunteer basis for professional, trade, or civic organizations.

2. Wholesalers or Brokers

Wholesalers or brokers are like middlemen (or -women) who represent your products and services. Traditionally, *wholesaler* refers to someone who would purchase a product from you at a discount and sell it to retailers. The concept of wholesaling, however, is now applicable to selling services as well as products. Many self-employed individuals are able to sell their services through brokers, referral services, registries, agents, or bureaus—who are, in essence, wholesalers. Such representatives are also "middlemen" between you and your clients. They market your services and mark up your price to provide their fee.

Using wholesalers or brokers of some kind can be a good idea for several reasons. First, using a wholesaler frees you from selling so you can spend your time actually delivering your product or service or developing new marketable skills. Also, wholesalers are ideal when you are homebound or don't have the personality to sell. Finally using a wholesaler or broker takes advantage of what we call using OPE—Other People's Energy!

Here are three tips for increasing your chances for selling through wholesalers or brokers:

Demonstrate a demand. Wholesalers or brokers are usually interested in products and services that already have a track record of success and a high demand, so to get a good wholesaler you will need to demonstrate that people do or will buy what you offer.

Develop a line of products or services. Wholesalers also often prefer representing a line of products, not just one. So consider developing a range or variety of products or services you can offer, i.e., consulting services, books, audiotapes.

Build a partnership. Make sure the wholesaler or broker you select believes in and will take a personal interest in your product or service. Remember: out of sight, out of mind. Develop a personal relationship with your wholesaler or broker and keep in regular contact with him or her. Also, don't leave everything to them. Use public relations to build your visibility so when the wholesaler or broker mentions you and what you offer, buyers will have heard about it, or better yet, will have had people asking for it.

3. Retail Sales

Placing your products or your materials in the right retail stores is one way to make sure the people who need what you offer will find it. Here are several tips even service businesses can use to make sales through retailers:

Make tie-ins with retailers. Don't overlook working with retailers just because you have a service business. Think of where your clients and customers shop. For example, a desktop publisher might tie in with a print shop. An organizer could affiliate with an office supply store, a Web site designer with an established design studio, or a computer repair service with a computer store.

Be willing to pay for such retailer arrangements. You can arrange to pay referral fees or you can let the customer pay the retailer directly and then pay you a percentage. Be sure, though, to set your "wholesale" fees high enough to cover your costs and still have a profit.

Don't undercut your retailers. If you want to develop good relationships with retailers, the ultimate customers should not be able to buy directly from you for a better price. For example, if you have a computer repair service, you should establish one fee for your services, not one fee if the customer goes through the computer store and a lower fee if they contact you directly.

4. Indirect Sales

Some of the most effective selling strategies for home-based businesses are indirect routes to putting OPE to work for you. Here are a few examples:

Develop a program to build referrals from existing clients. Referrals usually don't happen automatically. Let clients and customers know that their referrals are important to you and have a method through which they can make them. For example, you might give your client gift certificates for a free initial consultation they can give away to friends or associates or you might give them discount coupons to use or give away.

Make reciprocal referral arrangements with your competition. Let them know you will do overload work for them and send your overload their way. Offer to work with customers who have specialized needs. If appropriate, offer to pay them a referral fee.

Identify and build relationships with gatekeepers. As we indicated above, gatekeepers are those people who have ready access to your potential customers. A convention bureau is a gatekeeper for an event planner, for example. An event planner is a gatekeeper for a reunion planner. A commercial real estate agent is a gatekeeper for any number of business services because he or she knows about new businesses that will be opening soon. You can make reciprocal referral agreements with such gatekeepers and/or arrange to pay referral fees. See *Teaming Up,* our book with Rick Benzel, for the details of how to create these and other useful strategic alliances.

30. Under which form of business do you wish to operate?

_____ Sole proprietorship: a business owned and operated by one person

_____ Partnership: when two or more individuals operate a business as joint owners

_____ Limited liability company: the newest kind of business entity offering tax advantages and limited liability.

_____ Corporation (for profit or nonprofit): an association of individuals who form a legal entity which is independent of the individual members.

PROS AND CONS OF DIFFERENT FORMS OF BUSINESS

	Pros	Cons
Sole proprietorship	Easy to set up	Limited to owner's lifetime
	Costs little to start	Getting loans more difficult
	Few legal restrictions	All responsibility and risk
	Owner keeps all profits	resides with owner
		Not considered as prestigious
Partnership	Pooling of talent, time, and energy	Liability for partner's actions
	Sharing of expenses	Disagreements between
	Few legal regulations	owners common
	Easy to set up	Finding good partners
	Raising capital easier	difficult
Limited liability company	Limits liability	Most states require more than one person
	Less paperwork than for a corporation	Expense in forming and filing
	Taxed like a partnership	Annual informational tax returns

		Breakups common
Corporation	Creates stable impression	Much more expensive to start and operate
	May limit liability	Many regulations to meet
	Easier to sell	Can raise insurance costs
	Raising capital easier	Extensive recordkeeping
	Business survives owners	May be double taxed in some states

!!!! **RECOMMENDATION** !!!!

Unless you will be forming a partnership, starting a business that has a high risk of liability that you can be sued for, or one that you are developing in order to eventually sell, we recommend that people who want to start making money with their computer begin as a sole proprietorship in order to keep costs and technicalities to a minimum. If you are starting a partnership with anyone other than a spouse, however, we recommend that you incorporate, form a limited liability company, or have a lawyer draw up a partnership agreement. You might also look into a number of software products like Nolo's Partnership Maker available from Nolo Press that contain templates for partnerships in any state, as well as incorporation documents for California and New York. You can contact Nolo at 950 Parker Street, Berkeley, CA 94710, (510) 549-1976, or on the Web at *http://www*.nolo.com

31. Have you selected a name for your enterprise?

The name you select for your business activity can be one of your most important marketing decisions. The right name will get you business; the wrong name will cost you business. The right name, for example, will attract attention to you in the yellow pages. The right name can be enough to make sure someone keeps your card. The right name helps people remember you even when they didn't get or keep your card.

Here are four rules of thumb for selecting a name that will mean business:

Only use your own name as a business name if you are so well known in your field that your name will be immediately recognized and respected

(or if you are willing to spend the time and money it will take to make your name readily recognizable). Then make sure to use a tag line on your materials that tells what you do; e.g., "Rick Baily, Network Installation."

Make sure the name you select is easy to pronounce, understand, spell, and remember. Strange or unusual names may be interesting or clever, but if people can't pronounce them, understand them, spell them, or remember them, you'll miss business that otherwise could be yours.

Avoid names that don't convey what you do. Unless you plan to become or appear to be a large conglomerate like ITT or Textron, the more precisely your name relates to your service, the more of an asset your name will be.

Include a benefit in your name. If your name not only tells what you do but what's special about the way you do it, it becomes a mini-advertisement, reminding everyone who sees or hears it just how wise they would be to use your products or services.

!!!! **A L E R T** !!!!

If you plan to use a name other than your own, you will need to register and protect your business name.

Here are several examples of winning names we've seen recently:

THE FINANCIAL SOFTWARE COMPANY is Michael Cahlin's home-based business that produces a financial software package called *Finance 10.*

DR. DIGIT, operated by Randy Benham, offers services from simple bookkeeping to complex financial analysis, including computer upgrades with software support.

SHARP INFORMATION is an information research service operated by Seena Sharp of Los Angeles.

REEL 3-D is a mail-order business run by David Starkman and Susan Pinsky specializing in 3-D photography.

COMPLETE BILLING SERVICES is a billing service and more operated from home by Barry Schrock of Edgewater, Florida. When Schrock opened his billing service, he chose to name it Complete Billing Services for two reasons. First, it conveys two benefits: thoroughness and accuracy. Second, it piques people's curiosity about what "complete" billing is and allows him to explain the other related services he offers like mailing-list management.

CHECKING WHETHER A BUSINESS NAME IS AVAILABLE TO USE

To find out whether someone else is already using the name you are considering:

1. Check the yellow pages; call information for recent listings.

2. Do a search on the Internet to see if the name has already been registered as a "domain" name. (A domain name is the name that comes right after the "*http://www.*" part of a URL.) Use Inter-NIC (http://rs.internic.net) or one the many other domain name search engines available.

3. Contact your county courthouse for fictitious name registrations, also referred to as "DBAs"—"doing business as."

4. Write to the state office that handles corporate names, usually the secretary of state, to determine whether someone has reserved or taken the name for corporate use.

5. Search a computer database of company names, such as those discussed in chapter 6, compiled from all the nation's telephone directories.

6. Conduct a trademark search. A trademarks and patents attorney will advise you if your name can be registered and will conduct a trademark search for about two hundred dollars. An attorney checks for legally similar names and exact duplicates at the federal level in all fifty states. You can also do your own searches electronically (see chapter 6).

---

32. Have you opened a separate bank account and installed a separate business phone line?

For tax purposes and for financial planning, it's useful to have a separate bank account for your business, into which you deposit all the business income and from which you pay all your business expenses, including your salary. A separate business bank account is important even if your business is only part-time. For one thing, with a separate business account, if your business should be audited by the IRS, the audit won't necessarily need to involve your personal tax return.

In order to open a business bank account if you are using a name other than your own, your bank will usually need a copy of your fictitious name registration (commonly referred to as your DBA, "Doing Business As"), which you can arrange for through most small community newspapers.

A separate telephone line for your business is also important. First, a business line will enable you to have a yellow-page listing for your business. Enough people shopping for a computer-related service business look in the yellow pages that you don't want to cut yourself out of a possible source of business. Second, a business listing will make it possible for potential clients and customers to find you when they call information to get your telephone number. Third, a separate business line helps you manage your business from home more effectively. For example, with a separate line you can make sure you answer your business line with an appropriate business greeting. You can also put an answering machine or voice mail on the line you don't want to answer during particular hours of the day or night. And a separate line will help avoid phone conflicts and misunderstandings with others living in your household. Some local telephone operating companies have a special home business telephone service rate that costs somewhat more than a residential line, but less than a standard business line. Most phone companies are at least considering such a program, so ask for this service.

If you will be doing a lot of work by fax or modem, you may want a to have a third line installed. We will be describing other ideas for managing your phone communications in Part II.

33. Do you have the office equipment and supplies you need to work most productively?

Fortunately, prices for home-office equipment are coming down so substantially that by shopping carefully you can equip yourself with the equivalent of a *Fortune* 500 office, including a state-of-the-art computer with a fax/modem board, a large monitor, a laser printer, and a CD-ROM drive for under $3,000. And, as you will discover in Part II of this book, such cost-effective equipment and supplies can help you run your business more profitably.

Even if you don't have the money to buy it all right away, you need not despair. Most people begin by buying the most essential items and add to their office as their income increases. If you use the ideas presented in Part II, you'll find, however, that this equipment will pay for itself in increased productivity and added business.

34. Have you established a work schedule for yourself?

During what hours of the day and week do you plan to work? Customers, suppliers, clients, and family members need to know your hours, and you need to have at least a general work schedule in mind to make sure you don't inadvertently slack off or overwork.

!!!! **ALERT** !!!!

Eight hours a week is the minimum investment for a sideline venture. Sixty-one hours a week is the average for a full-time business (about the same number of hours a corporate executive puts in).

For those working part-time:

We advise against planning to do everything involving your sideline business on the weekends. Invariably, personal and family activities will arise to thwart such plans.

For those working full-time:

Make sure you don't schedule clients strictly at their convenience or you could find yourself working morning, noon, and night.

A rule of thumb for establishing your work schedule is to set up your week so that you will have either the morning, afternoon, or evening free.

35. If you have young children, have you made arrangements for needed supplementary child care?

Sometimes parents overestimate how much productive work they will be able to get done with young children at home. Although some men and women can work with toddlers playing underfoot, many parents simply can't concentrate sufficiently to complete certain tasks. Therefore, if you have children under six, we recommend that you arrange an alternate source of child care for those times of day or night when you need to work without interruption.

By working from home, you will have many more options for child care and much greater flexibility than when you are away at an office. In our book *Working from Home,* we outline seven child-care options to consider along with guidance for what level of supervision is required while working from home for children of various ages.

36. Have you lined up a team of professionals to whom you can turn for help if you need it?

Establish a relationship with the following professionals whom you can call upon when you need them:

___ Accountant or tax advisor, to help make sure you can qualify for and take all tax deductions to which you are entitled and to help you avoid or resolve any tax problems

___ Computer consultant, to help you install and get up and running with new equipment and software

___ Information researcher, to track down key information when you need it

___ Insurance agent, to assist you in finding the best insurance coverage at the lowest cost

___ Investment counselor, to help you make the most of the money you make

___ Lawyer, to advise you on legal matters such as contracts and collections

___ Marketing consultant, to help you make advertising and other marketing decisions that will result in the maximum amount of business for the lowest possible price

___ Professional organizer, to assist you in setting up your office so you will have a functional place for everything and will be able to find it when you need it

___ Public relations specialist, to assist you in achieving high visibility for yourself and your business

37. Do you have a support network of professional colleagues and friends?

Ninety-six percent of people who go out on their own to work from home are glad they did and say they would do it again. But there is one thing missing from most home offices, and that's other people—colleagues, mentors, co-workers, business associates, and peers. To keep from feeling isolated and to make sure you keep abreast of current developments, you'll need to take the initiative to make sure you have ample contact with colleagues, peers, and mentors. You'll need to duplicate the following types of social interaction that usually happen automatically when you're employed by an organization:

- the ability to brainstorm ideas with a colleague
- the chance to commiserate with a fellow worker who knows what you're up against
- the occasion to celebrate a victory with someone who can appreciate what you've accomplished
- access to a grapevine that will keep you abreast of the latest developments and inside scoop in your field or industry
- the ability to turn to a mentor who can show you the ropes, introduce you to the right people, cheer you on, and guide you to success

To meet these needs, we recommend joining or creating, and then participating actively in, one or more of the following four types of groups:

Trade and professional associations. You can join a professional association in your own field and/or the field to which you are marketing your product or services. Such associations are invaluable routes for meeting colleagues and peers, gatekeepers and mentors, keeping abreast of the latest developments and needs of the field, and building your reputation. Should you be one of the many people who are moving to less populated states or communities and find that there is no chapter in your area, consider establishing a chapter. Names and addresses of such associations are included whenever possible for the computer-based businesses we list in chapter 1 of this book. We also suggest getting involved in the online communities found in professional forums, newsgroups, listservs, and discussion groups found on the Internet and through online services like CompuServe and America Online.

Civic, business, and community organizations. If you are serving a local clientele, becoming active in civic and community organizations such as the chamber of commerce can become a valuable route for meeting potential clients, gatekeepers, and mentors, and for building business relationships. An increasing number of communities have home-based business associations. These groups are another route for self-employed individuals to meet peers, get referrals, and support one another. An up-to-date list of home business associations is available on the Working from Home Forum on CompuServe Information Service.

Referral networks. Today most communities have one or more networking organizations, the sole purpose of which is for members to refer business to one another. Such groups customarily meet for breakfast once a week and, to prevent competition, only one person from a given type of business can join. In this way, members become gatekeepers for one another.

NATIONAL NETWORKING ORGANIZATIONS

Business Network International
199 S. Monte Vista Avenue, Ste. 6
San Diego, CA 91713
(800) 825-8286 (outside
    Southern Calif.)
(909) 305-1818 (inside
    Southern Calif.)
http://www.bni.com

Leads Clubs
P.O. Box 279
Carslbad, CA 92018

(800) 783-3761 or (619) 434-
    3761
Fax: (619) 729-7797
E-mail: leadsclb@ix.netcom.com
http://leadsclub.com

LeTip, International
4901 Marina Blvd., Ste. 703
San Diego, CA 92117
(800) 255-3847
http://www.letip.org

WOMEN'S BUSINESS

Business and Professional
    Women/USA
2012 Massachusetts Ave NW
Washington, DC 20036
(202) 293-1100
http://www. bpwusa.org

Federation of Organizations
    for Professional Women
1825 'I' Street, N.W., Ste. 400
Washington, DC 20006
(202) 328-1415
Fax: (202) 429-9574

National Association for
    Female Executives
(800) 927-6233
http://www.nafe.com

National Association of
    Women Business Owners
1100 Wayne Avenue
Ste. 830
Silver Spring, MD 20910
(301) 608-2590
Fax: (301) 608-2596
http://www.nawbo.org/

Call or write to find out about the chapter nearest you of any of these organizations or for information on starting a new chapter.

One key to benefiting from such a referral network is to make sure the one you join has members who would come in frequent contact with your potential clients and customers. Another key is to be sure to give ample referrals yourself to people in your group. Your referrals to them will engender goodwill, and so they will want to return you the favor.

Peer mentoring groups. A peer mentoring group is a group of two to four fellow self-employed peers, colleagues, and associates who get together on a regular basis to support, advise, guide, and cheer one another on. Support groups like this often form spontaneously and are highly informal.

Mentor groups go one step beyond the valuable interaction you can get from attending monthly professional and business association meetings. They become a very personal group of supporters who share their goals and dreams with one another, meet often, and call one another spontaneously when they need someone to talk with. Such groups are highly committed to helping one another succeed and will go out of their way to assist one another in whatever ways they can through the ups and downs of being self-employed.

Because such groups are informal, you usually have to form your own group. However, many micro-loan programs throughout the country create such groups as part of the lending program. Also some home-business associations may have programs to help members form mentor groups, and we've developed a program to help people form local or online peer mentor groups through the Working from Home Forum on CompuServe Information Service. To obtain a copy of *A Guide to Peer Mentoring: Creating Your Own Support System,* send $5 to Here's How, P.O. Box 5091, Santa Monica, CA 90409.

We believe strongly:

Participating in professional, trade, civic, and business organizations can be an important source of support.

38. Are your cards and stationery designed and printed?

Your business cards and letterhead can serve as mini-billboards for your work. If they are done well, they will help you get business and be taken seriously. Therefore we suggest that you take the time and spend the money to create a professional overall graphic identity for your business and use this graphic image on all your printed materials.

You may be able to design and even print your cards, letterhead, and stationery yourself using software and equipment described in Part II of this book. If you do not have a keen design sense, however, or the right equipment, we suggest that you make the investment to use the services of fellow self-employed individuals who specialize in desktop publishing or graphic design. Once you have created your graphic image, you can use the same artwork to create invoices, mailing labels, proposal covers, Rolodex cards, postcards, etc., as your budget allows.

!!!! **ALERT** !!!!

To avoid the expense of having to reprint your materials prematurely, do not invest the several hundreds or even thousands of dollars that designing and printing high-quality letterhead and stationery can cost until you have settled on a business name that you know will work, as well as determined your permanent business address and installed your business telephone line or lines. You don't want to find yourself writing in by hand a new business phone number on your beautiful cards for which you spent several hundred dollars.

39. Do you have adequate insurance to protect your business property and liability?

When you set up your moneymaking venture in a home office, the cost of insuring your business from loss and liability should be minimal, or at least far less than setting yourself up in an outside office. Take the following chart (pp. 235–6) to your insurance agent and work out a cost-effective plan.

!!!! **ALERT** !!!!

Your homeowner's or renter's insurance usually will not cover business use of your home. But you can get usually get a rider added to your existing policy for a nominal fee to cover your business activities.

40. Have you made plans for obtaining health and disability insurance coverage if you are leaving behind employment benefits you had at a job?

Concern about how to get adequate health insurance for an affordable cost keeps many people from going out on their own full-time. Next to getting enough work, it is the major concern for self-employed individuals. We suffer more than most groups under our troubled health-care system. As many as one-third of the self-employed do not have health insurance.

The best health insurance option for many self-employed is to check out the group policies offered by local or state business, trade, or professional associations they can affiliate with. The following organizations are not insurance companies but do attempt to provide good-quality health insurance at affordable rates:

Co-op America
1612 K Street N.W., Ste. 600
Washington, DC 20006
(202) 872-5307

Small Business Service Bureau
    (operating in fourteen
    eastern states)
554 Main Street
P.O. Box 15014
Worcester, MA 01615
(800) 222-5678

Small Office and Home Office
    Association
1767 Business Center Drive
Reston, VA 20190
(703) 438-3060

Support Services Alliance
P.O. Box 130, Schoharie, NY
    12157
(518) 295-7966
http://www.ssainfo.com

Also consider taking a look at a health maintenance organization, such as the Kaiser and Pacificare plans if you are located in their areas of service. Pacificare has a hybrid plan that blends an HMO with fee-for-service and the resulting choices.

Before buying a policy, however, check it out thoroughly. Consumer Reports has done reader surveys of health insurance companies including HMOs. Because it is such a major concern, we are continually alert for workable solutions. In our book *Working from Home,* we provide further health insurance alternatives, along with what to look for in selecting a plan, how to check out if a company is reliable, and the merits of various health insurance plans for the self-employed.

Disability insurance protects you from loss of income when you are unable to work due to illness or injury. It's important if you are depending on your business as the sole source of your income and would have no other forms of income should illness or injury prevent you from carrying out your work for an extended period of time. Disability insurance premiums are based on age, income, and the condition of your body. Here are a few examples of the possible cost to you: If you are earning $35,000 a year and want to receive $2,000 a month in disability after ninety days, insurance costs could run something like $682 a year. If you are earning $100,000 a year and want to receive $5,000 a month, a disability policy might run something like $1,562 a year. Unfortunately, insurance companies are making disability insurance increasingly expensive and difficult for home-based self-employed individuals to get.

Discuss all these insurance needs with your agent.

HOME OFFICE INSURANCE WORK SHEET

Indicate below which types of insurance you think you Have Already (H); Don't Need (D); Should Get Now or in the Future (G). Use this Worksheet to review your insurance needs with your lawyer and/or insurance agent. (Prices are average estimates subject to many variables.)

Type of Insurance	Coverage	When Needed	Costs
_____ Liability Insurance	Covers costs of injuries occurring to business-related visitors while on your property	If you ever have delivery personnel, clients, or customers who come to your home.	$20/yr for $500,000 of coverage when added as a rider to homeowners policy.
_____ Business Property Insurance	Protects you from damage or loss to your business property.	If you have any equipment in your home/office that's used for business purposes.	$100/yr for $5,000–$7,000 of equipment.
_____ Small Business Insurance	Provides coverage for losses, or when you want an umbrella policy. It also covers general liability, business interruption and loss of earnings, errors and omission, and product liability, although these policies can be purchased separately as well.	When you have more extensive inventory or equipment than you can protect by adding a business endorsement or rider to your homeowners insurance.	$500 per year.
_____ General Liability Insurance	Covers damages from accidents occurring while you are on someone else's property	If you ever do some portion of your work on someone else's premises. (Included as part of Small Business Insurance.)	
_____ Business Interruption Insurance	Protects you against losses arising from not being able to do business due to damage from fire or another disaster.	If you would need to have income coming in should you not be able to do business due to these circumstances. (Included as part of Small Business Insurance.)	

Type of Insurance	Coverage	When Needed	Costs
_____ Special Computer Insurance	To cover risks related to your computer hardware, software, and data.	Applicable if computer-related losses can't be adequately covered under your property or small business insurance.	$90/yr for $5,000–$8,000; $110/yr for $8,000–$11,000; $130/yr for $11,000–$14,000.
_____ Malpractice, Errors & Omission, or Product Liability Insurance	To insure against claims or damages that arise out of the services or products you offer.	If the work you do could inadvertently inflict an injury or loss on your clients or customers.	Price varies by type of business.
_____ Worker's Compensation Insurance	Compensates you for costs of work-related injuries. Available primarily for employees.	State regulations vary. May be called State Disability Insurance.	Provides bare bones coverage for about $200/yr.
_____ Auto-Related Insurance	Covers loss of business property while in your car and costs of accidents arising while you or someone on your behalf is driving your car for business purposes.	If you use your car for business purposes other than driving to and from work. Especially if you transport equipment or merchandise in your car or have someone else driving the car for business purposes.	Could cost around $1600/yr.
_____ Partnership Insurance	Protects you against suits arising from the actions of any partners in your business when you have partners or do joint ventures.		

41. Have you written down specific measurable goals for your business with a target date and action plan for each goal?

Research sponsored several years ago by the Ford Foundation shows that people who write down specific goals are considerably more likely to achieve them. We believe this is particularly true when you are working from home in a business of your own. Use the following form to articulate your goals.

GOALS WORK SHEET

What is motivating you to make money on your own? Check all that apply:

_____ A better lifestyle

_____ Additional income

_____ Pay for my equipment

_____ Being home with children

_____ Be my own boss

_____ Do work I choose

_____ Pay for my hobby

_____ Other

Describe how you will know when you have achieved these goals. (Be specific: What will your life will be like? Precisely how much money will you make? What work will you be doing? etc.)

By what date would you like to have achieved your goals?_____

What are the first ten steps you need to take to achieve your goal and by when do you plan to have each completed:

Steps   *Date to be Completed*

1. _____
2. _____
3. _____
4. _____
5. _____
6. _____
7. _____
8. _____
9. _____
10. _____

42. Do you have realistic expectations?

A Canadian study of successful businesses found that people who have realistic expectations for themselves and their businesses have a higher success rate. For example, those who are realistic about how much money they can earn and how long it will take to build a client or customer list are more successful. They don't buy into the start-a-business hype that suggests they can quickly make tons of money with little work. They don't think of self-employment as utopia, a solution to all their problems from financial to family. They realize that building a business income and a new lifestyle takes time and that they will have to invest some money and lots of energy.

To help gain a realistic perspective of your expectations, think about what others with a background and experience similar to yours have been able to accomplish over what period of time. The experiences of others can serve as a baseline for what's realistic. Success is a process that has a schedule of its own, however, so if you can see a way to do things more quickly or better, don't limit yourself to what you've seen others do. On the other hand, if you're not progressing as quickly as someone else, don't necessarily throw in the towel. How long it will take you to succeed depends upon how ready the market is for what you offer and how ready you are to seize the opportunities that await you.

The following work sheet can help you determine how realistic your plans are.

HOW REALISTIC IS WHAT YOU EXPECT?

This work sheet is designed to assist you in assessing how realistic your estimations are as to what you will be able to accomplish over what period of time.

How Ready Are You?

Rate yourself on a scale of 0 to 10 for each of the following points. (0 = virtually none; 10 = abundant)

____ Your Experience Level. How much do you know about marketing and operating on your own? How familiar are you with the field you're entering?

____ Your Contacts. How many people do you know now who need and are ready to pay for your service? How many people do you know now who are in a position to refer business to you?

____ How Much Money You Have on Hand to Capitalize Yourself. Will you need to bootstrap all your costs? Will you need to finance some of your costs?

____ Your Credentials. What credentials do you have for doing what you're offering that establish you as qualified to do what you do in the eyes of potential clients or customers.

____ Your Results. How good are the results you produce for your clients? Just how vital or dramatic are they?

____ Time. How much time do you have before you need to be supporting yourself full-time?

Scoring: The higher your score, the more likely you are to succeed over a shorter period of time. The lower your score, the longer it could take you to establish yourself and therefore the more time you will need to build your business.

How Ready Is the Market?

Check the statements that apply to your situation. Is the product or service you're offering:

____1. Ahead of the market? Are you anticipating a trend or offering something so new, different, or unusual that people are as yet unaware of it and why they need it? If so, you will need to educate them about the benefits of what you offer. That will make getting clients and customers slower and more time-consuming.

____2. Right on the market? Is there a strong, unmet demand right now for what you are offering? If so, you may find getting business easier and quicker and the lower your own readiness score needs be.

____3. In a growing market? Are the number of people who need what you offer expanding beyond the ability of what is now available to handle it? If the market is expanding, your growth could be quick and easy even if your own readiness score is not particularly high.

Most of our unhappiness comes from comparing ourselves unfavorably to other people.

43. Are you willing to read, take courses, study, use consultants, and otherwise learn what you need to learn to succeed on your own?

Research studies show that those who are willing to make the investment in learning as much as they can about what it takes to succeed are more likely to do so. Those who succeed, for example, are more likely to spend from six to nine months planning what they're going to do and how they're going to do it. They use this time to test out the feasibility of their plans as well.

Those who succeed are also more likely to ask for and use the advice of experts. They don't assume they know everything they need to know, nor do they just blindly move ahead. And they educate themselves in aspects of business with which they are unfamiliar. They take courses, buy books and tapes, and attend conferences and seminars. One added benefit of taking seminars and courses is that you may find clients, mentors, and gatekeepers through the instructors or other students you meet.

44. Where will you turn to obtain the additional information and expertise you need?

Of course, your personal support network and various trade and professional organizations will be a source of much information and expertise, but there is a wealth of information available today for self-employed individuals. Here are just a few places you can turn to build your skills and knowledge about everything from marketing to tax issues.

Resources

BUSINESS@HOME, 610 S.W. Broadway, Ste. 200, Portland, OR 97205, (503) 223-0304, *http://www.gohome.com*. Focuses on the lifestyles of people working at home.

SMALL BUSINESS DEVELOPMENT CENTERS (SBDCs), funded by the Small Business Administration, offer counseling, courses, and written materials on all aspects of small business. For the SBDC nearest you, contact the nearest Small Business Administration office, or call the Small Business Administration Answer Line (below).

SMALL BUSINESS ADMINISTRATION ANSWER LINE provides information about SBA programs and materials. It's available both by voice phone (800) 827-5722 and online via modem at (800) 697-4636. For help on the online service, call (202) 205-6400. The SBA has a comprehensive Web site as well: *http://www.sbaonline.sba.gov/lynx/index-lynx.html*

THE WORKING FROM HOME FORUM on CompuServe Information Service is a twenty-four-hour online support network of over 25,000 self-employed individuals. You can get advice, usually within twenty-four hours, on virtually any topic from accounting and tax issues to sources of funding and zoning, and you can also consult with marketing and PR experts, accountants, lawyers, and others in your field.

SHAREWARE. *Small Business Advisor,* by Michael D. Jenkins, is a program that's loaded with business start-up information, help with legal matters, and tax information written for all fifty states: 3020 Issaquah-Pine Lake Rd., #36, Issaquah, WA 98027. Also available in Library 2 of Working from Home Forum.

HOME OFFICE COMPUTING magazine, 411 Lafayette St., New York, NY 10003, (800) 505-4220. *http://www*.smalloffice.com. Since 1988, this periodical has covered both business and technology.

45. Are you willing to experiment until you find the combination of products, services, and marketing methods that will work for you?

Ultimately, success on your own is not about how much money, experience, or contacts you begin with. Nor is it the result of carefully following a set of rules (unless you've purchased an already proven franchise or business system, and even then there is likely to be a learning curve). Making money is an experiment. It involves knowing what you want to accomplish, doing what you think you need to do, tracking the results you get, and modifying what you do accordingly until you get the results you want.

Ultimately, if you're providing a product or service that people need and you can offer them satisfying results as long as there are enough such people and you let them know about you, then, over time you will succeed. But let your results be your guide. If you're getting the results you want, keep doing what you're doing; if not, experiment further. Try different marketing methods, different pricing, different ways of describing what you do, different aspects of what you offer, until you start getting the results you want.

"Insanity is doing the same thing over and over and expecting to get different results."
Chellie Campbell, Financial Coach

46. Do you have or are you willing to develop the traits necessary to manage yourself and make your business a success?

We are frequently asked what kind of person is suited to self-employment. Having personally met thousands of successfully self-employed individuals, we can say with confidence that you do not need to be a born entrepreneur or even to have grown up in an entrepreneurial household. We have seen people succeed from all walks of life, all backgrounds, all ages, and various levels of education and experience. They are the living proof that anyone who is willing to learn, persevere, and experiment can ultimately succeed on her or his own. We've noticed that the most successful self-employed people tend to share several qualities they have already or develop along the way—all of which can be acquired by setting one's mind to it. How well do these qualities describe you? Are you:

___1. **Broad-minded.** On your own, you need to be able to let go of pre-conceived, limited notions and be open to a wealth of possibilities, both those you want to attain as well as those you want to avoid.

___2. **Competent.** Being good at what you do is a given when you're on your own. Nepotism or favoritism might get you started, but it won't keep you flying over time and mediocrity will stall you or keep you sputtering along.

___3. **Courageous.** Because most of us have been raised to believe economic security lies in having a paycheck, the act of going out on our own requires the courage to believe in ourselves and the value of our work.

___4. **Fair-minded.** Trust is at the core of most business transactions and to earn the trust of clients and customers, they must believe you will be fair-minded and consider their needs and circumstances.

___5. **Honest.** Honesty is another aspect of attaining trust. Clients and customers need to trust that you will be forthcoming and ethical in your business dealings.

___6. **Imaginative.** Since making it on your own is basically a matter of taking an idea and turning it into a living, you have to be able to see what could be in addition to what already is.

___7. **Inspiring.** When you're on your own, you need to be able to inspire your clients and customers to believe they will benefit from your products and services. You also must be able to inspire yourself to believe in your goals and keep yourself going.

___8. **Intelligent.** Sometimes people think intelligence means having a high IQ or doing well on standardized tests. Studies show that having an unusually high IQ is not necessary to succeed on your own, however. In fact, people with very high IQs don't always do well in business—possibly because they don't relate well to the perspective of their clients and customers. But the *Random House Dictionary* defines intelligence as "the capacity for learning, reasoning, and understanding." This we do believe is vital for making it on your own, and fortunately we all have the capacity to develop our abilities for learning, reasoning, and understanding.

___9. **Straightforward.** It's hard to make it on your own if your potential clients and customers can't understand what you do and how you operate. They need to be clear about who you are, where you stand, and what they can count on you for.

___10. **Self-directed.** To work on your own, you have to know where you want to go in life and what you want to accomplish. You can't wait for something to come along or for someone else to tell you what to do.

___11. **Goal oriented.** Not only do you need to have a clear idea of where you're going and what you want to accomplish; you also have to be able to make plans for how you will get there, then follow through on them.

___12. **Tenacious.** We've discovered there needs to be a little Scottish terrier in anyone who wants to succeed on his or her own. Scottish terriers are renowned for their ability to grab on to whatever they're chasing and never, never let go. Sometimes that's what you need when you go out on your own—the ability to relentlessly pursue your goals until you attain them.

47. Are you willing to stick it out and persevere until you succeed?

> *A goal is a dream*
> *with a deadline.*
>
> BRIAN TRACY,
> *The Psychology of Success*

PART II

Using Your Computer in Business

ACTUALLY, MAKING MONEY with your computer on a consistent, ongoing basis means that you're "in business." Even if your business is only part-time from your home, running a computer-based business successfully involves managing the same functions as a *Fortune* 500 company—administration, marketing, sales, customer service, and accounting—except that you are usually the only employee and therefore you must do all the work. How then can you possibly get everything done? How can you accomplish all the things you need to do to keep your business running smoothly and, at the same time, do the work that brings in the money?

The answer is: That's how you really make money with your computer! You put your computer, modem, and other high-tech office equipment to work doing as much of the work for you as it can. Indeed, a well-equipped office with a computer and an assortment of the most appropriate software gives you the capability of having a corporate executive team working with you. With you as the CEO, scheduling and calendar programs can become your administrative assistant; database, contact management software and your Web site can become your public relations staff, financial software can act as your accounting department; and online databases can carry out your R & D efforts.

Here's a partial list of the things your computer can do for you:

- keep track of your appointments and meetings
- maintain records on all your clients and contacts
- prepare brochures, slides, and many other presentation documents
- create and post a presence on the World Wide Web
- make and receive phone calls through the World Wide Web
- teleconference through the World Wide Web
- create reports, business proposals, and even book-length documents
- send and receive faxes
- send and receive E-mail
- store and file all or most of your important papers
- create artwork, drawings, graphs, tables, and maps
- calculate your income and expenses and manage your financial data

- print checks, log phone calls, visitors, transactions, and time spent on projects
- record and diagram the steps needed to manage a project and arrive at your goal
- prepare your business and personal taxes
- and much, much more!

What's also important to remember is that your computer works tirelessly, costs only pennies a day to operate, and is always open to new ideas and new ways of doing things. Even as we write this book, in fact, it is nearly impossible to predict what products or technologies might come along to further the recommendations we are now making. New tools for operating a business or accomplishing tasks are constantly developed by engineers and software programmers, faster, more powerful hardware is always one step around the corner, and the Internet and World Wide Web are still in their infancy.

In Part II of the book, we will show you in depth how you can use your computer, the Internet, and other home-office equipment to solve problems and manage many critical functions of your day-to-day operations. The approach we take in the next four chapters will be to identify one by one the most crucial routines and tasks that home businesses typically need to do or should be doing, and show you which technology exists in each case for improving the way you work.

Chapter 3 reviews how you can use your computer to manage your money, from check writing and accounting to doing your taxes. Chapter 4 shows how many kinds of software can assist you in keeping track of the dozens of administrative functions that inevitably fall on your shoulders as a home-based business.

Chapter 5 goes on to discuss how you can use your computer and other technology to market yourself and keep a steady stream of business coming to you. We'll examine several kinds of powerful programs that allow you to keep up-to-date information about your clients or your dealings with them and how you can use a variety of software packages to keep your name in the forefront of your clients' minds. You'll see, for example, how the newest generation of desktop publishing programs not only helps you create professional level brochures, ads, flyers, slides, and other presentation materials; they also do the groundwork for creating dynamic "home pages" you can post on the World Wide Web. All the tips and recommendations in this chapter help you stay in touch with your clients and create a professional image so that they will turn to you first when they need your product or service, or will hire you over competitors because you have impressed them with the way you do business.

Finally, chapter 6 will explore the world of online information and show how your computer can provide you with valuable strategic information to identify, get, and keep clients. We will discuss how you can verify financial information on potential contacts and how you can research any topic for which you need information, including how to track down money owed to you. You'll also get a primer on the Internet and the Web, tips on finding the right Internet service provider, and hints on how to use the World Wide Web to find, communicate, and network with clients, prospects, and colleagues for support and advice.

Clearly, the more computer literate you are, the easier it will be to implement these recommendations. But even if you consider yourself to be a novice at using computers, you needn't fear. In today's competitive world of hardware manufacturers and software vendors, the odds are in your favor that you can find a system and easy-to-learn programs that you will feel comfortable working with. Most programs, for example, come with "context-sensitive" help screens, meaning that you can push one key as you work on your computer, regardless of what function you might be doing, and the software will respond with a help screen indicating how that function works and what options you may have. Such features often reduce the amount of time it takes you to get up and running with a software package to less than two hours! In short, the benefits are enormous if you can learn to take advantage of the technology available to make your home office work for you.

The Ideal Home Office

When we discuss the "ideal" home office, we are referring to setting up a configuration of equipment and furnishings that makes your work space a place where you can be as productive, efficient, and professional as if you worked for a large company. While each person will have different needs—and so there is no single recommendation that applies to all—we believe that to operate a home business either part- or full-time, in the manner this book recommends, it is worthwhile owning as many of the pieces of equipment we review below as are appropriate for the business you run. Provisioning your office with these basic items will cost between $3,000 and $6,000, a small amount relative to the power and sophistication you can achieve. Naturally, some businesses will need more specialized equipment that will increase their investment. Some computer-aided design (CAD) services, for example, will need an oversize (seventeen inches or larger) monitor with high-resolution color capabilities, a desktop publishing service may require a sophisticated color scanner, and a Web designer will need all of the aforementioned, as well as extra hard drive memory and specialized software.

Here is a rundown of the essential and basic items we recommend most home offices should have. Of course, many people will not be able to purchase all this equipment at one time, but you don't need to. You can begin with those pieces that will make the greatest impact for you and invest in the rest as quickly as your business growth allows. The following describes the ideally equipped home office along with brief explanations of the important technical issues most often asked about when purchasing the item.

Personal Computer

We assume that most readers of this book already have a computer, but if you are considering upgrading an older machine in order to start your business, you undoubtedly are aware that you have a wide array of choices from which to pick. For many people, the decision about what to buy is very perplexing, or you may feel unsure about how much to pay since it always seems that if you wait another month, prices will come down.

On both counts, though, we recommend that you proceed cautiously but without delay, since postponing your upgrade or new computer costs you time and the opportunity to get into business. Prices will always change, but by waiting a few months to save a few hundred dollars, you might have possibly lost a few thousand dollars in income. If your dilemma is not knowing whether to buy a Windows-based or an Apple Macintosh computer, the choice is actually now much less problematic. The distinction between these two machines has greatly narrowed, making it largely a matter of personal taste and preference as to which platform you choose. (Note, though, that this book largely focuses on Windows-based computers, since more business software is available for PC-compatible machines, and Macintosh computers can be configured to run Windows-based programs.)

If you are buying or upgrading, your choice, at the time of this book's writing, is primarily a computer based on the 586 processor chip, also called Pentium by its manufacturer, Intel. There are still some 486 processor chip machines available at some very low prices, but we do not recommend buying one. The online and multimedia worlds are changing so quickly that you will most certainly have an obsolete system on your hands in a matter of months with a 486-based machine.

586 processor chip systems come in different speeds, such as 100 megahertz (MHz), 133 MHz, 160 MHz, 200 MHz, and higher. The larger the number, the faster the computer will operate, since it reflects the number of millions of cycles per second the system processes. The differences between the microprocessors and their speeds reflect two variables: how many millions of instruc-

tions they handle each second and how many bits of data they can handle at one time through their "data bus," the wires that connect the microprocessor with other system components. For example, the slowest processing chips are 486-based and start at around 60 MHz, and the fastest at the time of this writing is the 586 at 200 MHz. Developments, such as MMX, which allows 586 chips to process audio and video content more quickly, are being introduced so frequently it's sometimes hard to keep up.

The choice of which machine and microprocessor you buy should reflect how you expect to use your computer. In fact, it is generally recommended that you first have some awareness of the kind of software you will need to run before you purchase your hardware. You may not need the fastest machine for your business. This can save you a few hundred dollars on the basic computer setup and will leave you enough to buy a better printer, extra software, or a bigger monitor.

In addition to processor speed, you need to be aware of how much RAM (Random Access Memory) your computer has. RAM memory exists in the form of chips plugged in to your motherboard. You will need a minimum of 16MB of RAM to run any of the newer programs or operating systems currently available. If you are doing anything serious in the way of graphics, database management, sound, or video, 32MB would be the minimum.

PLEASE NOTE: There are many machines being sold today that meet the aforementioned minimums in terms of processor speed and RAM memory, but not all systems are created equal. Make sure the system you are looking at has an *external RAM cache* (also known as secondary or 1.2 memory) of at least 256Kb of *pipelined-burst* cache. Cheaper systems will feature 256Kb of *asynchronous* cache (or no cache at all) that won't perform as quickly or as well.

The microprocessor chip and memory on your motherboard are only two of the major components to consider in purchasing or upgrading your system. Other important basic items include the hard drive and monitor.

Hard Drive

There is no point in purchasing a computer without a hard drive large enough to store your programs and data files. In fact, with the variety of programs you will likely want to use, you will probably want to have at least a 1.6-gigabyte (1,600 megabytes) hard drive, although many professionals now consider 3 gigabytes or larger as the standard. One rule of thumb is to add up the hard disk memory required to store all the programs you expect to use in the future (and don't shortchange yourself, since you may want to use a graphics or database program down the road, even if you don't now), then add 50 percent of that figure to determine the space needed for your data files, and then double or triple that total to allow yourself room to grow. Also, if your business has any special needs, such as storing graphics files or large databases, you need to plan for some sort of external storage device.

Another feature of hard drives you should be aware of is the speed of the disk, called the "average access time," which is measured in milliseconds (ms). This speed reflects the amount of time that your hard disk needs to locate and begin retrieving a file or program from one of the hard disk platters. We recommend a minimum of twelve ms access time, but this number will undoubtedly go lower. These days hard disks are so cheap that its hardly worth buying a smaller disk just to save $100. Couple that with the trend toward larger programs (Windows 95 itself is over ninety MB!) and more size-intensive multimedia programming, and you have a clear case for buying the largest hard drive you can afford.

Monitor

The standard monitor on many systems is a fifteen-inch SVGA .28 dot pitch that allows for a number of colors and good text resolution. SVGA indicates that the monitor handles up to 800 x 600 pixels, or greater. There is also a "super" SVGA that shows 1,024 x 768 pixels and an "enhanced" SVGA that can show up to 1280 x 1024 pixels. In general, the higher the number of pixels, the sharper the image and the more you can see on the screen at once, although text shown on the super and enhanced SVGA is almost too small to look at comfortably for long periods of time.

Another factor to consider is the "dot pitch" of the pixels, meaning the distance between them. Monitors can have a "dot pitch" ranging, in general, from .28 mm to .51 or higher. It is generally recommended to get dot pitch of at least .28, since the lower number indicates a finer, less grainy resolution, which makes reading your screen easier.

When choosing a monitor, you also need to take into account the video card that drives the monitor's graphic capability. The video card is simply another circuit board that plugs in to the motherboard and determines the clarity, or resolution, of your screen. Video cards also come with their own RAM in which images are stored for even quicker access time. Look for a video card with at least two MB of RAM. If your business is based on graphics or multimedia applications, you may want more video RAM.

In short, the monitor is a very important item in your system and should not be overlooked. In fact, we even recommend that you purchase a seventeen-inch monitor if you have the extra money. This larger screen significantly reduces eyestrain, improves the amount of text you can see at once, and makes paging and moving around documents much easier. You will definitely want an even larger screen, such as a twenty-inch one, if you are doing desktop publishing and need to see large blocks of text all at once.

Fax Machine or Fax/Modem Board

The fax machine is a vital home-office item. Even people who do not expect to use a fax find that when they get into business, they send and receive more than a few faxes each week to and from potential clients, suppliers, vendors, and even colleagues. One might say that faxing is actually becoming a way of life in our information age, with over fifty million fax machines installed around the world.

There are essentially two options for fax technology. The first option is to purchase an external machine that allows you to fax paper documents, photos, drawings, and any other kind of preprinted material. You can purchase a fax machine for as little as $200 and still have the functionality you need for a home office, though most people are spending a few hundred dollars more and getting a multifunction or all-in-one machine The other option is a fax "board" that you insert internally into your computer's motherboard so that it is controlled by your computer. The advantage of an internal fax board is that you can type a document on your word processor and fax it directly from your computer without printing it out. You can also receive a document directly into your computer when the fax board is connected to your phone line. Then, using optical character recognition (OCR) software now included with many fax software programs, you can translate the fax from a graphic image into a word-processing text file and edit it to be included in your own documents.

The disadvantage of an internal fax board is that you cannot fax a printed item you haven't created in your computer, such as a newspaper article you might have clipped or an invoice from a company, without first scanning the item into your computer with a scanner. Alternately, the disadvantage with an external machine is that you often must stand at the fax machine to make sure multiple page transmissions are being fed smoothly, whereas the internal fax board lets you keep working while it faxes in the background.

Some people have both kinds of fax options, using the internal board to fax documents they've created themselves on their computer and the external machine to send and receive all other documents. Since fax boards are often combined with a modem, it's an easy and inexpensive way to supplement an external fax machine. We'll discuss modems in more detail below.

CD-ROM Drive

Almost every new computer comes with a CD-ROM drive configured into the system. Information is stored on CD discs through a process known as "sampling." The faster your CD-ROM drive samples and plays the material stored on the disk, the clearer the images and sound you will experience. Look for at least a 8X (eight time) sampling device, minimum. If you are using an older machine that doesn't include a CD-ROM drive, you can purchase one separately and install it into an empty disk slot on the front of your computer. If you don't have a CD-ROM drive, you are definitely missing out. Most important, many new software programs are being released on CD-ROM only. Without a CD drive, you won't even be able to load the programs. Additionally, there are so many excellent resources available on CD-ROMs such as encyclopedias, databases, national yellow and white pages, art files, sound files, and much, much more, that you are limiting your business's potential by denying yourself access to them.

Multimedia Equipment

Multimedia equipment is not absolutely essential to the basics of business computing, but it sure helps. A good sixteen-bit sound card, such as the industry standard Sound Blaster from Creative Technologies, and a pair of decent speakers will not only liven up your computing experiences; they take on a new level of importance when browsing the World Wide Web or running multimedia applications on your CD-ROM drive. Sound cards and speakers come standard with many computer systems these days. Buying a system with multimedia already bundled will save you money over buying and installing the components separately.

Printers

As recently as only a few years ago the options for printers were rather limited, but today, your choices are almost more diverse than computer systems themselves. Several advancing technologies have brought about these changes, including higher-quality ink-jet printers with color capabilities and laser printers, some of which also have color capability. Color-capable laser printers, however, start at about $3,500 and range to well over $10,000. Unless you have an extensive desktop publishing or graphic design business, the added benefit of color won't be cost-effective.

Ink-jet printers are of two kinds: aqueous, which heats up ink until it boils and sprays out of a nozzle onto the page; and solid ink jet, which is a wax-based system that melts the ink and jets it onto the page. Laser printers utilize a laser beam to electrostatically charge a drum that causes ink to transfer to the paper.

Of these two major technologies, the laser printer generally produces the highest quality, meaning that text and images are crisper and the blacks are blacker. You pay somewhat more for a laser printer than for other technology (except for thermal wax transfer printers now available, which are used for printing high-quality color), but we recommend the laser printer because the output adds a greater professional appearance to your correspondence, documents, proposals, and other printed materials. Laser printers are also very quiet and fast, printing from four to eight pages per minute.

We do, however, have to qualify our recommendation a bit. With the great strides made in ink-jet technology, the choice between ink jet and laser jet is not as clear as it once was. Ink jets now offer true 600 x 600 dots-per-inch resolution for black-on-white printing and 300 x 300 dots per inch in color modes. The real advantage ink jets offer is color. For less then $500 you can add rich, well-saturated colors (using special paper) to word-processing documents, reports, flyers, newsletters, etc. The downside of ink jets is that blacks aren't as crisp or even as from laser printers, and on regular paper, colors can appear washed-out or grainy and show banding. Color ink jets also cost more to operate, as colored inks need to be refilled often. As a rule, ink jets are good for adding color to reports and presentations, but for standard business functions such as letters, spreadsheets, and graphics, laser printers still offer the better output. We therefore recommend that you consider a color ink-jet printer as a second printer, after the purchase of a laser printer.

If your business produces multipart forms or invoices, or if you print spreadsheets and financial statements with many columns, you will probably benefit from having a dot matrix printer for your office. Some businesses own both a laser and a dot matrix printer, using the latter when they print multiple-part forms or draft documents and in-house materials in order to save the more expensive laser cartridges for important papers. Keep in mind that dot matrix and impact printers are noisy. You will find it difficult to print documents in your office while talking with clients on the phone.

Modems

Modems, which can be external devices or internal boards, are nothing more than devices that transmit signals via telephone from one computer to another. Internal boards are cheapest and usually provide fax capabilities as well. External modems are more expensive but do offer the advantage of providing you a series of indicator lights that are helpful in letting you know the status of your modem functions. A modem is your link to hundreds of thousands of valuable sources of online information through the Internet, bulletin boards, and online services such as CompuServe and America Online. Chapter 6 will examine in greater detail the benefits of the online world, including the Internet, E-mail, databases, and the "big four" online services.

It is absolutely essential for businesses to have and use a modem. A modem is your lifeline to the outside and online worlds. As more and more business migrates over to the online world, not having a modem will be like running a business without a telephone. Conveniently, modem prices have come down considerably over the past two years. Many of today's standard 36.6 Kbps (Kilobytes per second. This refers to the speed at which modems transmit and receive information. The higher the Kbps rate, the faster the modem) modems are available for less than $100.

Modems, like everything in the world of computers, change and evolve rapidly. Only a few years ago 9,600 Kbps modems were the standard. Then it was 14,400, quickly replaced by 28,800, now 36.6. Coming up is 54 Kbps You can still use slower modems, but the speed at which they operate is prohibitive. A good way to stay ahead of the curve in terms of modems is to purchase a model than can be upgraded via software at a later time to operate at the most current, faster speed. US Robotics, for example, offers a 36.6 model that can be quickly upgraded with software at a later time to 54 Kbps.

The most challenging issue of owning a modem is understanding and working with the communications software programs that operate them, although, even these once-daunting protocol crunchers have been tamed to operate reliably in the background.

Multifunction Machines

One of the most interesting developments in home office hardware over the last few years has been the introduction of multifunction machines. These units combine a printer, fax, copier, scanner, and telephone technology into one unit. Multifunctions have many advantages in the home-office setting. For one, they are compact. The largest models are about the size of an average laser printer. Second, they generally cost less than it would to purchase their components individually. Hewlett-Packard, Xerox, Sharp, Canon, and Brother are leading producers of multifunction machines. The third advantage of multifunctional units is that they save you the time and hassles involved in shopping for each of these technologies separately, then setting them up to run with your computer. Most multifunction units require only one or two connections.

Multifunctional units do have some limitations. If the scanner component isn't working and you have to send it in for repairs, you'll also be sending in your printer, fax, and scanner. If your requirements change over time and you need to upgrade your copier, for instance, you may find yourself locked in to some difficult choices: buying a new copier and duplicating your basic capabilities, buying a new copier and new scanner and a new printer, or making do with what you have for a while.

If you do decide to buy a multifunction unit, make sure each component has the following minimum specifications. Look for the printer to have at least 600 x 300 dpi (dots per inch) resolution and an output of at least three pages per minute. Make sure the fax has plain-paper capability and a document feeder that can accommodate a minimum of twenty pages. The copier should reproduce at 300 dpi, minimum, and be size scalable. Check that the scanner works at least 300 dpi resolution and has a TWAIN interface.

Other Peripherals

Among the other peripheral hardware equipment that makes up the ideal home office, depending on your needs, are:

Alternative Input Device: Instead of a traditional mouse and keyboard, some computer users turn to an alternative device for interacting with their machines. Track balls are a common substitute for a standard mouse. You might consider a mouse pen, which is easier to hold than a mouse, and so causes less wrist pain. There are several ergonomically designed keyboards that help alleviate the repetitive motion discomfort brought on by heavy use of traditional keyboards. In addition, we use a keyboard pillow onto which we place our keyboard to reduce keyboarding strain.

Backup Device: Many people don't consider buying a backup storage device when they first purchase their computer. Naturally, no one enjoys thinking about the fact that they could lose all their data or programs in one fell swoop from a disk crash or fire. Additionally, although computer processing speeds and amount of RAM have grown almost exponentially in the last few years, the standard 1.44MB floppy drive has remained the same. The amount of portable storage offered by the 1.44MB drive can be quite limiting, especially if your business revolves around images, sound, or video. The solution for high-capacity portable storage is digital versatile disk (DVD) among other technologies. DVD is a recent development. Write-once DVD devices are available, and rewritables based on phase change technology will be available soon. DVD is available as a 4.7GB single-sided, single-layered disk. DVDs will be available to store seventeen gigabytes on double-sided, double-layered disks that are the same size and shape as the 5.25-inch CD-ROM. Lower-capacity and lower-priced portable drives include Iomega's popular removable Zip drive. Slightly wider and thicker than a traditional floppy disk, a Zip disk stores up to 100MB of information on a thin, filmlike material. For greater storage capacity, there are several removable hard drive technologies available. Iomega's Jaz drive will store up to one GB of data. SyQuest, the inventor of removable hard disk technology, offers a number of different drives such as the SyQuest EZFlyer 230 which will store up to 230MB. You may also wish consider the tried and true DAT (Digital Audio Tape) tape backup technology. Hewlett-Packard's popular Colorado T4000/T4000es series allow you to store up to one GB in about thirty minutes.

Scanner: A scanner is useful if you are working in any field related to desktop publishing, Web design, graphics, or other businesses in which you may frequently need to use preprinted materials in your documents. If you intend to produce a newsletter or maintain a Web site as a marketing tool for your business, you also might want to invest in a scanner. With OCR (optical character recognition) software getting better all the time, any business should consider the purchase of a scanner. OCR software allows you to scan documents, such as incoming invoices, business correspondence, contracts, etc., into your computer where you store them as a database entry or word-processing document. This can greatly simplify your accounting and filing procedures.

Scanners vary considerably in terms of capability and price. Physically, there are three types of scanners: hand scanners, sheet fed, and flat bed. Hand scanners are generally the least expensive, yet they offer some distinct advantages. Hand scanners are aptly named, as they are handheld. You simply run them over the image or text you wish to scan. They are small, portable, and very easy to use. Color models, such as the Scanman Color 2000 by Logitech are available for less than $150. Sheet-fed scanners lie in the middle ground in terms of price. Compaq even makes a keyboard with a sheet-fed scanner built in. These scanners scan individual sheets that are fed through the unit itself, much the way a fax machine scans a document it is sending. Sheet-fed units have one disadvantage: You can't scan images from books, reports, or any other sources that are bound or otherwise inflexible. Flat-bed scanners are more expensive, but more versatile. They scan material that is placed on a platen, much like a standard copy machine. Hand scanners, such as Logitech's, are a less expensive alternative.

Any business that deals with printed material as its final product, such as graphic designers and desktop publishers, will need flat-bed scanners with the highest resolutions and that scan in color. Web designers and multimedia and desktop video professionals don't need as a high a resolution. Most twenty-four-bit, 600 x 300 color flat-bed scanners will do the trick. If your business doesn't involve image manipulation at all, you may consider a sheet-fed or flat-bed scanner, depending on your budget. In these cases, resolution and even color capability are more a matter of personal taste than a strict requirement. Any scanner you buy, no matter the price, should be TWAIN compatible and come with OCR software.

Copy Machine: Some home offices can benefit greatly from having a small copier or personal copy machine. If you end up going to a copy store every few days and wasting two to three hours per week in traffic and waiting for your copies, a copy machine pays for itself in just a few months.

Telephone System, Answering Machine, and Voice Mail and Computer Telephony: We will discuss a wide range of telephone systems, including voice mail and computer telephony, in greater detail in chapter 5. We believe strongly, though, that professional telephone hardware and components are critical to the success of a home-based business. From maintaining a separate line for your business to having a high-quality answering system for calls while you are away, and having a separate line for fax and modem, your phone system is an important link in your business.

EIGHT RESOURCES ON CD-ROM

Tens of thousands of CD-ROM titles are already available with more coming all the time. Here are just a few of the applications businesses can use by having a CD-ROM capability in their computer:

1. For accountants and those interested in keeping your own books, you can get access to the U.S. tax codes, rulings, and cases that enable you to get detailed, authoritative information quickly, available from Prentice-Hall, Research Institute, and CCH.

2. For writers and anyone else who must produce well-written documents, you can have ready access to many useful writing and research tools such as dictionaries, encyclopedias, almanacs, books of quotations, and other reference data. There are also many specialized dictionaries, including those for science, engineering, or medical terms.

Microsoft's Bookshelf for Windows, for example, contains seven reference tools all on one CD-ROM disk, including a dictionary, thesaurus, and atlas. You might also use *Compton's Multimedia Encyclopedia* on CD-ROM, which contains 32,000 articles, 15,000 images and maps, 5,000 charts and diagrams, and 60 minutes of sound. *The Time Magazine Compact Almanac,* updated annually, contains 10,000 *Time* articles from 1923 onward, 400 tables from U.S. Statistical Abstracts, the complete *Congressional Directory,* and the *CIA World Factbook.* And Software Toolwork's *World Atlas* contains 240 color maps, 4,400 statistical maps, and 300 articles.

3. For desktop publishers, you can obtain clip art and type via CD-ROM with such products as AgfaType with over 1,900 typefaces and Click Art from Broderbund with 125,000 images.

4. For anyone involved in extensive mailings or people in the mail-order business, you can get Arc Tangent's Zip++ on CD-ROM, which has every address in the U.S. and allows you to check your lists for accuracy and insert carrier route and zip +4 codes, both necessary components if you are seeking the lowest postal rates.

5. For programmers and computer consultants, you can use CD-ROM disks from Microsoft or Borland, each with listings of the company's databases of known bugs and their fixes.

6. Marketing campaigns can be conducted with Digital Directory Assistance, Inc's (800-284-8353) PhoneDisc series, which provides comprehensive national directories of business and residential phone numbers, addresses, even fax numbers. You can create lists by business type, zip codes, or geographical areas.

7. For people interested in software, *PC Magazine Select Demos* contains over 1,100 Windows software program demos.

8. Video and audio clip libraries, such as Soundstations from Softbit, can spruce up any Web site or computer presentation, or simply customize your home-office desktop.

Protecting Yourself from the Computer's Occupational Hazards

Unhappily, using a computer can be hazardous to your health. While millions of people are using their computers without noticeable distress, others are suffering from eyestrain, headaches, backaches, skin rashes, problems with fatigue and concentration and, most seriously, repetitive motion injuries. Fortunately, most of these ills can be prevented or reversed if caught early enough. To paraphrase an old saying, "A few dollars spent on prevention are worth months of lost income and medical bills."

Here are the key problems to be alert to. Remember, unlike in a company where an employer is concerned about health insurance claims, worker compensation costs, and OSHA requirements, the only person caring for you is you.

Repetitive Motion Injuries. The number of people afflicted with carpal tunnel syndrome continues to rise because using a computer requires as many as 40 percent more keystrokes than using a typewriter. Important to prevention is working at a desk that enables your keyboard to be between twenty-three and twenty-eight inches high. Ways to get your keyboard at the right height include placing it on an extension arm extending from your desk or putting it on your lap, resting on a keyboard pillow or wrist-support pad.

Posture and body position matter, too, so keep your feet flat on the floor or on a footstool or footrest; your thighs parallel to the floor; your back straight; your upper arms dropping almost straight down with your elbows to your sides and at the same height as the keyboard; your forearms also parallel to the floor; your wrists straight so that the backs of your hands and the tops of your forearms are in a straight line with your fingers drooping slightly to the keys. The backs of your hands should not slope upward from your forearms.

Devices that may help reduce stress on your wrists include wrist rests and ergonomically designed mice, all available at your local computer store. Chairs with armrests may also be helpful in avoiding repetitive motion injury unless your height forces the armrests to shrug or slump your shoulders.

Backaches. Your chair and desk are keys to avoiding back problems. Your chair needs to provide good low-back support and it should have an adjustable seat. More expensive chairs have armrests that are adjustable. A chair should also have five legs for greater stability. A Comfort Zone Cushion (708/325-0045) made from a NASA-developed material provides a super cushion for your seat or back. Your desk needs to provide you with adequate clearance for your knees.

Eyestrain, Blurred Vision, and Headaches. To avoid eye problems, first pay attention to the positioning of your monitor so that light sources are not producing glare and reflections. If your monitor does not have a built-in antiglare filter, you can add one or use a visorlike hood on your monitor that will protect against glare from overhead lighting. Indirect lighting is usually best, however.

Full-spectrum compact fluorescent lights and incandescent bulbs made with neodymium relieve eyestrain by being more like natural outdoor light and save on energy, too. Also, do not face an unshaded window because the difference in brightness between your screen and the window will be uncomfortable. The center of the screen should be from level with your eyes to twenty degrees below eye level. If you wear glasses, you may need a prescription that is adjusted for the distance to your screen. Make sure that your glasses, particularly bifocals, don't cause you to tilt your head into an uncomfortable position. If your eyes feel dry, blink, because staring at a computer monitor causes us to open our eyes more widely and to blink less frequently. It's also important to take frequent breaks.

Electronic Magnetic Radiation (EMR) and Ozone. Although how harmful this radiation may be is still being debated, by staying eighteen to twenty-eight inches away from your monitor, you can avoid the most potentially harmful rays. Be aware, too, that monitors vary in the amount of EMR they transmit, so it's wise to consider the EMR rating in choosing a monitor. You can also add a screen like a NoRad shield (800/262-3260) that blocks radiation or a plug-in device like a Clarus VDT Clear System (800/223-1998). Also, keep a five-foot distance between you and your laser printer and photocopier. Ozone is another hazard, so make sure exhaust ports are directed away from your work area and replace ozone filters regularly as prescribed by manufacturers.

Catalogs featuring ergonomic products are available from Action Computer Supplies (800/822-3132).

PURCHASING YOUR SYSTEM

If you are buying a computer system or upgrading to new equipment, we generally recommend that you purchase your computer from a vendor in your area who will answer your questions and provide you with immediate service in the event your machine needs any adjustments or repairs. You might even consider supporting a home-based computer consultant or sales consultant who could help you make your choices and design a system to fit your needs. This person could then become a useful ongoing contact for you, and you might jointly refer business to each other.

On the other hand, if you feel comfortable with purchasing by mail order, you can often save several hundred dollars over retail prices and get very good packages from such established original equipment manufacturers as Dell, Micron, and Gateway. The *Computer Shopper* (*http://www.cshopper.com*), a large monthly magazine available on most newsstands, is an extremely comprehensive resource for mail-order computer and equipment shopping. We recommend that you first examine the advertisements in at least several computer magazines to compare prices and promised services. Then keep a written record of what you ordered and make sure you receive the same equipment as advertised.

A Word About "Suites"

In the following chapters we will discuss how computers and computer software can make your life easier as a home-based business person. We've identified four major aspects of doing business in which computer technology can be of greatest help: Money Management, Administrivia (we'll define this term in chapter 4), Marketing and Promotions, and Communications.

We're not the first to have delineated these aspects of doing business. Corporate giants such as Microsoft and Corel have identified the same basic needs. Their way of addressing these needs has been the development of what are known in the industry as software "suites." A suite is simply a bundle of software programs that address the basic needs of doing business. Typically, a suite will include a word-processing program, a presentation-graphics program, a spreadsheet program, and a database management program, as well as a number of smaller helper programs such as organizers, communication programs, help programs, and the like. Suites generally come in two levels: a higher end for business, and a more consumer-oriented lower end. For example, Microsoft offers the Microsoft Works suite as their consumer-oriented package and Microsoft Office, in its several editions, as their high-end package. Lower-end suites usually contain scaled-back versions of a manufacturer's programs. Again, using Microsoft Works as an example, the word-processing program contained in the suite is not nearly as powerful as the full version of Microsoft Word, which is offered in the higher-end editions of *Microsoft Office*. Most computers sold today offer some sort of "bundled" software which will more than likely contain a lower-end version of one of the popular suites. You may find that these suites are all you need to take care of the basics. But, then again, you may not.

Currently, Microsoft, Corel, and Lotus are the dominant players in providing professional-level software suites. Upgrades from either consumer-oriented suites or older versions of professional-level suites are available at reasonable prices. To give you an idea just how comprehensive suite packages are, here is listing of the most recent professional-level suites offered by the big three and the major individual software packages included in each:

COREL PROFESSIONAL OFFICE: *Corel WordPerfect* (word processing/desktop publishing); *Paradox* (database); *Corel Quatro Pro* (spreadsheet); *CorelDraw* (illustration); *Corel Presentations* (presentation graphics); and more.

LOTUS SMARTSUITE: *Word Pro* (word processing/desktop publishing); *Approach* (database); *Lotus 1-2-3* (spreadsheet); *Freelance Graphics* (presentation graphics); *Organizer;* and more.

MICROSOFT OFFICE SMALL BUSINESS EDITION: *Microsoft Word* (word processing), *Microsoft Publisher* (desktop publishing); *Excel* (spreadsheet); *Outlook* (desktop organizer and contact manager); *Automap* (street maps for everywhere in the U.S.); and more.

MICROSOFT OFFICE PROFESSIONAL: *Microsoft Word* (word processing/ desktop publishing); *Access* (database); *Excel* (spreadsheet); *PowerPoint* (presentation graphics); *Outlook* (desktop organizer and contact manager); and more.

One of the wonderful advantages of all suite programs is their interoperability. Suites generally include a "shell" program that allows documents and data created in one program to be seemlessly imported to another. For example, you can enter a client's address into the database program. If you need to send the client some correspondence, you can import his or her address directly into the word processor where it can be used in the letterhead and printed on the envelope so you won't have to retype it. The address and other data on the client can also be used in your spreadsheet program for billing, job tracking, etc. There are countless time-saving scenarios that are possible due to the interoperability of suite software.

For the remainder of Part II, we will focus on the four areas of doing business where your computer will be of greatest help. These chapters will be equally helpful, whether you use individual programs to help you in each of these areas or if you use a suite.

CHAPTER 3

Using Your Computer to Manage Your Money

At the end of each month, Walter spends several hours paying bills for his Web writing business and another few hours sending out invoices. If there's time, he also balances his checkbook. If not, he lets that slide "until next time." Together, the three tasks consume nearly two days of his time.

Amanda, who owns a medical transcription service, devotes part of each Saturday to bookkeeping tasks—unless family commitments intervene. Then she has to find some time late at night during the week to catch up. Often she gets behind.

Charleen and Earl run a computer repair service, and although they are both working seven days a week, they nonetheless feel that there's never enough money left over each month.

Despite spending many hours paying bills and sending out invoices, none of these home-business owners knows what their overhead is and each wonders how he or she can be working so hard and still just be getting by.

Although Walter, Amanda, Charleen, and Earl all use computers to do their work, they're missing out on one of their computers' most valuable assets: the ability to help them organize, manage, and otherwise run the financial aspects of their businesses. These business owners have encountered what many people fear when they think about becoming their own boss—they don't enjoy doing the financial aspects of their business, and they're concerned about their ability to do it well. Concern about being able to handle financial issues like budget projections, overhead, income and expense accounts, and balance sheets is actually one of the most common reasons some people doubt their ability to be their own boss.

Unfortunately some home-business operators do fail or struggle along needlessly because they don't know how to handle the financial aspects of their businesses. In fact, a classic study of the reasons for small-business failures found that while some of the factors related to inadequate planning, such as starting the business without enough capital, or taking on a venture that was too risky, seven of the factors have to do with how people managed their money once they were in business, including:

- taking on too much debt
- poor budgeting
- bad cash management
- taking too much money out of the business
- confusing net income with cash flow (which was the problem with the couple above for whom the faster that they pedaled, the farther behind they got)
- not keeping up with billings
- errors in paying one's own bills

Fortunately, the right computer software can help you avoid all these problems and many more with surprisingly little effort on your part. In this chapter, we'll tell you how. We'll examine the most crucial money tasks you'll face and show how your computer can help you manage them.

#1. Finding a Simple Way to Manage Your Money

The Problem
Basically there are only five financial tasks most home-based businesses need to accomplish when it comes to managing their money:

1. Figure out how much money to charge for your product and service.
2. Keep track of your income and how much you are spending each month.
3. Analyze your profitability and see what products or services are producing the most income.
4. Keep track of your invoices and make sure your customers pay you on time.
5. Keep sufficient records to pay your estimated and year-end taxes accurately and on time while claiming all the deductions to which you are entitled.

Since most of us have little experience and background, and often little interest, in how to do such financial tasks, the problem is finding a way to do them that's simple enough that we don't have to go back to school, hire a bookkeeper, or spend hours of our time struggling to get them done and feeling awful if we don't.

Computer Solutions

In most cases, your computer can help you carry out these five financial tasks quickly, easily, and accurately. In fact, you can choose from three types of software that can help you perform nearly all your own financial record keeping, estimating, and analysis: check-writing software, general ledger accounting software, and spreadsheet accounting systems. Here is an overview of each.

Check-Writing Software: In general, most home-based businesses can use one of several easy-to-learn check-writing software programs such as *Quicken* (Intuit), *Managing Your Money,* CashGraf's *Checks Plus,* or *Microsoft Money* as the foundation for carrying out all their essential financial tasks. They make bookkeeping about as easy as writing checks and recording transactions in a checkbook register.

The benefit of these programs is that they handle money in the same way that most home businesses have been used to doing it by hand. Whereas large companies or businesses with inventories and employees need to use a "double-entry" or "accrual-based" bookkeeping system to reduce errors and catch improprieties, the home-based person most often can use a much simpler method. (See "An Accounting Primer" on page 268.) For most home-business owners, a check-writing financial software package contains all the features they need to maintain their records and do their business planning, budgeting, and analysis.

In general, check-writing software programs are very easy to learn to use, and most people can get one running within just a few hours of installing it. Here's an example of how easy it is: Let's say you choose to use *Quicken* (available for Windows and Macintosh) to manage your money. When you load *Quicken* and select "check register," you'll see a familiar lined checkbook register on the screen that looks just like the old-fashioned paper checkbook. This is the register onto which you will type your entries (see Figure 3-1).

You begin by putting in your starting balance—the amount of money you have in your business bank account. Then each time you get paid by a client or you pay a bill, you simply call up the check register and record the information just as you would do when recording a deposit or payment in your personal checkbook. After each entry, *Quicken* automatically recalculates your account balance. When you pay bills, you can choose to have *Quicken* display a visual of a check (just like one in a checkbook). Type in the name and amount on the check and then, by pressing a key, you can print out the check using your printer and blank checks that you purchase to work with the program. *Quicken* will automatically deduct the amount and update the balance in your check register. You don't need to type any entry twice!

By using a check-writing program on a daily basis, you will save the time involved in writing out your checks and balancing your books. You will also have an accurate running record of your business's cash flow from which the software can provide you with many informative reports.

AN ACCOUNTING PRIMER

Basically there are two methods of accounting and two methods of bookkeeping. Each meets different needs. Here's an overview of all four.

Two Accounting Methods

Accounting is essentially a process of determining and demonstrating the financial health of your business. There are two basic methods for doing this: accrual basis and cash basis.

Accrual Basis: In accrual-based accounting, income is recorded when a service is performed or when a product is sold, regardless of when the cash is received or paid. So, in using this method, if you perform a job today and mail out your invoice, you have "received" income even though you didn't get the money yet. Similarly, an expense is logged when services or goods are purchased, not when you actually pay for them. Accrual-based accounting is most frequently used by companies that have inventories because it allows them to manage their accounts better and recognize income and expenses on a more timely basis.

Cash Basis: In cash-basis accounting, income is recorded when you get paid, and expenses are incurred when you write a check or pay cash for them. Do not confuse "cash basis," however, with paying in cash; you can still write checks or use credit cards when using a cash-basis system. The terminology has to do with the method of accounting, not the method of payment. Cash-basis accounting is generally the preferred method for home businesses, since they seldom have extensive inventories or employees, and usually their financial picture

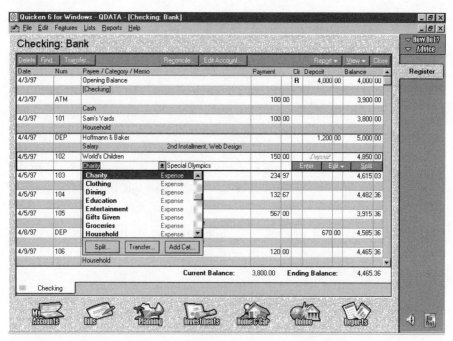

Figure 3-1: Two views of how Quicken helps to facilitate your bookkeeping needs. The top screen shows how Quicken simulates a standard check register where you can input your entries. The screen on the bottom shows how Quicken allows you to prepare a check as easily as writing it yourself. Filling out a check automatically makes an entry in your register and updates your balance.

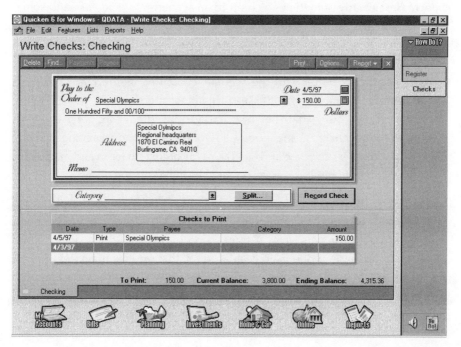

is most accurately determined from the balance of money that has come in and gone out rather than what's been billed or acquired.

Two Bookkeeping Methods

Bookkeeping is basically a method of recording information about your business's financial situation, and as such it is secondary to accounting. That is, first you choose the accounting method by which you want to demonstrate the value of your company; then you pick the method by which you will record the information. As with accounting, there are also two basic bookkeeping methods.

Double Entry: In using double-entry bookkeeping, there are dozens of accounts on which the business keeps separate records, and each account uses a two-sided grid as shown here:

<u>debit | credit</u>

For every transaction, you always need to log two accounts, with one recorded as a debit and the other as a credit. This is why the bookkeeping method is called double entry, and why the method is preferred for reducing errors and making sure that everything always balances out. What makes double-entry accounting confusing is that sometimes a debit is an increase and sometimes it is a decrease; similarly, sometimes a credit to an account is an increase and sometimes a decrease, depending on whether the account is an asset, a liability, or an owner's equity account.

Double-entry bookkeeping is useful because it makes it easier to track mistakes. It also works better with the accrual accounting method in which businesses are usually tracking their assets, liabilities, and equity in great detail to portray what they own, what they owe, and various intangibles such as depreciation, deferred charges, and goodwill. Double-entry bookkeeping can become quite complex, however, and can take a lot of time to learn and master. For this reason, most home businesses prefer the single-entry method.

Single Entry: In using single-entry bookkeeping, you only need to log each transaction of income or expense once, in the way *Quicken* and other check-writing software programs work. A transaction in this method is simply an increase or a decrease in one main cash account that you maintain. You do not track corollary accounts for the company's assets or liabilities. For example, if you were to buy inventory, you only record a payment to the vendor as an expense. You don't record both a payment to the vendor and an increase in the inventory asset account, as you would in a double-entry system. Single-entry methods are therefore most appropriate for small service businesses in which your primary objective is to track cash flow, not assets and liabilities of the company like inventory or debt.

Errors inevitably develop in a single-entry system, however, because even the most careful person makes mistakes, so it's important to reconcile a single-entry system regularly.

Congratulations on completing Accounting 101! In a nutshell, if you are like most home-based businesses, you can restrict yourself to using cash-basis accounting with a single-entry bookkeeping system and this is all you really need to understand.

General-Ledger Accounting Software: This kind of financial software is more sophisticated than a check-writing program and is useful for businesses that have inventory, employees on payroll, or that wish to use the accrual method of accounting because a simple cash-basis accounting method like the one we described is not appropriate for them. Some programs in this category require an understanding of double-entry bookkeeping and accrual-based accounting, programs like *DacEasy Instant Accounting* (DacEasy), *M.Y.O.B.* (Teleware), *Peachtree Complete Accounting* (Peachtree), or *Simply Accounting* (Computer Associates) make general-ledger accounting somewhat easier to do than in the past because they automate the posting functions from your individual journals of accounts to your general ledger. However, other programs such as *Quickbooks* (Intuit) and *One-Write Plus* (NEBS) are easy-to-use modified double-entry systems that essentially disguise the journaling aspects of double-entry accounting.

Note that accountants will often advise business clients to use general-ledger systems like these because these programs meet what is known as "generally accepted accounting standards." Accountants prefer this for two reasons: (1) such a system reduces the chances of posting errors, and (2) if you use an accountant for year-end work or to prepare a financial statement, your information will not have to be reentered by the accountant into such a system. Nevertheless, our recommendation is that often check-writing software is the most appropriate for home-based businesses.

Spreadsheet Accounting Systems: For people who prefer working with spreadsheet software, another alternative is simply to design your own spreadsheet to follow IRS Schedule C for sole proprietorships, in which your columns are the categories on Schedule C and your rows are your dated entries.

The advantage of using spreadsheet software to track your business finances is that you have access to more powerful analysis than a check-writing program offers, but obviously you will lack the ability to use your software to write checks!

#2. Determining What You Need to Charge and How Much Business You Need to Generate

The Problem

No doubt you know or can calculate how much money you need to bring in to support yourself and your family. What may be more difficult for you to figure out is how much you will need to charge and how much business you will actually need to generate each month in order to meet your income needs after paying your expenses and other costs involved in getting and doing business. Usually those of us who are used to living on a salary have never had the need to make such projections. But it doesn't take long to realize that because you have to spend money to make money, it's too often your living expenses that come up short when the month is too long for the money.

Computer Solution

You can use your computer to prepare a budget that will help you project how much you need to charge and how much business you will need to generate. Of course, you can do budget projections with pencil and paper, but using a computer to calculate expected income and expenses will save a lot of time in recalculating your projections and actually make your budget projections more accurate.

In fact, most check-writing programs like *Quicken* have budgeting capabilities that are tailored to help you make the projections you need. In general, you begin by identifying the recurring expenses you anticipate and establishing a category for each type such as those we listed on pages 203–4 in chapter 2 (salary, travel, office supplies, phone, insurance, and so on). *Quicken* even makes this easy because it has predefined categories for common business expenses that you can simply check off to include in your budget, or you can add your own categories if you have special expenses. When preparing your budget, be sure to include all three classes of expenses we mentioned in chapter 2: your personal living expenses, your direct costs, and your overhead. We find that many home-business owners do not account fully for their overhead expenses when setting their prices or fees, and that's why they may be working long hours but not making enough money.

Once you have selected your categories, you can estimate the amount of money you believe you will need to spend each month in each category. The software will then tally the numbers for you and give you a total budgeted expenditure. This then is the amount you will need to make that month to pay for your supplies, your overhead, and your salary. (See Figure 3-2.)

Then, if you are trying to determine how much you need to charge per hour for your services, you simply take the total amount from your budget and divide it by how many hours you expect to be able to bill that month. Your result is equal to how much per hour you will need to charge. For example, if you were to add up all your costs and saw that you would spend $4,000 per month including your salary, direct costs, and overhead, and you know you need to charge around $40 per hour to be competitive, then you know that you will have to bill out 100 hours to generate sufficient income, and you can develop your marketing efforts accordingly.

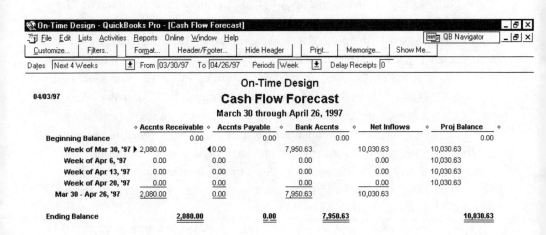

Figure 3-2: With a check-writing program, such as Quicken, *you can project your income and expenses using budgets. But you can go beyond that with a cash flow forecast that allows you to anticipate your cash flow needs for the coming month. In this example,* Quickbooks, *an accounting program, does that.*

We realize that sometimes new businesses must take whatever work they can generate or accept a smaller fee than they often desire, at least in the beginning. So, of course, your budget is simply a "projection." However, by creating a budget of estimated income and expenses, you benefit in three ways. First, the numbers you derive are useful in giving you a realistic idea of what to bid for a job when you have the chance to do so. Second, budget projections give you a clear target to aim for, and you can use them to motivate yourself to keep marketing aggressively until you have all the clients you need to cover your projections. Without budget projections, it's too easy to lull ourselves into thinking, "Well, I'm busy so I must be doing okay." And third, the budget projections provide a barometer by which you can measure your progress and evaluate how close you are to achieving your goals.

Some businesses may want to perform more sophisticated analyses on their budget projections than check-writing programs like *Quicken* or *Microsoft Money* allow. For example, you may want to see what would happen to your budget if you doubled your expenditures on advertising. Could you increase your billable hours by thirty? Such "what if" scenarios are more easily handled by the spreadsheet modules in *Lotus Works* or *Microsoft Works* or spreadsheet programs like *Lotus 1-2-3, Microsoft Excel* and *Quatro Pro* (Corel), which allow you to examine many different options at the same time. Spreadsheet programs are actually quite easy to learn to use, often incorporating an internal "intelligence" that does some of the work for you. For instance, in some spreadsheets, if you type in "January" in the first space of a row, the program will automatically type in the remaining months in the rest of the row.

Once you've used a spreadsheet to project various scenarios and selected your optimal projections, you can put the final data back into a budget in your check-writing program to track actual income and expenditures against your projections.

#3. Keeping Track of Your Money

The Problem

Many home businesses operate essentially with their bank statement as their only source of information about where they stand financially. In some cases (although we recommend against it), the home-business owner has not even set up a separate business bank account for the company and, instead, mixes his or her personal checking and savings with the money from the business. In either case, since the bank statement provides little useful information about how your business is really doing, without additional information you could find yourself making decisions in the dark and end up in debt or, under the assumption that you can't afford it, putting off making purchases that would actually increase your income.

Computer Solutions

By using a check-writing program such as *Quicken* or *Microsoft Money,* or a general ledger or spreadsheet program, you can monitor your financial situation in much greater detail than a bank statement can provide. In fact, by having identified categories for your projected income (i.e., types of projects, services, or clients) and expenses (i.e., marketing costs, insurance costs, etc.) when doing your budget, you have already done half the work of tracking your money.

From that point on, all you need to do when recording your income or paying your bills is to indicate which of your categories each deposit or payment applies to as you enter them in your check register. Then at month's end, you can request that the software prepare and print out a precise report clearly showing where you made your money and where you spent it, category by category. Some programs also allow you to establish subcategories for obtaining even more precise information such as tracking income or expenses by client name. Furthermore, you can also have the program print out a comparison of what you projected in each category against your actual income and expenses, and graphically display how well you did, where you may need to cut back, and where you could expand.

By creating a report of your income and expenses in this fashion, you are, in effect, examining your "cash flow"—how much is coming in versus how much is going out. Having a computerized record that compares your budget to actual expenses will provide a useful history you can call upon whenever you need to bid on a project or make an estimate for a flat fee.

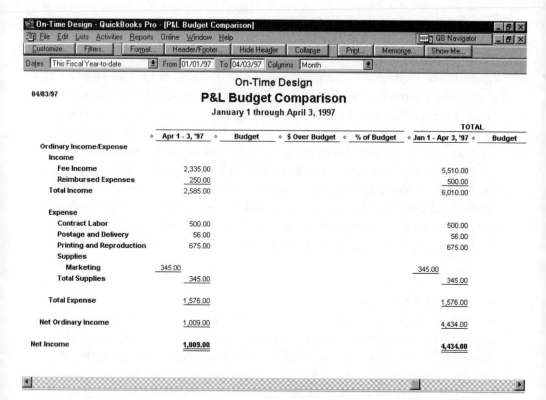

Figure 3-3: It is often useful to track your income and expenses for each project you work on. Here, Quickbooks allows you to print out a Budget Comparison for a specific period of time for each client.

You will no longer have to rely on guesstimates or intuition to estimate your costs, thus assuring that your projects are profitable. Such information can also help you make a case for turning down business that won't be profitable.

Additionally, once you get into the habit of recording your finances, you can easily move on to preparing the many other kinds of reports that most financial software programs will do. For instance, you can create a report that accounts for all the invoices you have sent out—that is, your accounts receivable—and track how long it takes to get them paid. Most of the software packages we discussed can create and print out account-receivable reports formatted either by client or by date showing which accounts are thirty, sixty, and ninety days overdue. And should you need one, you can also generate a "balance sheet," which shows your company's assets, liabilities, and owner's equity.

Finally, if you are visually oriented, as many people are, all these programs have charting and graphing capabilities that let you plot your data in various ways, and they let you export your data to a spreadsheet program that has a graphics module. Seeing where you are making money and where you are losing money on a bar graph can help you see patterns in your business, such as recurring seasonal downturns or relying too heavily on one client. It can also help you in making wise tax-planning decisions.

#4. Analyzing Your Profitability

The Problem

Most home businesses operate with limited resources. You only have so many hours you can bill out; you can only charge so much and still be competitive; and you only have so much money to spend for equipment, marketing, and other aspects of running your business. However, too many of us end up spending most of our time, money, and energy on the activities that demand the most attention, which are not necessarily the ones that will provide us with the best results. We get bogged down responding to the most bothersome clients, trying to break into the most difficult-to-penetrate fields, or going after the most complex projects. In fact, as many people discover, it often turns out that only 20 percent of your clients will be generating 80 percent of your money, or 20 percent of your services will be producing 80 percent of your income, or 20 percent of your marketing expenditures will be bringing in 80 percent of your clients. This phenomenon is evidence of the 80/20 Rule at work.

The problem is how do you know which markets, which marketing activities, which purchases, and which clients are actually going to be most worth your time and energy? For example, how do you know if you should take the time to submit a complex proposal for a shot at a big contract or if you would be better served devoting more time to your existing smaller ongoing clients? How do you determine if you will be better served by attending the upcoming national conference in your field or upgrading your laser printer? These are the kind of strategic decisions that challenge us all day in and day out.

Computer Solutions

By having computerized your finances, you can analyze the profitability of various activities and more easily correlate your efforts with what actually produces your income. By tracking your hours and expenses and compar-

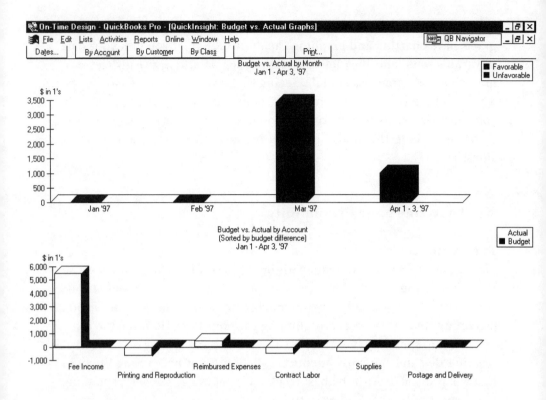

Figure 3-4: Many programs allow you to graph your financial results. In this screen, Quickbooks contrasts your budgeted vs. actual results. You can readily spot items you need to pay attention to.

ing them to your income, you can recognize when you have fallen prey to the 80/20 Rule and redirect your energies at once. For example, you can determine if the time you are spending on a particular project is worth the fee you're getting paid—or whether all the time and money you are putting into a particular marketing activity is paying off.

Programs like *TimeSlips* (TimeSlips Corporation) enable you to track every minute you spend on a job for up to 30,000 clients or jobs. *TimeSlips,* for example, works in either of two ways:

- You can record the time yourself by keeping track of and then logging in the exact hour each day when you started working on a particular project and the hour you stopped. *TimeSlips* will then tally the number of minutes for you and keep a record of your total project time.

- Or if the work you are doing is on your computer or the telephone, you can simply press a few keys that tell *TimeSlips* to start tracking time for you until you tell it to stop. *TimeSlips* is what's called a TSR (terminate and stay resident) program, meaning it works in the background in your computer's RAM memory. While you're using the computer to do other things, it's busy tallying the time you're devoting to whatever project you are working on. This feature can be especially useful when you need to keep track of time spent on the phone with clients so that you can bill them accurately.

When you have completed your work on a project, *TimeSlips* will calculate the total hours you spent on the project and prepare your invoice according to whatever hourly or per diem rate you specify. This invoicing feature alone could save you hours each week and improve your cash flow by enabling you to bill more quickly.

TimeSlips has many other features as well. You can arrange to have multiple billing schedules so one kind of work can be charged at one fee while another kind of work can be billed at a different fee. You can also record expenses billable to a certain project and add them to your invoice. In short, a program like *TimeSlips* provides you with the hard-and-fast facts and in-depth information you need to make decisions like when to raise your rates and what expenses you've been absorbing as overhead that you need to pass back to your customers.

Programs like *Quicken* and *Quickbooks Pro* can also be useful in helping you analyze your profitability. For example, having defined your income and expense categories (for example, type of client, type of expense), you can have *Quicken* print a Project or Client report that compares your Income and Expenses across all categories for clients and projects. This information will readily tell you the extent to which one project is worth more to you than others.

Let's say, for example, that it's time to renew your membership in a professional association and you must decide whether to rejoin or to use the $400 you would spend on your membership to expand your newsletter mailings. On the one hand, the phone always rings with new clients after your newsletter goes out and, on the other hand, you can't remember getting many new clients from networking at the association meetings. So you are leaning toward postponing or dropping the membership in favor of sending your newsletter to a larger mailing list. But by printing out a report of the sources of your income over the last year and another report of your marketing expenditures, you can find out which activity is really paying off. You could discover that while the newsletter brought in more clients, the clients you got through referrals from the association brought in larger sums and did more repeat business. In other words, the newsletter could actually cost more to produce per-client dollar than the dues for the professional association.

Or let's say that you have attended four trade shows every year because industry wisdom has it that "everyone needs to be at these shows." By analyzing the business produced from each show, however, you might learn that two of the shows have never actually paid for themselves and decide to cut back to only the two shows that are producing results.

#5. Making Sure You Get Paid

The Problem

Home-based business owners, especially new ones, can end up having to wait sixty or even ninety days or longer to get paid. This is especially true if your clients are large corporations that have long payment cycles. And even for home businesses with a track record, being a small sole proprietor can mean your invoices end up low on the priority list for getting paid. This means that unless you stay on top of your invoices you could spend hours on the phone tracking down your hard-earned money. When this happens, getting paid can actually cost you money, since you have to waste time finding out what's holding up the money you've already earned. And while many other businesses have a problem getting paid too, particularly in tough economic times, we think that one factor behind long delays is that some companies simply take advantage of small and home-based businesses to improve their own cash flow.

Computer Solutions

The good news is that we need not sit back and take it on the chin when it comes to demanding our fees. With a little help from your computer, you have many options that can give you clout in the battle to get paid promptly.

First, by keeping track of billable time on your computer by client as you go along or by building your invoice in the field by recording expenses as they occur on a laptop, you can make sure your invoice goes out the very moment you finish a job or are allowed to bill a partial fee. Then to increase the chances your clients will take your invoice seriously, you can create an "official," professional-looking invoice that commands the utmost respect.

SIX CHOICES FOR CREATING EFFECTIVE INVOICES

To easily create such a professional invoice, consider using one of these five options:

1. Dedicated time-tracking and invoicing software like *TimeSlips* and *WinVoice* (Good Software)

2. Invoicing software designed to work in conjunction with your money-management or accounting programs

3. Word-processing programs like *Microsoft Word* or *WordPerfect* that provide you with different templates that make it easy to design your own invoices

4. Professional form-design programs like *PerFORM Pro Plus* (Delrina/Symantec) or *BizForms* (JetForm) that contain many template forms as well as offering you the opportunity to custom-design your own forms

5. Add-on programs like *HotDocs* (Capsoft Development), which provides templates you can use with a spreadsheet

6. Accounting programs that include invoicing such *as M.Y.O.B., One-Write Plus, QuickBooks,* and *Peachtree Complete Accounting*

Should the day come when an invoice becomes overdue, you need not let the day pass without notifying the client of your concern. You can use a calendar software program such as *Lotus Organizer* to notify you automatically when an invoice is due. *Quickbooks Pro* also includes time tracking of invoices. When the day arrives, the moment you turn on your computer, the screen will flash a message indicating with whom you need to follow up.

For customers who say your invoice can't be found, you can instantly fax them another one. In fact, you can fax a second copy of any overdue invoice with a polite reminder. Doing this need not distract you from other work if you have an internal fax/modem board that lets you fax a document in the background while you're working on other things.

Finally, when you need to resort to sending a "dunning" letter to remind a client about an overdue bill, you can compose a series of collection letters to have on hand that become progressively more firm and quickly personalize them as the need arises. Such repetitive reminders are often the icebreaker in getting the client to know that you mean business. Programs like *Model Business Letters* from Model provide samples of collection letters you can modify for your own use. You can also use your computer to access online databases that can help you ascertain the financial stability of prospective clients and those who owe you money (see chapter 6).

#6. Preparing Estimated and Year-End Taxes

The Problem
Tax preparation can be time-consuming and frustrating when you're busy focusing on getting business and serving your clients and customers. But every quarter, you must take time out to calculate how much your net income has been over the past three months and pay your estimated taxes. Should you estimate incorrectly, you could face penalties. And, of course, you must take out time once again to tally your year-end totals and prepare your final tax return. You could end up spending several days working for the IRS or alternatively having to pay an accountant thousands of dollars of your hard-earned money to do it for you. And if you didn't take time out to prepare for your taxes throughout the year, you'll probably have to take out an even larger block of time preparing them in April. Then, Heaven forbid, you could be audited and have to document everything for the IRS!

Computer Solutions
Actually, preparing your taxes is one of the best reasons to use a bookkeeping and financial record-keeping program. Most of the programs described earlier make preparing your taxes almost routine. If in setting up your business categories you tailored them to correspond with IRS Schedule C for businesses and have logged your actual expenses and income throughout the year by category, then you have already laid the groundwork for quickly preparing your taxes.

Furthermore, many of the financial record-keeping or check-writing programs allow you to export your data directly to tax preparation software such as *TurboTax* (Intuit). If, in addition to entering expenses you've paid by check, you have entered deductible expenses paid in cash and with a charge card, the export procedure practically wraps up your taxes, and all you need to do is write a check. If you prefer, you can print out reports in conjunction with doing either quarterly estimates or year-end summaries, and then prepare your taxes by hand or give them to your accountant. In

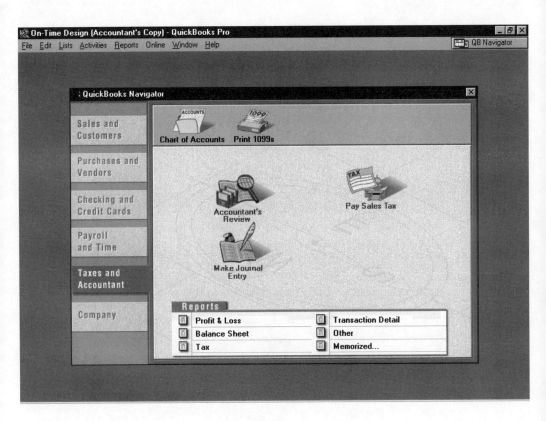

Figure 3-5: Tasks are made the basis for finding your way around with Quickbooks' *Navigator screen, enabling you to make choices quickly.*

either case, by using a tax program, you will save a lot of time and you may be able to save money on the amount of professional tax preparation help you will need.

No matter how computerized you become, however, remember that the expenses you deduct must be ones that are acceptable to the IRS, and since computer entries can be altered, you still must maintain a paper trail of all your receipts and other transactions.

SIX QUICK SECRETS FOR MANAGING YOUR MONEY

1. Group tasks such as writing checks into activities performed a few times a month. To maximize your cash flow, you can prepare checks at one time in advance and then mail them at the appropriate time throughout the month.

---

2. Set up a consistent template for preparing your invoices. You can design an invoice and simply save it as a permanent template.

3. Print your checks out directly from your financial software package. As long as you are taking the time to record an entry, you might as well use the program's ability to write the checks, and they will look more professional than handwritten or typewritten checks.

4. If you know a client chronically pays late, offer a small percentage off if the bill is paid within thirty days or charge such clients a higher price because you are offering them financing.

5. Enter charges and cash receipts at a regular time each week so you will have all information necessary at your fingertips for calculating your taxes and knowing where you stand.

6. Since you still need to have a paper record of business receipts, file receipts immediately after entering them by category so you won't need to sort them out later.

CHAPTER 4

Computerizing
Your Administrivia

Most home-business owners dislike "administrivia": filing, record keeping, scheduling, keeping track of appointments, deadlines, names, phone numbers, E-mail, notes and project details, making copies and getting things into the mail—the list seems endless—all the little detailed, repetitive things that someone has to take care of. Unfortunately, chances are that the only person who can do them now that you're on your own is YOU.

When we began working from home, the extent of the administrivia took us by surprise. We both had worked in large organizations: Sarah for the federal government, Paul for a nonprofit research and development foundation. Little did we realize how much we had come to rely on our secretaries and other administrative support staffs. So many things that had been simple because someone else took care of them for us suddenly became time-consuming roadblocks to getting our work done. When we needed a copy we had to go out to a copy store—there went thirty minutes to an hour, depending on how long the line was. Whatever we needed to do—send a letter, create a newsletter, make travel arrangements to meet with an out-of-town client—all these previously simple tasks could devour our days.

But today, we've turned over most of the tasks that slowed us down and drove us crazy to our computer, fax, online connections, laser printer, copy machine, telephone, and other home-office technology. One by one we've been able to streamline many of our administrative tasks to the point that they are no longer obstacles to getting our work done. Instead, they get done with the ease and speed of a well-trained staff. We don't have to run out to the paper store: we call up their Web site, place our order, and receive it by mail. We don't have to address mail by hand or even feed envelopes into our printer: we simply press a button, and the computer feeds in and prints out our envelopes or mailing labels. We don't have to wait for someone to tell us what airline flights we can take or book rooms over the phone: in minutes we can look it all up online.

By taking advantage of the many administrative tasks the computer can handle, you can free up hours and even days each month for income-producing activities instead of spending your time bogged down in administrative chores you don't enjoy anyway. In this chapter we'll address how you can use your computer to streamline four of the most time-consuming and frustrating types of administrivia that we all face.

#1. Organizing Tasks and Responsibilities

The Problem
In the hustle and bustle of operating a one- or two-person business, it's easy to feel overwhelmed as you try to keep up with the many demands of a given day. You may be trying to finish a project while responding to incoming calls or trying to make a key marketing arrangement while responding to an emergency with a new client—all right at the time your estimated taxes are due and your new printer is being delivered.

Often while trying to juggle all the various activities and information that come across your desk, you may wish you could be more productive and better organized. You may expect if you were more on top of things you could not only get more business but also do it more efficiently and have more time left over to play. Sometimes, of course, procrastination or too many distractions and interruptions keep us from being more productive, but more frequently it's a matter of simply having too much information to track and too many priorities to handle. Organizing these tasks and responsibilities is a perennial problem even for the most dedicated and committed home business.

Computer Solutions
Fortunately, many software programs are directly aimed at helping people better manage their time and information. Depending on your needs, you can select from among calendar and appointment tracking programs, often called personal organizers, or the powerful "personal information managers" (PIMs). Here's a brief description of these two types of technologies and how they can help take the hassles out of your day.

Calendar and Appointment Programs: These programs are particularly useful if you would like to automate your calendar, appointment schedule, and address book. They have a wide variety of features ranging in complexity from simple to highly sophisticated.

Many calendar programs that have been developed for Windows make use of the graphic interface to simulate a typical page from one of the popular appointment and calendar books. With such programs as *Organizer* (Lotus), *Outlook* (Microsoft), *Calendar Works* (Parsons Technology) and *Sidekick* (Starfish Software) your screen looks like an open appointment book with tabs along the edge, and you simply use your mouse to point to a tab you want and then go to the pages you need for addresses, phone numbers, to-do lists, appointments, schedules, and so on. Other programs allow you to view your calendar in different increments such as two days at a time, a week at a time, a month at a time, or a whole year at a time. Many of these programs link up to database programs and address-filing programs to help keep even greater track of whom you need to see, when, and where. Some will even interface with your E-mail and send out as well as receive scheduled E-mail correspondence.

If you have many tasks to do and are seeking a really powerful program, *Lotus Organizer,* for example, offers a broad range of useful additional options, such as being able to link an appointment in the Calendar to a task on your "To-Do" List or to a contact name in your Address Book, or to a flowchart stored in your Notepad. If you are double-checking an appointment with a client, for instance, once you find it in your Appointment Calendar, you can jump immediately to the address section of your book to locate the phone number of that person. *Calendar Quick* (Logic Pulse Software) is a shareware program that allows you to create calendars and timelines to track your tasks. By integrating it with other Windows applications, you can easily transfer any schedule displayed to your favorite word processor or desktop publishing program via the Clipboard. Like most shareware programs it's available on bulletin boards and through the Internet (*http://www*.download.com).

Many of these appointment and calendar programs also have an automatic alarm function to remind you of appointments by beeping at an assigned time. When you enter an appointment, you simply indicate that you want the alarm to alert you as the scheduled time approaches. A time-saving feature many of these programs also offer is auto dialing. When you access a phone number in the program's address book, you can tap a key or two and the software will dial the phone number for you. You need to have a modem connected to your computer for this feature to work.

These calendar programs can be more than convenient time-savers. They can also help you get focused and "stick to business" by helping you prepare "to-do" lists, set priorities, and outline and track your goals. Using an organizer consistently is almost like having a personal secretary to assist you in managing your day.

Calendar programs can also serve as your one central calendar and appointment schedule so you don't waste time trying to coordinate your various calendars. Many programs have the ability to print out your schedule on one of the popular paper formats such as *Dayrunner* or *Day Timer.* This feature lets you maintain your schedule on your computer but gives you the flexibility of carrying a printed version with you when you leave the office.

In addition, these programs can help you create permanent records that may prove useful if problems and misunderstandings arise. For example, you met two weeks ago to sign a contract for a new project, and the client now says that you are three weeks overdue on the project. Or perhaps you phoned a vendor last week, but now she can't remember if you called on Tuesday or Wednesday. By consistently keeping track of your appointments, and making notes of what transpired on an electronic notepad, you can often save yourself many headaches and possibly even the loss of a client or a lawsuit.

Personal Information Managers (PIMs): PIMs are essentially a step up from calendar and appointment programs. They offer many more powerful features. In fact, PIMs are actually specialized database programs that let you make "records" of information far beyond simple names, numbers, appointments, and dates, although the programs also have those capabilities as well. For example, with a PIM, you can take lengthy notes, write personal profiles, store references to magazine articles, make lists of all kinds, and link them all together in groups so you can correlate related topics. Then, whenever you need to find something, you can search through all the information you've stored using keywords or key phrases, and any record that contains those words will appear on your screen.

Ecco Pro (NetManage), and *Time & Chaos* (iSBiSTER International) are among the award-winning personal information managers listed by *Windows* magazine. Some of these programs are described as free-form databases, in that you are not restricted, as is the case with many database programs, to predefined fields for your entries. For example, *Infoselect,* a popular program by Micrologic, allows you to input information in any fashion you want, whether it's numbers or characters, one sentence, or forty sentences in length. To add information from E-mail correspondence, just drag it over and drop it in with your mouse. Many database programs require you to "define" each record in advance, telling the program the maximum length it should expect for any entry. This can be a considerable annoyance as your needs change and you want flexibility to include additional types of information. *InfoSelect* also has an alarm function.

We'll also discuss a related kind of software called "contact management programs" in the next chapter. Contact managers are better suited to keeping track of client and customers contacts while PIMs are best for storing, accessing, and using information.

Now That You Know about PIMs, How about PDAs? One of the only drawbacks to keeping your calendar, agenda, notes, etc., in your computer is that your trusty PC is a little awkward to carry to meetings. The last two years have seen the rise of "personal digital assistants" (PDAs) that are, in essence, much smaller versions of your office computer. Not to be confused with laptop or notebook computers, PDAs are even smaller, ranging in size from a credit card to about the size of an average frozen entree. PDAs are also not as powerful as notebooks or laptops. Although they won't run the full version of AutoCAD, PDAs do a great job of running specialized calendar and PIM-type programs. Popular models include the Pilot by Palm Computing and several from Hewlett Packard.

PDAs fit easily into a briefcase, purse, even a coat pocket, ready to be taken out, turned on, and used. Information entered into a PDA can be quickly downloaded into your office computer. For example, appointments can be streamed right into a calendar program, meeting notes converted into a word-processing document, and new addresses and phone numbers transferred into a database program. You can also import information the other way: from your office PC into your PDA. Many PDAs also come equipped with modems, and some even have a cellular phone circuit so you can send and receive faxes and E-mail and browse the Internet from anywhere you happen to be. Microsoft has even developed a version of Windows, called Windows CE for PDAs that allows you to run slightly scaled-down versions of Word, Excel, and other popular programs.

#2. Making Time to Do What Needs to Be Done

The Problem

Finding time to do everything that needs to be done is no less daunting than keeping track of what we need to do. We frequently have more to do than will fit into an eight-hour day. Chances are, in times like these, we either get diverted by the many administrative tasks that demand to be done, or, after having ignored them long enough, we get bogged down because they haven't been addressed.

Computer Solutions

Although some people dispute it, we believe technology is a time-saving tool when it comes to administrative matters such as typing letters, getting out a mailing, making phone calls, preparing faxes, and so on. Here's a list of ways technology can help you save time day in and day out by taking over and streamlining many common administrative tasks:

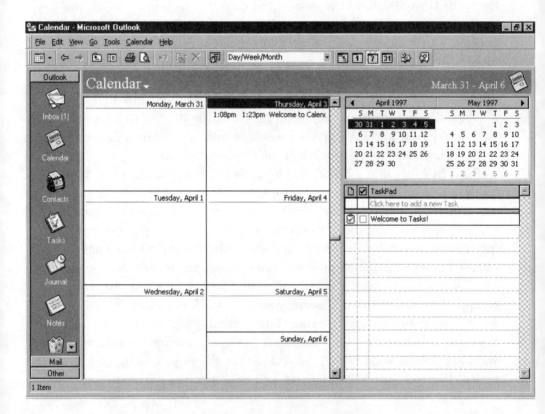

Figure 4-1: Personal information managers can greatly facilitate your ability to store and sort through the mountains of information and tasks that business owners need to schedule and track. This is the Calendar view of Microsoft's Outlook.

Twenty-one Ways to Save Time with Technology

1. Use integrated software (suites) when you need to make intermittent use of multiple software programs. With integrated software like *Microsoft Office Professional Suite* or *Lotus SmartSuite,* you get a word processor, a spreadsheet, presentation graphics, and a database program as well many other modules. All these components have similar command structures and tool bars so you can learn to use them more quickly. You also can move simply and easily from one to another and transport information or data among the various applications. (See our introduction to suites, p. 263.)

2. Find it online! No matter what you are looking for—a resource book, a marketing fact, a government agency or law, up-to-the second news, the latest version of a software program, where to stay in almost any city in the world, a replacement cartridge for that twelve-year-old dot matrix printer, what *not* to feed to a depressed horse—just about any fact or product is available online. Save time by using the Internet to actually buy items and make reservations, or just compare prices and features before you buy. We can't tell you how much time and effort has been in saved in research because of the Internet. Before you look anywhere else, log on and try to find it online.

3. Use macros. When using a word processor, macros save time by stringing together sequences of keystrokes that can be activated by entering one short command. Each sequence—be it several words, a sentence, or a paragraph—is associated with just one or two keys that you can press to get the entire sequence. For instance, you might program your word processor so that whenever you press the Alt and C key simultaneously, it writes out a standard closing for your letters, for example:

Sincerely,
Paul and Sarah Edwards

4. Automate as many functions as possible. Programs such as *AutoMate* from Unisyn Corp. allow you to set up a schedule of tasks the program will automatically perform for you, such as backups, close routines, or other tasks you routinely do.

5. Use templates for standardized documents. Programs like *Microsoft Word* and *WordPerfect* already have predefined templates or style sheets for things like business letters, faxes, memos, proposals, and more. Desktop publishing packages like *Microsoft Publisher* and *PageMaker* also have predefined templates for creating such documents as newsletters, cards, and catalogs. When you use one of these templates for a letter, for example, the program automatically inserts the date, sets up the "Dear . . ." salutation, lets you select from a library of names and addresses you've already keyboarded, and signs "Sincerely" and [Your Name], thereby saving you hundreds of keystrokes.

6. Use the outlining feature of a word-processing program that lets you move entire sections of a report around just by moving the title associated with that section.

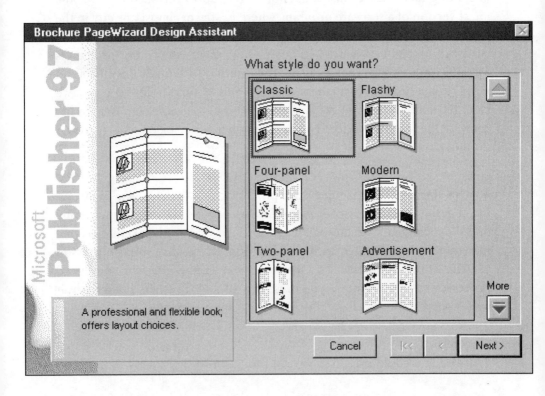

Figure 4-2: Wizards reduce the steps to creating marketing materials using a desktop publishing program like Microsoft Publisher. *Here you choose among alternative looks for a brochure. With desktop publishing you can easily test different approaches as well as individualize your marketing materials for particular prospective customers.*

7. Use a spell checker, grammar checker, dictionary, and electronic thesaurus that come with many word processors to save the time of looking up words in reference books.

8. Link documents if you are operating in a Windows environment. With linking, anytime you revise the numbers in one document like a spreadsheet, they will be automatically updated in your other documents like reports, overheads, or proposals that have incorporated those numbers.

9. Use the automatic addressing and envelope printing utility that comes with most word-processing programs or purchase an add-on utility, like *Office Accelerator,* with additional powers. These save keystrokes since you don't have to type a name and address twice or spend time setting up your printer for an envelope.

10. Use a separate label printer such as *Avery's Personal Label Printer* and *Label Pro* software to print rather than hand-type or write out individual mailing labels. These dedicated label printers also enable you to print out labels for file folders and make index tabs for proposals.

11. Use form design software for your standard business forms. A package like *PerFORM Pro Plus* (Delrina/Symantec) or *Formworx* (Power Up Software) includes predesigned form templates you can use either as is or customized to your needs. You can print out and use these forms or you can save paper by filling them out on your computer screen, for example, while interviewing or collecting information by phone. *PerFORM Pro Plus* enables you to do calculations while filling out a form, look up information in a database, or turn the data you've collected into a database file that can be used in programs like *Microsoft FoxPro* and *Paradox.* Using electronic forms is saving some companies over 70 percent of what they would be spending to print paper forms.

12. E-mail documents instead of mailing, if possible. If the document contains only text, you can attach it as a file to any E-mail transmission and send it to any E-mail address in the world. This saves a great deal of time and expense for approving terms and conditions on contracts, approving content for publications, and any form of business or personal correspondence.

13. Add an internal fax board or fax/modem so you can fax directly from your computer instead of having to print out a document and manually feed it into your fax machine. (Fig. 4.3)

14. Turn incoming faxes into text files so you can edit and revise them or capture them to use in your own documents. Software like *WordScan Plus* from Caere Corp. or *WinFax* (Delrina) have optical character recognition capability (OCR) that translates fax images into text files. Without this capability, your computer simply considers a fax to be a graphic image, like a piece of art, and you cannot manipulate it, edit it, or use it in a document of your own.

15. Use your fax machine as a copier. If you don't have a copy machine, you can make one or two quick copies of important documents with your fax machine and save the time of having to run out to a copy shop. Most fax machines can make small numbers of copies, and with plain paper faxes now priced at less than $500 you can get decent copies through your fax on plain paper. Even if you have a copy machine, you can use your fax machine as a backup if the copy machine goes out of commission.

16. Speed up your printer with a print enhancement software program like *SuperPrint* by Zenographics.

17. Eliminate the need to manually load or feed envelopes, letterheads, or other special papers into your printer by investing in an envelope and/or paper feeder that will do it for you.

18. Use special precut and preprinted papers to speed up making indexes, printing brochures, and creating reports. Such special paper products and printing supplies are available from mail-order supply houses like Paper Direct (Call 800-A PAPERS for a free catalog) or in self-help paper stores in many metropolitan areas. See chapter 5 (p. 324) for additional information on sources of specialty papers.

19. Speed up backing up your hard disk with a program like *Cheyenne Backup.* Those who are most dedicated to backing up their work tend to be those who have lost their work. The cause of such a loss may arise from your hard disk crashing, a fire, water damage, theft, electrical problems, computer viruses—so many things can go wrong. But you can protect your files by backing up in one of multiple ways.

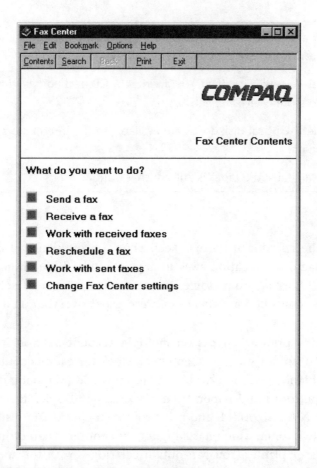

Figure 4-3: Save time and paper by faxing directly from your computer. This particular "fax center" software came bundled with the computer. You can also separately install capable software that comes with multi-function devices that serve as your printer, copier, fax, PC fax, scanner, telephone and digital answering machine.

HERE ARE YOUR BACKUP OPTIONS

- Small amounts of data can be backed up on floppy disks.

- An extra hard drive or hardcard can back up material several times during a day.

- Tape drives quickly store up to 1 gigabyte and more of information per tape.

- Removable drives such as Iomega's Jaz Drive and Syquest Technologies can store up to 1 gigabyte on removable disks.

- Digital VersatileDisk (DVD) is a writable CD technology that allows you to store over 4.5 gigabytes on a disk.

- Magneto-Optical disk drives are available for long-term storage of all your data.

- DAT (digital audio tape) is still another option.

To be on the safe side, it's wise to keep a copy of your data in a safe deposit box or some other location away from your office. Steve Thomas, a member of the Working from Home Forum on CompuServe, wisely and succinctly observes, "PC's are cheap; software, expensive; your data, priceless."

20. Simplify printing checks on multiple accounts. If you have a laser printer and do not want to keep check stock for each account, you can purchase blank check stock, which requires MICR (Magnetic Ink Character Recognition) bond paper, from a source like Duplex Products, 8565 Dempster, Niles, IL 60714, and print your own checks. You will also need special MICR toner, which has a higher iron content than ordinary toner, for your laser printer. You can obtain cartridges with the special MICR from companies such as Black Lightning (800/BLACK99) that recharge laser cartridges. You can expect to reduce your cost of printing checks in the process. You will also avoid accidentally printing a check with the wrong preprinted number. Shareware is available for printing checks with *Quicken* on the IBM Applications Forum on CompuServe Information Service in the Personal Accounting Library with the file name LQ121.ZIP.

21. Cut down on the time and difficulty involved in drawing up business contracts by using software that contains pro forma contracts that you can customize to your needs. For example, you can find such contracts for writing partnership agreements, engaging professional service, employee agreements, nondisclosure agreements, permission to use copyrighted material, and consignment agreements. Sources of such contracts include *Quickform Contracts* (Invisible Hand Software), *Business Law Partner* (Intuit), and PC-FORMS Document Drafting System available in Library 5 as shareware under the file names PCFMS1.ZIP and PCFMS2.ZIP of the

LAWSIG Forum on CompuServe. Also check shareware sites on the Web such as *http://www*.jumbo.com

#3. Planning Large Projects

The Problem

If, like event planners, catalog publishers, or professional practice managers, you are involved in large or complex projects that involve many steps or components, inevitably something can go wrong if you miss a step or forget a task. Such mistakes can cost you money and time, and even future business.

Computer Solutions

Project-planning and flow-charting software can help you manage many of the problems associated with large projects. Programs like *ABC Flow-Charter* (Micrografx), *Project Scheduler* (Scriptor Associates), *Microsoft Project, Visio* (Visio Corporation), and *Primavera Project Planner* contain predefined flow-charting capabilities for planning projects. You can use different shapes (triangles, boxes, rectangles, etc.) to visually represent individual aspects of a project and sequence or arrange them into timelines or action plans. Then you can track your progress along these chains with the confidence of knowing that you won't miss an important step. These programs also provide analysis capability to notify you of time or resource conflicts you may have mistakenly assigned to the project. Good project-management software should also be able to actually provide you options to the problems that data analysis points out. Many also allow you to quickly and easily send memos and write reports on a given project's status, and even connect to the Internet so these communications can be instantly sent wherever they need to go.

#4. Managing Your Computer

The Problem

Like many computer users you may find that your computer soon becomes overstuffed with multiple programs, each with its own files and data, along with hundreds of Windows files and other UFOs (unidentified file objects) you can't remember creating. A quick scan through your file manager may reveal several trees of directories more confusing than the genealogies of European monarchy.

When your computer gets to this stage of clutter, it can become as self-defeating as a hopelessly disorganized desk or an overstuffed file cabinet. What you thought would save time now eats away at your time as you try to figure out how to access what you need, remember what you named it, or locate where you put it on your disk. Upgrading your operating system can exacerbate this problem to the point of madness. The best way to think about computer management is that in running a business, your computer becomes your staff in a box. Instead of managing people, you must start effectively managing the contents of your computer to get the most out of them.

Computer Solutions

Fortunately, the problems the computer has created it can also help solve. In fact, frustrated and confused computer users have created a substantial market for good "computer management" software. The best known of these programs are *Norton Utilities* and *Norton Desktop* (Symantec). The Norton programs arose from the imperfect beginnings of DOS and then Windows, and allow users to simplify the way the computer performs many operations such as opening up an application, copying files, formatting disks, backing up, and setting preferences. Other popular management programs for your computer include *PC Tools* (Central Point Software).

Some of these programs use the metaphor of the "desktop," so when you turn on your computer your "desktop" pops up on the screen. From your desktop, you can then move quickly into any program or file you want, transfer from one application to another, and have your fax/modem and printer always at the ready. Some desktop managers use other metaphors to simplify how you visualize and access your computer files. One called *Dashboard* (Hewlett-Packard) resembles a car dashboard, complete with clock and other various icons that represent your applications or files. Another, called *Tabworks* by Xerox Corporation, gives your screen the appearance of notebook with each program area represented as a clickable tab.

The dream of the paperless office is greatly helped by a group of programs known as document managers. Well-reviewed packages such as *GreenDesk* (GreenSoft Corp.), *PageMaster* (DocuMagix), and *Presto Page-Manager* (NewSoft) help you organize electronic files such as reports, faxes, diagrams, E-mail, and any other kind of stored document. Files can be searched for and imported into an "inbox" where you can organize them any way you see fit.

The good news on the horizon is that the future of all such file management for Windows-based machines is quickly moving in the direction of what is called object-oriented operating systems more like Macintosh computers. The latest version of Windows, as matter of fact, is giving desktop organizers a run for their money.

Once you invest the money and take the time to select and learn to use the types of software and other products available today, your computer can provide you with the same capabilities as a talented and dedicated support staff, freeing you from hours of drudgery to do the work you do best. But there is more, because not only can your computer help you administer your business more easily, it can also, as you will find out in the next chapter, help you bring business in the door without breaking your budget.

CHAPTER 5

Using Technology to Market Yourself and Increase Your Business

T he minute you decide to start making money on your own, your thoughts will undoubtedly shift to how to get your first customers or clients . . . the survival instinct at work! Of course you want to get these clients as quickly as possible. Then as soon as you get some business, your next interest becomes how to turn that business into a steady flow. This means that somehow you have to make yourself and what you have to offer known to those who need it and are willing to pay for it. And then you have to keep yourself in the top of their minds so that when they do need you, you'll be the first person they'll call. Finally, you need to make sure that they can reach you when the moment comes that they do call.

As eager as you are to get business, you probably have limited funds to spend on business acquisition and little expertise or interest in marketing and sales. Nonetheless, whatever business-generating activities you go about doing, you'll probably need to do them yourself and you'll probably need to do them on a shoestring budget. Furthermore, to keep business coming your way, you'll need to remain active at marketing, even after you're busy working with your new clients or customers. And somehow prospective customers will need to be able to reach you even while you're out marketing and serving your clients.

Fortunately, your computer and other wisely selected home-office equipment and services, from Internet Service Providers (covered in Appendix I) to the latest telephones to voice mail systems, faxes, modems, copiers, and scanners, can become your marketing partners, enabling you to produce affordable, cost-effective, high-quality marketing materials and maintain communications to virtually anywhere. In our book written with Laura Clampitt Douglas, *Getting Business to Come to You,* we describe thirty-five of the most effective, low-cost marketing methods used by successful home businesses. While this chapter won't explain the ins and outs of using these methods, it will show you how your computer and other technology can assist you in using almost every one of those marketing methods more easily and effectively. Just as your computer can help you manage your money and office administrivia, this chapter will demonstrate how your computer can be an invaluable tool for getting and keeping plenty of customers and clients.

Once again, we've organized this chapter to address the most pressing issues home businesses typically face then suggest technological solutions for each issue. First we'll address how you can use hardware and software to initiate and expand your client and customer base, and then we'll discuss how to equip yourself so you can make sure that you're accessible to your clients and don't miss key business phone calls. We have included a specific emphasis on the telephone because it is the umbilical cord that connects your home office to the business world. Home businesses spend more time using telephone, fax, voice, and electronic communication than any other single activity.

THE BEST MARKETING METHODS

Getting Business Fast

- Turn your ex-employer into a client.

- Ethically take business with you when you leave your job.

- Do overload and get referrals from your competitors for work they don't want or are unable to do.

- Respond to classified ads and convince prospective employers that you could do a better job as an independent professional.

- Directly solicit business by phone or in person whenever you have free time. The worst thing that can happen is that you will make a new contact who doesn't need your services at this time.

Generating a Steady Flow of Business

Getting business is an active endeavor. You can't just sit back and wait for customers to come to you. You must take action to identify and get to know potential clients and their needs. You must attract them to your product or service and keep them coming back to you. Although such marketing efforts take time and energy initially, the momentum they generate can get business coming to you with only a minimal amount of on-going effort. Your computer can help you launch your initial marketing effort and then make a regular habit of continuing to reach out and stay in touch.

For example, as you will discover in this chapter, you can use desktop publishing, Web publishing, and powerful word-processing software to create your own display ads, newsletters, flyers, Web sites, brochures, cards, and stationery. You can use brain-extending software like *IdeaFisher* to develop creative and effective ad and brochure copy. You can use contact management software to communicate with prospective clients every month so you are never "out of sight, out of mind." In this section we will outline how you can use your computer to accomplish the three most time-consuming and challenging administrative tasks involved in getting and maintaining a steady flow of business. They are the key ways we believe everyone should put their computer to work to get more business with less effort and less time.

#1. Keeping Track of Business Contacts

The Problem

Each day you're in business puts you in contact with many people who represent potential business or access to business. This ever-growing base of contacts can be your most valuable resource. It can be your lifeline to a steady flow of business. Unfortunately, however, many people find themselves too busy and too disorganized to take advantage of the contacts they are making. For example, you might meet 20 or 30 interested contacts at a speech, trade show, or exhibit and while some of these contacts will turn into business from that first contact, a much larger number could become clients at some later time—if you continue to make contact with them. Or you might run an ad and receive 100 phone calls that turn into 5 new clients, but many of the other 95 callers could become clients later if you were set up to send them a mailing at regular intervals in the future. You may periodically meet someone while interacting online who could refer many clients to you, but will they actually make a referral if they never hear from you again? For most people, out of sight equals out of mind.

Because you most likely don't have a full-time secretary or sales and marketing staff, it's easy for business cards, brochures, and other notes that represent the valuable contacts you've made to become strewn throughout your filing cabinets, Rolodex cards, appointment books, business card holders, and other repositories of names, addresses, and phone numbers. But if you could keep track of all the contacts you've already made and stay in touch with them regularly, you could increase your business manyfold and reduce the time and energy you need to exert continually trying to make new contacts.

Computer Solutions

The most valuable marketing function your computer can perform is to enable you to create a complete record of all your vital business contacts—potential clients, present clients, past clients, gatekeepers, and other referral sources, vendors, media, etc.—so you can easily and simply identify and contact them regularly by phone, E-mail, or regular mail in any desired combination whenever you wish to. There are many ways you can do this. You can use personal organizer software or a personal information manager program like those described in chapter 4. You might consider using mailing list software, or contact management software, or even a full-fledged database program. We'll describe each of the additional methods here so you can decide which will best meet your needs.

MAILING-LIST SOFTWARE

The simplest way to create a contact list is to use a mail list manager, such as *Address Book Plus* (Learning Company), *My Deluxe Mail List* (MySoftware Co.), *Address Book* (Parsons Software), *LabelPro* (Avery-Dennison), or *Labels Unlimited* (SoftKey). These programs are actually simplified database programs that are "preformatted" with only ten or twelve items, called fields, to fill out for each person, such as Name, Address, City, State, Zip, Phone, and so on.

One of these mailing-list programs, for example, *My Deluxe Mail List,* has a built-in word processor and mail-merge capability that enables you to write brief letters to send to all the names on your mailing list (see box below). The software also enables you to print out the letters and mailing labels, complete with Zip bar codes. It also sorts first-class and third-class mail to save you money with bulk mailings.

When looking for a mailing-list program, make sure it has the capability to export data into word-processing documents for mail merges (discussed below) and into larger database programs. If you feel you don't need these capabilities right now, that's okay. You don't have to use them. But next year, as your needs grow, you'll be thankful that all the hard work you put into compiling your mailing lists won't be stuck, immovable in your mailing list program.

PERSONALIZING MAILINGS WITH MAIL MERGE

Mail merge refers to the ability to link your mailing list to letters and other documents so that you can send the same letter to individuals on your list but each one will be personally addressed. What happens is that the mail-merge function automatically goes through your mailing list and inserts the proper name, address, salutation, and other information into a template document you have designed. This allows you to personalize and customize your letters rather than sending them all out saying "Dear Sir/Madam," or some other impersonal reference. In essence, the template document is a form letter, with personalized return address, salutation, possible references in the letter itself, and closing.

Full-scale word-processing programs such as *Microsoft Word* and *Word-Perfect* have mail-merge capabilities that may make it easy for you to create your customer lists and write letters without even purchasing a mailing-list program. (See Figure 5-1.)

Here is a sample of how you can use mail merge to personalize your mailings:

$SANAME$RL
$SAADDRESS$RL
$SACITY$RL, $SASTATE$RL, $SAZIP$RL

$SADATE$RL

Dear $SANAME$RL,
Thank you for the opportunity to have worked with you on $SALAST WORK DATE$RL. We appreciate doing business with you and hope you were satisfied with our prompt attention to resolving your computer problems.

We would like to take this occasion to let you know that we are currently offering a special to our former customers, good until $SAFUTURE DATE$RL. Please feel free to give us a call to learn more about our current discount.
Sincerely,
John L. Jacobs

The limitation of mailing-list programs, however, is that they don't provide the alternatives to create and sort your list by your own categories, nor do they have such features as calendars for scheduling activities, alarms that alert you to whom you need to follow up with, or notepads for recording salient points of discussions you have with those on your list. But if your needs are primarily to send out regular mailings of various kinds to your entire list, a mailing-list program may be your best bet.

CONTACT-MANAGEMENT SOFTWARE
A second alternative for setting up and maintaining a list of your clients and contacts is to use another specialized type of database program: contact-management software. Contact-management programs combine

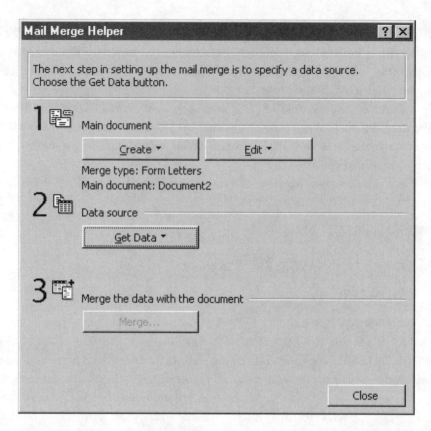

Figure 5-1: Word processing programs have built-in mail merge capabilities. On this screen, Microsoft Word shows you the steps needed to create or edit a list of names, then merge them into documents, creating individualized letters quickly.

mailing-list management and mail-merge capabilities with other features such as calendar and appointment logs, notepads, automatic phone dialing, record keeping of calls, alarms that alert you when to follow up with a contact, daily to-do lists with priority settings, and even faxing and E-mail capabilities. The power of contact managers is that all these functions are integrated and linked in an easy-to-use format. Here's an example of how contact managers can save you time.

Let's say it's Monday, and you decide to begin the week by filling in a calendar with your to-do list for the upcoming two days. As you fill in the list, you indicate for each item if it has an A, B, or C priority. When you are finished with your planning, you then select one of your upcoming appointments with a certain person. The program will show you the history of all previous appointments you've had with that person and the notes that you've made about what transpired during each contact (see Figure

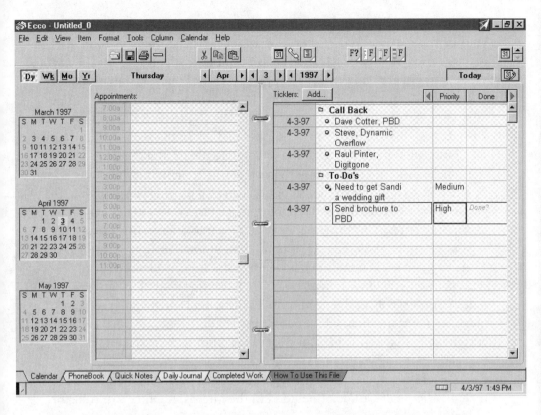

Figure 5-2: Contact management software, such as the program Ecco Pro from Netmanage shown above, lets you keep track of all your activities as well as send and store E-mail, faxes, and letters. You can also type in memos about phone calls and meetings you have, and maintain a complete history of your contacts with clients. With Ecco Pro you can also manage projects.

5-2) such as letters, E-mail, faxes, appointments set, mail messages sent, and any modification made.

You might then hit a key or use your mouse to point to the auto-dial command, and the software will automatically dial the person's phone number. As you talk on the phone, you can make additional notes on a "notepad," and these will automatically be added to the contact history for that person.

After the conversation is over, you then decide to send the person a standardized E-mail letter such as an acknowledgment or thank-you note that you've already written and stored. With the push of a few keys, you have one of these letters sent to the person, complete with a personalized greeting and perhaps a comment related to the conversation you've just held.

Contact-management software will also allow you to contact those in your database through the Internet via E-mail. Many programs even offer features such as "docking," which allows you to work off-line (in the car, planes, hotels, etc.) and then use docking to synchronize databases, mail, and appointments when reconnecting to the Internet through your office computer. Another powerful feature will allow you to record timed events such as customer calls or consulting time either in the record history or on a notepad. When the scheduled appointment date and time is reached, the software will send an audio or visual "alarm," reminding you of the appointment. A click of your mouse button can also provide you with a snapshot overview of your day with appointments, tasks due, unread mail, next alarm, and more. Many programs even allow you to drag an E-mail message to your calendar and create an appointment automatically.

As you can see, contact management software can increase your productivity and efficiency in many ways. Because this kind of software originated in order to meet the needs of sales personnel and telemarketers who must keep logs on their sales appointments and telephone sales calls, its advantage is that it provides an easy-to-use approach to making, managing, and recording your contacts.

Some of the popular and well-regarded contact-management packages include *Microsoft Outlook* (included in the Microsoft Office Pro suite, or available as a stand-alone program), *Act!* (Symantec) and its simpler and less-expensive version *1st Act!, OfficeTalk,* (Sareen Software), *Maximizer* and *Maximizer Light* (Maximizer Technologies, Inc.), and *TeleMagic* (Telemagic Corp.). Each of these differs in the modules they offer, and some, like *TeleMagic,* are particularly helpful for businesses that rely heavily on telephone contacts as when you're making dozens of phone calls each day. For example, *TeleMagic* can automatically generate a list each morning of the people you've tagged to call after ten days and print out many kinds of reports based on the hundreds of phone calls you may have made over the past month. The Phonelink module adds full telephone support, including answer, hold, conference, dial, redial, transfer calls, caller ID, and screen synchronization.

Janna Contact Personal (Janna Systems, Inc.) provides many powerful features in one compact, easy-to-use program that costs less than $100. Features include searchable contact lists that can be displayed side by side. *Telemagic* now works in conjunction with your telephone and Caller I.D. When someone calls who is listed in your contact base, the program will automatically identify the caller and display their contact record on the screen so you have all pertinent information in front of you while you talk. Developments in contact managers include Internet connectivity such as Now Software's *Now Up-to-Date & Contact,* which allows you to drag information from Web pages and drop it right into the program.

Most of the contact-management programs also offer features such as mail merge for quickly sending out customized letters, quick label and envelope printing using addresses already stored in the records, and alarm mechanisms you can program to beep at a given time if you need to be reminded about an upcoming appointment or call.

DATABASE SOFTWARE

A third way to keep track of all your contacts is to use a full-fledged database program. Mailing-list-management and contact-management software are actually specialized database programs that provide a predefined structure for keeping track of client contacts. Today's powerful database programs have become so much easier to learn and use, however, that you can now use them to develop your own customized format for tracking your contact records. Popular database programs include *Paradox* (Corel), *Approach* (Lotus), *Microsoft Access, FileMaker Pro* (Claris), *Alpha Five* (Alpha Software), and *Microsoft FoxPro.* You can also use the database modules associated with Microsoft Works, Lotus Works, or other integrated packages.

To use a database program for contact management, begin by defining what you want each client "record" to contain. Because many database programs are now graphically oriented, this process is quite easy and simply requires laying out the different "fields" or types of information you want to store; i.e., Name, Address, Phone, E-mail, Fax, Notes, etc., on an on-screen index card. After you've defined your fields of data, you then keyboard in the information for each contact you have and continue updating your database as you encounter new people.

The advantage of using graphically oriented database programs is that you can input nearly any category of information regardless of whether it's numbers, dates, or text, and you can easily add fields at a later date if you discover you left out important categories of information you need for each client. Also, database programs are typically far more powerful than mailing-list management or contact managers in that they offer many specialized sorting and searching functions. And while some databases are "flat-file" programs, most programs available these days are considered "relational" databases, which means that you can join several files together to simplify how you construct your database. For example, rather than trying to create one database that includes all your customers and then leaves enough extra fields for all the orders that each customer might make in the future (which you usually can't predict), you can instead create one database of customers and their addresses, and another database for orders, and then link the two files together.

Last, there's also a kind of database software known as "free-form," in which you do not need to specify your fields in advance. Imagine that rather than the database program showing you an index card on which is already written Name, Address, Phone, and so on for you to fill in, instead you see a totally blank screen onto which you can write anything you want in any order, and call it a record. Then when you want to look something up, you can search through your records using easy commands such as "Get Fred Smith," and the program will find all the records that contain the name Fred Smith. Many people find these kinds of database programs much easier to use, since they don't have to remember any specific method of keying in information or searching. Popular programs of this nature include *InfoSelect* (Micro Logic), which is used by some people variously as both personal information managers and contact management programs.

WHICH SOFTWARE TO USE: PERSONAL ORGANIZER, PERSONAL INFORMATION MANAGER, MAILING LIST MANAGER, CONTACT MANAGER, OR DATABASE?

If you are uncertain about which type of software would best help you build and track your business contacts, here are some tips to help you decide.

First, ask yourself which of the following statements your needs are more heavily weighted toward:

A. Sending mailings to your contact list

B. Locating and contacting various categories of contacts by mail, E-mail, or phone

C. Keeping basic information on individuals you deal with, such as addresses, phone numbers, and some personal and business information for use in a variety of sales and marketing efforts

D. Keeping extensive records about not just the people but also each transaction you have with the person, including meetings and phone calls

E. Keeping records not so much on people but on pieces of information, such as summaries of news articles you've read or notes to yourself.

If your answer is

A. You can probably get by with a simple mailing-list program.

B. A database program like the one in *Works for Windows* might best meet your needs.

C. You might want to use a simpler personal organizer such as the *Lotus Organizer* or *Amaze.*

D. You may wish to have the power and sophistication offered by a contact management program such as *ACT!*

E. You may want to look into a free-form information manager such as *InfoSelect.*

Also, note that the distinction between all these kinds of programs is blurring more and more as software companies in this field are eager to make their programs serve as many needs for contact management as possible. We strongly suggest that to make your decision you read as much information as you can about any program you're considering, and get a demonstration of it as well. Only then will you know if the program fits the specific needs of your business.

No matter which type of software you select, the biggest hurdle to using it effectively may be finding the time and making the effort to enter the information you want to keep track of into it. Some people bite the bullet and do the data entry themselves; others hire someone else to do it for them. But once that initial work is done, you can update your data and expand it with ease as each day goes by. One way or the other, it's worth the effort because, in time, you will have built yourself an invaluable asset that can assist with any marketing program you initiate.

#2. Making Sure Clients Keep You in Mind

The Problem

Almost without exception, there are far more people who will need what you're offering sometime in the future than there are people who need you at any given moment. As a result, when the moment comes that someone does need what you offer, chances are they will turn to whoever comes to mind. You have to make sure that it's you. We call this "top of the mind marketing," and we know firsthand just how important it can be. Here's just one example.

One week, you contact a company to discuss some work you might do. They're interested but not at this time. Of course, you tell them that you'll be glad to work with them when they are ready and you leave feeling optimistic about having them as a client sometime in the future. A few months later, however, you hear that one of your competitors is working with that company, doing exactly what you were proposing to do.

In cases like this you may actually have done the sales job for someone else who walked in at just the right moment. And the most frustrating thing about this is that it happens all too often—more than you know—but, of course, you can't be everywhere at once. You have to devote the majority of your time to working on income-producing business. You can't spend all your time trying to keep track of whom you need to follow up with from last month or last year so that you can be there at that magic moment.

Technology Solutions

If you've created a database of all your business contacts and selected the right software for it, you can use your computer, laser printer, fax, and modem to do "top of the mind" marketing for you. You can make sure that every person on your list receives something from you by phone, fax, E-mail, or regular mail as often as necessary with minimal time and energy on your part. Your software can track and inform you of who needs follow-up. You can then use the computer to design and produce materials you can easily reproduce and mail to everyone on your list or just to select categories; for example, new clients, past clients, people you met at the trade show last month. You can even customize the mailing individually so it appears you have sent it just to them.

Here are nine ways you can use your computer hardware, software, and supplies that enable you to do "top of the mind" marketing without breaking your budget or your work schedule:

Customize Your Brochures and Flyers. You can use your computer to send your past or potential clients a professional-looking brochure tailor-made to address their needs. Preprinted papers formatted for brochures, flyers, certificates, and letterhead like those available from Paper Direct allow you to produce full-color items using a printer or copier. These papers have good-quality designs printed in color on them. Used with a high-quality laser printer like the 600 x 600 dot-per-inch Hewlett-Packard LaserJet or other laser printer, what you produce is virtually indistinguishable from an expensive full-color print job from the best printer in town.

Figure 5-3: Preprinted papers make it easy for you to create professional-looking brochures and flyers on full-color letterhead, business cards and envelopes, as well as other items. With Paper Direct products, you use your computer to add your name and address.

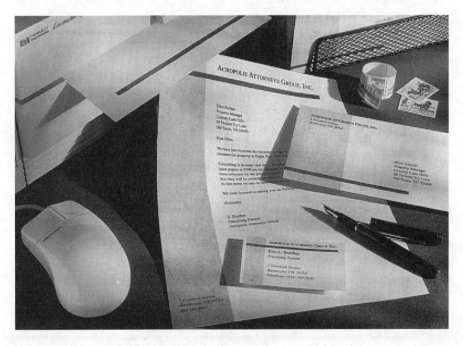

Figure 5-4: You can get printed products including all types of checks, invoices and forms, and stationery that have a consistent logo, typeface, and color scheme from NEBS.

Catalogs with preprinted papers are Idea Art, P.O. Box 291500, Nashville, TN 37229, (800) 433-2278; Paper Direct, 3660 Victoria Street North, Shoreview, MN 55126 (800-A-PAPERS); and Queblo Images, 131 Heartland Blvd., Brentwood, NY 11717, (800) 523-9080.

For a truly special effect, use your word processor and its mail-merge function to customize the language on the brochure, flyer, or envelope for each individual or company you wish to contact. Vary the greeting, the price, the services you indicate as your specialty—whatever you think will best demonstrate what you can do and appeal most to their needs.

Create Special Postcards. You can send your clients and potential customers a quick postcard every six to eight weeks to remind them about your services or to let them know about any specials you may be offering. You can create these postcards yourself for just pennies apiece using your laser printer, desktop publishing software, and Avery's Laser Post Cards. Many desktop publishing packages like *Microsoft Publisher* and *Adobe PageMaker* have predesigned templates for postcards and most of the other marketing materials described in this chapter. You just fill in the copy and any additional art you wish to use. Then, using your contact-management software, organizer, or mailing-list software and your laser printer, you can quickly print out the cards and the mailing labels to send off dozens of cards in just a few minutes.

Avery's Laser Post Cards come in page-size sheets that are perforated, which makes them easy to print out, tear apart, and pop in the mail. Avery also has laser-ready sheets of a wide variety of standard labels. Using their *Label Pro* software, you can add art or your logo to the mailing labels, and with a personal label printer you can even do single labels easily and quickly.

Send Personalized Messages via Regular Mail. You can create and send personalized announcements, thank-you notes, greeting cards, and other attention-getting messages to clients, prospects, and referral sources. For example, Idea Art (800/433-2278) offers a variety of laser papers preprinted with cartoon and graphic word art such as "Thanks," "For Your Information," "News," and "Attention." Paper Direct has a line of attractive, blank, prefolded holiday greeting cards that you can run through your laser printer with your own message on the inside. *Microsoft Publisher* has a template for creating your own attractively designed thank-you note or greeting cards.

Send Personalized Messages via E-mail. These days, people check their E-mail more frequently than their regular (snail) mail. Sending personalized, informal E-mail messages is an effective way to keep potential customers thinking of you. People hate getting "spam" messages (overtly commercial offers), so we don't recommend sending E-mail to someone unless you have already established contact in some other way. With E-mail, the more personalized, the better. If your contact has a particular interest or hobby, use PointCast or a digital "clipping service" to provide you with the latest news on the subject, then attach the article to your E-mail message and send it. Almost all contact-management software allows you to E-mail right from their programs (if you have an Internet Service Provider), so it is relatively easy to keep track of what you sent to whom when.

Publish Periodic Newsletters. Other than a check or an order, nothing is more likely to stand out amid the volume of postal and electronic mail every business receives each day than a newsletter that's chock full of important information or free advice. Whether your newsletter is a single-sided sheet or an eight-page folded and stapled magnum opus, using inexpensive desktop publishing programs like *OmniPage Pro* (Caere Corp.), *Master Publisher Suite* (IMSI), or *Microsoft Publisher,* you can produce this valuable marketing tool fairly easily. Most desktop publishing programs also include HTML templates or easy-to-use HTML coding so you can quickly convert your printed newsletter into an online version for the Web. If you plan to send an online version of a newsletter, look for a contact-management or mailing program that will allow you to do mass E-mailings.

To make producing your newsletter even easier, several desktop publishing and even word-processing programs come with preformatted newsletter templates, complete with headline type, multiple-column format, and boxes where you can insert art and text. All you need to do is enter your text, and import a piece of clip art or scan in a photo, and there you go . . . an amazingly professional-looking newsletter ready to print out on your laser printer or at your local print shop. And once again, you can quickly print mailing labels from your contact-management, database, or mailing-list program and get your newsletter in the mail.

What was once an expensive and highly time- and skill-intensive process has become a practical do-it-yourself marketing method that any small business can use to update clients and potential clients on developments in your field, to share information about people and events, or to show off your professional knowledge. While it may cost you a few hundred dollars to produce and mail each issue, a newsletter can not only pay for itself with the first call it generates but may also bring in thousands of dollars of additional business. At the very least, it keeps you in mind for future business.

Send Timely Fax Messages. Faxes are great for getting immediate results or action, and for top-of-the-mind marketing campaigns. You can use your fax to send a quick thank-you to a client for giving you past business. You can dash off a flyer announcing a special offer you are making or to remind a client that you are available. Some fax machines enable you to send the same materials simultaneously to multiple recipients, so you could even fax a monthly newsletter to key gatekeepers with just one push of the button.

Actually you can use your fax for any number of other marketing needs as long as you are faxing to people who already know you and would want to receive material from you. Unsolicited faxes are not only often poorly received; in some states they are also illegal. We also suggest that you not overuse faxes as their impact diminishes with frequency of use. You might vary sending a fax with postcards, newsletters, flyers, and other mailed marketing pieces.

You can also design your own fax forms using form design programs such as *PerForm* (Delrina/Symantec). Most popular word-processing programs provide several fax cover sheet templates to choose from as well.

Communicate via Users' Groups, Bulletin Boards, and the Internet. Online gathering places such as users' groups, newsgroups, Web sites with "chat" rooms, and discussion groups often serve as important connections to your colleagues, customers, and potential clients. Through these sources you can obtain news and updates on trends in your business by communicating with other people online. The online world is really just a series of small communities that gather around common interests and concerns. If you are a financial planner, for example, you can find literally hundreds of places online to talk with your peers, discuss trends with providers of financial products, find out about the latest productivity tools, market your services. You name it, and it's probably out there. The information you gather online may prove valuable in obtaining intelligence regarding your market and industry. You may find new ways to target new clients or get the edge you will need in a competitive situation. Networking online is also a great way to obtain leads for new business. The growth of the online virtual world is shrinking the size of the actual business world. Networking online frees you from the confinements of geographic markets. Among the phone, the fax, and the modem, most home-based computer businesses can service clients anywhere in the country, or even the world.

Online gathering places also include the Working from Home Forum on CompuServe, which is dedicated to all kinds of home-based businesses like information brokers, independent writers, accountants, and book-keepers. Large online services also offer specialized bulletin boards and discussion areas, such as CompuServe's computer consultants' section sponsored by the International Computer Consultants Association; a desktop publishing forum hosted by Tom Hartmann, founder of the Newsletter Factory; a broadcast professionals' forum; and one for public relations and marketing professionals. Other high-traffic home-office and small-business locations include America Online's discussion groups found at Keyword: YOUR BUSINESS. Many larger commercial sites on the Web have their own "chat" rooms where you can interact on a real-time basis. Look up manufacturers of the products your business might use— for example, a video animator might search for the Silicon Graphics or Adobe site—and see if there are chat rooms or discussion areas on the site. (If you are a little unclear as to the difference between a chat room, a discussion group, and a newsgroup, we'll discuss these more fully in the following chapter.) Search for newsgroups that cater to your industry or expertise, as well as the technologies you use. Read through them and see where the discussions have been going. If someone has posted a question you can answer, go ahead and answer it. That's instant recognition for you as an expert in your field. There is still a plethora of private, specialized bulletin board services for people with a specific mutual interest in an industry such as medical, legal, engineering, writing, programming, and many other areas.

Most professional associations now have a site on the World Wide Web. Check out the associations related to your business and see what's happening on their sites.

Obviously, to use online resources you will need a modem and a subscription to an Internet Service Provider. Most ISPs offer fairly inexpensive base monthly rates; however, you will often need to pay additional fees to log on to private bulletin boards.

Send Out Professional News Releases. Public relations (PR) entails doing what it takes to obtain editorial coverage in the media about you, your service, or your product. PR can be a very effective marketing tactic. If a publication does cover or feature you, you have the double benefit of, first, "free" (not counting the expense of producing and mailing the kit, see below) exposure, and second, a recommendation from a trusted impartial source. People give far more credence to the judgments of a publication's editorial content over its advertising content.

Until somewhat recently, creating your own publicity kit and news release was a major undertaking, as was gaining access to the names and addresses of the key media people you wanted to receive your kit. As a result, anyone who wanted to use public relations as a marketing technique either had to pay out thousands of dollars to hire professionals to produce and distribute materials about them or they had to develop the needed expertise themselves, which, of course, is a time-consuming and expensive process. Now, however, your computer can help you do your own PR. While it will still take some practice and time, it is now possible to produce a top-notch media kit yourself from your home office.

You must begin with a clear understanding of what it is about what you offer that will be perceived as newsworthy. Keep the emphasis on news. If your kit looks like an overt marketing presentation about your business, no one will want to pick up your story. Concentrate your press release on how your product or service will help people. Answer questions like: Whom will it help? How will it help? Is it part of a trend? Is it trendsetting? When you've determined the content of your news release and media kit, then use your word processor to write the news release, along with a desktop publishing program, clip-art software, graphic design software, and a scanner if needed to add any graphs, illustrations, or photos that might enhance your presentation. You can either print out your materials on your own laser printer, transmit the material via modem, take a diskette to a service bureau for higher-quality printing.

Finally, you can package your news release and accompanying material in a professional-looking folder such as those available in office supply stores from companies like Avery Dennison or by mail from companies like Paper Direct. If you print out your own news release, you can design the form or you can purchase preprinted, multicolored news release sheets from Paper Direct or Idea Art.

To learn how to write effective news releases and create a successful media kit, see Part Two of *Getting Business to Come to You*, which we wrote with Laura Clampitt Douglas.

The next step is getting your kit or news release into the hands of the right people. But this is also at your fingertips. You can have your news release distributed via fax by PR Newswire (806 Plaza 3, Harborside Financial Center, Jersey City, NJ 07311, 212/832-9400, Web: *http://www. prnewswire.com*), and Business Wire (40 East 52d St., 19th Floor, NY, NY 10022, Web: *http://www.businesswire.com* or 800/221-2462). You can also E-mail your release to both of these services and they will distribute it, for a fee, to hundreds of online news-gathering organizations such a America Online, CompuServe, Cnet, PointCast, and many more.

Bacon's Press Distribution Service, publisher of Publicity Checker and Radio/TV Directory, also offers mailing labels as well as printing and distribution for news releases. You can contact them at 332 S. Michigan Avenue, Chicago, IL 60604, (800) 621-0561, Web: *http://www.*baconsinfo. com. Gale's Directory of Publications & Broadcast Media has detailed information on 65,000 newspapers, magazines, journals, periodicals, directories, newsletters, and radio, television, and cable stations and systems. It's available online on Dialog.

You can also obtain database software such as *News Release Lists* from Mailer Software Corporation (800/443-8834). This software is available in three configurations: *Computer Magazine Editors, Computer Newspaper Columnists,* and *Business Magazine Editors,* and each list contains a thousand or more names and addresses that you can use to generate your own mailing labels.

#3. Creating a Professional Image for Your Business

The Problem

Many home-based businesses report that being taken seriously is one of their top concerns. They fear that clients, vendors, and business institutions may discount home-based businesses or automatically assume that someone who works from home cannot do as good a job as a larger company. In fact, succeeding in today's fast-paced, competitive economy means that you must command respect and convey a positive professional image at all times. Even though you don't rent an office or have an administrative assistant or a corporate bureaucracy behind you, and you may operate on a shoestring, you nonetheless need to project the image of a professional business that will get the job done with the highest quality possible. To overcome any stigma associated in people's minds with your being a home-based business, you must demonstrate that you take your business seriously and that others should take you seriously too.

Technology Solution

Once again, home-office technology comes to the rescue. Fortunately, today's technology makes it possible for you to ensure that everything you produce is indistinguishable from what comes out of a *Fortune* 500 corporation. With the right equipment, you can achieve the same sophistication as just about any company. There is an onslaught of technology and resources you can use for every job you do that will enhance your professional image and add a glow to your business. Whether it's a computer-based slide presentation, a memo, or a final report, that glow will go a long way toward capturing your client's attention and making sure he or she feels that you have gone to the end of the road for them.

Here's a list of cost-effective suggestions for how you can use your computer, software, and printer to give your work a 100 percent professional image:

CREATE A DISTINCTIVE GRAPHIC IDENTITY FOR YOUR BUSINESS

Design Your Own Logo. Whatever business you are in, don't settle for simply putting your company name in sixteen-point Helvetica with a rule beneath it across the top of your stationery. It pays to have a smartly designed letterhead and/or company logo that distinctively identifies your business and makes people take notice. Your distinctive graphic identity should appear on your stationery, envelopes, business cards, Web site, and just about anything else you present to the public. Every letter, every report, and every brochure is a walking billboard for your company. An appealing, dynamic letterhead or logo for your company solidifies your unique professional identity and adds to the positive impression clients will have about your company.

Of course, you can get your letterhead professionally designed, but you can also do it yourself using any of several easy-to-learn desktop publishing programs like *Microsoft Publisher, OmniPage Pro,* or *Master Publisher Suite,* along with the clip art from these or other programs to create your own typography and artwork. If you have a freelance designer do the work for you, be sure to get the image scanned and saved as a graphic file so that you can take it home and add it into your own computer where you can use it with your word processor or desktop publishing program on everything you produce. In this way, you can put your company logo on every document that leaves your printer, even your mailing labels, invoices, notes, postcards, and memos.

Don't Forget Your Business Card! Even in today's complex cyberworld, face-to-face contacts are still among your most important encounters. Giving your business cards to people you meet while networking, at sales meetings, etc., will act as your ambassador long after you've left the room. Put a great deal of time and consideration into their design and production. Make sure that they are consistent with your stationery in terms of design elements and "feel." There are specific software packages available that will help you design your own cards, if you are so inclined. *Microsoft Publisher* comes with predesigned templates that you can modify to create your own unique business cards.

And speaking of business cards, there are even software packages that help you keep track of all the cards others give you. Corex's *CardScan 200 Plus* (800) 942-6739, *http://www.*cardscan.com) can be bought as a stand-alone and is packaged with many scanners. This program allows you to scan in business cards and integrate them with your database, contact-management or list-management software. IRIS America's CardIRIS and NewSoft's Presto Biz Card are also well-regarded programs that scan business cards right into your database and other programs.

Custom-design your forms. Use desktop publishing or form design software to produce distinctive invoices and other forms that make your company stand out from the rest. Add an inspiring message or thank-you to standard forms using an intriguing typographic element that lets your clients know you appreciate their business. Today you can create your own custom multipart order forms and invoices and print them on carbonless paper with your laser printer. Such forms can be ordered from distributors like Laser Label Technologies (800/882-4050).

Give envelopes and mailing labels a distinctive look. Use your software to print envelopes and labels on your laser or ink-jet printer. The more individualized your envelope appears when it arrives, the less likely it is apt to be thrown away without being opened. You can add an envelope feeder to many printers so you do not have to feed envelopes one-by-one. For large mailings, you can use clear mailing labels like Avery's Clear Laser labels that are much less obvious than customary labels on white stock. You may also wish to get the larger die-cut mailing labels, such as Avery's 5577, printed with your logo at a local printer.

Print your checks. When you pay suppliers or vendors, print your checks with your laser printer using customized checks available with programs like *Quicken* or *Money*. As mentioned in chapter 3, *Quicken* will fill in the check with the name of the payee and the amount. (See page 267.)

CREATE MEMORABLE MARKETING MATERIALS

Use special fonts and clip art. There's no longer any reason to produce bland, boring documents that look as if they had come from a typewriter

Figure: Use your printer to print out attention-getting collateral materials such as these from Avery as shown above.

when most word processors and desktop publishing software offer scores of font choices. (If you're unsure—and many people are, including manufacturers—about the difference between a font and a typeface, here's the lowdown: a typeface is a printing term and refers specifically to physical "type" that must be set by a machine; a "font" is simply the digital equivalent of a typeface. Computers and computer printers use fonts, not typefaces.) You can use special fonts on your brochures, flyers, and other marketing materials to capture attention and enhance your company image. Consider getting one or two inexpensive software type packages such as *True Type Font Packs* (Bitstream) that provide literally thousands of special fonts in scalable point sizes. These font add-ons work with Windows' print manager and can be output on any brand or type of printer you may use. *Font F/X* (DCSi) offers 3-D fonts that can be used on Web pages and in text documents and presentations.

Use a high-quality printer. Your marketing documents represent your company identity, and so quality printing announces that you are a professional who takes business seriously. If at all possible, spiff up your marketing materials by using a high-quality printer such as a laser printer printing at 600 dpi x 600 dpi minimum, or take them to a service bureau with professional equipment. As Karen French, an independent home-based publicist consultant in Los Angeles says about her promotional materials, "People see my brochures and other collateral materials and think that anyone who invests that much time and effort in producing them has to be serious about what they do."

Add color. You can produce color documents inexpensively in several ways. The easiest way to add spot color to your documents is to use plastic color foils like those available from LaserColor and available through the Paper Direct catalog. Here's how they work: First you print out your page with a laser printer. Then apply the small strips of shiny colored foil to the text or graphic areas you'd like to highlight with color. Finally, run the page through the laser printer again. The printer's heat causes the foil to stick to the area of type or art you selected. This kind of spot color is perfect for short runs of fliers, cards, brochures, or report covers. LaserColor can also be applied using a copy machine.

Alternatively, you can also substitute a cartridge with color toner for the black cartridge in your laser printer or copier. Color cartridges are available by mail from BlackLightning (800/252-2599, Web: *http://www.flashweb.com*) and come in blue and brown. These cartridges can print your color letterhead or artwork, and then you can print the same page again using black or another second color.

Or, you can purchase a color printer, ink jet or laser. We discussed printers at greater length in chapter 3 (p. 254), but to recap some color options: the low end, in terms of quality and price, is the realm of ink-jet printers. For well under $500, you can find a plethora of color ink-jet printers that will print up to 600 x 300 dpi on regular paper. As we mentioned, these printers are fine for reports, letters, and presentations, but we do not suggest using them to create business cards, brochures, mailers, or anything else that will represent your business to a large audience. The quality just isn't there. Color laser printers do a much better job at resolution but will cost you substantially more. Even a $5,000 color laser printer's output does not match that of your local quick print business and will cost you a great deal in consumables (color toner and drum wear).

Please note: Inappropriate use of color or special effects can actually detract from the professionalism of your materials. A good cook knows just how much salt to use to make a recipe taste great. Too much salt will kill the flavor of any dish. If you are the least bit unsure of your color choice or design sense, skip the color or effect. If you are not a visually oriented person, we recommend you give the business to a fellow home-based designer or desktop publisher.

The impression we hope to be making on you in this section is that image is everything, at least in terms of getting your foot in the door with a prospective client or customer. Generally, your promotional materials (stationery, business card, brochure, etc.) will have preceded you there. For this, materials printed by a professional printer usually make the best impression, although printers affordable for home offices are getting better and may soon match the work done in many print shops. You can save money on professional print jobs if you have your pre-press work completed. Most desktop publishing software packages allow you not only to design your materials, but also to prepare your work for the printing press. Your desktop publishing program may also allow you to "separate" the colors into individual "sheets." The program should then allow you to save each sheet into an integrated file, which you can take right to your local printer for production.

One additional way to add color to flyers is to bring them to a copy shop where you can have your originals photocopied using color inks or colored papers. You can even print out selected words in color by masking text on the first pass, then sending it through the photocopier again on a second pass in a different color.

You can also have files you have created on your computer printed in full color in print runs of less than 500 pieces. What makes this affordable is Raster Image Processor equipment. This equipment accepts both Mac and IBM Encapsulated Postscript files. Shop for a local printer who offers this service.

Use special paper. Don't limit yourself to plain white paper. You can print your marketing materials on special papers from mail-order companies like Paper Direct (800/A-PAPERS), Queblo (800/523-9080), and Moore (800/323-6230). Today's laser papers come with colorful frames, exotic designs, background patterns, and "faux finishes" like parchment, marble, and granite. Paper Direct offers many specially formatted items for brochures and flyers that already include color borders and designs around which you can place your text for an instant professional look. Some of their brochure papers also include a prepunched, perforated section that becomes a Rolodex card or business card on which you can print your company name, address, phone number, and so on. Sometimes such papers are also available from self-help paper houses and local office-supply stores (Fig. 5-3).

Consider alternatives to printed materials. Some people can be better reached through other media, such as E-mail with attached files, audio-cassettes, and videocassettes. So why not produce an electronic brochure? Presentation software like Microsoft *Powerpoint* and *Corel Presentations* allow you to create dynamic, interactive slide show–like presentations and save them to a disk which you can send out. (You can even E-mail these presentations if the receiver has the same presentation software as you.) To add even more punch, attention-grabbing disk and cassette labels are available from Paper Direct and Laser Label Technologies that you can make with your laser printer and color-coordinate with your letterhead and stationery, including "hot" colors and metallic foils which you can print, cut, and stick on anything.

Freelance Graphics (Lotus) and many other programs allow you to pub-lish in HTML so your slide show can be posted to your Web Site, or sent to an FTP (File Transfer Protocol) site where it can downloaded by a prospec-tive client.

You can also create premiums and other gift incentives ranging from T-shirts to mouse pads that you can customize with your company logo or motto, using laser printer transfer toners and metallic foils available from BlackLightning (800/BLACK99) or clear labels that are available in uncut sheets for easy customizing to desired sizes and shapes (Paper Direct).

MAKE IMPRESSIVE PROFESSIONAL PROPOSALS, REPORTS, AND PRESENTATIONS

Format your documents for distinction. Whenever you need to give a client a written document such as a proposal or report, use your software to format and lay it out so that pages are attractive, easy to read, and in-corporate useful graphics, charts, and even artwork. If you need to write many such documents, we recommend using a word-processing program like *Microsoft Word, WordPerfect* (Corel), or *WordPro* (Lotus) that allows you greater flexibility in formatting. For very lengthy documents with lots of charts or graphics, you might want to port your word-processed file over to one of the desktop publishing software packages discussed earlier in the chapter. These programs give you even greater flexibility in laying out text across pages, as well as in formatting them if you need to vary the fonts, margins, columns, and other components of text-heavy documents.

To add borders or artwork to your proposals and reports, you can buy any number of clip-art programs that will provide you with thousands of images from which to choose to integrate into your report. You can also draw your own artwork using drawing programs like *CorelDraw, Adobe Illustrator,* or any number of useful shareware art programs (check out *http://www.*jumbo.com), all of which let you download your art into a word processor or desktop publishing program. These drawing programs also give you hundreds, sometimes thousands, of clip-art pieces you can use as is or customize for your presentations. *Art Explosion 125,000* (Nora Development) is a package that includes 125,000 pieces of clip art on a CD-ROM. *Key Photo Gallery* (SoftKey) offers over 2,100 royalty-free photos that you can include in your documents and presentations.

Add visuals for impact. If you are preparing a slide presentation or proposal requiring many bulleted charts and graphs, use a software program like *Freelance Graphics* (Lotus), *Corel Presentations,* or *Microsoft Power-Point* to create high-impact, colorful slides and charts quickly and easily. You can then print out overheads for your presentation on your laser or color printer using special laser transparencies or you can transmit your output by modem to special photo labs like Chroma Copy (800/548-8558) that will make up color slides for you and ship them to you with a twenty-four-hour turnaround.

Present proposals, reports, and samples in elegant folders and bindings. Avery Dennison and Paper Direct have excellent selections of plastic sleeves and envelopes, presentation folders, binders, slipcases, notebooks, and other supplies for presentations. Paper Direct has one catalog devoted entirely to products for presentations, called *Wow! What a Great Presentation,* which you can obtain by calling Paper Direct, (800/A PA-PERS. Also Avery Dennison offers several kits for producing professional-looking divider pages and tabs (800/525-7064).

To protect samples, catalogs, price lists, and spec sheets that people will be frequently handling, you may want to use a desktop bindery that will bind, laminate, and mount your material. If you will be showing these items in a three-ring binder, you can use paper with a tear-proof mylar strip that reinforces the edge with the punched holes that can be used in laser printers and copiers. Available from Queblo (800/523-9080).

Making Sure Clients and Customers Can Reach You

Your home office is unlike a retail shop, in that your prospective clients most likely will not be dropping by. This means that no matter how great your marketing efforts are, if your potential and existing clients and customers can't reach you by phone when they need you, you won't get their business. Considering the fact that your fax machine and online access also utilize phone lines, your telephone connection will most likely be your lifeline to getting and doing business. So it's no wonder most home-based, self-employed individuals use phone line communication, also known as telephony, more frequently than any other technology.

No matter how people initially learn about you, chances are that when they are ready to do business with you, they will contact you via the telephone. And whether you're needing to follow up on an overdue invoice or negotiate a new contract, chances are many of the key transactions with your clients once you have them will be by phone.

Somehow you will need to make sure you don't miss incoming calls from clients and customers, even though you may frequently be away from your office marketing or providing services to others. And you won't want to miss calls coming in while you're talking with others, which could be quite often. If you are working from home, you will need to decide how you will manage personal and business calls as well as how to deal with your fax machine's and modem's need to use the phone lines as well. In addition, your clients and customers should be able to look up your phone number in the telephone book or get it by calling information, and they most likely will not think to look under your name or to request a residential listing.

When we were starting out on our own, managing these telephone issues was a challenge because there were very few options. We could hire an answering service or plug in an answering machine, which half the callers hung up on, and that was about it. Phone company tariffs didn't permit using a residential line for business purposes, but having a business line was much more expensive and offered little other than a yellow-pages listing. Today, all that's changed. You now have a wealth of options for staying in touch with your clients and customers by phone. Most phone companies are eager to help small and home-based businesses find solutions to all their telephone needs, and they have developed a wide variety of services to meet almost every conceivable need. Some companies even have trained special "home-office" customer representatives whose role is to help you solve whatever telephone needs you have. Business lines offer a variety of services not available on residential lines, and some phone companies are obtaining new tariffs from state utility commissions to allow residential phones to be used for home businesses. Even companies that have not established separate home-office services and representatives have largely stopped playing the role of "telephone cops" or "tariff sheriff."

Today, there is no need for you to miss calls. You can be available to your clientele as often and as quickly as you wish. You can, in effect, be in two places at the same time. In fact, your callers need not know you are a one-person operation, or that you may be working from home in blue jeans and a sweatshirt. Your telephone system can make you virtually indistinguishable from a *Fortune* 500 company. Today the choice is yours, and the only problem becomes finding out about and selecting among the many telephone options open to you.

Here are a variety of telephone solutions to the five biggest challenges involved in making sure that you don't miss calls for new business and that your clients and customers can reach you when they need you. You can review these various options and then consult with your local telephone operating company about the best way to meet your needs. Not all these services are available from every telephone company and some call the services we describe by different names, but if you describe what you need the service to do, they will most likely be able to tell you how they can meet that need.

#1. Taking Messages When You're Busy or Out of the Office

The Problem

Missing a call can mean missing the opportunity to sign up a new client or the chance to serve a current customer. But the typical, home-based businessperson spends fewer than twenty hours each week actually in her or his home office, according to a recent study. Having a reliable way to get calls or take messages while you're out is crucial. In addition, there will undoubtedly be times when you don't want to be interrupted by incoming calls, times when you're meeting with a client, working on a deadline, or completing a highly demanding project.

In these situations, you need your telephone system to serve as a dependable receptionist, capturing your messages reliably and accurately. Unfortunately the most common solutions—having an answering machine or an answering service—have significant limitations. Although it is now considered rude in most parts of the country not to at least have an answering machine, some callers consider having one to be a signal that you're not a substantial business. Also, as we all know, answering machines sometimes break down unexpectedly, cut off the caller's message, or simply have poor sound quality. On the other hand, hiring a traditional answering service can be equally frustrating, as many services are impersonal, distant, and prone to making mistakes.

Another drawback of both of these options is that you will most likely end up spending time playing telephone tag with your contacts and clients, because busy people can spend days leaving messages for each other without ever talking personally. In short, chances are neither solution may serve your business needs.

TELEPHONE SOLUTIONS
The following is a list of more versatile options for taking messages so you can return calls when it is most practical and productive.

Voice mail. Voice mail answers your calls and takes messages like a sophisticated answering machine, but it offers additional advantages. First, since most large companies use voice mail, a home business with voice mail becomes virtually indistinguishable to callers from a *Fortune* 500 company. And in many ways voice mail is like having a receptionist because it can carry out so many of the tasks a receptionist would provide. For example, in addition to simply leaving a message, callers can choose from among a variety of options. They can listen for a list of your services, get directions for getting to your office, or obtain instructions for ordering a product. Having such information available on a prerecorded message saves you the time of returning such calls and provides your callers with immediate access to frequently requested information.

Also, voice mail systems usually offer the ability to set up different outgoing messages that can be programmed to run at various times of the day. Voice mail also enables you to set up individual "mailboxes" where you can leave private messages for different people in addition to your generic greeting. Each mailbox has its own ID-coded extension, which you can assign to people who call you frequently. The value of mailboxes is that you can leave detailed messages for any individual with whom you may need to communicate and thereby avoid playing phone tag with hard-to-reach people.

As with an answering machine, you can pick up your voice mail messages from wherever you are by dialing into your own number. And as you will see below, voice mail can also take calls while you're talking on the phone, forward selected calls to you at other locations, or even have you paged so you can call into to receive a message.

Here are three different ways you can set up a voice mail system for your business:

Voice mail through your phone company. Most local telephone companies are now offering voice mail service for a modest monthly charge through your existing phone and phone number. Most of these services include the ability to set up a number of mailboxes and take messages while your on the line. For example, Bell Atlantic has Answer Call, which for under $10 a month provides the ability to record thirty to forty-five minutes of voice messages. As with an answering machine you can access your messages from a remote location, save some of the messages to replay at a later time, and erase others. Similarly, GTE's voice mail is called Personal Secretary; US WEST offers Voice Messaging; Pacific Bell's service is called Message Center; Ameritech's is Call Minder; and Bell South's is Memory Call. Note, though, that the voice mail systems offered through specific phone companies may not have all the features described above.

Private voice mail services. If voice mail is not an option through your phone company or they don't offer the features you need, another choice is to sign up with a private voice mail service. In fact, in chapter 1 of this book, you'll note that we have described Answering/Voice Mail Services as one of the computer businesses you might even start.

In the short term, using one of these two methods is probably the most simple, effective, and least expensive option for most home businesses, with one exception which we'll discuss directly. You will pay from around $5 to $20 a month, depending on the number of mailboxes and other options you select.

Voice mail on your computer. A more versatile and cost-effective solution over the long haul might be to set up a voice mail system on your own computer using specialized software and a voice mail card that you install in your computer. Many new computers sold today come with simple voice mail software packages included as part of their "bundle." As with any other computer technology, there is a wide range of voice mail products offered with a wide variety of prices and capabilities. Those systems that come bundled with computer systems are generally at the lower end of the spectrum in terms of capability and price, but, depending on your needs, just may do the job.

A voice mail package that you buy separately will generally be more powerful in terms of features, but it will cost more. Such packages include software that runs the system and a voice mail card that digitizes incoming and outgoing messages so that they can be stored on your hard drive just as computer data is. When a call comes in, it is picked up by the voice mail card, the caller hears your greeting, and the person's message is recorded on your hard disk.

Inexpensive packages like Symantec's *CommSuite* and *PROCOMM Plus* from Quarterdeck combine fax, E-mail, telephone answering, and pager communications right through your modem. These systems handle only one line, however, so you might want to select a more expensive and capable system like one from companies like Dialogic and Rhetorex that will handle multiple lines. Since, like an answering machine, your voice mail system will need several seconds to reset between incoming calls, a system that will handle two lines is an advantage for people receiving a heavy volume of incoming calls.

To accommodate any of these systems you will need a large-capacity hard drive, because the outgoing greeting or messages you leave combined with any incoming messages from callers require about ten megabytes per hour of high-quality speech. While some voice mail systems offer a low-quality recording speed that doesn't take as much disk space, if you will want to be using voice mail while you are working at your office, you will probably want to buy a computer that you can dedicate to your voice mail system.

George Walther of Seattle, Washington, author of the books *Phone Power* and *Power Talking,* has installed a voice mail system in his home office. Walther uses his system to provide his callers with three choices. They can (1) hear specific prerecorded information about his products and services, (2) leave a message, or (3) retrieve a personal message Walther has prerecorded just for them. The latter option, called an extension, enables Walther to assign some clients personalized mailboxes where he can leave messages for them. Walther says of this feature, "I can leave a message for someone exactly as I would have if I had reached them in person. It enables me to avoid telephone tag by having a 'nonsimultaneous' telephone conversation." Walther notes that voice mail is a productivity tool, because, as with most of us, many of his business callers do not need to talk with him personally.

On the desktop, the latest developments in voice mail have been in terms of integration. For example, *COMMUNICATE* by 01/Communiqué, Inc., was designed specifically for the home office and combines voice, fax, imaging, E-mail, paging, and data communications through one integrated package. In other words, you use the same card with a scanner to capture images into your computer, act as a voice mail system that automatically routes calls to either its fax or voice mailboxes, and serve as a modem for electronic mail and accessing the online world.

!!! VOICE MAIL TIP !!!

You can avoid the hassle of having to remember to see if you have any voice mail messages waiting by using a telephone that has a Message Waiting indicator light.

Call forwarding to a homebound assistant. Another option for taking your phone messages is to have your calls forwarded to a reliable individual who will take your messages for a reasonable charge. Consultant and professional speaker Tom Winnenger of Waterloo, Iowa, for example, has his calls forwarded to the residence of a homebound person whom he pays to answer his phone in person.

Fax in or fax back. Since callers often want either to leave or obtain information of some kind, you might want to consider using your fax to respond to certain calls when you can't answer the phone. For example, your voice mail or answering machine message can inform callers that they can fax certain information to you that you can respond to upon your return. Or by using a fax-back service, your callers can select an option to have information like a price list or service descriptions faxed to them automatically. US Robotics offers the PM 336 which is an integrated voice/data/fax modem that also includes fax-on-demand capabilities which you can configure so that your callers can use their telephone keypad to select from a menu of documents that are then faxed to the number they indicate.

Caller ID. If you have too high a percentage of hang-ups when callers get your recorded message, Caller ID is an ideal service, because by obtaining a simple device that records the phone numbers of callers (even those who have hung up), you can call these individuals back to ascertain interest in your service. For example, if you are a computer repair service, you can call back your hang-ups and ask if they ever have a need for computer repair services. You can also use a fax-on-demand service. For a comparison of such services, TechProse, a company operated by Sarah Stambler, an authority on marketing with technology, publishes a *Comparison Table of*

Fax-on-Demand Service Bureaus, 370 Central Park West, #210, New York, NY 10025 (212) 222-1765. TechProse also publishes a report entitled *Selecting an in-House Fax-on-Demand System.*

DO YOU NEED VOICE MAIL?

If you answer "yes" to any of these questions, you probably will benefit from voice mail:

1. Is it important that you disguise the fact that you are a small, one-person, or home-based business? Voice mail makes you virtually indistinguishable from a *Fortune* 500 company.

2. Do you have an aversion to call waiting but believe you are missing calls while you are talking on the phone? Voice mail will take messages while you're on the phone.

3. Do you find yourself frequently playing telephone tag? Voice mail can allow you to leave personalized messages for people who would otherwise be hard to reach.

4. Do you spend a considerable amount of time conveying the same information to caller after caller? Voice mail can allow your caller to select a prerecorded message containing frequently requested information.

5. Could your clients place an order or request information without talking with you personally? Voice mail allows callers to receive instructions for placing orders or requesting written materials like a catalog or product list.

6. Do you need to have a variety of messages for different types of callers? Voice mail allows your callers to select specific types of messages.

#2. Receiving Calls When You're Out of the Office

The Problem

Sometimes taking a phone message, no matter how reliably, is not enough. There may be times when you need to get your calls immediately even though you are not in your office. This is particularly true if, like consultants, cleaning services, sales reps, and psychotherapists, you need to make appointments, take orders, handle emergencies, or respond to customer needs on demand. At such times, you can't afford to pick up your messages later.

TELEPHONE SOLUTIONS

Today's telephone services and equipment enable you to be available to your business callers literally anytime, almost anywhere, no matter what you are doing. So if you cannot afford to miss calls or your clients need to have immediate access to you while you're working elsewhere, here are a variety of ways to have your calls follow you when you're out of the office:

Call forwarding. Call forwarding sends your calls to another telephone number wherever you are. So, for example, you can have your calls forwarded to a meeting you're attending, to a client site where you're working, or to a cellular phone. Carlton MacBeth of Burbank, California, the sole proprietor of Bridge Publications, a home-based publishing company, has call forwarding provided to him by his local phone company. When he's out of the office, he has his calls forwarded to his cellular phone. "I never miss an order," says Carlton. "My customers don't know that I'm a one-man operation, probably stuck in traffic on I-5, when they call. They just know that someone is always here, ready to take their orders."

A number of other options may also be available if you subscribe to call forwarding. For example:

Delayed call forwarding will automatically forward your calls to another number after four rings, so you don't need to take the time to program your phone for call forwarding each time you leave the office.

Remote call forwarding is an added feature offered by some phone companies that enables you to program call forwarding remotely from one location to another, so you do not need to be in your office to direct your calls elsewhere.

Priority call forwarding, offered by some phone companies, allows you to program your phone to forward calls only for specific phone numbers you designate. In other words, you may not want to have all your incoming calls forwarded, but you can give priority to particular calls you don't want to miss. For example, you might forward a particular call you've been waiting for, calls from your partner, or calls from key clients, but not others.

If you use call forwarding frequently, you might want to get a telephone that has a Call Forwarding Indicator light so that when you return to your office you'll be reminded to cancel the forwarding.

A cellular phone. If you routinely work at various client sites during the day, travel a lot in your work, or spend considerable time making deliveries or sales calls, a cellular phone is practically a necessity for conducting business. The prices for cellular equipment are, fortunately, declining rapidly. And by having your calls forwarded to your cellular phone, you won't need to give people two phone numbers: one for your office and one for your cellular phone. If you do this, however, you may want to use priority call forwarding (described above) to keep your cellular costs down. And if you think you will be spending a lot of time talking on your cellular phone, call waiting may be available for cellular so you won't miss incoming forwarded calls while you're talking to someone else. You may even find that by having your calls forwarded to you while you are out of town and using your cellular's ability to "roam," you can get calls forwarded without an additional long-distance charge either to you or your caller.

700 number. With a 700 number from AT&T, you can remotely forward calls made to you on your 700 number to virtually any phone you're near. It can be a cellular phone or a pay phone. You can also make this a toll-free call for your clients and customers and you can be selective about whom you give your 700 to or you can print it on your business card.

A paging system. Another alternative for remaining accessible to your clients and customers is to use a paging service, which takes your calls and then pages you through a remote unit that you carry with you. The pager service provides you with a telephone number for your pager that you can give out to your clients and have put on your business cards so they can call your pager directly. By entering their phone number when they reach the pager, you can see the number on the pager screen and can call them immediately back without having to call the service.

Of course, you can combine several of these technologies to arrive at the best solution for your business. For example, you can leave a voice mail message that includes instructions to call your pager or cellular number in case of an emergency. You can refer callers to a homebound assistant to take orders or schedule service. Some phone companies even offer a call forwarding service that first forwards a call to your cellular phone (or any other number you designate). If the call is not picked up in a certain number of rings, it is forwarded again, this time to your pager, or other number. You can add several numbers in this chain.

Bernard Otis, whose company the Otis Group provides a sales and marketing support service from his Woodland Hills, California, home, uses voice mail and a paging service. Even though he calls in regularly to pick up his messages, Otis believes that voice mail is not sufficient in a consulting business like his. "People need to be able to reach you when they need you," he says. Therefore, Otis carries his pager with him even into client meetings. When the meeting begins, he takes the beeper out of his pocket, turns the beeper off, and sets it on the table in front of him. He then explains his philosophy of being available to clients to the very people he's meeting with and finds that this level of service is a tremendous selling point. Should Otis receive a call during the meeting, a red light flashes on the pager with the caller's phone number and message on the screen. At this point, Otis can determine whether the call is an emergency or if it can be returned after the meeting.

OTHER HANDY AND HELPFUL PHONE FEATURES

1. **Automatic redial.** Tired of dialing a busy number over and over? Automatic redial will do it for you. You hang up your phone and you're notified when the number you're calling is available.

2. **Three-way calling.** This is the residential version of conference calling. This feature allows you to connect with one party, flash the switch hook to call a second party, and after the second party answers, flash the switch hook again to allow all three parties to be connected on the same line. But you can enlarge the conference to up to thirty parties if the people you call also have three-way calling because they can also add people to the conference.

3. **Call Wake-up.** While this service is designed for wake-up calls, it can equally be used as a reminder for telephone appointments and prearranged conference calls that can be programmed up to

---

twenty-four hours in advance. The phone will ring to remind the subscriber to initiate the conference call.

4. **Call Timer.** Do you want to know how much telephone time to bill to a particular client? It's easy to underestimate how much time you've spent on the phone. Call Timer will provide that information for you when you're talking on the phone. While you can do this with software like *TimeSlips* or have it as a feature on your phone, you can also get it as a service from the phone company.

5. **Call Blocking.** Tired of being hounded by a particular salesman or other frequent, but uninvited caller? Some phone companies allow you to specify originating numbers that will not be able to get through to your number.

#3. Handling Incoming Calls While You're on the Line with Someone Else

The Problem

A repeated busy signal can turn away potential business and frustrate existing clients and customers. But if you spend a considerable part of each day on the phone, your phone line could be tied up when others need to reach you. And if you have only one phone line (which we don't recommend, but sometimes necessity dictates that you do) between your voice calls, fax use, and computer online time, your phone will probably be busy most of the time. Of course you don't want to be in the predicament of having to stay off the line just in case someone calls. You need a way to pick up calls while you're tying up the line.

Technology Solutions

Fortunately, you don't need to miss other calls while you're on the phone. Here are a variety of ways to pick up incoming calls.

Voice mail. One of the best features of voice mail is that it will pick up incoming calls while you are on the phone, so your callers will never get a busy signal. Most systems these days provide you with an audio cue, such a subtle beep similar to call waiting, to let you know that there's a call coming in. This feature is available with phone-company-provided voice mail as well. Some systems, however, do not give such a cue. With these, you wouldn't know you had a second call coming in until you'd completed your call and checked to see if any calls had come in while you were on the phone. But if you have a message waiting indicator light on your phone, you'll know immediately.

Call waiting, cancel call waiting, and three-way calling. Call waiting allows you to hear when another call is coming in so that you can interrupt the call you're on to answer an incoming one. Essentially, you are putting your first caller on hold while you find out who is calling. You can then either handle that call or put the second caller on hold while you wrap up your initial call. The problem with call waiting is that it does not interact well with online communications. If you are online and a call comes in, the call waiting audio cue, that friendly little beep, will often knock you offline. This can be especially upsetting if you're communicating with someone online or downloading a file.

Some people find taking another call in the midst of a phone conversation to be rude and disruptive, but if you generally like call waiting except under certain circumstances, you might want to use a feature called **Cancel Call Waiting.** It enables you to punch in a code that will cancel call waiting prior to placing a call or while you are in the midst of an important phone call—or while online!

Three-way calling enables you to talk to two people in different locations at the same time—no matter who placed the call. For example, you might be on the phone with a client and realize that you'd like to include another party in the conversation. You simply place the first call on hold, dial the other person, and then depress the hook switch or flash button to connect all parties.

Using these three features together gives you the equivalent of having two incoming lines and two outgoing lines all with one telephone line, and the monthly charges for these services are minimal.

Call return. This feature will automatically redial the number of the last person who tried to phone you. So if you're in the middle of a vital conversation and don't want to interrupt it by responding to call waiting, you can still let the incoming call go by and call return will call the number of the call you missed when you hang up.

Busy call forwarding. If you don't want to use call waiting, you can use busy call forwarding to forward your incoming calls to a second phone line when you are on the phone. For example, you can send incoming calls to your residential line or to a second business line, and by placing an answering machine on your residential line during working hours, you can be assured that your business callers will never get a busy signal. Not all phone companies have busy call forwarding available for forwarding to a residential line, however.

Call forwarding of call waiting. If you want to use call waiting under some circumstances, but not others, call forwarding of call waiting will forward your call waiting callers to a second line when you don't pick up on the call waiting signal.

Call hunting. If you have more than two lines, you may be interested in call hunting, a service that will seek out or hunt for the free line when an incoming line is busy. By having voice mail or an answering machine on the lines you can avoid missing incoming calls. This hunting feature is not always available for crossing over to a residential line, however.

Susan Fassberg discovered this solution for her public relations firm after calling her local phone company in sheer desperation. She spends the majority of her time on the phone either with clients or the media, and the busier she got the less likely she was to finish any phone conversation without multiple interruptions from call waiting. The hunting feature solved the problem.

Screening Calls While You Are on the Phone

If you had a full-time secretary and two lines, she could screen your calls while you were busy talking on the phone. Well, you can do almost as well without the secretary by using several phone services in conjunction with one another. By having **Call Forwarding of Call Waiting** and **Caller ID**, along with a telephone that has a message waiting indicator light, you can see the phone number of incoming calls and pick up special calls before they are forwarded to your voice mail.

Incoming phone calls, as vital as they are, can be highly interruptive when you are needing to stay focused on income-producing work. Many, if not most, calls can easily be responded to at a later time without unduly inconveniencing the caller. But we usually feel compelled to take our calls because any call could be "the" important one. Screening calls while you work is an excellent solution to this dilemma. Here are two ways you can screen calls while you're working:

Use an answering machine. Turn on the answering machine; set the volume to a tolerable level, and listen to the incoming callers as they leave their messages. If a call is a "must-take," pick it up. Allow the others to complete their messages so you can return their calls later at a more convenient time.

Special Call Acceptance. Some phone companies offer this service as a way to screen calls. To use this service, you enter a list of selected numbers that you want to have reach you even when you're not taking other calls. When you receive a call from one of these numbers, the call will ring through to you while other callers will hear a recording which requests that they leave a message.

VIP Alert. Another feature that enables you to screen for priority calls is VIP Alert, which announces with a short-long-short ring that someone is calling from a list you have designated. Usually up to twelve numbers may be chosen for this treatment.

#4. Not Enough Telephone Lines

The Problem

For those of you are starting out in your first home-based business let us say at the outset: If you only have one phone line, you don't have enough phone lines! Think of all the personal phone calls you get, not to mention make. Then add the business calls. The more your business succeeds, the more calls you're going to get. Then add the faxes you will need to send—and, of course, those you will receive. Finally, compute your online time. How much time you spend online will depend on your business, but chances are that it will be significant. Never underestimate the importance of being connected to the world via phone lines.

To ensure that there are enough adequate connections, many home businesses simply pay the price of extra lines—several for business, one for residential, a spare line for a teenager, and so forth. But often it's not that simple. Some homes are not wired for multiple lines. Multiple lines are more expensive, and a business line is more costly than a residential line. And, of course, you don't want to go running around the house from room to room answering various phone lines. Nor do you want to have your desk loaded down with multiple phones, answering machines, and faxes.

Technology Solutions

Today's technology offers an amazing variety of solutions to these problems. If you want to start out handling multiple types of calls on one line, there are practical options for doing that. If you're ready to go for two or even three lines, that's possible too. Here is a checklist of options.

1. PUT ONE LINE TO MULTIPLE USE

Here are a variety of ways you can get multiple uses from your one line:

Mixing Personal and Business

Distinctive ringing. Although different companies call this service by different names, distinctive ringing enables you to use one line for up to three different incoming phone numbers. For example, if you have only one phone line coming into your home, your family might use one phone number, while your business uses another. This way, your teenager won't need to pick up your business calls when he or she hears the distinctive ring. Or if you and your partner have separate businesses, you can give each one a separate number and a distinctive ring. You could also use a separate number for different aspects of your business as larger companies do; i.e., one number to reach your "order line," another to get your "business office."

Of course, since you still have only one physical line coming into your house in this arrangement, distinctive ringing has a definite drawback: You can't do two things on the one line at once. So you can't send a fax while you're talking on the phone. And callers to one of the numbers will still get a busy signal whenever the other line is being used, unless you have call waiting on both phone numbers, in which case each of your numbers has a distinctive call-waiting beep, so you will be able to tell which number has a call.

So while this can be a good stopgap measure, getting a separate business line is still truly the best arrangement for most home-based businesses, because having a separate line assures your business callers privacy and also makes it easier to track phone expenses for tax purposes. But if you do decide to use this option, talk to your phone company about how you could make sure that the distinctive ring number you're using for your business could be transferred to a business line in the future if need be.

Mixing Voice, Fax, and Modem

There are six options for using one line for receiving all types of business calls:

1) Use programs like Quarterdeck's *PROCOMM* or Symantec's *Comm-Suite* to manage phone, fax, and modem communications easily and efficiently.

2) Distinctive ringing. You might use distinctive ringing on your business line, assigning one ring to your business voice calls and the other ring to fax calls so you will be prepared to receive a fax if your phone setup requires that your fax machine be answered manually.

3) Use line-sharing devices such as Command Communication's *ComShare* that direct incoming traffic from a single phone to three, four or five different devices.

4) Fax/phone/voice-processing combination. With this combination, you can have one line serving three purposes. What's best is that when you are unavailable to answer your phone, the machine answers incoming calls and detects if it's a fax to receive or a voice call. Voice calls trigger the answering machine, and, of course, if it's a fax, the fax machine receives it. This type of technology is available as a stand-alone system or can be integrated into your home computer. Many modem cards now come with software that allows for fax/phone/voice-processing combinations.

5) Fax/modem switches. If you already own a fax machine or are using an internal fax/modem board inside your computer, the combination unit described above won't help you. Instead, you can buy a "fax/modem switch" that will enable you to use the same phone line for both voice and fax/modem transmissions. There are three types of these switches:

   - Voice priority sits in waiting, listening to hear if a fax or modem call is coming in. The incoming caller doesn't have to key in or otherwise notify your system of which type of call is coming in.
   - Machine priority requires that the incoming caller instruct the switch as to which type of call is coming in. If you've ever called someone and had their answering machine message tell you

either to leave a voice message or punch in a number if you are sending a fax, then you've encountered one of these devices.

- Answer and detect devices cannot detect manual dialing fax machines or automatic machines used in manual mode.

Having tried multiple fax/modem switches that have not worked consistently with our manual fax, it appears that voice priority is the best system. Fax/modem switches do have two drawbacks, however, compared to having two separate lines for voice and fax/modem: 1) You cannot send or receive a fax AND talk on the phone at the same time since you have only one line; 2) we have never heard of a fax/modem switch that functions with 100 percent accuracy. Some calls or faxes will be lost, but the more expensive switches do offer greater reliability.

6) Use the Internet to make inexpensive long-distance and local calls. If your modem is at least 28.8 kbps and you have an SLIP/PPP connection to the Internet, and have a soundcard, microphone, and speakers, you can use the Internet to make long-distance calls for the price of a local call. Several software packages are available for under $50, such as *Web Phone* by Netspeak (*http://www*.netspeak.com), *Internet Phone* from Vocaltec (*http://www*.vocaltec.com), and *Webtalk* by Quarterdeck (*http://www*.qdeck.com) that allow you to send voice communications over the Internet. Most versions also offer voice mail capabilities and video conferencing as well. The software is not exceedingly easy to install and set up, but once you're up and running you can save considerable amounts of money on your long-distance phone bill while reducing the amount of time you spend tying up your telephone line.

2. ADDING ADDITIONAL PHONE LINES: BUSINESS VERSUS RESIDENTIAL

We strongly recommend adding a separate line for your business as soon as you can and, for many reasons, we believe your second line should be a business line, as opposed to a second residential line. Here's why: Yes, installing and using a second "residential" line is much less expensive than having a "business" line installed. But without a business line in most states, you usually can't get a yellow-pages listing and when clients call information for your phone number, the operator may not think to look for you in the residential directory. And in some states utility commission tariffs preclude you from using a residential number in business advertising, including on your business cards, letterhead, and stationery.

But the regulations governing this area seem to be changing rapidly, with the growth of more and more home-based businesses. One phone company, Ameritech, told us they are tolerant of home businesses using residential phone lines for business purposes. "We're not interested in playing the role of phone police," a spokesperson explained. Similarly, the people at GTE Public Affairs told us that within five to ten years, their different rates for residential and business lines will disappear. In the future, all phone lines we believe will simply be charged based on usage like an electricity bill.

US WEST is an excellent example of how phone companies across the U.S. have changed, or are in the process of changing, how they deal with home-based businesses. Gone are the days when a phone company would require you to be in a commercial location in order to get a business phone line. U.S. WEST has gotten the tariffs in states in which it operates changed to give home business operators a "choice" of whether they use a residential line or a business line for their work. The phone companies we spoke with treat home businesses the same as any other enterprise. Business rates have come down considerably as well. According to Bell Atlantic, a home business can expect to pay only about 50 percent more than residential rates for basic line service.

TIP

ANSWERING MULTIPLE LINES IN MULTIPLE PLACES

Once you get two or more lines, you don't want to have to be running back and forth from home to office to answer them. Here are three solutions for being able to pick up your lines wherever you are in your home.

1. **Multiple extensions.** Identify the places where you expect to be spending major blocks of time and install extensions in these locales.

2. **Two-line phones.** Install a two-line phone on each floor or area of your home so you can pick up either business or residential calls without going far from wherever you are.

3. **Call pickup.** This service ties two or more lines together, enabling you to answer an incoming business call at the closest residential phone by entering a one- or two-digit code. Some companies like Pacific Bell offer this service, which they call their Comstar 2 service, along with the ability to transfer calls between your residential and business lines should, for example, your children's friends call in on your business line. And your phone line can also be used as an intercom between the various phones in the home.

3. INTEGRATED EQUIPMENT

Between business and personal lines, fax/modem lines, answering machines, and fax machines your home office could start looking more like an electronics store than a residence. But today's phone equipment is getting smaller and smaller, and one piece of equipment may do what it once took two, three, or more pieces to do. Using such integrated equipment can save you money as well as desk space.

While integrated equipment doesn't save you the cost of installing a second or third phone line, it does reduce clutter on your desk, improve your efficiency, and save you the cost of buying multiple pieces of equipment. You can choose from a growing selection of space-saving integrated telephone equipment such as:

- two-line phones and two-line cordless phones
- speakerphones, single or two-line
- telephone/answering machines
- fax phones, some with built-in answering machines
- computer phones utilizing sound or fax cards, speakers, and microphones

When public relations consultant Daylanne Jackson found she needed a multifeatured fax and telephone, she decided to get one integrated piece of equipment to meet both needs. She was delighted when she found a versatile model from AT&T which offered a two-line telephone and fax with a speakerphone. She especially likes having the built-in speakerphone feature and the fact that with the two lines, she can still talk on one while she's receiving or sending a fax on the other.

By shopping at office superstores such as Office Depot, Office Max, and Staples that sell home-office electronics, you'll find a rich array of these space-saving integrated products. It's important to think about your needs in advance of buying, though, as the variety of options is almost overwhelming, and each choice has its own advantages and disadvantages. To benefit most from one device or another, you may also need to have other options such as those we discuss throughout this section.

4. ONE HOUSE-WIDE PHONE SYSTEM

Few home offices want the expense or complication of having the entire house wired for a phone system like what you would find in most office buildings. Who wants fat, gray wires snaking throughout their home, and who has an extra closet or small room just to house the "brain" such a system requires? But once you've grown to the point of needing multiple phones with three or more lines, you may well yearn for the convenience of a system that links all your phones. When you get to that point, a system like the AT&T Partner offers an all-modular alternative, without the unwanted drawbacks.

The Partner can link all the phones and all the lines (up to four) in your home without requiring a special closet or room for the "brain." The control unit can be desk mounted or wall mounted, and you add lines simply by adding cards. It can usually be run off regular home wiring. (There's also The Partner Plus, which can be expanded up to eight lines.)

The Partner has a speakerphone and hands-free intercom. (The intercom system enables you to call a room and overhear what's happening in the room without anyone answering. This can be a valuable feature for a working parent who wants to monitor a child's or baby's room.) An added feature for anyone who has employees coming into their home is that the Partner can be programmed to restrict the use of phones by personnel making outgoing calls (long distance calls, 900 calls, etc.).

Jim Richards chose a Partner Plus system after going to the expense of installing and replacing three different phone systems in the course of two years. His company, High Tech Medical, provides doctors with a radiographic private-label brand of medical X-ray film and has grown 200 percent each year since he opened in 1987. His business is conducted principally by phone and through the mail, and so he quickly outgrew first a two-line and then a three-line phone system.

Richards told us: "I wanted a phone system that could keep up with me." He now has five lines: three incoming 800 lines, one local outgoing line, and a fax line—all handled now by the Partner Plus—and he still has room to grow. The Partner Plus control unit (19 inches tall by 11½ inches wide by 12 inches deep) is mounted on a wall in his kitchen by the back door—the least obtrusive place they could find for it. Richards tells us he's happy, although he says, "I would like it to be a little more user friendly. It's like learning a new software program; it takes time to learn how to use it." He's especially pleased, however, with it's ability to play music while the caller is on hold and the fact that all his phones can be answered by one answering machine after hours.

Richards leases the Partner Plus, which costs over $4,000. His payments on a lease purchase plan run around $175 per month. AT&T offers a variety of leasing arrangements.

On a smaller scale, Alycia Enciso purchased an AT&T Spirit to run her interior design company, Alycia Enciso & Associates, which provides space planning and design services. At first she had only one phone line, but as her home-based company grew, she expanded her office space in a unique way: she leased additional apartments in the building where she lives. She now has four employees and three apartments: one for her home and two for her business.

At that point she needed to coordinate her three phone lines among these apartments. "I was too busy for call waiting and I needed to have an intercom between the phones too." So the Spirit enables her to have her three lines on a rotary (that is, if one is busy it will ring over to the next one), and with call waiting it's like having five lines. Like Richards, she especially likes being able to have music playing while people are on hold. Some home offices with heavy traffic are using the even more capable and expensive Merlin system.

Cathy Teal, a graphic designer based in Los Angeles, has seen her home-studio-based business grow from a single-person operation to having four employees. She has had to deal with the disruption of reconfiguring her phone system twice. Based on her hard-won experience, she offers these tips for any home business ready to install a new phone system:

- Buy a system that's too big so you can grow into it.
- Make sure to get a warranty.
- Make an actual drawing or plan of which lines you want where. This helps when coordinating with phone companies.
- If the manufacturer of the phone system offers training on how to operate the system, take it!
- Try find a system that is easy to upgrade to digital (ISDN). Don't buy an analog phone system unless it's upgradable.
- Leasing is strongly recommended as opposed to buying.
- Used equipment is available, but be very wary.
- Buy a two-line phone, and get separate lines for fax and for modem.

After reading about these many telephone solutions, you may feel as we did in discovering them, both delighted and somewhat overwhelmed by the many options we have. While some of these services may not yet be available in your area, at least you know that phone companies and manufacturers are spending a lot of time and money to come up with innovative and creative solutions to the phone problems that plague home businesses. And there will undoubtedly be more to come.

To select options that will truly work for you, we suggest beginning with a call to your local telephone operating company. Most likely they have their own version of the services we've mentioned either up and running or on the drawing board, and we found all the companies we spoke with ready, willing, and eager to help home businesses. Also Hello Direct is a comprehensive catalog of telephone products (5884 Eden Park Place, San Jose, CA 95138, (800/444-3556).

5. GET AN ISDN LINE IF YOUR PHONE COMPANY OFFERS IT TO RESIDENCES
One ISDN line can be used for two telephone numbers simultaneously. It also enables fast communication over the Internet and videoconferencing.

As you can see from this chapter, your computer is a valuable tool in marketing yourself and your business. From contact managers and other kinds of specialized database programs that help you track the people who will make a difference in your business to top-of-the-mind marketing techniques and software programs that will help you establish and maintain a professional image, getting full use of your computer is like having an entire corporate staff working for you.

CHAPTER 6

Using Your Computer to Go Online to Find Customers, Collect Money, and Get the Information You Need to Compete

O nce only sovereigns and chief executives of large organizations could get instant answers to their questions because they alone had a retinue or staff of runners and experts at their beck and call. Now you, too, have the power to get the same quick and often comprehensive answers. With the tremendous growth of the Internet, most people know that there is a wealth of information out there, yet they don't truly utilize this revolutionary resource. Now, at your fingertips, the computer instantly makes available information that large companies have long spent thousands, often millions, of dollars to gather to help in making key financial and marketing decisions. For example, you can use your computer and the Internet to gather the key information you need to:

- select a name for your business that will attract the right customers;
- evaluate what to charge and set your prices to maximize your profits without turning potential clients away;
- study your customer base to learn what media they use most often so you can plan your advertising or promotional campaign;
- figure out what and how well your competition is doing;
- learn about new developments in your field so you can be prepared for the future;
- stay abreast of general business trends that affect the economy as a whole; and
- advertise, broadcast, and otherwise communicate to and with local, national, and international communities through the Internet and the World Wide Web.

Until just a few years ago, the traditional way most small and home-based businesses gained access to such information amounted to what we might call the "ear-to-the-ground" method. They would read business and marketing books, peruse some general trade and professional magazines, and talk with other people whom they considered to be in the know. Today, however, information is moving too fast for the ear-to-the-ground method to be truly effective. There is too much information now and too many new developments that change dramatically from one week to the next, and sometimes from one day to the next.

Fortunately, much of the sophisticated information you need to make key business decisions is available through your computer and over countless online databases that are accessible through thousands of information services such as CompuServe, America Online, Cnet, Mead Data Central, and ZDnet, among many others. And you won't need to have an MBA or hire an expensive marketing consultant to use these resources. There is a vast sea of information to be found in online databases that can help you make the most of your key business decisions right from your desk. Utilizing information is an essential element of what we call a "marketing mindset." Whether you are just starting out in business or have been self-employed for years, understanding the nuances of your market is an important function in the equation for attaining success and maintaining it. This chapter will provide online solutions to nine common problems for making contacts and obtaining information. It will show you how to tap into valuable online information sources to gather the key information you need to make many of the most important decisions all businesses make. If you are not yet online you can refer to Appendix I for a basic online lexicon for how to access the rich variety of electronic resources described in this chapter.

#1. Finding Out If the Name You Want for Your Company Is Taken

The Problem

You no doubt remember reading or hearing about businesses that have had to change their name or that of their product because their name was the same or too much like one belonging to another company. This is an expensive mistake that can cause a business to go out of business. In choosing a new name for a business you want to be certain that the name you've chosen is not being used by anyone else whose rightful claim would force you to stop using that name.

Online Solutions

Checking a name for conflict with other business or product names is made easier using online resources. The extent and kind of searching you do will depend on whether you're establishing a local business, a national business, international business, or whether you're naming a product instead of a business.

Checking out a local business is the easiest thing to do. The first step is to find out if someone else is using the name you want or one that sounds like it, even though spelled differently or is so similar that a problem might arise. Check your local phone book. If the name's clear, now check the World Wide Web. Since most businesses with Web sites use their business name as their domain name, you should run a search through InterNIC to see if the name you're considering is already taken. There are many sites on Web that will allow you to conduct such a search. Why not start at the source: *http://*rs.internic.net. In the near future, there will be other companies like InterNIC.

While on the Web, check its "white and yellow page" directories. These include BigBook (*http://www.*bigbook.com), Bigfoot (*http://www.*bigfoot.com), Four11 (*http://www.*four11.com), GTE SuperPages (*http://www.*superpages.gte.net) ON'VILLAGE (*http://www.*onvillage.com), and Who Where? (*http://www.*whowhere.com).

If you're a CompuServe subscriber you can tap into Biz*File, a database from American Business Information containing over ten million U.S. and Canadian business establishments that are listed in phone books throughout both countries. You can use Biz*File to find out if the name you want is in use and where that business is located. The database also includes additional information such as the length of time a business has been listed in the yellow pages. Biz*File is available on CompuServe and carries a small surcharge. A search for a specific company can be done in less than a minute. Note that you can also get the same information from American Business Information Business Infoline via phone at (900) 896-0000. The cost for this service is $3 for the first minute and $1.50 for each additional minute. ABI also offers a toll-free number through which you can charge your search to your credit card (800/638-7171). ABI offers a more limited service on its Web site located at *http://www.*lookupusa.com. For the Web, you need to know the state in which the number you are seeking is located.

Another online resource is Dun & Bradstreet's Electronic Business Directory (described more fully under Problem #2), available on CompuServe. This database includes listings from over 5,000 yellow pages nationwide, but it also contains some names that may not be listed in telephone directories. America Online offers, among other resources, Hoover's Directory of Businesses (keyword: HOOVER'S). Another great resource is the many national yellow-pages directories available on CD-ROM, such as PhoneDisc PowerFinder (Digital Directory Assistance, Inc.). Also, perform some general searches on the Web with a few of the major search engines.

Checking more thoroughly will involve making sure your candidate for a name does not violate someone's claim on it as a trademark or service mark. A trademark is a word or logo that identifies a product; a service mark offers the same protection to a service that a trademark provides a product. For this, you can use Trademarkscan, available on CompuServe, containing over 1.2 million federally registered trademarks and 950,000 trade and service marks registered with the states, a description of the service or product, the status of the trademark, and the registration date and date of first use.

A variety of databases is also available to check company names and trademarks in other countries.

!!! **NOTE** !!!

To be sure that the name or trademark you want to use is available, you still need to check with the state office, usually the secretary of state's office, that handles corporate name registration to determine if a name is reserved or newly registered. Nexis offers a database called Corporate Filings, which contains the corporate name information on file in the secretary of state's offices in all fifty states. To be on even more certain ground, consult with an attorney, especially if you are seeking a trademark, who specializes in intellectual property. However, if you provide the attorney with the results of your online searches, you can save a lot of the legal fee normally charged.

#2. Identifying Prospects for a Mailing List or Direct Solicitation

The Problem

Every business needs new customers, so being able to locate names, addresses, and telephone numbers of companies, professionals, or businesses that might need your services can be key to your survival and growth. To obtain such information, many businesses buy mailing lists from mailing-list brokers. Yet, buying such lists can be expensive and generally can be used only once.

Computer Solutions

By going online, you can locate names, addresses, telephone numbers, and a great deal of other information about potential clients to contact by phone, mail, or E-mail. Here is a list of some of the resources available to you:

AMERICAN BUSINESS INFORMATION, INC.

ABI is a leading provider of business-to-business marketing information on more than ten million businesses in the United States and one million businesses in Canada. The database is compiled and updated from the following sources: yellow pages and business white pages, SEC information, federal, state, and municipal government data, business magazines, newsletters and newspapers, postal service information, bankruptcy records, and legal filings. The database is searchable by business type. ABI also provides printed lists, CD-ROM products, mailing labels, and more. The database is available through America Online (keyword: YELLOW PAGES) and on the Web: *http://www.*abii.com. You can also call (800) 336-8349 for more information.

COMMERCIAL SITES INDEX

A comprehensive list of the companies who have a presence on the Internet. The site is updated frequently, but things change fast in cyberspace and this is by no means the definitive source. Web: *http://www.*directory. net

DUN'S ELECTRONIC BUSINESS DIRECTORY

Formerly called the Electronic Yellow Pages by its prior owner, it contains information on over 8.5 million businesses and professionals in the U.S., including both public and private companies of all sizes and types. The information available about a company includes the name, address, telephone number, type of business, number of employees, and its Standard Industrial Code (called the SIC, a seven-digit number developed by the Office of Management and Budget and the Census Bureau, although some databases have modified the last few digits since the codes have not been updated regularly and therefore do not include some new technologies.) You can search according to a specific company name, or by product or service, SIC code, city, county, SMSA (Standard Metropolitan Statistical Area) code, geographic location, telephone number, zip code, or number of employees. There is a small per-record charge for each company. Available on CompuServe and Dialog.

DUN'S MARKET IDENTIFIERS

This database is a subset of Dun's Electronic Business Directory with more detailed information on over 6.7 million U.S. establishments, both public and private, derived from the compilation of credit information collected by Dun & Bradstreet. Each record includes the name, address, and telephone number, as well as various company characteristics such as sales figures, number of employees, net worth, date and state of incorporation, and names of key executives. You can search with either a specific company name or according to geographic location, product or service, executive name, number of employees, or sales as your search criteria. Currently each company record costs $3. Available on CompuServe, Dialog, and the World Wide Web: *http://www*.dialog.com/dialog/databases/html2.0/bl0276.html.

EDGAR

This is the online database of the Securities and Exchange Commission. The site allows you to obtain federal filings for thousands of public companies. Web: *http://www*.sec.gov/edgarhp.htm

MOODY'S CORPORATE PROFILES

Moody's Corporate Profiles provides in-depth descriptive and financial information on over 5,000 companies listed on the New York Stock Exchange and the American Stock Exchange plus companies traded over the counter on NASDAQ. The information is derived by this Dun & Bradstreet company from required filings to the Securities and Exchange Commission (SEC), annual company reports, newspaper articles, and other information both by and about each corporation. Available on Dialog and the World Wide Web: *http://www*.corp.dialog.com/dialog/databases/html2.0/bl0555.html

STANDARD & POOR'S CORPORATE DESCRIPTIONS

Financial and business information on over 9,500 of the largest publicly owned U.S. and non-U.S. corporations is provided. Available on Lexis and Nexis.

THOMAS REGISTER ONLINE

Thomas Register Online contains information on over 152,000 U.S. and Canadian manufacturers and service providers. Each record includes the company name, address, telephone number, and products or services provided; and some listings also include other useful information such as the number of employees, exporter status, names of parent or subsidiary companies, and executive names and titles. You can retrieve company records by entering the company name, words describing its line of business, product, trade name, city, state, zip code, or telephone area code. Available on CompuServe, America Online and on the World Wide Web: *http://www.*thomasregister.com

USENET AND NEWSGROUPS

Another comprehensive resource for mailing lists of any sort is the Usenet/Usegroups on the Internet. The list below is the first ten listings the of over *6,180* hits we got for the search phrase: "marketing mailing lists." The newsgroups offer an incredible wealth of information, if you can sift through the "spam" (outright advertising). All the major Internet Service Providers include search engines for newsgroups as do all the major Web search engines such as Yahoo (*http://www.*yahoo.com) and Altavista (*http://www.*altavista.com), Lycos (*http://www.*lycos.com), and LookSmart (*http://www.*looksmart.com).

1. General business mailing lists: *alt.business.multi-level*
2. General business mailing lists: *misc.entrepreneurs*
3. General business mailing lists: *alt.business.misc*
4. General business mailing lists: *alt.business*
5. Mailing lists for manufacturing, etc.: *sci.engr.manufacturer*
6. General business for manufacturing, etc.: *biz.marketplace*
7. Mailing lists for export: *alt.manufacturing.misc*
8. Mailing lists for electronics: *alt.electronics.manufacturing*
9. Mailing lists for sport rowing: *rec.sport.rowing*

!!! C D - R O M S O L U T I O N S !!!

You can also obtain a plethora of information for developing mailing lists through several exciting CD-ROM sources such as the ten million companies taken from multiple databases, including the American Business Directory and Biz*File, which are available on CD-ROM from American Business Information (ABI), Web: *http://www.*abii.com. You can also call (800) 336-8349 for more information. PhoneDisk USA Business contains 9.5 million business listings and PhoneDisk USA Residential contains nearly 80 million listings. Updates are available quarterly. Digital Directory Assistance, Inc., 5711 S. 86th Circle, Omaha, NB 68127, (800) 284-8353.

#3. Obtaining Credit Information about Clients and Those Who Owe You Money

The Problem

Before you undertake work for a client, you want to feel assured that the client will be able to pay you. You need to determine whether a customer is a good credit risk and gather other financial information about a company that might help you make a decision whether or not to work for them, or under what conditions. Likewise, if you have collection problems, you may need to locate people and determine vital financial information about them.

Computer Solutions

You can often get information about a company's creditworthiness and financial track record through several online sources, including:

DUN & BRADSTREET

Three types of D&B reports will tell you a lot about over nine million public and private U.S. companies. These include:

1. The Business Information Report provides perspective on a firm's operations, profitability, and stability, including general financial information, public filings, suits, officers, and so on.
2. The Payment Analysis Report compares the company's payment habits over two years.
3. The Family Tree Service shows corporate ties that exist among a company and its parent, headquarters, branches, divisions, and subsidiaries. Available on NewsNet and Westlaw.

NCI TELE-TRACE NETWORK

NCI provides instant investigative information and enables you to do skip tracing online. NCI derives a portion of its information from the three major credit bureaus, including TRW, though you may not qualify under federal law to get the full credit information available. NCI screens you to determine the level of information you are qualified to get. Among the typical searches NCI can perform are motor vehicle licenses, crisscross directories, public records (judgments, tax liens, bankruptcies, Uniform Commercial Code filings), changes of address, corporate records, criminal records, and tracing by Social Security number. NCI charges a one-time fee, usually around $500, plus a charge for each report. Note that if you qualify to obtain credit information from individual credit bureaus and you use a large volume of credit information, you can obtain credit reports at a lower rate than NCI charges. NCI can be reached at WDIA Corporation, P.O. Box 31221, 7721 Hamilton Avenue, Cincinnati, OH 45231, (513) 522-3832.

TRW BUSINESS CREDIT PROFILES

TRW is one of the nation's three major credit bureaus. Online it offers credit and business information on more than thirteen million companies. The information available in a report includes such items as credit histories, financial information and ratios, key business facts like size, ownership, products; and Uniform Commercial Code filings, tax liens, judgments, and bankruptcies. The report for a specific company may not include all this information. You retrieve reports by entering a company name and either the state or ZIP code of the specific company or location you desire. The database-search software for this product is very sophisticated. If no company name exactly matches the name you entered, it will try to retrieve and display up to twenty-four companies with similar names. Likewise, if you enter a ZIP code, it will also retrieve similarly named companies from adjacent ZIP areas. Available on CompuServe, Dialog, and on the Web at: *http://www*.trw.com

#4. Finding Facts Fast for Business Plans, Proposals, Reports, and Decisions

The Problem

You are in the middle of writing a business plan or proposal for a potential major client. Suddenly, you realize that you are missing an important piece of information, and yet you must prove that you know your field from top to bottom. You may need to gather the most current information about a new development you read about a few months ago, or you may need information about a new competitor. Many such circumstances require that you stay abreast of late-breaking news in your industry. And in the press of deadlines, you need to gain this information without spending endless hours at the library.

Online Solutions

Online research is truly your answer to this problem. In fact, it is the only way to operate when it comes to obtaining timely information quickly and cost effectively. Whatever your needs, you can find a universe of facts and information about specific companies, product lines, market trends, and potential clients in many different kinds of databases to be found online.

Here's a rundown of databases and online sources that may be useful to you for finding the pertinent information you need to have at your fingertips.

INTERNET/WEB SEARCH ENGINES

The World Wide Web is now *the* information source and clearinghouse. Before going anywhere else for information, chances are you can find it on the Web first, and for free! To locate the information you need from the fifty-million-plus Web sites you will need to use one of the many search engines available. Search engines are provided free of charge by a number of companies. Their job is to continuously find and compile the ever-growing information on the Web and the Internet and index it so you can find just what you want when you search. Contrary to popular belief, search engines don't search the entire Internet; they search through their own extensive databases of Web sites, FTP sites, newsgroups, etc. To keep their databases current, they send out "spiders," little software agents, to search the Internet and bring back new information. Here is a list of ten of the most frequently used search engines:

1. Altavista: *http://www*.altavista.com
2. ComFind: *http://www*.comfind.com
3. DejaNews (for newgroups searches): *http://www*.dejanews.com
4. Excite: *http://www*.excite.com
5. HotBot: *http://www*.hotbot.com
6. Infoseek: *http://www*.infoseek.com
7. Lycos: *http://www*.lycos.com
8. Magellan: *http://www*.magellan.com
9. WebCrawler: *http://www*.webcrawler.com
10. Yahoo: *http://www*.yahoo.com

TIPS FOR BETTER INTERNET SEARCHES

Like everything else, the Internet contains its share of chaff with its wheat. A typical Internet search will reveal a great deal of information, of which only 5 percent may be of use. For example, we just conducted a search using Altavista for the phrase "Best Home Businesses." The search came back with 400,000 "hits," sites containing references to

---

"Best Home Businesses." Can you imagine reading through each one of these sites to find the exact information you require? And you thought the Internet would make things easier!

The Internet can, and does, make finding information faster and easier. The trick is knowing the right way to ask the questions. Search engines allow you to enter a word or phrase, called the search phrase, to specify what you're looking for. The following tips will help you formulate the best search phrases and get you right to the information you need while excluding the superfluous. They will work with any of the major search engines.

- Every search engine offers its own help section, tips and answers to frequently asked questions (FAQ). Take the time to read these over. The time and frustration you save will be immeasurable.

- Many search engines also offer enhanced, pro, or advanced versions. Use these whenever possible.

- Be as specific as possible in your search phrase. Avoid generalities such as *marketing,* or *graphic design.* Specific phrases such as *"1997 sales Mercedes statistics, Los Angeles,"* or *"graphic design accounting software"* will get you to the information you're looking for much faster.

- Use specifiers such as locations, dates, brand names, company names, etc., to make the search as exact as possible.

- Use quotation marks around phrases that shouldn't be separated. Search engines look for occurrences of the words you enter. Being mere software, they don't know the meanings of those words, or that they even belong together. For example, if you are looking for medical software billing programs, put quotation marks around the entire phrase. This tells the search engine to find just those words in just that order. Without the quotation marks, the search will turn up every occurrence of the word *medical,* every occurrence of the *billing,* and— you get the picture.

- Use quotation marks around inseparable phrases, and use the plus sign (+) to distill the search even further. For example, to find a good deal on 33.6 kbps modems and ISDN modems, type **"modems for sale" + 33.6 + ISDN.**

- When in doubt as to case, use lower-case characters.

For Statistical Information

If the data you are seeking is statistical or factual in nature, examine the databases available from Data Resources, Inc., a McGraw-Hill subsidiary, or from Chase Econometrics/Interactive Data. Data Resources maintains more than sixty fact databases covering a variety of industries and financial markets. You can also use CENDATA on CompuServe, a database derived from the Census Data, which includes information on housing starts, population, agriculture, and more. Some of the data is delivered in raw tabular form, while other data is condensed into reports that compare business information. Another database of interest is called Neighborhood Report, available on CompuServe, which contains a summary of the demographic makeup of any ZIP code in the U.S. You can obtain information about the population, race, and age breakdowns as well as income distribution, the types of households, and the occupations of the residents.

MARKETPLACE RESOURCE CENTER

This site offers free demographic information on major U.S. markets, business performance by line, and business consumer trends. The site is operated by MarketPlace Information Corp., a software company that specializes in developing direct marketing tools. Web: *http://www. mktplace.com/home1022*

STOCKS AND COMMODITIES

Financial and business information with comprehensive links to many leading information providers, including Lexis-Nexis Small Business Service. Web: *http://www.onr.com/stocks/smallbus.html*

For Reports, Articles, Abstracts

If the data you are seeking is more analytical or contextual, such as that published in a business or trade journal, there are many databases available on America Online, CompuServe, Microsoft Network, and Prodigy, as well as the Web.

ABI/INFORM

ABI/Inform is considered one of the best business databases with over 675,000 two-hundred-word abstracts and citations from an extensive assortment of 900 general business and management periodicals going back to 1971. You can find company histories, competitive intelligence, and new-product development information. Available on BRS, BRS/After Dark, CompuServe Marketing Management Research Center, Dialog, Knowledge Index, Orbit, and NEXIS. Also on CD-ROM.

BUSINESS RESEARCHER'S INTERESTS
This Meta-site is the most comprehensive resource we have yet found on the Web. The site contains links to cutting-edge business research, trends, technological developments, business theory, international business, business and technology publications, and that's just for starters. Before looking anywhere else for info, we recommend you start here. Web: *http://www.*bint.com.

Libraries on the Net

The following library sites offer exhaustive informational resources and links to a wide variety of businesses and other topics. They also offer links to hundreds of online databases.

- Berkeley Public Library, Web: *http://www.*ci.berkeley.ca.us/bpl/bkmk/index.html
- Chicago Public Library, Web: *http://*cpl.uic.edu/
- Clearinghouse of Subject-Oriented Internet Resource Guides, Web: *http://www.*lib.umich.edu/chhome
- The Internet Public Library, Web: *http://*pl.sils.umich.edu/
- Carol's Guide to Reference Sources, Web: *http://*cyclops.edbsu.edu
- Louisiana State Webliography, Web: *http://www.*lib.lsu.edu/weblio.html
- The Mansfield Cybrarian, Web: *http://www.*mnsfld.edu/~library/
- University of Indiana Research Collection & Service Department Home Page, Web: *http://www.*lib.indiana.edu.8080/

AIRMEDIA LIVE INTERNET BROADCAST NETWORK
The AirMedia Live Internet Broadcast Network is a unique new wireless broadcast network that brings the online world to home and office PCs across the country, even while the computer is off-line. This extends the reach of the Internet to connected and nonconnected users alike. With an AirMedia Live–enabled receiver, you can receive wireless alerts of breaking headline news, scores from every professional and college sport, timely financial market updates, online chats, interactive game challenges, and even E-Mail alerts from a wide variety of online sources. These alerts con-

tain embedded URLs and provide single-click access to the full source of the information on the Internet or commercial online service.

THE POINTCAST NETWORK

PointCast is a Web tool that provides continuous updates on any subject area or topic you specify. It's like having your own personal search engine constantly searching the Web for the latest news and bringing it back to you automatically. Web: *http://www*.pointcast.com

PR NEWSWIRE

This database contains the complete text of news releases prepared by companies, PR agencies, trade associations, and government agencies. News releases often contain valuable information not found in newspaper or magazine articles. Available on America Online, Dialog, Dow Jones News/Service, Knowledge Index, NewsNet, and NEXIS.

PTS PROMT

PTS PROMT, produced by Predicasts Terminal System, is known for the depth of its coverage on marketing and technology news. It contains over 2.8 million abstracts of business journals, magazines, and newspapers. The same company also produces several subsidiary databases, including one covering new-product announcements. Available on CompuServe, Dialog, and NEXIS.

ZD NET DATABASES

The following four databases from Ziff are all available on CompuServe: Business Database Plus contains full-text articles from more than 450 regional, national, and international business and trade publications. You can search the database through any one of seven methods to locate articles that can provide you with sales and marketing ideas, product news, industry trends, and analyses. Web: *http://www*.ZDNet.com

#5. Keeping Current in Your Field

The Problem

Whatever field you are in, chances are the pace of change is constant, and keeping up with it can occupy half your time. New developments are occurring constantly. New leaders and industry gurus emerge. New inventions and products are introduced. New companies come to prominence as old ones change or decline. To stay competitive and keep the confidence of your clients, you need to keep up with all the news in your field without having to subscribe to dozens of journals or newspapers and spend your days reading instead of working.

Online Solutions

Many of the databases mentioned in the previous problem can also fulfill your need to stay abreast of general news in your profession. Most major daily newspapers, magazines and journals now have sites on the Web that you can browse through for subjects of interest in your field for free, or at minimal cost.

Here's a list of some additional online solutions that you may wish to explore.

CLIPPING SERVICES

You may wish to explore the electronic clipping services. With an electronic service, you enter in advance a group of keywords that you want the service to track for you, after which any article containing those keywords is automatically collected for you. When you access the service, a file of articles is waiting for you to review. The major electronic clipping services include:

America Online AOL monitors Associated Press, United Press International, Reuters, and OTC NewsAlert and PR Newswire. (You must be an AOL subscriber to use the clipping service.)

CompuServe, Inc. CompuServe Executive News Service monitors the Associated Press, United Press International, Reuters, and OTC NewsAlert. (You must be a CompuServe subscriber to use the clipping service.)

Datatimes, 14000 Quail Springs Parkway, Ste. 450, Oklahoma City, OK 73134, (405) 751-6400, (800) 642-2525. DataTimes monitors regional and international newspapers and major wire services. Web: *http://*www.datatimes.com

Dow Jones News Services, P.O. Box 300, Princeton, NJ 08540-0300, (800) 522-3567. Dow Jones's Facts Delivered clipping service covers the *Wall Street Journal, Barron's, Business Week,* and other newspapers and publications. Also available is an online news retrieval service with over 3,400 publications and 55 million articles. Web: *http://*bis.dowjones.com

LEXIS-NEXIS, 9393 Springboro Pike, P.O. Box 933, Dayton, OH 45401, (800) 227-4908. The Eclipse electronic clipping service provides full-text from more than 750 magazines, newspapers, government reports, news wires, and newsletters. Web: *http://*www.lexis-nexis.com

NewsNet, 945 Haverford Road, Bryn Mawr, PA 19010, (610) 527-8030, (800) 345-1301. NewsNet's Newsflash tracks 1,000 national and international wire services. Web: *http://www.newsnet.com*

NEXIS. Includes the full text of the *New York Times* since 1980 as well as the full text from hundreds of magazines, worldwide newspapers, wire services, and industry newsletters that range from the *ABA Banking Journal* to the Xinhua English Language News Service.

NEW PRODUCTS TRACKING

Thomas New Industrial Products: produced by the same company as the Thomas Register Online, and contains the latest technical information on over 277,000 industrial products manufactured worldwide. Updated weekly, this database is always current and it covers a wide variety of products. The information in each record includes the product name, any applicable product synonyms, SIC codes, trade name, model number, product use, attributes and specifications, plus the manufacturer's name, address, and telephone number. An individual record may not contain all this information. You can retrieve product records by entering the company name, company location, product name, trade name, model number, SIC code, or publication date. Available on CompuServe, America Online, and Dialog.

ZDNET

ZDNet is one of the Web's leading sources of new information on computer and technology products. Web: *http://www.zdnet.com*

#6. Finding Names and Titles for Your Mailings and Sales Calls

The Problem

As you prepare to do a mailing to a few dozen or a few hundred companies, you may discover that you do not know the names of the people to whom you should send your materials. When this happens, you need a reliable, speedy way to find out who the key people are in the companies you want to reach so that you won't find yourself sending out an expensive mailer impersonally addressed to a title like "Dear Chief Financial Officer."

Online Solutions

Many of the databases we've already cited such as Dun's Market Identifiers and Dun's Electronic Business Directory can be used to find out the names of the officers and executives in millions of American companies. You can also use:

Biz*File (CompuServe): Includes over eighty million U.S. households and contains the name, home address, phone number, and length of residence. You can search the listings in many ways, knowing either the name or the telephone number. The database is derived from public records, such as the white pages and public documents.

Hoover's Online Service: Search over 10,000 companies. Each company profile includes a list of company officers. Web: *http://www.*hoovers.com

Marquis Who's Who (CompuServe): This database provides information on key North American professionals, including date of birth, education, positions held during career, civic and political activities, memberships, awards, and other affiliations.

#7. Finding a Supplier for Hard-to-Find Items and Locating Good Prices

The Problem

Selecting the most cost-effective business equipment, accessories, and supplies can be a difficult decision, given the plethora of products from which to choose. You may need to find reliable information and reviews of office equipment, computer supplies, and other items required to run your business.

Online Solutions

AIRMEDIA LIVE INTERNET BROADCAST NETWORK
See page 361.

CNET
Cnet is a news-gathering and -reporting organization that disseminates the latest news concerning computing and technology issues. Information on their Web site (*http://www.*cnet.com) is updated twice daily.

CONSUMER REPORTS
Most businesses can make occasional use of the recommendations made by Consumer Reports on business and office equipment, as well as on various financial products. Consumer Reports is available on America Online, CompuServe, Microsoft Network, and Prodigy.

THOMAS REGISTER
See page 354.

THE WEB!
The World Wide Web was created for the purpose of helping people and businesses find one another. Use any of the search engines listed on pages 358–59 to search for the product or technology you are looking for.

ZDNET
This service includes several databases useful for finding hard-to-find items and suppliers. Notable among these is the Computer Directory, which provides information on over 70,000 computer-related products and more than 8,500 manufacturers of hardware, software, peripherals, and data communications equipment. Information includes pricing, phone numbers, fax numbers, and key specifications. Available on CompuServe and Prodigy.

#8. Overcoming Isolation

The Problem

In a rural area or even an urban one, no longer having colleagues or co-workers in an office down the hall to sound out an idea or share opinions or experiences with can leave you feeling isolated and alone when you work from home. Throughout the day, week, or month, you may well feel the need to get suggestions and support from colleagues and want to avoid feeling trapped or stuck to your home office.

Online Solutions
Nearly every information service offers special-interest-group forums and "chat" rooms that allow you to converse electronically with other people around the country. For example, CompuServe has over 1,000 forums or special-interest groups, including the Working from Home forum we began in 1983, which has over 200 messages a day from people discussing a variety of topics of interest to those of us who work from home on our own. The big-four online service providers all offer a wide scope of discussion groups and chat rooms. These forums and discussions include a large assortment of specific computer user groups, users of various software products, and hobbyists of all kinds who are interested in sharing information. Taking an online coffee break can often be just the thing to give yourself a boost or to help you relax in the midst of a strenuous project.

Don't forget about E-mail. E-mail is a convenient and quick way to stay in touch with colleagues across the country, share information, or learn about new developments. Most people these days check their E-mail before checking on phone messages or regular mail.

The Internet also offers a mind-bending array of sites with chat rooms and discussion groups, not to mention the thousands of Usenet Newsgroups. Participating in online discussion not only alleviates the feeling of isolation all at-home entrepreneurs eventually experience; it's also an essential way to network, meet new colleagues, and perhaps even generate some new business.

#9. Getting Business Online

The Problem

Many people feel that if they spend time online, they should be able to develop clients or customers out of the contacts they make by letting people around the country know they are available for work and soliciting for business. For people who have chosen to live in rural areas and small towns and need to derive their income from distant cities, making new contacts may only be possible through online services short of expensive travel. However, most vendors discourage or prevent people from directly soliciting business unless they actually pay to advertise on the service. Also, just as people don't look in the want ads for a CPA or an attorney, ads don't usually work for professional and technical services.

Online Solution

Actually, many people do get business online as a result of meeting people, sharing information, and developing friendships. This works extremely well for programmers, computer consultants, and Web-based businesses who provide thoughtful advice to others online. A management consultant shared the following secrets for successfully developing business online:

> I have acquired eight clients who met me or were introduced to me through CompuServe. Three of these people have been very worthwhile, and have paid me well over the years. I follow several rules that I set up for myself in this regard, and they seem to work: 1) Give away all the help you can when you are online in a forum. 2) Don't expect to gain clients; anything that comes along is a bonus. 3) Consider what you do not as marketing but as

fun. You always get back much more than you give. I recommend that you give away your expertise here. You'll love the results!

Additionally, you can access databases that might lead you to a government contract. For example, Commerce Business Daily—available on CompuServe, Dialog, and NewsNet as well as the Web: http://cbdnet.access.gpo.gov/—is the online version of the print document published by the Commerce Department listing opportunities for contracts from the U.S. government. Civilian procurements over $25,000 and military procurements over $100,000 are listed. Procurements reserved for small businesses are also indicated.

Since trade shows are another route to business, you can find the dates and locations for trade shows, international conferences, conventions, and exhibitions worldwide using the Fairbase and Eventline databases available from Knight-Ridder Information Services: (800) 221-7754, Web: *http://www*.krinfo.com

CREATE YOUR OWN WEB SITE

The World Wide Web is one of your best resources for getting the word out about your business. A well-designed Web site can also attract business for you as well. It is beyond the scope of this book to provide all the details of how to create a Web site, but the following information should point you in the right direction.

There are three basic steps involved in creating and posting a successful site on the World Wide Web:

1. *Creating the Site Itself*—Your first step is designing and creating the site and all its component parts. You have two choices here: You can do it yourself, or you can have a professional Web site designer do it for you. Unless you have some extra time on your hands, understand how to write well for the Web, know the current tools and technologies, and are visually oriented, we recommend using a professional designer. Consider giving the work to a fellow home-based businessperson. If you really want to do it yourself, there are many excellent books available entirely devoted to the process of creating Web sites. See the resources section of the Web Site Design profile in section 1, page 159.

2. *Finding a Server/Host*—When the site itself is finished, you will need to find a server/host service that will actually store your site and serve it to the Web. There are literally thousands of companies who do this. Your best bet is to research several and find the best one most suited to your needs. You may want to start with your own ISP or Online Service Provider. Nearly

every ISP provides Web hosting services. *Please Note: Many ISPs offer free Web site hosting for personal use. We recommend that you do not take advantage of this for your business. The URL you will receive will indicate that your site is a personal site and will detract from the professional appearance and perception of your business. We recommend that you pay the extra money and list your site as a business site for the same reasons that we recommend that you obtain a business phone line so that your business will be listed as business in the phone directory.* Then call at least three to four other hosting services. You can find hosting services by asking your colleagues whom they use, conducting searches on the Web itself, and looking through computer and Web-oriented magazines. Compare issues such as price per month, speed, bandwidth, size of the site (listed in megabytes), how long the company has been in business, and their list of services. Ask any company you are considering to provide a list of their current business customers, then contact a few names at random from the list. Ask them if they're happy with the service.

3. *Publicizing Your Web Site*—Once your site is securely nestled on a server to the World Wide Web, you will need let the world know about it. Many businesses make the mistake of assuming that the cyber community will just find them, then wonder why their site is lonelier than the Maytag repairman. To get people to visit your site, you have to tell them it's there. We suggest you hire the services of a home-based Web Site Publicist. Their business is building up the traffic on your site. If want to do some publicity yourself, start by submitting your site to all the major search engines. There are several online tools that can help you do this, including SubmitIt (Web: *http://www.*submitit.com). You should also write a press release and send it out electronically and via regular mail to trade magazines, newsletters, and any other organizations your industry and customers turn to for information. Also, ask colleagues, trade organizations, and any other relevant entities to include a link to your site on their site.

Eleven Tips for Saving Time and Money Online

One of the prime deterrents to going online is concern about the cost of connect time, which can run from around 3 cents to more than $20 a minute. But you can substantially lower your connect costs by following these guidelines, which are distilled from our own experience and from that of other users of online services.

Tip #1. Know What You Are Looking For

As we have indicated, there is a vast sea of information out there, and many people can literally drown in it when they don't know specifically what they want to find. Before you do any searching, think clearly about what you are looking for and which vendor and database are likely to have what you want. For example, if you want a brief overview of a topic from a magazine like *Time* or *Newsweek* or a newspaper, you would search in the kind of database that offers such full-text articles. However, if you are seeking more in-depth business information, complete with financial analysis, ratios, and other quantitative information, you can log onto a database that is more oriented toward that specific information.

#Tip 2. Scope Out Your Territory

Familiarize yourself with how each online service you use works so you don't spend needless time reading menus or using help files. The best way to do this is to read the manual or go to the practice area if there is one offered, since most vendors allow you to work there for free or at little cost in the beginning. On CompuServe, for example, there is a Practice Forum (type GO PRACTICE) where you can learn to use the traditional commands and menus. Also check out the rates for using the service at different times of the day and night. Some services like CIS charge the same rate twenty-four hours a day. Others charge a premium for daytime use.

Tip #3. M.Y.O.B. (Mind Your Online Baud)

Many vendors let you work at 14,000 baud (also know kbps), but this transmission rate is half as fast a 28,000-baud modem, which is half as slow as 33.6. Invest in the highest-speed modem you can afford. It will more than pay for itself if your online service charges hourly rates. Even if you pay a flat rate, a faster modem will save a great deal of your own time!

Tip #4. Automate Your Usage if Possible

As soon as you know how to download files, the most important money-saving action you can take is to get a software program designed to automate your use of the service if available. On CompuServe, for example, you can use AutoSig, Navigator, OzCIS, TapCis, or the CompuServe Information Manager. Use "Flash sessions" to compose new E-mail and read E-mail off-line. The big four online services also offer tools that allow you to download information quickly, then read it off-line.

Tip #5. Select the Best Phone Line

Most ISPs have a network of local phone numbers through which you will access their service. Make sure that the number you have chosen to use is indeed a local call, and that the number is located in the zone closest to you.

Tip #6. Perform Efficient Searches

Review the section in this chapter on conducting better Internet searches on pages 358–59. The better your search results, the less time you will be spending sifting through information you don't need. If you are using one of the big-four services, take the time to learn their internal structure so you can use the right keywords to go where you want without having to perform time-consuming searches.

Tip #7. Search Multiple Databases at the Same Time

If the service you are using offers you the ability to search multiple databases at the same time instead of one at a time, you will usually save time and money by doing this. Some services allow you to store the commands you use in making a search (your search strategy). Doing this will enable you to repeat a search in another database or at another time more quickly, saving you money.

Tip #8. Use Bookmarks

Both Netscape Navigator and Microsoft Explorer allow you to build and store a list of "bookmarks." Bookmarks are the Internet addresses of your favorite and most frequently accessed sites. Once a bookmark is created you can click on it any time and be taken to the site immediately, thereby saving you the time of having to search for it again.

Tip #9. Know When to Sign Off

Once you get involved in the online world, you might find yourself spending more time there than necessary. Actual addiction to the Internet is a growing phenomenon. Always have an idea of what you wish to accomplish online before logging on. Once you have found what you were looking for, contacted the people you needed to, or otherwise accomplished what you set out to do, log off.

Tip #10. Save Your Search to a File

To minimize the time you spend online, download your entire session to a file in your computer so that you can review it when you are done. Not only do you save time by not reading while online, but if you make a mistake you can review your commands and see where you went wrong. Most communications software allows you to "capture" your online sessions to a file on your hard drive or on a floppy disk.

Tip #11. Learn More

You can find a lot of specific information and software that will help you take full advantage of any database and vendor. If you are serious about making online resources your business partner, check into any of these resources:

Finding It on the Internet: The Internet Navigator's Guide to Search Tools and Techniques, by Paul Gilster, 2d rev. and exp. ed. Wiley, New York, 1996, ISBN: 0471126950.

Gale Directory of Databases, published by Gale Research, Company, Book Tower, Detroit, MI 48226. This two-volume set is a consolidation of the Cuadra Associates' *Directory of Online Databases* and several Gale online directories. Brief descriptions are provided for 8,100 databases, 3,100 providers, and 800 online services. The second volume covers databases available on CD-ROM, diskette, handheld, and batch access data products.

Harley Hahn's Internet and Web Yellow Pages 1997 (4th ed.), by Harley Hahn, Osborne McGraw-Hill, 1997, ISBN: 0078822580.

How to Get the Most Out of CompuServe, by Charles Bowen and Dave Peyton, New York, Bantam. Regularly updated. Also to learn to use CompuServe, self-study and classroom training are offered by Mentor Technologies. Mentor's toll-free number is (800) 227-5502. The firm's address is 1266 East Broad Street, Columbus, OH 43205.

Official Netscape Guide to Internet Research, by Tara Calishain, Ventana Communications Group, Inc., ISBN: 1566046041.

Online Market Research: Cost-Effective Searching of the Internet and Online Databases, by John F. Lescher, Reading, MA, Addison-Wesley, ISBN: 0201489295.

The Prentice-Hall Directory of Online Business Information 1997, by Scott Grimes and Christopher Engholm, Englewood Cliffs, NJ, Prentice Hall Trade, ISBN: 0132552825.

Web Search Strategies, by Bryan Pfaffenberger, Mis Press, ISBN: 1558284702.

Appendix I
Getting Online

When the first version of this book came out not so long ago, there were two paragraphs in this section. A few short years later, we've added over twenty new Internet-based careers to Part 1, and nearly every business, organization, and institution referenced in these pages is followed by an Internet address. Due in large part to the Internet, and the World Wide Web in particular, the online world has grown from just another resource for the home-based business to an absolutely essential connection to the world around you.

If you are not already online, you are placing your business at a real disadvantage. Information that your online peers, allies, and competition have at their fingertips will take you hours, perhaps days, to access—if you can find it at all. With all the press and excitement "cyberspace" has been generating these past few years, you don't really need us to tell you that the Internet is the fastest-growing communications medium in the past fifty years. And unlike television and radio before it, the Internet is a truly worldwide phenomenon that is connecting people, business, information, and human communication like nothing we've seen before.

Okay. If you're still not online, you know you have to be. Read on—it's much easier than you think. The only hardware you will need is a modem. Most computer systems sold during the past two years include a modem as standard, so chances are you have one already. If you don't have a modem, or are thinking about upgrading your current one, get the fastest-speed model you can afford. For more details on modems, go to page 255 in chapter 3.

To get access to the Internet, you will need an Internet Service Provider (ISP). For either a straight monthly fee or a per-hour charge, depending on the company or plan, ISPs provide you with a gateway to the Internet. With an ISP, you use your modem to make a local call into their system. Their computer will then connect you to the Internet itself. This is done so quickly and easily it will appear seamless to you. There are basically two kinds of ISPs:

1. Straightforward ISPs—these companies provide no-frills access to the Internet and give you an E-mail account. They are often very easy to use and are generally cheaper per month than the online services. However, they don't offer nearly the informational and networking resources of Online Service Providers. Well known ISPs include Earthlink (Web: *http://www*.earthlink.net, phone: 800-395-8425), MindSpring (Web: *http://www*.mindspring.com, phone: 800-719-4660), and NTR.NET Corporation (Web: *http://www.* ntr.net, phone: 800-962-3750).

2. Online Service Providers—Online Service Providers offer a gateway into the Internet in addition to a plethora of their own information resources, discussion groups, bulletin boards, and much more. Online Service Providers are part library, part newsstand, part broadcast network, and part town square and meeting place. The original content they provide is unique and separate from the Internet itself and can only be accessed by "members." Monthly fees and hourly charges tend to be higher for Online Service Providers than ISPs.

The "big four" Online Service Providers are:

America Online (Web: *http://www*.aol.com, phone: 800-827-6364)

CompuServe (Web: *http://www*.compuserve.com, phone: 800-848-8990)

Microsoft Network (Web: *http://www*.msn.com, phone: 800-386-5550)

Prodigy (Web: *http://www*.prodigy.com, phone: 800-776-3449)

Choosing the Right Internet Service Provider (ISP)

There are over 500 ISPs offering connections to the Internet, and the number is growing all the time. Choosing the right ISP for your needs is just as important a decision as which accounting program or office suite package to buy. The right ISP can make your online life much easier and give you the most conducive set of services for the money you have to spend. How do you begin? The first thing to do is to identify your own needs in terms of services. Then determine how much you can comfortably afford to spend each month on your connection. Your ISP answer lies between these two points.

Use the following criteria when assessing the merits of national and local ISPs:

1. Price—There are almost as many pricing plans as there are ISPs. First and foremost, make sure the ISP offers you a local access phone number, or toll-free number, to dial the service. If the dial-up access number is a long-distance or toll call, look elsewhere. Second, consider the ISP's price plan carefully. Many ISPs offer something like five hours for $9.95 and $2.95 for each additional hour. If you only plan to spend five hours a month online, these are good plans. If you think your time online will probably be more, you may wish to consider a plan that offers more hours or, better yet, unlimited hours for a single monthly fee.

2. Online Resources—Many local and national ISPs offer unlimited access time for generally lower monthly fees. The interfaces they provide are usually not as complete or user-friendly as those of the big four. If you are fairly computer savvy, these plans might be right for you. You will enjoy looking for the additional software required to fully access all of the Internet, such as a browser, browser "plug-ins" for multimedia, etc., E-mail program, newsgroup reader, FTP, and more. If you are new to computers or don't have the time to configure your online environment, you may want to turn to one of the big four Online Service Providers. They provide easy-to-use, all-in-one interfaces that include all the software required to handle Internet navigation and E-mail. They also provide extensive original content as described in the above section. As competition for your online dollars becomes fiercer, we predict the monthly and hourly fees of the big four will come down.

3. Dependable Connection—Look for an ISP that provides connections at a number of modem speeds. The current standard of 28,800 kbps is quickly being replaced by the fast 33.6 kbps, and many telephone companies are offering good rates for home-based ISDN (an even faster connection, up to 128 kbps, that requires a special phone line) lines. An ISP should offer connections at any of these rates. Ask the ISP how many subscribers they have and what their "customer-to-modem" ratio is. This refers to how many customers are routed through each modem in the company's system. The more customers per modem, the slower your access time will be and the more frequently you will encounter a busy signal when trying to access the provider. Look for a customer-to-modem ratio of no higher than twelve to one.

4. Service—Find out about the ISP's customer service logistics. Do they have an 800 phone number for technical support? Do they

have online support where you can ask technical questions of a live support person. The big four have comprehensive support logistics as do the larger, national ISPs like Earthlink.

Once you've found an ISP that's right for you, a simple phone call will allow you to open an account with them. The company will usually then ship you a software package which you will install. You will then be ready to conquer the online world.

Some of the Most Commonly Used ISPs

The following is a list of nineteen of the most commonly used Internet Service Providers. This list includes the big four Online Service Providers as well some highly regarded national Internet providers. Although each company listed has received favorable reviews from its own subscribers, as well as *PC* magazine and Cnet, as they say about all things Internet: your mileage may vary.

1. AMERICA ONLINE
VIENNA, VA
(800) 827-6364
WEB: *http://www*.aol.com
The biggest of the big four, America Online (AOL) offers in-depth databases and original content, thousands of chat rooms and discussion groups, E-mail, Web and Internet access, and much more.

2. AT&T WORLDNET SERVICE
PARSIPPANY, NJ
(800) 967-5363
WEB: *http://www*.att.com/worldnet
Easy to install and use, WorldNet includes a customized version of Netscape Navigator for Web browsing, E-mail, and other basic Internet services and tools.

3. COMPUSERVE INFORMATION SERVICE, INC.
COLUMBUS, OH
(800) 524-3388
WEB: *http://www*.compuserve.com
Another member of the big four, CompuServe Information Service serves the needs of many kinds of people: business, professional, and consumer. Its over 1,000 special-interest forums in which people exchange information with other members about mutual interests also have exten-

sive libraries of information and software. CompuServe provides Web access with the Microsoft Explorer browser, E-mail, and access to Dialog's Knowledge Index databases, ZiffNet services, and IQuest, which offers menu searching access to over 850 databases from ten database vendors.

4. CONCENTRIC NETWORK
CUPERTINO, CA
(800) 939-4262
WEB: *http://www*.contric.net
Concentric Network provides straight Internet access, E-mail, as well as access to BBS Direct, a nationwide system of bulletin board systems. The Web browser provided is Netscape Navigator.

5. EARTHLINK NETWORK
PASADENA, CA
(800) 395-8410
WEB: *http://www*.earthlink.net
Earthlink is a fast-growing access provider that offers its own databases of business, technology, and lifestyle resources. It includes the Netscape Navigator browser and E-mail.

6. EPOCH NETWORK/HLC
IRVINE, CA
(714) 474-4950
WEB: *http://www*.hlc.net
Epoch Network is a business-oriented site that provides many business services and a high-speed connection to the Net.

7. GTE INTERNET SOLUTIONS
IRVING, TX
(800) 363-8483
WEB: *http://www*.gte.net
This service is easy to install and is a straightforward Internet access service. Includes E-mail and the Netscape Navigator browser.

8. IBM INTERNET CONNECTION SERVICE
WHITE PLAINS, NY
(800) 455-5056
WEB: *http://www*.ibm.net
A straightforward, no-nonsense Internet access service, IBM offers good speed and reliability. This service is geared toward business customers and comes with the Netscape browser.

9. IDT INTERNET SERVICES
HACKENSACK, NJ
(800) 245-8000
WEB: *http://www*.idt.net
Includes E-mail, the Netscape Navigator, and other Internet software tools.

10. MCI INTERNET
ARLINGTON, VA
(800) 550-0927
WEB: *http://www*.mci2000.com
A business-oriented service that includes E-mail, Netscape Navigator, and a package that allows you to combine long-distance phone service, paging, and access fees in one bill.

11. MICROSOFT NETWORK
REDMOND, WA
(800) 386-5550
WEB: *http://www*.msn.com
The third member of the big four, the Microsoft Network (MSN) software comes standard in any version of Windows later than Windows 95. The service can also run under Windows 3.1. With news features, databases, and a teeming host of original programming, MSN is an excellent and growing resource. It comes, of course, with the Microsoft Explorer browser.

12. MINDSPRING
ATLANTA, GA
(800) 719-4332
WEB: *http://www*.mindspring.com
A comprehensive software interface with E-mail and the Netscape Navigator make this a popular ISP.

13. NETCOM
SAN JOSÉ, CA
(800) 638-2661
WEB: *http://www*.netcom.com
The seamless NetCruiser interface and Netscape Navigator make Netcom one of the most widely used ISPs in the country.

14. PRODIGY
WHITE PLAINS, NY
(800) 776-3449
WEB: *http://www.*prodigy.com

The fourth member of the big four on our list. Prodigy offers access to several specialized business databases, mentioned earlier, as well as most of the other resources and services offered by its competitors

15. SPRINT INTERNET PASSPORT
KANSAS CITY, KS
(800) 359- 3900
WEB: *http://www.*sprint.com/sip/

Basic Internet access that includes E-mail and the Netscape Navigator.

16. SPRYNET
BELLEVUE, VA
(800) 777-9638
WEB: *http://www.*sprynet.com

This is CompuServe's Internet-only access service. Includes E-mail and Microsoft's Internet Explorer browser.

17. USA NET
COLORADO SPRINGS, CO
(800) 592-1241
WEB: *http://www.*usa.net

Multiple payment plans and the Netscape Navigator browser make USA Net a popular ISP.

18. UUNET TECHNOLOGIES
FAIRFAX, VA
(800) 488-6383
WEB: *http://www.*uu.net

A business-oriented ISP that offers a wide range of plans and options. Basic service includes E-mail and the Netscape Navigator browser.

19. WHOLE EARTH NETWORKS
SAN FRANCISCO, CA
(415) 281-6500
WEB: *http://www.*wenet.net

This service started the highly regarded WELL, one of the first cyber communities. Whole Earth offers a number of different access plans.

Online Lexicon

In case you are not familiar with the terminology frequently used in discussing online systems, this short glossary is intended to clarify the most frequently used terms.

Browser—Browsers are software programs that allow you to navigate the Internet, especially the World Wide Web. Browsers are really a seamless interface that read HTML, JAVA, and other Web languages and translate the information into the exciting graphics and text combinations that make the Web unique. Browsers can be enhanced by using "plug-in" applications such as Streamworks by Xing Technologies, which allows you to view real-time video, and RealAudio, which allows you listen to live audio streams. Plug-ins are easily downloaded from the Web. The leading browsers today are Netscape Navigator and Microsoft Explorer. Many ISPs provide a browser as part of their initial software package. CompuServe and America Online offer their own browsers, or allow you to use either the Netscape or Microsoft browser.

Database—A database is a collection of records, each of which may be the full text of an article from a magazine, journal, or newspaper, or it may be simply a brief summary (called an abstract) of an article along with a listing of the original author, the name of the publication in which the article appeared, the date of publication, and several key words that the computer uses to classify the article for searches. Other databases may also be composed of factual and statistical information, such as tables and lists of numbers, rather than text, such as CENDATA, which is a database based on U.S. Census data. Note that a database may be compiled from either just one publication or from articles originally printed in hundreds of publications.

Database Vendor or Information Service—As online services continue to expand the amount of information they offer, Database Vendors have grown increasingly specialized. Generally vendors offer extremely comprehensive databases of information focused on a particular topic or service. Such vendors include Lexus/Nexus (financial and business data) and Mead Data Central (news service).

Internet—The Internet is really a vast network of computers (servers) that store and serve information. The network is connected through a complex system of routers and switching devices. The most common areas on the Internet are:

- *World Wide Web:* A series of "sites" that share a common protocol which allow viewers to experience text and graphics, as well as video and audio simultaneously on one screen. Sites are searchable through powerful "search engines" such as Yahoo (*http://www*.yahoo.com), Infoseek (*http://www*.infoseek.com), Altavista (*http://www*.altavista.com), and over 200 more.
- *Gopher and WAIS:* A large collection of databases that can be searched with rather interestingly named search tools such as "Archie," "Veronica," and "Jughead." This part of the Internet is older than the World Wide Web and is still primarily used by universities and research institutions. There is an incredible amount of useful information here, without the commercialism that is rampant on the Web.
- *FTP* **(File Transfer Protocol):** FTP allows you to both download files from FTP sites on the Internet and upload files to computers to which you have access. Files can consist of software, text, and graphics from the Internet.
- *Newsgroups* **(also called Usenet):** Newsgroups allow you to find communities of people interested in specific topics and to participate in discussions on a wide range of subjects with millions of people around the world.

Internet Service Provider (ISP)—An ISP generally provides you with a straight connection to the Internet and an E-mail account. ISPs don't offer as many unique services and resources as Online Services, but they are generally less expensive.

Information Provider (IP)—a company that compiles or puts together the content of a database but isn't necessarily the same as the company that makes the database available online to the public.

Online Services—Online services offer you a host of online resources including Internet access, E-mail, and a wide range of other services exclusive to the provider. These services typically include news, a series of chat and discussion rooms and forums, reference material, and much more. The most popular Online Services include CompuServe, America Online, Microsoft Network, and Prodigy.

Since the World Wide Web has grown to be such an integral part of business communications, here's a general lexicon of its main terms:

Bandwidth—The biggest technological issue concerning the Web today is bandwidth. Bandwidth is simply the amount of digital "space" transmissions take up. Bandwidth, like most things digital, is measured in bytes. A small Web site with few graphic images takes up relatively little bandwidth and can be quickly accessed by viewers. The really exciting stuff on the Web, like video, audio, animation, and high-resolution images takes up much more bandwidth.

Domain Name—The domain name is the most important part of the URL. The *http://www* component is easy to remember, but the domain is tricky. Having a memorable domain name for your site is like having a memorable phone number; more people will be able to find you more quickly. Most businesses use their business name, for example: *http://www.* microsoft.com. You can obtain your own unique name by registering it with interNIC (*http://*rs.internic.net), the official registrar of domain names. There is a small one-time registration fee and an even smaller annual registration to keep your domain name current and exclusive.

URL (User Resource Location)—Every Web site has a unique address that allows it to be found on the network. This address is the URL. For example, the URL of our site is *http://www.*workingfromhome.com. The *http://* component of the URL signifies that the file uses in Hypertext Transfer Protocol (the protocol that allows you to see text, image, and sound simultaneously). The *www.* component signifies World Wide Web. The *workingfromhome* component is the Domain Name (see above) and the *.com* signifies that ours is a commercial site. Other common extensions include *.org* for organization, *.edu* for educational and *.gov* for government related. More extensions will soon be available.

Web Site—A site on the World Wide Web is basically a file that contains text, graphics, and sometimes video, audio, and animation. The site itself resides on a server that is part of the World Wide Web network.

To find out more about what exactly goes into a Web site and the Web in general, read through the profiles for Web Designer, Web Specialty Programming (CGI. JAVA, HTML), Web Publicist, Web Publication, and the other Web-related business in Part I of this book.

Appendix II
Additional Helpful
Web Sites

BUYSMART
*http://www.*buysmart.com
Advice ranging from how to buy a color printer to how to choose the best long-distance carrier. A free service from the publishers of *Business Consumer Guide* magazine.

ELECTRONIC COMMERCE RESOURCE CENTER
*http://www.*ecrc.ctc.com
A federally funded organization dedicated to promoting electronic commerce, this online center is a good place to start when researching an entrepreneurial online business.

IDEA CAFE
*http://www.*ideacafe.com
This site is operated by an Internet service provider as a showcase of its skill. It offers business gossip, horoscopes, and valuable help for entrepreneurs and owners.

INTERNAL REVENUE SERVICE
*http://www.*irs.ustreas.gov/prod/
The IRS's Web site allows business owners to download tax forms and tax preparation educational documents, and much more.

INTERNATIONAL SMALL BUSINESS CONSORTIUM
*http://www.*sbc.com
Contacts and discussion on the prospects for international and multicultural business development. A good source of information on establishing business relationships in developing nations.

QUICKBOOKS SMALL BUSINESS ONLINE
*http://www.*intuit.com/quickbooks
An offshoot of the *Quicken* Financial network from Intuit, Inc., a software provider, this Web page features articles on management and accounting. Also

provides interactive links to the Better Business Bureau and Dow Jones News Service.

SMALLBIZ NET
http://www.lowe.org
Web page of the Edward Lowe Foundation, a nonprofit organization dedicated to developing and conducting research on small business and entrepreneurship.

SMALL BUSINESS ADMINISTRATION ONLINE
http://www.sbaonline.sba.gov
A listing of SBA resources such as documents and links to Web pages for individual SBA offices, the White House, and the U.S. House of Representatives.

SMALL BUSINESS LAW CENTER
http://www.courttv.com/legalhelp/business
Legal discussions and online help for locating a lawyer by location and specialty. The site is operated as a public service by Court TV. A good source to find out how telecommunications reform affects small business.

SMALL BUSINESS RESOURCE CENTER
http://www.webcom.com/%7eseaquest/welcome.html
A listing of sites relevant to small business on the Internet, including online newsletters, venture capital firms, publishers, and trade associations.

WOMENBIZ
http://www.frs.com/womenbiz
Discussion, networking, and entertainment for female business owners. Allows users to post bulletin board notes and share ideas with other female entrepreneurs.

VENTURE CONNECT
http://www.texel.com
A gathering place for entrepreneurs and venture capitalists looking to invest. The site is a good starting place for an online fund-raising search.

Index

Do You Have Questions or Feedback?

The authors of this book, Paul and Sarah Edwards, want to answer your questions. They can respond to you directly, usually within twenty-four hours, if you leave a message for them on the Working From Home Forum on CompuServe Information Service. If you have a computer and access to CompuServe, simply type "GO WORK" at any "!" prompt; their ID is 76703.242. You can also visit Paul and Sarah's resources offered on the Internet's World Wide Web at *http://www*.workingfromhome.com

If you do not have a computer, you can write to Paul and Sarah in care of "Q&A," Home Office Computing magazine, 411 Lafayette Street, New York, NY 10003. Your question may be selected to be answered in their monthly column or they may respond to it on their radio or TV show. However, they cannot respond to every letter.

If you want advice on selecting or setting up the right business for you, the Perfect Work Network offers coaching by phone, online, and in person. For names and information regarding fees, write Network, Box 5091, Santa Monica, CA 90409.

Other Books by Paul and Sarah Edwards

Use the table below to locate other books that contain the information you need for your business interests.

Subject	Best Home Businesses for the 90s	Finding Your Perfect Work	Getting Business to Come to You	Home Businesses You Can Buy	Secrets of Self-Employment	Teaming Up	Working From Home
Advertising			Yes				
Business opportunities				Yes			Yes
Business planning							
Children and child care							Yes
Closing sales			Yes		Yes		
Credit							Yes
Employees							Yes
Ergonomics							Yes
Failure					Yes		
Family and marriage issues						Yes	Yes
Financing your business					Yes		Yes
Franchise							Yes
Getting referrals			Yes	Yes			Yes
Handling emotional/ psychological issues					Yes		
Housecleaning							Yes
Insurance							Yes
Legal issues						Yes	Yes
Loneliness, isolation							Yes
Managing information							Yes
Marketing	Specific techniques by business		Yes Focus of book		Yes Attitude	Yes	Yes
Marketing materials			Yes				
Money					Yes	Yes	Yes
Naming your business			Yes				
Negotiating						Yes	
Networking			Yes			Yes	Yes
Office space, furniture, equipment							Yes
Outgrowing your home							Yes
Overcoming setbacks					Yes	Yes	
Partnerships	Yes					Yes	
Pricing	Yes Specific						Yes Principles
Profiles of specific businesses	Yes				Yes		
Public relations and publicity			Yes				Yes
Resource Directory				Yes	Yes		
Selecting a business/ career/business opportunity	Yes	Yes Focus of book		Yes			Yes
Software							Yes
Speaking			Yes				
Start-up costs	Yes						
Subcontracting						Yes	
Success issues					Yes	Yes	
Taxes						Yes	Yes
Time management					Yes	Yes	Yes
Zoning							Yes

Complete Your Library of the Working from Home Series by Paul and Sarah Edwards

These books are available at your local bookstore or wherever books are sold. Ordering is also easy and convenient. To order, call 1-800-788-6262, prompt #1, or send your order to:

Jeremy P. Tarcher
Mail Order Department
PO Box 12289
Newark, NJ 07101-5289

For Canadian orders:
PO Box 25000
Postal Station 'A'
Toronto, Ontario M5W 2X8

			Price
_____	The Best Home Businesses for the 90s, Revised Edition	0-87477-784-4	$12.95
_____	Finding Your Perfect Work	0-87477-795-X	$16.95
_____	Getting Business to Come to You	0-87477-629-5	$11.95
_____	Home Businesses You Can Buy	0-87477-858-1	$13.95
_____	Making Money with Your Computer at Home	0-87477-898-0	$15.95
_____	Secrets of Self-Employment	0-87477-837-9	$13.95
_____	Teaming Up	0-87477-842-5	$13.95
_____	Working from Home	0-87477-764-X	$15.95

Subtotal _____
Shipping and handling[*] _____
Sales tax (CA, NJ, NY, PA) _____
Total amount due _____

Payable in U.S. funds (no cash orders accepted). $15.00 minimum for credit card orders. [*]Shipping and handling: $3.50 for one book, $1.00 for each additional book. Not to exceed $8.50.

Payment method:

☐ Visa   ☐ MasterCard   ☐ American Express
☐ Check or money order
☐ International money order or bank draft check

Card # _____ Expiration date _____

Signature as on charge card _____

Daytime phone number _____

Name _____

Address _____

City _____ State _____ Zip _____

Please allow six weeks for delivery. Prices subject to change without notice. Source key WORK

About the Authors

PAUL and SARAH EDWARDS have been researching, studying, and analyzing the trend toward home-based business for twenty years. Paul, an attorney, and Sarah, a licensed clinical social worker, have written eight best-selling books, as well as hundreds of articles that have earned them the titles "gurus of the home office" and "self-employment experts." Paul and Sarah are also the hosts of TV's *Working from Home with Paul and Sarah Edwards.* They provide advice about self-employment and home businesses in their *Los Angeles Times* syndicated column, and on NPR's "Marketplace," CompuServe, the Business News Network, and in *Home Office Computing* magazine. They live in California.